Thomas Boston

Human nature in its four-fold state of primitive integrity

Thomas Boston

Human nature in its four-fold state of primitive integrity

ISBN/EAN: 9783337102586

Printed in Europe, USA, Canada, Australia, Japan

Cover: Foto ©Thomas Meinert / pixelio.de

More available books at **www.hansebooks.com**

OF

Primitive Integrity, entire Depravity, begun Recovery, and Confummate Happinefs or Mifery;

SUBSISTING IN

The Parents of Mankind in Para⸺, the Unregenerate, the Regenerate, and all Mank⸺ in the Future State.

IN SEVERAL

PRACTICAL DISCOURSES.

By the Reverend and Learned
Mr. THOMAS BOSTON,
Late Minifter of the Gofpel at ETTRICK.

John ii. 24, 25. *But Jefus did not commit himfelf unto them, becaufe he knew all men; and needed not that any fhould teftify of man; for he knew what was in man.*

Luke ix. 55. *Ye know not what manner of fpirit ye are of.*

Prov. xxvii. 19. *As in water face anfwereth to face: fo the heart of man to man.*

LONDON:

Printed and Publifhed by J. CHALMERS, OLD-STREET.

Sold alfo by J. MATHEWS, *Strand*; M. TRAPP, No. 1, J. PARSONS, No. 21, W. SIMMONS, No. 64, and W. BUTTON, No. 24, *Pater-Nofter-Row*; G. OFFOR, *Poftern-Row, Tower-Hill*; T. THOMAS, No. 29, *Houndfditch*; and J. FENLEY, *Briftol*.

M DCC XCIII.

PREFACE.

IT is a maxim among wife men, that the knowledge of perfons is of as great ufe in the conduct of human life, as the knowledge of things: and it is moft certain, that he who knows the various tempers, humours, and difpofitions of men, who can find out their turn of thought, and penetrate into the fecret fprings and principles of their actings, will not be at a lofs to find out proper means for compaffing his aims, will eafily preferve himfelf from fnares, and either avoid or overcome difficulties. But the knowledge of human nature, morally confidered, or, in other words, of the temper and difpofition of the foul, in its moral powers, is of much greater value; as it is of ufe in the concerns of an unchangeable life and world: he who is poffeffed of fo valuable a branch of knowledge, is thereby capacitated to judge aright of himfelf, to underftand true Chriftianity, and to conceive juftly of perfect happinefs and confummate mifery.

The depravity of human nature is fo plainly taught, yea, inculcated in facred Scripture, and is fo obvious to every thinking man's obfervation, who fearches his own breaft, and reflects duly on his temper and actings, that it is furprifingly ftrange and wonderful, how it comes to pafs, that this important truth is fo little underftood; yea, fo much difbelieved by men, who bear the name of Gofpel Minifters. Are there not perfons to be found in a neighbouring nation, in the characters of preachers, appearing daily in pulpits, who are fo unacquainted with their Bibles and themfelves, that they ridicule the doctrine of original fin, as unintelligible jargon? If they are perfons of a moral life and converfation, they feem to imagine that they cannot become better than they are: if they are immoral, they feem to indulge a conceit that they can become virtuous, yea, religious, when they pleafe. Thefe are the men who talk of the dignity of human nature, of greatnefs of mind, noblenefs of foul, and generofity of fpirit: as though they intended to perfuade themfelves and others, that pride is a good principle; and do not know that pride and felfifhnefs are the bane of mankind, productive of all the wickednefs, and much of the mifery, to be found in this and the other world; and is indeed that wherein the depravity of human nature properly confifts.

Upright Adam's nature faintly adumbrated the Divine, in a moderated felf-efteem, an adequate felf-love, and delightful reflection on his own borrowed excellency, regulated by a juft efteem of, and fupreme love to, his adorable Creator: whence a peaceful ferenity of mind, a loving, compaffionate, and benevolent difpofition of foul, a depth of thought, and brightnefs of imagination, delightfully employed in the rapturous contemplation of his beloved Maker's infinite perfections: thus bearing the Divine image, and resembling God that made him. But no sooner did he disobey the divine probatory command, than the scales were cast, his moderated self-esteem degenerated into pride, his adequate self-love shrunk into mere selfishness, and his delightful reflections on his own excellency, varied into the tickling pleasures of vanity and conceit; he lost view of the author of his being, and thenceforth, instead of delighting in him, first dreaded, and then despised him.

The modest, and therefore hitherto anonymous Author of the following discourses, Mr. THOMAS BOSTON, having handled this subject, in preaching to his own obscure parochial congregation of Ettrick, in the Sheriffdom of Selkirk, had a particular view to their benefit, in printing and publishing them; and therefore the stile and method is plain and simple, and the first edition printed on coarse paper; but the subject is so comprehensive and important, so well managed, and the book has been so well received, that it now appears in the world more embellished, as well as better corrected, than formerly.

Let it suffice to recommend it to those who have a right taste of genuine Christianity, that all the Author's notions flow so directly from the sacred Fountain, that it is to be doubted if he has had much recourse to any other helps than his Bible and his God for assistance. In the mean time, I am aware of an exception, from those who rank themselves among the polite part of mankind, that there is the same harsh peculiarity of dialect in it, which is commonly found in books of practical divinity. But I beg leave to observe, that the dialect which they except against, is borrowed from sacred Scripture: and as it has pleased God, by the foolishness of preaching, to save them that believe, so also to countenance what they are displeased with, by the operations of his Spirit, on the minds of true Christians, as their common experience witnesseth. However, I heartily wish, that the exception were altogether removed, by some persons digesting into a methodical Treatise, the views of human nature in its primitive perfection, in its depraved condition, and its retrieved state, who is master of modern stile, and thoroughly understands the subjects discoursed in this book, that, by becoming all things to all men, some, *viz.* of all ranks and kinds of men, may be gained.

I am not to declaim at large in favour of religion; this were to write a book by way of preface. Many able pens have been employed in recommending it to the world, by strong arguments drawn from its usefulness to society, its suitableness to the dignity of the Divine nature, and the advantages arising to men from it, in this and the other world. But, after all, may not one be left to doubt, if religion be rightly understood by all its patrons? May not the beauties and excellencies of a precious gem be elegantly described by a naturalist or jeweller, who never saw the particular one he talked of, and knows little of its nature, less of the construction of its parts, and nothing of its proper use? Are there not men of bright parts, who reason excellently in defence of religion, and yet are so much strangers to it, that they brand the persons, who are so happy as to be possessed of it, with the hard name of spiritu-

PREFACE.

alists, reckoning them a kind of enthusiasts, unworthy of their regard. The truth is, Christianity is a mystery; mere reason does not comprehend it. There is a spiritual discerning necessary, to its being rightly understood, whence it comes to pass, that men of great learning and abilities, though they read the Scriptures with attention, and comment learnedly upon them, yet do not, yea, cannot, enter into the vein of thought peculiar to the inspired penmen, because they share not of the same Spirit; therefore it is, that the apostle Paul asserts, that the natural, or the unregenerate man, doth not know the things of God, neither indeed is capable of knowing them, because they are spiritually discerned.

From what has been said, it is easy to conclude, that no pedantic apology, on the part of the Author, for appearing in print, or fawning compliments to the courteous reader, on the part of the Prefacer, are to be expected. The truth is, both the one and the other, are rather little arts, vailing pedantry and conceit, than evidences of modesty and good sense. It is of more use to recommend the perusal of the book to persons of all ranks and degrees, from a few suitable copies, and to shew wherein this edition differs from, and excels the first.

That all mankind, however differenced by their rank and station in the world, have an equal concern in what is revealed concerning another and future world, will be readily owned; and it must be as readily granted, that however allowable it may be, for men of learning and parts, to please themselves with fineness of language, justness of thought, and exact connection in writing, upon other subjects, yet they ought not to indulge themselves in the same taste in discourses on divine things, lest they expose themselves to the just censure of acting with the same indiscretion, as a person in danger of famishing by hunger would be guilty of, if he perversely rejected plain wholesome food, when offered to him, for no other reason than the want of palatable sauce, or order and splendour in serving it up.

The sacred Book, which we call the Bible, has a peculiar sublimity in its vailed and unusual dialect and seeming inconnection; but is not therefore to be rejected, by men who bear the name of Christians, as uncouth or unintelligible: true wisdom dictates quite another thing; it counsels us, by frequent reading, to acquaint ourselves with it, become accustomed to its peculiar phrases, and search into its sublimities: upon this ground, that the matters contained in it are of the utmost consequence to us, and, when rightly understood, yield a refined delight, much superior to what is to be found in reading the best written books on the most entertaining subject. What pleads for the parent is a plea for the progeny; practical discourses upon divine subjects are the genuine offspring of the sacred text, and ought therefore to be read carefully, and with attention, by persons of all ranks and degrees, though they are indeed calculated for, and particularly adapted to, such as move in low spheres of life.

Let it, however, be a prevailing argument, with persons of all denominations, carefully to read books of practical divinity, that many of them are not written on the same motives and principles as other books are; the authors have often a peculiar divine call to publish them, and well-founded hope of their being useful to advance Christianity in the world. In consequence whereof it is, that great numbers have reaped benefit by reading them, especially in childhood and youth; many have been converted by them; and it may be questioned, if ever there was a true Christian, since the art of printing made these books common, who has not in some stage of life reaped considerable advantage from them. This book recommends itself in a particular manner, by its being a short substantial system of practical divinity, insomuch that it may with truth be asserted, That a person who is thoroughly acquainted with all that is here taught, may, without danger to his eternal interest, remain ignorant of other things which pertain to the science called Divinity. It is therefore earnestly recommended to the serious and frequent perusal of all, but especially of such as are in the stage of life called youth, and are so stationed in the world, as not to have frequent opportunities to hear sermons, and read commentaries on the sacred text.

It is doubtless incumbent on masters of families, to make some provision of spiritual as well as bodily food for their children and servants: this is effectually done by putting practical books into their hands: and therefore this book is humbly and earnestly recommended as a family-book, which all the members of it are not only allowed, but desired to peruse.

As to the difference between this and the first edition, which gives it preference, it lies chiefly in the Author's not only having revised the stile, but the thoughts in many places, and corrected both, so as to set several important truths in a clearer light, and make the stile of the book now uniform, which formerly was not so, because of the explications of peculiar words and phrases in use amongst practical divines, especially of the church of Scotland, which were interspersed throughout the first edition, and introduced by another hand, for the sake of such persons as are not accustomed to them. It remains that the Prefacer not only subjoin his name, which was concealed in the first edition, as a testimony that he esteems the Author, and values the book, but that he may thereby recommend it in a particular manner to the perusal of persons of his own acquaintance. If, in his assisting towards its being published, and in prefacing both editions, he has not run unsent, he has what will bear him up under all censures. The charitable will think no evil, and others will do as they please.

ROBERT WIGHTMAN, M. D. G. E.

Edinburgh,
March 18, 1729.

The Rev. Mr. HERVEY's Recommendation of this Work, in the firſt Volume of his Dialogues.

"SEE this Work of grace, and procedure of converſion, more copiouſly diſplayed, in a valuable piece, en-
"titled, *Human Nature in its Four-fold State*, by Mr.
"BOSTON, which, in my opinion, is one of our beſt books
"for common readers. The ſentences are ſhort, and the
"compariſons ſtriking: the language is eaſy, and the doc-
"trine evangelical: the method proper, the plan compre-
"henſive, the manner ſearching, yet conſolatory. If an-
"other celebrated treatiſe is ſtiled, *The whole Duty of*
"*Man*; I would call this, *The whole of Man*; as it com-
"priſes—what he *was*, originally:—what he *is*, by tranſ-
"greſſion:—what he *ſhould be*, through grace:—and then
"what he *will be*, in glory."

THE CONTENTS.

I. The State of INNOCENCY, or PRIMITIVE INTEGRITY, difcourfed from Ecclef. vii. 29.

Of man's original righteoufnefs,	Page 4
The qualities of this righteoufnefs,	8
Of man's original happinefs,	10
Doctrine of the ftate of innocence applied,	18

II. The State of NATURE, or State of Entire DEPRAVITY.

Head I. The Sinfulnefs of Man's natural State, difcourfed from Gen. vi. 4. — p. 22

That man's nature is corrupted,	27
Of the corruption of the underftanding,	42
Of the corruption of the will,	60
Of the corruption of the affections,	91
Of the corruption of the confcience,	92
Of the corruption of the memory,	93
The body partaker of this corruption,	ib.
How man's nature was corrupted.	94
The doctrine of the corruption of nature applied,	97
Evidences of men's overlooking original fin,	104
How to get a view of the corruption of nature,	110

Head II. The Mifery of Man's natural State, difcourfed from Eph. ii. 3. — 112

Man's natural ftate a ftate of wrath,	114
What this ftate of wrath is,	116
The qualities of that wrath,	123
The doctrine of the ftate of wrath confirmed and vindicated,	125
Several inftructions from it,	130
Inftances of the wrath of God,	139
How to flee from wrath,	141
A few words to the faints,	142
A word to all,	145

Head III. Man's Utter Inability to recover himself, discoursed from Rom. v. 6. John vi. 41. - - p. 146
Man unable to recover himself in the way of the law, - 147
He cannot keep the commands perfectly, - 148
He cannot satisfy the justice of God for his sin, - 150
Object. God is merciful: we hope to be saved, if we do as well as we can. Answered, - - 152
Man unable to recover himself in the way of the gospel; to embrace and use the help offered for his recovery, proved by several arguments, - - - 154
Object (1.) If we be under utter inability to do any good, how can God require us to do it? Answered, - - 156
Object. (2.) Why do you then call us to believe, repent, and use the means? Answered, - - - 157
Object. (3.) The use of means needless, seeing we are utterly unable to help ourselves out of the state of sin and wrath. Answered, - - - 159
Quest. Has God promised to convert and save them who, in the use of means, do what they can towards their own relief? Answered, - - - - 160

The State of GRACE, or begun Recovery.

Head I. Regeneration, discoursed from 1 Pet. i. 23. - p. 163

Of the nature of regeneration, - - 164
Partial changes mistaken for this change, - - ib.
The change made in regeneration, what it is, - - 167
The mind is illuminated, - - 170
The will renewed, - - 174
The affections are changed, rectified, and regulated, - 177
The conscience renewed, - - 180
The memory bettered by regenerating grace, - - 181
The body changed in respect of use, - - 182
The whole conversation changed, - - 183
The resemblance between natural and spiritual generation, in nine particulars, - - - 186
Trial of one's state, whether born again or not, - 190
Some cases of doubting Christians resolved, - 194
The necessity of regeneration shewn, - - 203
Advice to the unregenerate, - - - 212

Head II. The Mystical Union between Christ and Believers, discoursed from John xv. 5. - - p. 213

A general view of the mystical union, - - 215
The natural stock of all men, Adam, - - 218
The supernatural stock, into which the branches are ingrafted, Jesus Christ, - - - 226
What branches are taken out of the natural stock, and grafted into the supernatural stock, - - 228

How they are cut off from the natural stock, in twelve particulars, — 229
How ingrafted into Christ, — 241
How one may know one's self to be apprehended of Christ, 244
The benefits flowing to believers from their union with Christ, in some particulars, — 246
The duty of saints as united to Christ, — 278
A word to sinners, — 282

IV. The ETERNAL STATE, or State of Consummate Happiness or Misery.

Head I. Death, discoursed from Job xxx. 23. — p. 283

The certainty of death, — 248
Man's life vanity, — 286
A short lived vanity, — 288
A flying vanity, — 290
Improvement of the doctrine of death, — 291

Head II. The Difference between the Righteous and the wicked in their Death, discoursed from Prov. xvi. 32. 300

The wicked dying are driven away, — 301
The hopelessness of their state at death, 306
Caution against false hopes of heaven; characters of those hopes, 309
The state of the godly in death, a hopeful state—Why? 313
Object.—Many of the godly, when dying, full of fears, and have little hope. Answered, — 318
Death uncomfortable to them in three cases, — 320
Ten Cases of saints concerning death. Answered, 321
Considerations to bring saints in good terms with death, 325
Directions how to meet Death, — 327

Head III. The Resurrection, discoursed from John v. 28, 29. p. 332

The certainty of the Resurrection, — 333
Who shall be raised, — 339
What shall be raised, — 340
How the dead shall be raised, — 341
The difference between the godly and the wicked, in their resurrection, — 342
The qualities of the raised bodies of the saints, 347
The qualities of the raised bodies of the wicked, 359
Improvement of the doctrine, — 351

CONTENTS.

Head IV. The General Judgment, difcourfed from Mat. xxv. 31. 32, 33, 34. 41. 46. — — P. 356

That there fhall be a general judgment, proved, 357
Jefus Chrift the Judge, 360
The coming of the Judge, 361
The fummons given, 362
The Judge's fitting down on the tribunal, 363
The appearance of the parties, 365
The feparation between the Righteous and the wicked, 366
The trial of the parties, 369
The books opened, 371
Sentence pronounced on the faints, 375
The faints judge the world, 377
Sentence of damnation on the ungodly, 378
The execution, 382
Improvement of the doctrine, 385

Head V. The Kingdom of Heaven, difcourfed from Matth. xxv. 34. — — — p. 390

The nature of the kingdom of heaven, 392
The faints kingly power and authority. ib.
Their enfigns of royalty, 393
The country where this kingdom lies, 400
The temple in this kingdom, 403
The fociety there, 404
The faints admiffion to the kingdom, 420
The quality in which they are introduced, 422
Trial of the claim to the kindom of heaven, 424
Duty and comfort of the heirs of the kingdom, 425
Exhortation to thofe who have no right to it, 428

Head VI. Hell, difcourfed from Matth. xxv. 41. 429

The curfe under which the damned fhall be fhut up, 431
Their mifery under that curfe, 434
The punifhment of lofs, feparation from God, 435
The horror of feparation from God, proved by feveral confiderations 436
The punifhment of fenfe, departing into fire, 442
Hell-fire more vehement and terrible than any other, proved by feveral confiderations, 443
Six properties of the fiery torments in hell, 446
Three inferences from this doctrine, 450
Society with devils in this miferable ftate, 452
The eternity of the whole, 453
What eternity is, ib.

CONTENTS.

What is eternal in the ſtate of the damned, - 455
Reaſonableneſs of the eternity of the puniſhments of the damned, - - 458
A meaſuring reed to meaſure out time and endeavours for ſalvation by, - - 460
A balance to diſcover the lightneſs of what is falſely thought weighty, and the weight of what is falſely thought light, 461
Exhortation to flee from the wrath to come, - 463

STATE I.

NAMELY,

The STATE of INNOCENCE, or PRIMITIVE INTEGRITY, in which MAN was created.

ECCLES. vii. 29.

Lo, this only have I found, that God hath made man upright: but they have sought out many inventions.

THERE are four things very neceſſary to be known by all who would ſee heaven; 1ſt, What man *was* in the ſtate of innocence, as God made him. 2*dly*, What he *is* in the ſtate of corrupt nature, as he hath unmade himſelf. 3*dly*, What he *muſt be* in the ſtate of grace, as created in Chriſt Jeſus unto good works, if ever he be made a partaker of the inheritance of the ſaints in light. And, *laſtly*, What he *will be* in his eternal ſtate, as made by the Judge of all, either perfectly happy, or compleatly miſerable, and that for ever. Theſe are weighty points, that touch the vitals of practical godlineſs, from which moſt men, and even many profeſſors, in theſe dregs of time, are quite eſtranged. I deſign, therefore, under the divine conduct, to open theſe things, and apply them.

I begin with the firſt of them, namely, the *ſtate of innocence:* that beholding man, poliſhed after the ſimilitude of a palace, the ruins may the more affect us; we may the more prize that matchleſs Perſon, who n the Father has appointed the repairer of the breach; and that we may, with fixed reſolves, bet ke ourſelves to that way which leadeth to the city that hath unmoveable foundations.

In the text we have three things;

1. The state of innocence wherein man was created. *God hath made man upright.* By man here we are to understand our first parents; the archetypal pair, the root of mankind, the compendized world, and the fountain from whence all generations have streamed; as may appear by comparing Gen. v. 1, 2. "In the day that God created man, in the likeness of God made he him, male and female created he them, and blessed them, (as the root of mankind) and called their name Adam." The original word is the same in our text. In this sense, man was made right (agreeably to the nature of God, whose work is perfect), without any imperfection, corruption, or principle of corruption, in his body or soul. He was made upright, that is, straight with the will and law of God, without any irregularity in his soul. By the set it got in its creation, it directly pointed towards God, as his chief end; which straight inclination was represented, as an emblem, by the erect figure of his body, a figure that no other living creature partakes of. What David was in a gospel sense, that was he in a legal sense; one according to God's own heart, altogether righteous, pure and holy. God made him thus. He did not first make him, and then make him righteous: but in the very making of him, he made him righteous. Original righteousness was con-created with him; so that in the same moment he was a man, he was a righteous man, morally good; with the same breath that God breathed in him a living soul, he breathed in him a righteous soul.

2. Here is man's fallen state; but *they have sought out many inventions.* They fell off from their rest in God, and fell upon seeking inventions of their own, to mend their case; and they quite marred it. Their ruin was from their own proper motion; they would not abide as God had made them; but they sought out inventions, to deform and undo themselves.

3. Observe here the certainty and importance of these things, *Lo, this only have I found,* &c. Believe them;

they are the result of a narrow search, and a serious inquiry, performed by the wisest of men. In the two preceding verses, Solomon represents himself as in quest of goodness in the world: but the issue of it was, he could find no satisfying issue of his search after it; though it was not for want of pains; for he counted one by one to find out the account. *Behold, this have I found*, saith the preacher—to wit, *That* (as the same word is read in our text) *yet my soul seeketh, but I find not*. He could make no satisfying discovery of it, which might stay his inquiry. He found good men very rare, one, as it were among a thousand; good women more rare, not one good among his thousand wives and concubines, 1 Kings xi. 3. But could that satisfy the grand query, Where shall wisdom be found? No, it could not: (and if the experience of others in this point run counter to Solomon's, as it is no reflection on his discernment, it can as little decide the question, which will remain undetermined till the last day.) But amidst all this uncertainty, there is one point found out, and fixed: *This have I found*. Ye may depend upon it as a most certain truth, and be fully satisfied in it: *Lo, this*; fix your eyes upon it, as a matter worthy of most deep and serious regard; viz. That man's nature is now depraved; but that depravity was not from God, for he *made man upright*; but from themselves, *they have sought out many inventions*.

DOCTRINE, God made man altogether righteous.

This is that state of innocence in which God placed man in the world. It is described in the holy Scriptures with a running pen, in comparison of the following states; for it was of no continuance, but passed as a flying shadow, by man's abusing the freedom of his will. I shall,

I. Enquire into the righteousness of this state wherein man was created.
II. Lay before you some of the happy concomitants and consequences thereof.

Lastly, Apply the whole.

Of Man's Original Righteousness.

First, As to the righteousness of this state, consider, that as uncreated righteousness, the righteousness of God, is the supreme rule, so all created righteousness, whether of men or angels, hath respect to a law as its rule, and is a conformity thereto. A creature can no more be morally independent of God, in its actions and powers, than it can be naturally independent of him. A creature, as a creature, must acknowledge the Creator's will as its supreme law; for as it cannot be without him, so it must not be but for him, and according to his will: yet no law obliges, until it be revealed. And hence it follows, that there was a law which man, as a rational creature, was subjected to in his creation; and that this law was revealed to him. *God made man upright*, says the text. This supposeth a law, to which he was conformed in his creation; as when any thing is made regular, or according to rule, of necessity the rule itself is presupposed. Whence we may gather, that this law was no other than the eternal, indispensible law of righteousness, observed in all points by the Second Adam; opposed by the carnal mind; some notions of which remain yet among the Pagans, who having not the law, are a law unto themselves, Rom. ii. 15. In a word, this law is the very same which was afterwards summed up in the ten commandments, and promulgated on mount Sinai to the Israelites; called by us the Moral Law: and man's righteousness consisted in conformity to this law or rule. More particularly, there is a two-fold conformity required of man; a conformity of the powers of his soul to the law, which you may call habitual righteousness; and a conformity of all his actions to it, which is actual righteousness. Now God made man habitually righteous; man was to make himself actually righteous: the former was the stock which God put into his hand; the latter was the improvement that he should have made of it. The sum of what I have said is, that the righteousness wherein man was created, was the conformity of all the faculties and powers of his soul to the moral law. This is what

State I.   *Man's Original Righteoufnefs.*   5

we call Original Righteoufnefs, which man was originally endowed with. We may take it up in thefe three things.

Firft, Man's underftanding was a lamp of light. He had perfect knowledge of the law, and of his duty accordingly: he was made after God's image, and confequently could not want knowledge, which is a part thereof, Col. iii. 10. *The new man is renewed in knowledge after the image of him that created him.* And indeed this was neceffary, to fit him for univerfal obedience; feeing no obedience can be according to the law, unlefs it proceed from a fenfe of the commandment of God requiring it. It is true, Adam had not the law written upon tables of ftone; but it was written upon his mind, the knowledge thereof being concreated with him. God impreffed it upon his foul, and made him a law to himfelf, as the remains of it among the Heathen do teftify, Rom. ii. 14, 15. And feeing man was made to be the mouth of the creation, to glorify God in his works, we have ground to believe that he had naturally an exquifite knowledge of the works of God. We have a proof of this in Adam's giving names to the beafts of the field, and the fowls of the air, and thofe fuch as exprefs their nature: *Whatfoever Adam called every living creature, that was the name thereof,* Gen. ii. 19. The dominion which God gave them over the creatures, foberly to ufe and difpofe of them according to his will (ftill in fubordination to the will of God) feems to require no lefs than a knowledge of their natures. And, befides all this, his perfect knowledge of the law proves his knowledge in the management of civil affairs, which, in refpect of the law of God, a good man will guide with difcretion, Pfal. cxii. 5.

Secondly, His will in all things agreeable with the will of God, Eph. iv. 24. There was no corruptions in his will, no bent nor inclination to evil; for that is fin, properly and truly fo called: Hence the apoftle fays, Rom. vii. 7. *I had not known fin, but by the law; for I had not known luft, except the law had faid, Thou fhalt not covet.* An inclination to evil is really a fountain of fin, and therefore inconfiftent with that rectitude and uprightnefs which, the text exprefly fays, he was endued with at his creation. The will of man then was directed, and naturally inclined, to God and goodness; though mutable. It was disposed, by its original make, to follow the Creator's will, as the shadow does the body; and was not left in an equal balance to good and evil: For, at that rate, he had not been upright, nor habitually conformed to the law; which in no moment can allow the creature not to be inclined towards God, as his chief end, more than it can allow man to be a god to himself. The law was impressed upon Adam's soul: Now this, according to the new covenant, by which the image of God is repaired, consists in two things (1.) Putting the law into the mind; denoting the knowledge of it. (2.) Writing it in the heart; denoting inclinations in the will, answerable to the commands of the law, Heb. viii. 10. So that as the will, when we consider it as renewed by grace, is, by that grace, naturally inclined to the same holiness, in all its parts, which the law requires; so was the will of man, when we consider him as God made him at first, endowed with natural inclinations to every thing commanded by the law. For if the regenerate are partakers of the divine nature, as undoubtedly they are; for so says the Scripture, 2 Pet. i. 4. and if this divine nature can import no less than inclinations of the heart to holiness: Then surely Adam's will could not want this inclination; for in him the image of God was perfect. It is true, it is said, Rom. ii. 13, 14. *That the Gentiles—shew the work of the law written in their hearts*: but it denotes only their knowledge of that law, such as it is; but the apostle to the Hebrews, in the text cited, takes the word *heart* in another sense, distinguishing it plainly from the mind. And it must be granted, that when God promiseth, in the new covenant, *To write his law in the hearts of his people*, it imports quite another thing than what Heathens have: for though they have notions of it in their minds, yet their hearts go another way; their will has got a set and a bias quite contrary to that law: therefore the expression suitable to the present purpose must needs import, besides these notions of the mind, inclinations of the will going along therewith; which inclinations, though mixed with corruption in the regenerate, were pure and unmixed in upright Adam. In a word, as Adam knew his Master's pleasure, in the matter of duty, so his will stood inclined to what he knew.

Thirdly, His affections were orderly, pure and holy, which is a necessary part of that uprightness wherein man was created. The apostle has a petition, 2 Thess. iii. 5. *The Lord direct your hearts into the love of God;* that is, The Lord straighten your hearts, or make them lie straight to the love of God: and our text tells us that man was made thus straight. *The new man is created in righteousness and true holiness,* Eph. iv. 24. Now this holiness, as it is distinguished from righteousness, may import the purity and orderliness of the affections. Thus the apostle, 1 Tim. ii. 8. will have men to *pray, lifting up holy hands, without wrath and doubting:* because, as troubled water is unfit to receive the image of the sun; so the heart, filled with impure and disorderly affections, is not fit for divine communications. Man's sensitive appetite was indeed naturally carried out towards objects grateful to the senses: for seeing man was made up of body and soul, and God made man to glorify and enjoy him; and, for this end, to use his good creatures in subordination to himself: it is plain, that man was naturally inclined both to spiritual and sensible good; yet to spiritual, the chief good, as his ultimate end. Therefore his sensitive motions and inclinations were subordinate to his reason and will, which lay straight with the will of God, and were not in the least contrary to the same. Otherwise he would have been made up of contradictions; his soul being naturally inclined to God, as the chief end, in the superior part thereof; and the same soul inclined to the creature as the chief end in the inferior part thereof, as they call it; which is impossible; for man, at the same instant, cannot have two chief ends. Man's affections, then, in his primitive state, were pure from all defilement, free from all disorder and distemper; because, in all their motions, they were duly subjected to his clear reason, and his holy will. He had also an executive power, answerable to his will; a power to do the good which he knew should be done, and which he was inclined to do; even to fulfil the whole law of God. If it had not been so, God would not have required of him perfect obedience; for to say that the Lord gathered where he had not strawed, is but the blasphemy of a wicked heart, against so good and bountiful a God, Mat. xxv. 24. 26.

From what has been said, it may be gathered, that the original righteousness explained was universal, and natural, yet mutable.

First, it was universal; both with respect to the subject of it, the whole man: and the object of it, the whole law. Universal, I say, with respect to the subject of it, for this righteousness was diffused through the whole man: it was a blessed leaven, that leavened the whole lump. There was not one wrong pin in the tabernacle of human nature, when God set it up; however shattered it is now. Man was then holy in soul, body and spirit: while the soul remained untainted, its lodging was kept clean and undefiled; the members of the body were consecrated vessels, and instruments of righteousness. A combat between flesh and spirit, reason and appetite, nay the least inclination to sin, lust of the flesh in the inferior part of the soul, was utterly inconsistent with this uprightness in which man was created; and has been invented to vail the corruption of man's nature, and to obscure the grace of God in Jesus Christ: it looks very much like the language of fallen Adam, laying his own sin at his Maker's door, Gen. iii. 12. *The woman whom thou gavest to be with me, she gave me of the tree, and I did eat.* But as this righteousness was universal in respect of the subject, because it spread through the whole man, so also it was universal in respect of the object, the holy law. There was nothing in the law but what was agreeable to his reason and will, as God made him; though sin hath now set him at odds with it: his soul was shapen out, in length and breadth, to the commandment, though exceeding broad; so that his original righteousness was not only perfect in its parts, but in degrees.

Secondly, As it was univerſal, ſo it was natural to him, and not ſupernatural in that ſtate. Not that it was eſſential to man as man: for then he could not have loſt it, without the loſs of his very being: But it was connatural to him. He was created with it: and it was neceſſary to the perfection of man, as he came out of the hand of God; neceſſary to his being placed in a ſtate of integrity. Yet,

Thirdly, It was mutable; it was a righteouſneſs that might be loſt, as is manifeſted by the doleful event. His will was not abſolutely indifferent to good and evil: God ſet it towards good only: yet he did not ſo fix and confirm its inclinations, that it could not alter. No, it was moveable to evil: and that only by man himſelf, God having given him a ſufficient power to ſtand in this integrity, if he had pleaſed. Let no man quarrel with God's work in this: for if Adam had been unchangeably righteous, he muſt have been ſo either by nature, or by free gift: by nature he could not be ſo, for that is proper to God, and incommunicable to any creature; if by free gift, then no wrong was done to him, in withholding of what he could not crave. Confirmation in a righteous ſtate is a reward of grace, given upon continuing righteous through the ſtate of trial; and would have been given to Adam, if he had ſtood out the time appointed for probation by the Creator; and accordingly is given to the ſaints, upon account of the merit of Chriſt, who was obedient even to the death. And herein believers have the advantage of Adam, that they can never totally nor finally fall away from grace.

Thus was man made originally righteous, being created in God's own image, Gen. i. 27. which conſiſts in the poſitive qualities of knowledge, righteouſneſs, and true holineſs, Col. iii. 10. Eph. iv. 24. All that God made was very good, according to their ſeveral natures, Gen i. 31. And ſo was man morally good; being made after the image of him who is good and upright, Pſal. xxv. 8. without this he could not have anſwered the great end of his creation, which was to know, love, and ſerve his God, according to his will. Nay, he could not be created otherwiſe: for he muſt either be conformed to the law, in his powers, principles, and inclinations, or not: if he was, then he was righteous; and if not, he was a sinner, which is absurd and horrible to imagine.

Of Man's Original Happiness.

SECONDLY, I shall lay before you some of those things which did accompany or flow from the righteousness of man's primitive state. Happiness is the result of holiness; and as this was a holy, so it was a happy state.

First, Man was then a very glorious creature. We have reason to suppose, that as Moses's face shone when he came down from the mount; so man had a very luminous and pleasant countenance, and beautiful body, while as yet there was no darkness of sin in him at all. But seeing God himself is glorious in holiness, (Exod. xv. 11.) surely that spiritual comeliness which the Lord put upon man at his creation, made him a very glorious creature. O how did light shine in his glorious conversation, to the glory of the Creator! while every action was but the darting forth of a ray and beam of that glorious unmixed light which God had set up in his soul: while that lamp of love, lighted from heaven, continued burning in his heart, as in the holy place; and the law of the Lord put in his inward parts, by the finger of God, was kept by him there, as in the most holy. There was no impurity to be seen without: no squint look in the eyes after any unclean thing; the tongue spoke nothing but the language of heaven: and, in a word, the King's Son was all glorious within, and his cloathing of wrought gold.

Secondly, He was the favourite of heaven; he shone brightly in the image of God; who cannot but love his own image wherever it appears. While he was alone in the world, he was not alone, for God was with him. His communion and fellowship was with his Creator, and that immediately: for as yet there was nothing to turn away the face of God from the work of his own hands; seeing sin had not as yet entered, which alone could make the breach.

By the favour of God he was advanced to be confederate with heaven, in the firſt covenant, called, The Covenant of Works. God reduced the law, which he gave in his creation, into the form of a covenant, whereof perfect obedience was the condition : life was the ·thing promiſed, and death the penalty. As for the condition, one great branch of the natural law was, That man believe whatſoever God ſhall reveal, and do whatſoever he ſhall command : accordingly, God making this covenant with man, extended his duty to the not eating of the tree of knowledge of good and evil; and the law, thus extended, was the rule of man's covenant obedience. How eaſy were theſe terms to him, who had the natural law written on his heart, and that inclining him to obey this poſitive law, revealed to him, it ſeems, by an audible voice, (Gen. ii. 16.) the matter whereof was ſo very eaſy? And indeed it was highly reaſonable, that the rule and matter of his covenant-obedience ſhould be thus extended ; that which was added being a thing in itſelf indifferent, where his obedience was to turn upon the preciſe point of the will of God, the plaineſt evidence of true obedience : and it being in an external thing, wherein his obedience or diſobedience would be moſt clear and conſpicuous.

Now, upon this condition, God promiſed him life, the continuance of natural life, in the union of ſoul and body ; and of ſpiritual life, in the favour of his Creator : he promiſed him alſo eternal life in heaven, to have been entered into, when he ſhould have paſſed the time of his trial upon earth, and the Lord ſhould ſee meet to tranſport him into the upper paradiſe. This promiſe of life was included in the threatening of death mentioned, Gen. ii. 17. For while God ſays, *In the day thou eateſt thereof, thou ſhalt ſurely die* ; it is, in effect, If thou do not eat of it, thou ſhalt ſurely live. And this was ſacramentally confirmed by another tree in the garden, called therefore the *tree of life*, which he was debarred from when he had ſinned, Gen. iii. 22, 23. *Leſt he put forth his hand and take alſo of the tree of life, and eat and live for ever : therefore the Lord God ſent him forth from the garden of Eden.* Yet it is not to be thought, that man's life and death did hang only on this matter of the forbidden fruit, but on the whole law: for so says the apostle, Gal. iii. 10. *It is written, Cursed is every one that continueth not in all things which are written in the book of the law, to do them.* That of the forbidden fruit was a revealed part of Adam's religion; and so was necessary expresly to be laid before him: but as to the natural law, he naturally knew death to be the wages of disobedience; for the very Heathens were not ignorant of this, *Knowing the judgement of God, that they which commit such things are worthy of death,* Rom. i. 32. Moreover, the promise included in the threatening, secured Adam's life, according to the covenant, as long as he obeyed the natural law, with the addition of that positive command; so that he needed nothing to be expressed to him in the covenant, but what concerned the eating of the forbidden fruit. That eternal life in heaven was promised in this covenant, is plain from this, that the threatening was of eternal death in hell; to which when man had made himself liable, Christ was promised, by his death, to purchase eternal life: and Christ himself expounds the promise of the covenant of works of eternal life, while he proposeth the condition of that covenant to a proud young man, who, though he had not Adam's stock, yet would needs enter into life in the way of working, as Adam was to have done under this covenant, Mat. xix. 17. *If thou wilt enter into life,* (*viz.* eternal life by doing, ver. 16.) *keep the commandments.*

The penalty was death, Gen. ii. 17. *In the day that thou eatest thereof, thou shalt surely die.* The death that was threatened was such as the life promised was, and that most justly, to wit, temporal, spiritual, and eternal death. The event is a commentay on this: for that very day on which he did eat thereof, he was a dead man in law: but the execution was stopped, because of his posterity then in his loins; and another covenant was prepared: however, that day his body got its death-wound, and became mortal. Death also seized his soul: he lost his original righteousness, and the favour of God; witness the gripes and throes of conscience, which made him hide himself from God. And he became liable to eternal death, which would have actually followed of course, if the Mediator had not been provided, who found him bound with the cords of death, as a malefactor ready to be led to execution. Thus you have a short description of the covenant, into which the Lord brought man in the state of innocence.

And seemeth it a small thing unto you that earth was thus confederate with heaven? This could have been done to none but him, whom the King of heaven delighteth to honour. It is an act of grace, worthy of the gracious God, whose favourite he was; for there was grace, and free favour in the first covenant, though the exceeding riches of grace, as the apostle calls it, Eph. ii. 7. were reserved for the second. It was certainly an act of grace, favour, and admirable condescension in God, to enter into a covenant; and such a covenant with his own creature. Man was not at his own, but at God's disposal. Nor had he any thing to work with, but what he received from God. There was no proportion between the work and the promised reward. Before that covenant, man was bound to perfect obedience, in virtue of his natural dependence on God: and death was naturally the wages of sin; which the justice of God could and would have required, though there had never been any covenant between God and man: but God was free; man could never have required eternal life as the reward of his work, if there had not been such a covenant. God was free to have disposed of his creatures as he saw meet: if he had stood in his integrity to the end of time, and there had been no covenant promising eternal life to him upon his obedience, God might have withdrawn his supporting hand at last, and so made him creep back into the womb of nothing, whence almighty power had drawn him forth. And what wrong could there have been in this? for God would have only taken back what he freely gave; but now the covenant being made, God becomes debtor to his own faithfulness: if man will work, he may crave the reward on the ground of the covenant. Well might the angels, then, upon his being raised to this dignity, have given him this salutation, *Hail thou that art highly favoured! the Lord is with thee.*

Thirdly, God made him Lord of the world, prince of the inferior creatures, universal lord and emperor of the whole earth. His Creator gave him dominion over the fish of the sea, and over the fowl of the air, over all the earth, yea, and every living thing that moveth on the earth : he put all things under his feet, Psalm vii. 6, 7, 8. He gave him a power soberly to use and dispose of the creatures in the earth, sea, and air. Thus man was God's deputy governor in the lower world; and this his dominion was an image of God's sovereignty. This was common to the man and to the woman; but the man had one thing peculiar to him, to wit, that he had dominion over the woman also, 1 Cor. xi. 7. Behold how the creatures came unto him, to own their subjection, and to do him homage as their Lord! and quietly stood before him, till he put names on them as his own, Gen. ii. 19. man's face struck an awe upon them : the stoutest creature stood astonished, tamely and quietly owning him as their lord and ruler. Thus man was crowned with glory and honour, Psal. viii. 5. The Lord dealt most liberally and bountifully with him, *put all things under his feet :* only he kept one thing, one tree in the garden out of his hands, even the tree of knowledge of good and evil.

But you may say, And did he grudge him this ? I answer, Nay ? but when he had made him thus holy and happy, he graciously gave him this restriction, which was, in its own nature, a prop and stay to keep him from falling. And this I say, upon these three grounds. (1.) As it was most proper for the honour of God, who had made man lord of the lower world, to assert his sovereign dominion over all, by some particular visible sign; so it was most proper for man's safety. Man being set down in a beautiful paradise, it was an act of infinite wisdom, and of grace too, to keep from him one single tree, as a visible testimony that he muſt hold all of his Creator, as his great landlord; that ſo, while he ſaw himſelf lord of the creatures, he might not forget that he was ſtill God's ſubject. (2.) This was a memorial of his mutable ſtate given in to him from heaven, to be laid up by him, for his greater caution. For man was created with a free-will to good, which the tree of life was an evidence of: but his will was alſo free to evil, and the forbidden tree was to him a memorial thereof. It was, in a manner, a continual watch-word to him againſt evil, a beacon ſet up before him, to bid him beware of daſhing himſelf to pieces on the rock of ſin. (3.) God made man upright, directed towards God as his chief end. He ſet him like Moſes, on the top of the hill, holding up his hands to heaven: and as Aaron and Hur ſtayed up Moſes's hands, (Exod xvii. 10, 11, 12.) ſo God gave man an erect figure of body, and forbid him the eating of this tree; to keep him in that poſture of uprightneſs wherein he was created. God made the beaſts looking down towards the earth, to ſhew that their ſatisfaction might be brought from thence; and accordingly it does afford them what is commenſurable to their appetite. But the erect figure of man's body, which looketh upward, ſhewed him, that his happineſs lay above him, in God; and that he was to expect it from heaven, and not from earth. Now this fair tree, of which he was forbidden to eat, taught him the ſame leſſon, that his happineſs lay not in enjoyment of the creatures, for there was a want even in paradiſe: ſo that the forbidden tree was, in effect, the hand of all the creatures, pointing man away from themſelves to God for happineſs. It was a ſign of emptineſs hung before the door of the creation, with that inſcription, This is not your reſt.

Fourthly, As he had a perfect tranquillity within his own breaſt, ſo he had a perfect calm without. His heart had nothing to reproach him with; conſcience then had nothing to do, but to direct, approve and feaſt him: and without there was nothing to annoy him. The happy pair lived in perfect amity; and though their knowledge was vaſt, true and clear, they knew no shame. Though they were naked, there were no blushes in their faces; for sin, the seed of shame, was not yet sown. Gen. ii. 25. And their beautiful bodies were not capable of injuries from the air: so they had no need of cloaths, which are originally the badges of our shame. They were liable to no diseases nor pains: and, though they were not to live idle, yet toil, weariness, and sweat of the brows were not known in this state.

Fifthly, Man had a life of pure delight, and undreggy pleasure, in this state. Rivers of pure pleasure ran through it. The earth, with the product thereof, was now in its glory; nothing had yet come in to mar the beauty of the creatures. God placed him not in a common place of the earth; but in Eden, a place eminent for pleasantness, as the name of it imports; nay, not only in Eden, but in the garden of Eden; the most pleasant spot of that pleasant place: a garden planted by God himself, to be the mansion-house of this his favourite. When God made the other living creatures, he said, *Let the water bring forth the moving creature*, Gen. i. 20. and, *Let the earth bring forth the living creature*, ver. 24. But when man was to be made, he said, *Let us make man*, ver. 26. So when the rest of the earth was to be furnished with herbs and trees, God said, *Let the earth bring forth grass—and the fruit-tree*, &c. ver. 11. But of paradise it is said, *God planted it*, ch. ii. 8. which cannot but denote a singular excellency in that garden, beyond all other parts of the then beautiful earth. He was provided with every thing necessary and delightful; for there was every tree that is pleasant to the sight, and good for food, ver. 9. He knew not those delights which luxury has invented for the gratification of lusts: but his delights were such as came out of the hand of God, without passing through sinful hands, which always leave marks of impurity on what they touch. So his delights were pure, his pleasures refined. Yet may I show you a more excellent way: wisdom had entered into his heart; surely, then, knowledge was pleasant unto his soul. What delight do some find in their discoveries of the works of nature, by those scraps of knowledge which they have gathered ! but how much more exquisite pleasure had Adam, while his piercing eyes read the book of God's works, which God laid before him, to the end he might glorify him in the same; and therefore he certainly fitted him for the work! But above all, his knowledge of God, and that as his God, and the communion which he had with him, could not but afford him the most refined and exquisite pleasure in the inmost recesses of his heart. Great is that delight which the saints find in those views of the glory of God, which their souls are sometimes let into; while they are compassed about with many infirmities: and much may well be allowed to sinless Adam; who no doubt had a peculiar relish of those pleasures.

Lastly, He was immortal. He would never have died, if he had not sinned; it was in case of sin that death was threatened, Gen. ii. 17. which shews it to be the consequence of sin, and not of the sinless human nature. The perfect constitution of his body, which came out of God's hand very good; and the righteousness and holiness of his soul, removed all inward causes of death: nothing being prepared for the grave's devouring mouth but the vile body, Phil. iii. 21. and those who have sinned, Job xxiv. 19: and God's special care of his innocent creature secured him against outward violence. The apostle's testimony is express, Rom. v. 12. *By one man sin entered into the world, and death by sin.* Behold the door by which death came in ! Satan wrought with his lies till he got it opened, and so death entered; therefore is he said to have been a *murderer from the beginning*, John viii. 44.

Thus have I shewn you the holiness and happiness of man in this state. If any shall say, What is all this to us, who never tasted of that holy and happy state? They must know, it nearly concerns us, as Adam was the root of all mankind, our common head and representative, who received from God our inheritance and stock, to keep it for himself, and his children, and to convey it to them. The Lord put all mankind's stock (as it were) in one ship; and as we ourselves would have done, he made our common father the pilot. He put a blessing in the root, to have been, if rightly managed, diffused into all the branches. According to our text, making Adam upright, he made man upright: and all mankind had that uprightness in him; for, if the root be holy, so are the branches. But more of this afterwards. Had Adam stood, none would have quarrelled with the representation.

The Doctrine of the State of Innocence applied.

USE I. For information. This shews us, (1.) That not God, but man himself, was the cause of his ruin. God made him upright; his Creator set him up, but he threw himself down. Was the Lord's directing and inclining him to good, the reason of his woeful choice? Or did heaven deal so sparingly with him, that his pressing wants sent him to hell to seek supply? Nay, man was, and is the cause of his own ruin. (2.) God may most justly require of men perfect obedience to his law, and condemn them for their not obeying it perfectly, though now they have no ability to keep it. In so doing, he gathers but where he has strawed. He gave man ability to keep the whole law; man has lost it by his own fault: but his sin could never take away that right which God hath, to exact perfect obedience of his creature, and to punish in case of disobedience. (3.) Behold here the infinite obligation we lie under to Jesus Christ, the second Adam, who with his own precious blood has bought our freedom, and freely makes offer of it again to us, Hos. xiii. 9. and that with the advantage of everlasting security, that it can never be altogether lost any more, John x. 28, 29. Free grace will fix those whom free-will shook down into a gulf of misery.

USE II. This conveys a reproof to three sorts of persons. (1.) To those who hate religion, in the power of it, wherever it appears; and can take pleasure in nothing but in the world, and their lusts. Surely those men are far from righteousness: they are haters of God, Rom. i. 30. for they are haters of his image. Upright Adam in Paradise would have been a great eye-sore to all such persons; as he was to the serpent, whose seed they prove themselves to be, by their malignity. (2.) It reproves those who put religion to shame, and those who are ashamed of religion, before a graceless world. There is a generation, who make so bold with the God who made them, and can in a moment crush them, that they ridicule piety, and make a mock at seriousness. *Against whom do ye sport yourselves? Against whom make ye a wide mouth, and draw out the tongue?* Isa. lvii. 4. Is it not against God himself, whose image, in some measure restored to some of his creatures, makes them fools in your eyes? *But be ye not mockers, lest your bands be made strong*, Isa. xxviii. 22. Holiness was the glory which God put on man when he made him: but now the sons of men turn that glory into shame, because they themselves glory in their shame. There are others that secretly approve of religion, and in religious company will profess it; who, at other times, to be neighbour-like, are ashamed to own it: so weak are they, that they are blown over with the wind of the wicked's mouth. A broad laughter, an impious jest, a scoffing jeer out of a profane mouth, is, to many, an unanswerable argument against religion and seriousness; for, in the cause of religion, they are as silly doves without heart: O! that such would consider that weighty word, Mark viii. 38. *Whosoever, therefore, shall be ashamed of me, and of my words, in this adulterous and sinful generation, of him also shall the Son of Man be ashamed, when he cometh in the glory of his Father, with the holy angels.* (3.) It reproves the proud self-conceited professor, who admires himself in a garment of rags, which he hath patched together. There are many who, when once they have gathered some scraps of knowledge of religion, and have attained to some reformation of life, swell big with conceit of themselves; a sad sign that the effects of the fall lie so heavy upon them, that they have not as yet come to themselves, Luke xv. 17. They have eyes behind, to see their attainments; but no eyes within, no eyes before, to see their wants, which would surely humble them: for true knowledge makes men to see, both what once they were, and what they are at present; and so is humbling, and will not suffer them to be content with any meafure of grace attained; but inclines them to prefs forward, forgetting the things that are behind, Phil. iii. 13, 14. But thofe men are fuch a fpectacle of commiferation, as one would be that had fet his palace on fire, and were glorying in a cottage which he had built for himfelf out of the rubbifh, though fo very weak, that it could not ftand againft a ftorm.

Use III. Of lamentation. Here was a ftately building; man like a fair palace, but now lying in afhes: let us ftand and look on the ruins, and drop a tear. This is a lamentation, and fhall be for lamentation. Could we avoid weeping, if we faw our country ruined, and turned by the enemy into a wildernefs? if we faw our houfes on fire, and our property perifhing in the flames? But all this comes far fhort of the difmal fight; Man fallen as a ftar from heaven! Ah! may we not now fay, *O that we were as in months paft!* when there was no ftain in our nature, no cloud on our minds, no pollution in our hearts *! Had we never been in better cafe, the matter had been lefs: but they that were brought up in fcarlet, do now embrace dunghills. Where is our primitive glory now? once no darknefs in the mind, no rebellion in the will, no diforder in the affections. But ah! *How is the faithful city become an harlot? righteoufnefs lodged in it; but now murderers. Our filver is become drofs, our wine mixed with water.* That heart which was once the temple of God, is now turned into a den of thieves. Let our name be Ichabod, for the glory is departed. Happy waft thou, O man! who was like unto thee! no pain, no ficknefs could affect thee, no death could approach thee, no figh was

* The author means this as the language of thofe who have nothing but the fall and its mifery in view. But the believer in Chrift may fay, *My lines are fallen to me in pleafant places,* Pfal. xvi. 5, 6. I am now more exalted than I fhould have been, had I retained my primitive innocency: for though a finner by nature and practice, and, while I continue on earth, fubject to the confequent miferies of fin, yet I am bone of his bone, and flefh of his flefh, who is God over all, blefled for ever. Had I kept my firft ftate, I fhould have had only my own righteoufnefs; now I have the righteoufnefs of God, and his Spirit as my portion and eternal inheritance.

heard from thee, till thefe bitter fruits were plucked from the forbidden tree. Heaven fhone upon thee, and earth fmiled: thou waft the companion of angels, and the envy of devils. But how low is he now laid, who was created for dominion, and made lord of the world! *The crown is fallen from our head: wo unto us that we have finned.* The creatures that waited to do him fervice, are now, fince the fall, fet in battle array againft him; and the leaft of them, having commiffion, proves too hard for him. Waters overflow the old world; fire confumes Sodom; the ftars in their courfes fight againft Sifera; frogs, flies, lice, &c. turn executioners to Pharaoh and his Egyptians; worms eat up Herod: yea, man needs a league with the beafts, yea, with the very ftones of the field, Job v. 23. having reafon to fear that every one that findeth him will flay him. Alas! how are we fallen! how are we plunged into a gulf of mifery! The fun has gone down on us; death has come in at our windows; our enemies have put out our two eyes, and fport themfelves with our miferies. Let us then lie down in the duft; let fhame and confufion cover us. Neverthelefs, there is hope in Ifrael concerning this thing. Come then, O finner! look to Jefus Chrift, the fecond Adam: quit the firft Adam, and his covenant; come over to the Mediator and Surety of the new and better covenant; and let your hearts fay, *Be thou our ruler, and let this breach be under thy hand.* Let your *eye trickle down, and ceafe not, without any intermiffion, till the Lord look down, and behold from heaven,* Lam. iii. 49, 50.

STATE II.

NAMELY,

The STATE of NATURE, or of ENTIRE DEPRAVITY.

HEAD I.
The SINFULNESS of MAN's Natural State.

GENESIS vi. 5.

And God saw that the wickedness of man was great in the earth, and that every imagination of the thoughts of his heart was only evil continually.

WE have seen what man was, as God made him; a lovely and happy creature: let us view him now, as he hath unmade himself; and we shall see him a sinful and miserable creature. This is the sad state we were brought into by the fall; a state as black and doleful as the former was glorious: and this we commonly call, *The state of nature*, or, *Man's natural state*, according to that of the apostle, Eph. ii. 3. *And were by nature the children of wrath, even as others.* And herein two things are to be considered: 1*st*, The *sinfulness*; 2*dly*, The *misery* of this state, in which all the unregenerate live. I begin with the *sinfulness* of man's natural state, whereof the text gives us a full, though short account; *And God saw that the wickedness of man was great*, &c.

The scope and design of these words are to clear God's justice in bringing the flood on the old world. There are two particular causes taken notice of in the preceding verses. (1.) Mixed marriages, ver. 2. *The sons of God*, the posterity of Seth and Enos, professors of the true religion, married with *the daughters of men*, the profane curſed race of Cain. They did not carry the matter before the Lord, that he might chuſe for them, Pſalm xlviii. 4. But without any reſpect to the will of God, they choſe not according to the rules of their faith, but of their fancy; they *ſaw that they were fair:* and their marriage with them occaſioned their divorce from God. This was one of the cauſes of the deluge, which ſwept away the old world. Would to God that all profeſſors in our day could plead not guilty: but though that ſin brought on the deluge, yet the deluge hath not ſwept away that ſin; which, as of old, ſo in our day, may juſtly be looked upon as one of the cauſes of the decay of religion. It was an ordinary thing among the Pagans, to change their gods, as they changed their condition into a married lot: many ſad inſtances the Chriſtian world affords of the ſame, as if people were of Pharaoh's opinion, That religion is only for thoſe that have no other care upon their heads, Exod. v. 17. (2.) Great oppreſſion, ver. 4. *There were giants in the earth in thoſe days,* men of great ſtature, great ſtrength, and monſtrous wickedneſs, *filling of the earth with violence,* ver. 11. But neither their ſtrength, nor treaſures of wickedneſs, could profit them in the day of wrath. Yet the gain of oppreſſion ſtill carries many over the terror of this dreadful example. Thus much for the connexion, and what particular crimes that generation was guilty of. But every perſon that was ſwept away with the flood could not be guilty of theſe things; and ſhall not the Judge of all the earth do right? Therefore, in my text, there is a general indictment drawn up againſt them all, *The wickedneſs of man was great in the earth,* &c. and clearly proved, for God *ſaw it.* Two things are here laid to their charge.

Firſt, Corruption of life, *wickedneſs, great wickedneſs.* I underſtand this of the wickedneſs of their lives; for it is plainly diſtinguiſhed from the wickedneſs of their hearts. The ſins of their outward converſation were great in the nature of them, and greatly aggravated by their attendant circumſtances: and this not only among thoſe of the race of curſed Cain, but thoſe of holy

Seth ; the wickedness of man was great. And then it is added, *in the earth:* (1.) To vindicate God's feverity, in that he not only cut off finners, but defaced the beauty of the earth, and fwept off the brute creatures from it, by the deluge ; that as men had fet the marks of their impiety, God might fet the marks of his indignation on the earth. (2.) To fhew the heinoufnefs of their fin, in making the earth, which God had fo adorned for the ufe of man, a fink of fin, and a ftage whereon to act their wickednefs, in defiance of heaven. God faw the corruption of life ; he not only knew it, and took notice of it ; but he made them to know that he took notice of it, and that he had not forfaken the earth, though they had forfaken heaven.

Secondly, Corruption of nature, *Every imagination of the thoughts of his heart was only evil continually.* All their wicked practifes are here traced to the fountain and spring-head : a corrupt heart was the fource of all. The foul, which was made upright in all its faculties, is now wholly difordered. The heart, that was made according to God's own heart, is now the reverfe of it, a forge of evil imaginations, a fink of inordinate affections, and a ftore-houfe of all impiety, Mark vii. 21, 22. Behold the heart of the natural man, as it is opened in our text ! The mind is defiled ; the thoughts of the heart are evil ; the will and affections are defiled ; the imagination of the thoughts of the hearts, (*i. e.* whatfoever the heart frameth within itfelf by thinking, fuch as judgement, choice, purpofes, devices, defires, every inward motion,) or rather, the frame of thoughts of the heart (namely, the frame, make, or mould of thefe, 1 Chron. xxix. 18.) is evil. Yea, and ever imagination, every frame of his thoughts, is fo. The heart is ever framing fomething ; but never one right thing : the frame of thoughts in the heart of man is exceeding various ; yet are they never caft into a right frame. But is there not, at leaft, a mixture of good in them ? No, they are only evil ; there is nothing in them truly good, and acceptable to God : nor can any thing be fo that comes out of that forge ; where not the Spirit of God, but the prince of the

Head I. *The Explanation of the Text* 25

power of the air worketh, Eph. ii. 2. whatever changes may be found in them, are only from evil to evil: for the imagination of the heart, or frame of thoughts, in natural men, is evil continually, or every day. From the firſt day to the laſt day in this ſtate, they are in mid-night darkneſs; there is not a glimmering of the light of holineſs. in them: not one holy thought can ever be produced by the unholy heart. O what a vile heart is this! O what a corrupt nature is this! The tree that always brings forth fruit, but never good fruit, whatever ſoil it be ſet in, whatever pains be taken with it, muſt naturally be an evil tree: and what can that heart be, whereof every imagination, every ſet of thoughts, is only evil, and that continually? Surely that corruption is engrained in our hearts, inter-woven with our very natures, has ſunk into the marrow of our ſouls, and will never be cured but by a miracle of grace. Now, ſuch is man's heart, ſuch is his nature, till regenerating grace change it. God, that ſearcheth the heart, ſaw man's heart was ſo, he took ſpecial notice of it: and the faithful and true witneſs cannot miſtake our caſe; though we are moſt apt to miſtake ourſelves in this point, and generally overlook it.

Beware that there be not a thought in thy wicked heart, ſaying, What is that to us? Let that generation of whom the text ſpeaks ſee to that. For the Lord has left the caſe of that generation on record, to be a looking-glaſs to all after-generations; wherein they may ſee their own corruption of heart, and what their lives would be too, if he reſtrained them not: for, *as in water face anſwereth to face, ſo the heart of man to man*, Prov. xxvii. 19. Adam's fall has framed all men's hearts alike in this matter. Hence the apoſtle, Rom. iii. 10—18. proves the corruption of the nature, hearts, and lives of all men, from what the Pſalmiſt ſays of the wicked in his day, Pſal. xiv. 1, 2, 3. Pſal. v. 9. Pſal. cxl. 3. Pſal. x. 7. Pſal. xxxvi. 1. and from what Jeremiah ſaith of the wicked in his day, Jer. ix. 3. and from what Iſaiah ſays of thoſe that lived in his time, Iſa. lvii. 7, 8. and concludes, ver. 19. *Now we know, what things ſoever the law ſaith, it ſaith to them who are* under the law: *that every mouth may be stopped, and all the world may become guilty before God.* Had the history of the deluge been transmitted unto us, without the reason thereof in the text, we might from thence have gathered the corruption and total depravity of man's nature: for what other quarrel could the holy and just God have, with the infants that were destroyed by the flood, seeing they had no actual sin? If we saw a wise man, who having made a curious piece of work, and heartily approved of it when he gave it out of his hand, as fit for the use it was designed for, rise up in wrath, and break it all in pieces, when he looked on it afterwards; should we not thence conclude, that the frame of it had been quite marred, since it came out of his hand, and that it does not serve for the use it was at first designed for? How much more, when we see the holy and wise God destroying the work of his own hands, once solemnly pronounced by him *very good*, may we not conclude, that the original frame thereof is utterly marred, that it cannot be mended, but must needs be new-made, or lost altogether? Gen. vi. 6, 7. *It repented the Lord that he had made man on the earth, and it grieved him at his heart: and the Lord said, I will destroy man,* or blot him out; as a man doth a sentence out of a book, that cannot be corrected, by cutting off some letters, syllables, or words, and interlining others here and there; but must needs be wholly new-framed. But did the deluge carry off this corruption of man's nature? Did it mend the matter? No, it did not. God, in his holy providence, *that every mouth may be stopped, and all the new world may become guilty before God,* as well as the old, permits that corruption of nature to break out in Noah, the father of the new world, after the deluge was over. Behold him, as another Adam, sinning in the fruit of a tree, Gen. ix. 20, 21. *He planted a vineyard, and he drank of the wine, and was drunken, and he was uncovered within his tent.* More than that, God gives the same reason against a new deluge, which he gives in our text, for bringing that on the old world: *I will not* (saith he) *again curse the ground any more for man' sake, for the imagination of man's heart*

Head I. *The Explanation of the Text.*

is evil from his youth, Gen. viii. 21. whereby it is intimated, that there is no mending of the matter by this means; and that if he should always take the same course with men that he had done, he would be always sending deluges on the earth, seeing the corruption of man's nature remains still. But though the flood could not carry off the corruption of nature, yet it pointed at the way how it is to be done; to wit, that men must be born of water and of the Spirit, raised from spiritual death in sin, by the grace of Jesus Christ, who came by water and blood; out of which a new world of saints arise in regeneration, even as the new world of sinners out of the waters, where they had long laid buried (as it were) in the ark. This we learn from 1 Pet. iii. 20, 21 where the apostle, speaking of Noah's ark, saith, *Wherein few, that is, eight souls, were saved in water: the like figure whereunto even baptism doth also now save us.* Now the waters of the deluge being a like figure to baptism, it planly follows, that they signified (as baptism doth) the washing of regeneration, and renewing of the Holy Ghost. To conclude, then, those waters, though now dried up, may serve us still for a looking-glass, in which we may see the total corruption of our nature, and the necessity of regeneration.

From the text, thus explained, ariseth this weighty point of doctrine, which he that runs may read in it, *viz.* Man's nature is now wholly corrupted. There is a sad alteration, a wonderful overturn, in the nature of man: where, at first, there was nothing evil, now there is nothing good. In prosecuting this doctrine, I shall,

First, Confirm it.
Secondly, Represent this corruption of nature in its several parts.
Thirdly, Shew you how man's nature comes to be thus corrupted.
Lastly, Make application.

That Man's Nature is corrupted.

First, I am to confirm the doctrine of the corruption of nature; to hold the glass to your eyes, wherein you may see your sinful nature; which, though God takes particular notice of, many quite overlook. Here we shall consult, 1. God's works. 2. Men's experience and observation.

I. For Scripture-proof, let us consider,

First, How the Scripture takes particular notice of fallen Adam's communicating his image to his posterity, Gen. v. 3. *Adam begat a son in his own likeness, after his image, and called his name Seth.* Compare with this ver. 1. of that chapter, *In the day that God created man, in the likeness of God made he him.* Behold here, how the image after which man was made, and the image after which he is begotten, are opposed! Man was created in the likeness of God: that is, the holy and righteous God made a holy and righteous creature: but fallen Adam begat a son, not in the likeness of God, but in his own likeness; that is, corrupt sinful Adam begat a corrupt sinful son. For as the image of God bore righteousness and immortality in it, as was shewn before; so this image of fallen Adam bore corruption and death in it, 1 Cor. xv. 49, 50. compare ver. 22. Moses in the fifth chapter of Genesis, giving us the first bill of mortality that ever was in the world, ushers it in with this, that dying Adam begat mortals. Having sinned, he became mortal, according to the threatening; and so he begat a son in his own likeness, sinful, therefore mortal. Thus sin and death passed on all. Doubtless he begat both Cain and Abel in his own likeness, as well as Seth. But it is not recorded of Abel, because he left no issue behind him, and his falling the first sacrifice to death in the world, was a sufficient document of it: nor of Cain, to whom it might have been thought peculiar, because of his monstrous wickedness; and, besides, his posterity was drowned in the flood: but it is recorded of Seth, because he was the father of the holy seed; and from him all mankind, since the flood, has descended, and fallen Adam's own likeness with them.

Secondly, It appears from that text of Scripture, Job xiv. 4. *Who can bring a clean thing out of an unclean? not one.* Our first parents were unclean, how then can we

Head I. *Man's Nature corrupted, proved.* 29

be clean? How could our immediate parents be clean? how can our children be so? The uncleanness here aimed at, is a sinful uncleanness; for it is such as makes man's days full of trouble: and it is natural, being derived from unclean parents: *Man is born of a woman,* ver. 1. *And how can he be clean that is born of a woman?* Job xxv. 4. The omnipotent God, whose power is not here challenged, could bring a clean thing out of an unclean; and did so, in the case of the man Christ: but no other being can. Every person that is born, according to the course of nature, is born unclean. If the root be corrupt, so must the branches be. Neither is the matter mended, though the parents be sanctified ones: for they are but holy in part, and that by grace, not by nature; and they beget their children as men, not as holy men. Wherefore, as the circumcised parent begets an uncircumcised child; and after the purest grain is sown, we reap corn with the chaff; so the holiest parents beget unholy children, and cannot communicate their grace to them, as they do their nature; which many godly parents find true in their sad experience.

Thirdly, Consider the confession of the Psalmist David, Psal. lvi. 5. *Behold I was shapen in iniquity, and in sin did my mother conceive me.* Here he ascends from his actual sin, to the fountain of it, namely, corrupt nature. He was a man according to God's own heart; but from the beginning it was not so with him. He was begotten in lawful marriage: but when the lump was shapen in the womb, it was a sinful lump. Hence the corruption of nature is called the *old man*; being as old as ourselves, older than grace, even in those that are sanctified from the womb.

Fourthly, Hear our Lord's determination of the point, John iii. 8. *That which is born of the flesh is flesh.* Behold the universal corruption of mankind—all are flesh! Not that all are frail, though that is a sad truth too; yea, and our natural frailty is an evidence of our natural corruption; but that's not the sense of this text: the meaning of it is,—all are corrupt and sinful, and that naturally: hence our Lord argues, that because they are flesh, therefore they must be born again, or else they cannot enter into the kingdom of God, ver. 3. 5. And as the corruption of our nature evidenceth the absolute necessity of regeneration; so the absolute necessity of regeneration plainly proves the corruption of our nature; for why should a man need a second birth, if his nature were not quite marred in his first birth? Infants must be born again; for that is an exception, John iii. 3. which admits of no exception. Therefore they were circumcised under the Old Testament; as having the body of the sins of the flesh (which is conveyed to them by natural generation) to put off, Col. ii. 11. And now, by the appointment of Jesus Christ, they are to be baptized; which says they are unclean, and that there is no salvation for them, but by the washing of regeneration, and renewing of the Holy Ghost, Tit. iii. 5.

Fifthly, Man certainly is sunk very low now, in comparison of what he once was. God made him but a little lower than the angels; but now we find him likened to the beasts that perish. He hearkened to a brute, and is now become like one of them. Like Nebuchadnezzar, his portion (in his natural state) is with the beasts, minding only earthly things, Phil. iii. 19. Nay, brutes, in some sort, have the advantage of the natural man, who is sunk a degree below them. He is more witless, in what concerns him most, than the stork, or the turtle, or the crane, or the swallow, in what is for their interest, Jer. viii. 7. He is more stupid than the ox or the ass, Isa. i. 3. I find him sent to school, to learn of the ant, which has no guide or leader to go before her; no overseer or officer to compel or stir her up to work; no ruler, but may do as she lists, being under the dominion of none; yet provideth her meat in the summer and harvest, Prov. vi. 6, 7, 8. while the natural man has all these, and yet exposeth himself to eternal starving. Nay, more than all this, the Scripture holds out the natural man, not only as wanting the good qualities of those creatures, but as a compound of the evil qualities of the worst of the creatures; in whom the fierceness of the lion, the craft of the fox, the unteachableness of the wild ass, the filthiness of the dog and swine, the poison of the asp, and such like, meet. Truth

Head I. *Man's Nature corrupted, proved.*

itself calls them *serpents, a generation of vipers*; yea, more, even *children of the devil*, Mat. xxiii. 33. John viii. 44. Surely, then, man's nature is miserably corrupted.

Lastly, *We are by nature children of wrath*, Eph. ii. 3. We are worthy of, and liable to the wrath of God; and this by nature: therefore, doubtless, we are by nature sinful creatures. We are condemned before we have done good or evil: under the curse, before we know what it is. *But will a lion roar in the forest, while he hath no prey?* Amos iii. 4. that is, will the holy and just God roar in his wrath against man, if he be not, by his sin, made a prey for his wrath? No, he will not, he cannot. Let us conclude, then, that, according to the word of God, man's nature is a corrupt nature.

II. If we consult experience, and observe the case of the world, in those things that are obvious to any person who will not shut his eyes against clear light, we shall quickly perceive such fruits as discover this root of bitterness. I shall propose a few things, that may serve to convince us in this point.

First, Who sees not a flood of miseries overflowing the world? Whither can a man go, where he shall not dip his foot, if he go not over head and ears in it? Every one, at home and abroad, in city and country, in palaces and cottages, is groaning under some one thing or other ungrateful to him. Some are oppressed with poverty, some chastened with sickness and pain, some are lamenting their losses; none wants a cross of one sort or another. No man's condition is so soft, but there is some thorn of uneasiness in it. At length death, the wages of sin, comes after these, its harbingers, and sweeps all away. Now, what but sin has opened the sluice? There is not a complaint or sigh heard in the world, nor a tear that falls from our eye, but it is an evidence that man is fallen as a star from heaven; for God distributeth sorrows in his anger, Job xxi. 17. This is a plain proof of the corruption of nature: forasmuch as those that have not yet actually sinned, have their share of these sorrows; yea, and draw their first breath in the world weeping, as if they knew this world, at first sight, to be a Bochim, the place of weepers.

There are graves of the smallest, as well as of the greatest size, in the church-yard; and there are never wanting some in the world, who, like Rachel, are weeping for their children, because they are not, Matth. ii. 18.

Secondly, Observe how early this corruption of nature begins to appear in young ones. Solomon observes, that *even a child is known by his doings*, Prov. xx. 11. It may soon be discerned what way the bias of the heart lies. Do not the children of fallen Adam, before they can go alone, follow their father's footsteps? What a vast deal of little pride, ambition, curiosity, vanity, wilfulness, and averseness to good, appears in them? And, when they creep out of infancy, there is a necessity of using the rod of correction, to drive away the foolishness that is bound in their hearts, Prov. xxii. 15. which shews, that, if grace prevail not, the child will be as Ishmael, *a wild ass-man*, as the word is, Gen. xvi. 12.

Thirdly, Take a view of the manifold gross out-breakings of sin in the world: the wickedness of man is yet great in the earth. Behold the bitter fruits of the corruption of our nature, Hos. iv. 2. "By swearing, and lying, and killing, and stealing, and committing adultery, they break out (like the breaking forth of waters) and blood toucheth blood." The world is filled with filthiness, and all manner of lewdness, wickedness, and profanity. From whence comes the deluge of sin on the earth, but from the breaking up of the fountains of the great deep, the heart of man; out of which proceed evil thoughts, adulteries, fornications, murders, thefts, covetousness, &c. Mark vii. 21, 22. Ye will, it may be, thank God with a whole heart, that ye are not like other men; and indeed ye have more reason for it than, I fear, ye are aware of; for, as in water face answereth face, so the heart of man to man, Prov. xxvii. 19. As, looking into clear water, ye see your own face; so looking into your heart, ye may see other men's there: and looking into other men's, in them ye may see your own. So that the most vile and profane wretches that are in the world, should serve you for a looking-glass; in which you ought to discern the corruption of your own nature: and if you were to do so, ye would,

Head I. *Man's Nature corrupted, proved.*

with a heart truly touched, thank God, and not yourselves, indeed, that ye are not as other men in your lives; seeing the corruption of nature is the same in you as in them.

Fourthly, Cast your eye upon these terrible convulsions which the world is thrown into by the lusts of men. Lions make not a prey of lions, nor wolves of wolves; but men are turned wolves to one another, biting and devouring one another. Upon how slight occasions will men sheath their swords in one another's bowels? The world is a wilderness, where the clearest fire which men can carry about with them will not fright away the wild beasts that inhabit it (and because they are men, and not brutes), but one way or other they will be wounded. Since Cain shed the blood of Abel, the earth has been turned into a slaughter-house; and the chase has been continued since Nimrod began his hunting; on the earth, as in the sea, the greater still devouring the lesser. When we see the world in such a ferment, every one stabbing another with words or swords, we may conclude there is an evil spirit among them. These violent heats among Adam's sons, speak the whole body to be distempered, the whole head to be sick, and the whole heart faint: they surely proceed from an inward cause, James vi. 1. lusts that war in our members.

Fifthly, Consider the necessity of human laws, fenced with terrors and severities; to which we may apply what the apostle says, 1 Tim. i. 9. That *the law is not made for a righteous man, but for the lawless and disobedient, for the ungodly and for sinners,* &c. Man was made for society; and God himself said of the first man, when he had created him, that it was *not meet he should be alone:* yet the case is such now, that in society he must be hedged in with thorns. And that from hence we may the better see the corruption of man's nature, consider, (1.) Every man naturally loves to be at full liberty, to have his own will for his law; and if he were to follow his natural inclinations, he would vote himself out of the reach of all laws, divine and human. Hence some (the power of whose hands has been answerable to the natural inclination) have indeed made themselves abso-

F

lute, and above laws; agreeable to man's monſtrous deſign at firſt, to be as gods, Gen. iii. 5. Yet, (2.) There is no man that would willingly adventure to live in a lawleſs ſociety: therefore, even pirates and robbers have laws among themſelves, though the whole ſociety caſts off all reſpect to law and right. Thus men diſcover themſelves to be conſcious of the corruption of nature; not daring to truſt one another, but upon ſecurity. (3.) How dangerous ſoever it is to break through the hedge, yet the violence of luſts makes many daily adventure to run the riſk. They will not only ſacrifice their credit and conſcience, which laſt is lightly eſteemed in the world; but for the pleaſure of a few moments, immediately ſucceeded with terror from within, they will lay themſelves open to a violent death, by the laws of the land wherein they live. (4.) The laws are often made to yield to men's luſts. Sometimes whole ſocieties run into ſuch extravagancies, that, like a company of priſoners, they break off their fetters, and put their guard to flight; and the voice of laws cannot be heard for the noiſe of arms. And ſeldom is there a time wherein there are not ſome perſons ſo great and daring, that the laws dare not look their impetuous luſts in the face; which made David ſay, in the caſe of Joab, who had murdered Abner, *Theſe men, the ſons of Zeruiah, be too hard for me*, 2 Sam. iii. 39. Luſts ſometimes grow too ſtrong for laws, ſo that the law is ſlacked, as the pulſe of a dying man, Hab. i. 3, 4. (5.) Conſider what neceſſity often appears of amending old laws, and making new ones; which have their riſe from new crimes, that man's nature is very fruitful of. There would be no need of mending the hedge, if men were not like unruly beaſts, ſtill breaking it down. It is aſtoniſhing to ſee what a figure the Iſraelites, who were ſeparated unto God from among all the nations of the earth, make in their hiſtory: what horrible confuſions were among them, when there was no king in Iſrael? as you may ſee from the 18th to the 21ſt chapter of Judges: how hard it was to reform them, when they had the beſt of magiſtrates! and how quickly they turned aſide again, when they got wicked rulers! I cannot but think, that one grand design of that sacred history, was to discover the corruption of man's nature, the absolute need of the Messiah, and his grace; and that we ought, in the reading of it, to improve it to that end. How cutting is that word which the Lord has to Samuel concerning Saul, 1 Sam. ix. 17. *The same shall reign over* (or, as the word is, *shall restrain*) *my people?* O the corruption of man's nature! The awe and dread of the God of heaven restrains them not; but they must have gods on earth to do it, to put them to shame, Judges xviii. 7.

Sixthly, Consider the remains of natural corruption in the saints. Though grace has entered, yet corruption is not expelled; though they have got the new creature, yet the old corrupt nature remains: and these struggle together within them, as the twins in Rebekah's womb, Gal. v. 17. They find it present with them at all times, and in all places, even in the most retired corners. It a man has an ill neighbour, he may remove; if he has an ill servant, he may put him away; if a bad yoke-fellow, he may sometimes leave the house, and be free of molestation that way: but should the saint go into a wilderness, or set up his tent in some remote rock in the sea, where never foot of man, beast, nor fowl, had touched, there will it be with him. Should he be, with Paul, caught up to the third heavens, it will come back with him, 2 Cor. xii. 7. It follows him, as the shadow doth the body: it makes a blot in the fairest line which he can draw. It is like the fig-tree on the wall, which how nearly soever it was cut, yet it still grew, till the wall was thrown down: for the roots of it are fixed in the heart, while the saint is in the world, as with bands of iron and brass. It is especially active when he would do good, Rom. vii. 21. then the fowls come down upon the carcases. Hence often in holy duties, the spirit of a saint (as it were) evaporates; and he is left before he is aware, like Michal, with an image in the bed instead of an husband. I need not stand to prove to the godly, - the corruption of nature in them; for they groan under it; and to prove it to them, were to hold out a candle to let them see the sun: as for the wicked, they are ready to account mole-hills in the saints as big as mountains; if not to reckon them all hypocrites. But consider thefe few things on this head. (1.) If it be thus in the green tree, how muft it be in the dry? The faints are not born faints; but made fo by the power of regenerating grace. Have they got a new nature, and yet the old remains with them? How great muft that corruption be in others, in whom there is no grace. (2.) The faints groan under it as a heavy burden: hear the apoftle, Rom. vii. 24. *O wretched man that I am! who shall deliver me from the body of this death!* What though the carnal man lives at eafe and quiet, and the corruption of nature is not his burden; is he therefore free from it? No, no; it is becaufe he is dead, that he feels not the finking weight. Many a groan is heard from a fick-bed; but never any from a grave. In the faint, as in the fick man, there is a mighty ftruggle; life and death ftriving for the maftery: but in the natural man, as in the dead corps, there is no noife; becaufe death bears full fway. (3.) The godly man refifts the old corrupt nature; he ftrives to mortify it, yet it remains; he endeavours to ftarve it, and by that means to weaken it, yet it is active: how muft it fpread, then, and ftrengthen itfelf in that foul, where it is not ftarved, but fed! And this is the cafe of all the unregenerate, who make provifion for the flefh, to fulfil the lufts thereof. If the garden of the diligent afford him new work daily, in cutting off and rooting up; furely that of the fluggard muft needs be all grown over with thorns.

Laftly, I fhall add but one obfervation more, and that is, that in every man naturally the image of fallen Adam appears. Some children, by their features, and lineaments of their face, do, as it were, father themfelves: and thus we refemble our firft parents. Every one of us bears the image and impreffions of their fall: and to evince the truth of this, I appeal to the confciences of all, in the following particulars.

Firft, Is not finful curiofity natural to us? And is not this a print of Adam's image? Gen. iii. 6. Is not man naturally much more defirous to know new things, than to practife old known truths? How much like old Adam we look in this, itching after novelties, and difrelifhing old folid doctrines! We feek after knowledge rather than holinefs; and ftudy moft to know thofe things which are leaft edifying. Our wild and roving fancies need a bridle to curb them, while good folid affections muft be quickened and fpurred up.

Secondly, If the Lord, by his holy law and wife providence, puts a reftraint upon us, to keep us back from any thing, doth not that reftraint whet the edge of our natural inclinations, and make us fo much the keener in our defires? And in this do we not betray it plainly, that we are Adam's children? Gen. iii. 2, 3. 6. I think this cannot be denied; for daily obfervation evinceth, that it is a natural principle, *that ftolen waters are fweet, and bread eaten in fecret is pleafant*, Prov. ix. 17. The very heathens were convinced, that man was poffeffed with this fpirit of contradiction, though they knew not the fpring of it. How often do men let themfelves loofe in thofe things, in which, if God had left them at liberty, they would have bound up themfelves! but corrupt nature takes a pleafure in the very jumping over the hedge. And is it not a repeating of our father's folly, that men will rather climb for forbidden fruit, than gather what is fhaken off the tree of good providence to them, when they have God's exprefs allowance for it.

Thirdly, Which of all the children of Adam is not naturally difpofed to hear the inftruction that caufeth to err? And was not this the rock our firft parents fplit upon? Gen. iii. 4. 6. How apt is weak man, ever fince that time, to parley with temptations! *God fpeaketh once, yea twice, yet man perceiveth it not*, Job xxxiii. 14. But readily liftens to Satan. Men might often come fair off, if they would difmifs temptations with abhorrence, when firft they appear; if they would nip them in the bud, they would foon die away: but, alas! though we fee the train laid for us, and the fire put to it, yet we ftand till it run along, and we are blown up with its force.

Fourthly, Do not the eyes in your head often blind the eyes of the mind? Was not this the very cafe of our firft parents? Gen. iii. 6. Man is never more blind than when he is looking on the objects that are moſt pleaſing to ſenſe. Ever ſince the eyes of our firſt parents were opened to the forbidden fruit, men's eyes have been the gates of deſtruction to their ſouls; at which impure imaginations and ſinful deſires have entered the heart, to the wounding of the ſoul, waſting of the conſcience, and bringing diſmal effects ſometimes on whole ſocieties, as in Achan's caſe, Joſh. vii. 21. Holy Job was aware of this danger, from theſe two little rowling bodies, which a very ſmall ſplinter of wood will make uſeleſs; ſo that (with the king who durſt not, with his ten thouſand, meet him that came with twenty thouſand againſt him, Luke xiv. 31, 32.) he ſendeth and deſireth conditions of peace. Job xxxi. 1. *I have made a covenant with mine eyes*, &c.

Fifthly, Is it not natural to us, to care for the body, even at the expence of the ſoul? This was one ingredient in the ſin of our firſt parents, Gen. iii. 6. O how happy might we be, if we were but at half the pains about our ſouls that we beſtow on our bodies! if this queſtion, *What muſt I do to be ſaved?* (Acts xvi. 30.) ran but near as oft through our minds as theſe queſtions do, *What ſhall we eat? what ſhall we drink? wherewithal ſhall we be cloathed?* (Matt. vi. 31.) many a (now) hopeleſs caſe would become very hopeful. But the truth is, moſt men live as if they were nothing but a lump of fleſh: or as if their ſoul ſerved for no other uſe but, like ſalt, to keep the body from corrupting. They are fleſh, John iii. 6. They mind the things of the fleſh, Rom. viii. 5. and they live after the fleſh, ver. 13. If the conſent of the fleſh be got to an action, the conſent of the conſcience is rarely waited for: yea, the body is often ſerved, when the conſcience has entered a diſſent againſt it.

Sixthly, Is not every one, by nature, diſcontented with his preſent lot in the world, or with ſome one thing or other in it? This was alſo Adam's caſe, Gen. iii. 5, 6. Some one thing is always wanting; ſo that man is a creature given to changes. If any doubt this let them look over all their enjoyments; and after a review of them, liſten to their own hearts, and they will hear a secret murmuring for want of something; though, perhaps, if they considered the matter aright, they would see that it is better for them to want, than to have that something. Since the hearts of our first parents flew out at their eyes, on the forbidden fruit, and a night of darkness was thereby brought on the world, their posterity have a natural disease, which Solomon calls, *The wandering of the desire* (or, as the word is, *the walking of the soul*), Eccl. vi. 9. This is a sort of diabolical trance, wherein the soul traverseth the world; feeds itself with a thousand airy nothings; snatcheth at this and the other created excellency, in imagination and desire; goes here and there, and every where, except where it should go: and the soul is never cured of this disease, till conquering grace bring it back, to take up its everlasting rest in God, through Christ: but till this be, if man were set again in paradise, the garden of the Lord, all the pleasures there would not keep him from looking, yea, and leaping over the hedge a second time.

Seventhly, Are we not far more easily impressed and influenced by evil councils and examples, than by those that are good? You will see this was the ruin of Adam, Gen. iii. 6. evil example, to this day, is one of Satan's master-devices to ruin men. Though we have, by nature, more of the fox than of the lamb; yet that ill property which some observe in this creature, *viz.* that if one lamb skip into a water, the rest that are near will suddenly follow, may be observed also in the disposition of the children of men; to whom it is very natural to embrace an evil way, because they see others on it before them. Ill example has frequently the force of a violent stream, to carry us over plain duty; but, especially, if the example be given by those we bear a great affection to: our affection, in that case, blinds our judgment; and what we would abhor in others, is complied with to humour them. Nothing is more plain, than that generally men chuse rather to do what the most do, than what the best do.

Eighthly, Who of all Adam's sons needs to be taught the art of sewing fig-leaves together, to cover their nakedness? Gen. iii. 7. When we have ruined ourselves, and made ourfelves naked, to our fhame, we naturally feek to help ourfelves by ourfelves: many poor fhifts are fallen upon, as filly and infignificant as Adam's fig-leaves. What pains are men at, to cover their fin from their own confciences, and to draw all the fair colours upon it that they can! And when once convictions are faftened upon them, fo that they cannot but fee themfelves naked, it is as natural for them to attempt to fpin a cover to it out of their own bowels, as for fifh to fwim in water, or birds to fly in the air. Therefore, the firft queftion of the convinced is, *What fhall we do?* Acts ii. 27 How fhall we qualify ourfelves? What fhall we perform? Not confidering, that the new creature is God's own workmanfhip, (or deed, Eph. ii. 10.) more than Adam confidered and thought of, being cloathed with the fkins of facrifices, Gen. iii. 21.

Ninthly, Do not Adam's children naturally follow his footfteps, in hiding themfelves from the prefence of the Lord? Gen. iii. 8. We are every whit as blind in this matter as he was, who thought to hide himfelf from the prefence of God among the fhady trees of the garden. We are very apt to promife ourfelves more fecurity in a fecret fin, than in one that is openly committed. *The eye of the adulterer waiteth for the twilight, faying, No eye fhall fee me,* Job xxiv. 15. Men will freely do that in fecret, which they would be afhamed to do in the prefence of a child; as if darknefs could hide from the all-feeing God. Are we not naturally carelefs of communion with God? aye, and averfe to it? Never was there any communion between God and Adam's children, where the Lord himfelf had not the firft word. If he were to let them alone, they would never inquire after him. Ifa. lvii. 17. *I hid me.* Did he feek after a hiding God? Very far from it: *He went on in the way of his heart.*

Tenthly, How loth are men to confefs fin, to take guilt and fhame to themfelves? Was it not thus in the cafe before us? Gen. iii. 10. Adam confeffeth his nakednefs, which he could not get denied; but fays not one word of his fin: the reafon of it was, he would fain have hid it if he could. It is as natural for us to hide sin as to commit it. Many sad instances thereof we have in this world; but a far clearer proof of it we shall get at the day of judgement, the day in which God will judge the secrets of men, Rom. ii. 16. Many a foul mouth will then be seen, which is now wiped, and saith, I have done no wickedness, Prov. xxx. 20.

Lastly, Is it not natural for us to extenuate our sin, and transfer the guilt upon others? When God examined our guilty first parents, did not Adam lay the blame on the woman? and did not the woman lay the blame on the serpent? Gen. iii. 12, 13. Now Adam's children need not be taught this hellish policy; for before they can well speak (if they cannot get the fact denied) they will cunningly lisp out something to lessen their fault, and lay the blame upon another. Nay, so natural is this to men, that, in the greatest sins, they will lay the fault upon God himself; they will blaspheme his holy providence, under the mistaken name of misfortune, or ill-luck, and thereby lay the blame of their sin at Heaven's door. And was not this one of Adam's tricks after his fall? Gen. iii. 12. *And the man said, The woman whom thou gavest to be with me, she gave me of the tree, and I did eat.* Observe the order of the speech. He makes his apology, in the first place; and then comes his confession: his apology is long; but his confession very short; it is all comprehended in a word, *And I did eat.* How pointed and distinct is his apology, as if he was afraid his meaning should have been mistaken! *The woman*, says he; or *that woman*; as if he would have pointed the Judge to his own work, of which we read, Gen. ii. 22. There was but one woman then in the world; so that, one would think he needed not to have been so nice and exact in pointing at her: yet she is as carefully marked out, in his defence, as if there had been ten thousand: *The woman whom thou gavest me:* here he speaks as if he had been ruined with God's gift: and, to make the gift look the blacker, it is added to all this, *Thou gavest to be with me, as my constant companion, to stand by me as a helper.* This looks as if Adam would have fathered an ill design upon the Lord in giving him this gift. And, after all, there is a new demonstrative here, before the sentence is compleat: he says not, *the woman gave me*; but *the woman, she gave me*, emphatically; as if he had said, *she*, even *she* gave me of the tree. Thus much for his apology. But his confession is quickly over, in one word (as he spoke it) *and I did eat*. There is nothing here to point to himself, and as little to shew what he had eaten. How natural is this black art to Adam's posterity! He that runs may read it. So universally doth Solomon's observation hold true, Prov. xvi. 3. *The foolishness of man perverteth his way; and his heart fretteth against the Lord.* Let us then call fallen Adam Father; let us not deny the relation, seeing we bear his image.

To shut up this point, sufficiently confirmed by concurring evidence, from the Lord's word, our own experience, and observation. Let us be perswaded to believe the doctrine of the corruption of our nature; and to look to the Second Adam, the blessed Jesus, for the application of his precious blood, to remove the guilt of our sin; and for the efficacy of his holy Spirit, to make us new creatures, knowing, that except we be born again, we cannot enter into the kingdom of God.

Of the Corruption of the Understanding.

SECONDLY, I proceed to enquire into the *corruption of nature*, in the several parts thereof. But who can comprehend it? Who can take the exact dimensions of it, in its breadth, length, height, and depth? *The heart is deceitful above all things, and desperately wicked: who can know it?* Jer. xvii. 9. However, we may quickly perceive as much of it as may be matter of deepest humiliation, and may discover to us the absolute necessity of regeneration. Man, in his natural state, is altogether corrupt: both soul and body are polluted, as the apostle proves at large, Rom. iii. 10—18. As for the soul, this natural corruption has spread itself through all the faculties thereof; and is to be found in the *understanding*, the *will*, the *affections*, the *conscience*, and the *memory*.

I. The *understanding*, that leading faculty, is despoiled of its primitive glory, and covered over with con-

Head I. *Corruption of the Understanding.* 43

fusion. We have fallen into the hands of our grand adverſary, as Samſon into the hands of the Philiſtines, and are deprived of our two eyes. *There is none that underſtandeth,* Rom. iii. 11. *Mind and conſcience are defiled,* Tit. i. 15. The natural man's apprehenſion of divine things is corrupt, Pſal. l. 21. *Thou thoughteſt that I was altogether ſuch an one as thyſelf.* His judgment is corrupt, and cannot be otherwiſe, ſeeing his eye is evil: therefore the Scriptures, to ſhew that man does all wrong, ſays, *Every one did that which was right in his own eyes,* Judges xvii. 6. and xxi. 25. And his imaginations, or reaſonings, muſt be caſt down, by the power of the word, being of a piece with his judgment, 2 Cor. x. 5. But to point out this corruption of the mind, or underſtanding, more particularly, let the following things be conſidered.

Firſt, There is a natural weakneſs in the minds of men, with reſpect to ſpiritual things. The apoſtle determines, concerning every one that is not endued with the graces of the Spirit, *That he is blind, and cannot ſee afar off,* 2 Pet. i. 9. Hence the Spirit of God, in the Scriptures, cloaths, as it were, divine truths with earthly figures, even as parents teach their children, uſing ſimilitudes, Hoſ. xii. 10. which, though it doth not cure, yet doth evidence this natural weakneſs in the minds of men. But there are not wanting plain proofs of it from experience. As, (1.) How hard a taſk is it to teach many people the common principles of our holy religion, and to make truths ſo plain as they may underſtand them? There muſt be *precept upon precept, precept upon precept; line upon line, line upon line,* Iſa. xxviii. 9. Try the ſame perſons in other things, they will be found wiſer in their generation than the children of light. They underſtand their work and buſineſs in the world, as well as their neighbours; though they be very ſtupid and unteachable in the matters of God. Tell them how they may advance their worldly wealth, or how they may gratify their luſts, and they will quickly underſtand theſe things; though it is very hard to make them know how their ſouls may be ſaved; or how their hearts may find reſt in Jeſus Chriſt. (2.) Conſider thoſe who have many advantages beyond the generality of man-

G 2

kind; who have had the benefit of good education and inftruction; yea, and are bleffed with the light of grace, in that meafure wherein it is afcribed to the faints on earth; yet how fmall a portion have they of the knowledge of divine things! What ignorance and confufion ftill remains in their minds! How often are they mired even in the matter of practical truths, and fpeak as a child in thefe things! It is a pitiful weaknefs, that we cannot perceive the things which God has revealed to us; and it muft needs be a finful weaknefs, fince the law of God requires us to know and believe them. (3.) What dangerous miftakes are to be found amongft men, in concerns of the greateft weight! What woeful delufions prevail over them! Do we not often fee thofe who, in other things, are the wifeft of men, the moft notorious fools with refpect to their foul's intereft? Mat. xi. 25. *Thou haft hid thefe things from the wife and prudent.* Many that are eagle-eyed in the trifles of time, are like owls and bats in the light of life. Nay, truly, the life of every natural man is but one continued dream and delufion; out of which he never awakes, till either, by a new light darted from heaven into his foul, he come to himfelf, Luke xv. 17. or in hell he lift up his eyes, chap. xvi. 23. Therefore in Scripture account, though he be ever fo wife, yet he is a fool, and a fimple one.

Secondly, Man's underftanding is naturally overwhelmed with grofs darknefs in fpiritual things. Man, at the inftigation of the devil, attempting to break out a new light in his mind, (Gen. iii. 5.) inftead of that, broke up the doors of the bottomlefs pit; fo as, by the fmoke thereof, to be buried in darknefs. When God firft made man, his mind was a lamp of light; but now when he comes to make him over again, in regeneration, he finds it darknefs, Eph. v. 8. *Ye were fometimes darknefs.* Sin has clofed the windows of the foul, darknefs is over all the region: it is the land of darknefs, and fhadow of death, where the light is as darknefs The prince of darknefs reigns there, and nothing but the works of darknefs are framed there. We are born fpiritually blind, and cannot be reftored without a mi-

Head I. *Corruption of the Understanding.*

racle of grace. This is thy cafe, whoever thou art, that art not born again. That you may be convinced in this matter, take the following evidences of it.

Evidence 1. The darkness that was upon the face of the world before, and at the time when Chrift came, arifing as the Sun of Righteoufnefs upon the earth. When Adam, by his fin, had loft that primitive light with which he was endued at his creation, it pleafed God to make a glorious revelation of his mind and will to him, touching the way of falvation, Gen. iii. 15 ! This was handed down by him, and other godly fathers before the flood : yet the natural darknefs of the mind of man prevailed fo far againft that revelation, as to carry off all fenfe of true religion from the old world, except what remained in Noah's family, which was preferved in the ark. After the flood, as men multiplied on the earth, the natural darknefs of the mind prevailed again, and the light decayed, till it died away among the generality of mankind, and was preferved only among the pofterity of Shem. And even with them it had nearly fet, when God called Abraham from ferving other gods, Joſh. xxiv. 15. God gives Abraham a more clear and full revelation, which he communicates to his family, Gen. xviii. 19. yet the natural darknefs wears it out at length, fave that it was preferved among the pofterity of Jacob. They being carried down into Egypt, that darknefs fo prevailed, as to leave them very little fenfe of true religion : and there was a neceffity of a new revelation to be made to them in the wildernefs. And many a cloud of darknefs got above that, now and then, during the time between Mofes and Chrift. When Chrift came, the world was divided into Jews and Gentiles. The Jews, and the true light with them, were within an incloſure, Pfal. cxlvii. 19, 20. Between them and the Gentile world, there was a partition wall of God's making, namely the ceremonial law ; and upon that there was reared up another of man's own making, namely a rooted enmity between the parties, Eph. ii. 14, 15. If we look abroad without the inclofure (and except thofe profelytes of the Gentiles, who, by means of fome rays of light breaking forth upon them from within the inclosure, having renounced idolatry, worshipped the true God, but did not conform to the Mosaical rites), we see nothing but dark places of the earth, full of the habitations of cruelty, Psal. lxxiv. 20. Gross darkness covered the face of the Gentile world, and the way of salvation was utterly unknown among them. They were drowned in superstition and idolatry, and had multiplied their idols to such a vast number, that above thirty thousand are reckoned to have been worshipped by those of Europe alone. Whatever wisdom was among their philosophers, the world by that wisdom knew not God, 1 Cor. i. 21. and all their researches in religion were but groping in the dark, Acts xvii. 27. If we look within the inclosure, and, except a few that were groaning and waiting for the consolation of Israel, we shall see a gross darkness on the face of that generation. Though to them were committed the oracles of God, yet they were most corrupt in their doctrine. Their traditions were multiplied, but the knowledge of those things wherein the life of religion lies was lost. Masters of Israel knew not the nature and necessity of regeneration, John iii. 10. Their religion was to build on their birth-privilege, as children of Abraham, Mat. iii. 9. to glory in their circumcision, and other external ordinances, Philip. iii. 2, 3. And to rest in the law, (Rom. ii. 17.) after they had, by their false glosses, cut it so short, as they might outwardly go well nigh to the fulfilling of it, Mat. v.

Thus was darkness over the face of the world, when Christ the true light came into it; and so is darkness over every soul, till he, as the day-star, arise in the heart. The latter is an evidence of the former. What, but the natural darkness of men's minds, could still thus wear out the light of external revelation, in a matter upon which eternal happiness depends? Men did not forget the way of preserving their lives; but how quickly they lost the knowledge of the way of salvation of their souls; which are of infinite more weight and worth! When patriarchs and prophets teaching was ineffectual, it became necessary for men to be taught of

Head I.   *Corruption of the Understanding.*   47

God himself, who alone can open the eyes of the understanding. But that it might appear, that the corruption of man's mind lay deeper than to be cured by mere external revelation, there were but very few converted by Christ's preaching, who spoke as never man spake, John xii. 37, 38. The great cure remained to be performed, by the Spirit accompanying the preaching of the apostles; who, according to the promise (John xiv. 12.) were to do greater works. And if we look to the miracles wrought by our blessed Lord, we shall find, that by applying the remedy to the soul, for the cure of bodily distempers, (as in the case of the man sick of the palsy, Mat. ix. 2.) he plainly discovered that his main errand into the world was to cure the diseases of the soul. I find a miracle wrought upon one that was born blind, performed in such a way, as seems to have been designed to let the world see in it, as in a glass, their case and cure; John ix. 6. *He made clay, and anointed the eyes of the blind man with the clay.* What could more fitly represent the blindness of men's minds, than eyes closed up with earth? Isa. vi. 1. *Shut their eyes*; shut them up by anointing, or *casting them with mortar*, as the word will bear. And chap. xliv. 18. *He hath shut their eyes:* the word properly signifies, he hath plaistered their eyes; as the house in which the leprosy had been was to be plaistered, Lev. xiv. 42. Thus the Lord's word discovers the design of that strange work; and by it shews us that the eyes of our understanding are naturally shut. Then the blind man must go and wash off this clay in the pool of Siloam : no other water will serve this purpose. If that pool had not represented him, whom the Father sent into the world to open the blind eyes, Isa. xlii. 7. I think the evangelist had not given us the interpretation of the name, which, he says, signifies *sent*, John. ix. 7. So we may conclude, that the natural darkness of our minds is such, as there is no cure for, but from the blood and Spirit of Jesus Christ, whose eye-salve only can make us see, Rev. iii. 18.

Evid. 2. Every natural man's heart and life is a mass of darkness, disorder, and confusion; how refined soever he appear in the sight of men. *For we ourselves also*, saith the apostle Paul, *were sometimes foolish, disobedient, deceived, serving divers lusts and pleasures*, Tit. iii. 3. and yet, at the time which this text looks to, he was blameless touching the righteousness which is in the law, Phil. iii. 6. This is a plain evidence that the eye is evil, the whole body being full of darkness, Mat. vi. 23. The unrenewed part of mankind is rambling through the world, like so many blind men, who will neither take a guide, nor can guide themselves; therefore are falling over this and the other precipice, into destruction. Some are running after their covetousness, till they be pierced through with many sorrows; some sticking in the mire of sensuality; others dashing themselves on the rock of pride and self-conceit; every one stumbling on some one stone of stumbling or other: all of them are running themselves upon the sword-point of justice, while they eagerly follow whither their unmortified passions and affections lead them: and while some are lying along in the way, others are coming up, and falling headlong over them. Therefore, wo unto the blind world because of offences, Mat. xviii. 7. Errors in judgment swarm in the world, because it is night, wherein all the beasts of the forest do creep forth. All the unregenerate are utterly mistaken in the point of true happiness: for though Christianity hath fixed that matter in point of principle; yet nothing less than overcoming grace can fix it in the practical judgement. All men agree in the desire of being happy: but among unrenewed men, touching the way to happiness, there are almost as many opinions as there are men; they being turned every one to his own way, Isa. liii. 6. They are like the blind Sodomites about Lot's house, all were seeking to find the door, some grope one part of the wall for it, some another; but none of them could certainly say he had found it: so the natural man may stumble on any good but the chief good. Look into thine own unregenerate heart, and there thou wilt see all turned up-side down; heaven lying under, and earth a-top. Look into thy life, there thou mayest see how thou art playing the mad-man, snatch-

Head I. *Corruption of the Understanding.* 49

ing at shadows, and neglecting the substance: eagerly flying after that which is not, and slighting that which is, and will be for ever.

Evid. 3. The natural man is always as a workman left without light; either trifling or doing mischief. Try to catch thy heart at any time that thou wilt, and thou shalt find it either weaving the spider's web, or hatching cockatrice-eggs, (Isa. lix. 5.) roving through the world, or digging into the pit; filled with vanity, or else with vileness; busy doing nothing, or what is worse than nothing. A sad sign of a dark mind.

Evid. 4. The natural man is void of the saving knowledge of spiritual things. He knows not what a God he has to do with; he is unacquainted with Christ; and knows not what sin is. The greatest graceless wits are blind as moles in these things. Ay, but some such can speak of them to good purpose: so might those Israelites of the temptations, signs and miracles, which their eyes had seen, (Deut. xxix. 3.) to whom, nevertheless, the Lord had *not given an heart to perceive, and eyes to see, and ears to hear, unto that day*, ver. 4. Many a man that bears the name of a Christian, may make Pharaoh's confession of faith, Exod. v. 2. *I know not the Lord*, neither will they let go what he commands them to part with. God is with them as a prince in disguise among his subjects, who meets with no better treatment from them than if they were his fellows, Psal. l. 21. Do they know Christ, or see his glory, and any beauty in him for which he is to be desired? If they did, they would not slight him as they do: a view of his glory would so darken all created excellency, that they would take him for, and instead of, all, and gladly close with him, as he offereth himself in the gospel, John iv. 10. Psal. ix. 10. Mat. xiii. 44, 45, 46. Do they know what sin is, who nurse the serpent in their bosom, hold fast deceit, and refuse to let it go? I own, indeed, that they may have a natural knowledge of those things, as the unbelieving Jews had of Christ, whom they saw and conversed with: but there was a spiritual glory in him, perceived by believers only, John i. 14. and in respect of that glory, the (unbelieving) world

H

knew him not, ver. 10. the spiritual knowledge of them they cannot have; it is above the reach of the carnal mind, 1 Cor. ii. 14. *The natural man receiveth not the things of the Spirit of God, for they are foolishness unto him: neither can he know them, for they are spiritually discerned.* He may indeed discourse of them; but no other way, than one can talk of honey or vinegar, who never tasted the sweetness of the one, nor the sourness of the other. He has some notions of spiritual truths, but sees not the things themselves, that are wrapt up in the words of truth, 1 Tim. i. 7. *Understanding neither what they say, nor whereof they affirm.* In a word, natural men fear, seek, confess they know not what. Thus you may see, man's understanding naturally is overwhelmed with gross darkness in spiritual things.

Thirdly, There is in the mind of man a natural bias to evil, whereby it comes to pass, that whatever difficulties it finds, while occupied about things truly good, it acts with a great deal of ease in evil; as being in that case in its own element, Jer. iv. 22. The carnal mind drives heavily in the thoughts of good; but furiously in the thoughts of evil. While holiness is before it, fetters are upon it: but when once it has got over the hedge, it is as a bird got out of the cage, and becomes a free-thinker indeed. Let us reflect a little on the apprehension and imagination of the carnal mind; and we shall find incontestible evidence of this woeful bias to evil.

Evidence 1. As when a man, by a violent stroke on the head, loseth his sight, there ariseth to him a kind of false light, whereby he seems to see a thousand airy nothings; so man being struck blind to all that is truly good, and for his eternal interest, has a light of another sort brought into his mind; his eyes are opened, knowing evil, and so are the words of the tempter verified, Gen. iii. 5. The words of the prophet are plain, *They are wise to do evil, but to do good they have no knowledge*, Jer. iv. 22. The mind of man has a natural dexterity to devise mischief: there are not any so simple, as to want skill to contrive ways to gratify their lusts, and ruin their souls; though the power of every one's

Head I. *Corruption of the Understanding.*

hand cannot reach to put their devices in execution. None needs to be taught this black art; but as weeds grow up, of their own accord, in the neglected ground, so doth this wisdom (which is earthly, sensual, devilish, Jam. iii. 15.) grow up in the minds of men, by virtue of the corruption of their nature. Why should we be surprised with the product of corrupt wits; their cunning devices to affront heaven, to oppose and run down truth and holiness, and to gratify their own, and other men's lusts? They row with the stream; no wonder that they make great progress: their stock is within them, and increaseth by using of it: and the works of darkness are contrived with the greater advantage, that the mind is wholly destitute of spiritual light, which, if it were in them, in any measure, would so far marr the work, 1 John iii. 9. *Whosoever is born of God doth not commit sin;* he does it not as by art, wilfully and habitually; for *his seed remaineth in him.* But on the other hand, *it is a sport to a fool to do mischief: but a man of understanding hath wisdom,* Prov. x. 23. *To do witty wickedness nicely* (as the word imports) *is* as *a sport* or *a play to a fool;* it comes off with him easily; and why, but because he is a fool, and hath not wisdom, which would marr the contrivances of darkness? The more natural a thing is, the more easily it is done.

Evid. 2. Let the corrupt mind have but the advantage of one's being employed in, or present at some piece of service for God; that so the device, if not in itself sinful, yet may become sinful, by its unseasonableness: it will quickly fall on some device or expedient, by its starting aside; which deliberation in season could not produce. Thus Saul, who wist not what to do, before the priest began to consult God, is quickly determined when once the priest's hand was in: his own heart then gave him an answer, and would not allow him to wait an answer from the Lord, 1 Sam. xiv. 18, 19. Such a devilish dexterity hath the carnal mind, in devising what may most effectually divert men from their duty to God.

Evid. 3. Doth not the carnal mind naturally strive to grasp spiritual things in imagination; as if the soul were quite immersed in flesh and blood, and would turn every thing into its own shape?. Let men who are used to the forming of the most abstracted notions, look into their own souls, and they shall find this bias in their minds; whereof the idolatry which did of old, and still doth, so much prevail in the world, is an incontestible evidence. For it plainly discovers, that men naturally would have a visible deity, and see what they worship; and therefore they *changed the glory of the incorruptible God into an image*, &c. Rom. i. 23. The reformation of these nations (blessed be the Lord for it) hath banished idolatry, and images too, out of our churches: but heart-reformation only can break down mental idolatry, and banish the more subtile and refined image-worship, and representations of the Deity, out of the minds of men. The world, in the time of its darkness, was never more prone to the former, than the unsanctified mind is to the latter. Hence are horrible, monstrous, and mis-shappen thoughts of God, Christ, the glory above, and all spiritual things.

Evid. 4. What a difficult task is it to detain a carnal mind before the Lord! how averse is it to the entertaining of good thoughts, and dwelling in the meditation of spiritual things! if a person be driven, at any time, to think of the great concerns of his soul, it is no harder work to hold in an unruly hungry beast, than to hedge in the carnal mind, that it get not away to the vanities of the world again. When God is speaking to men by his word, or they are speaking to him in prayer, doth not the mind often leave them before the Lord, like so many idols that have eyes, but see not, and ears, but hear not? The carcase is laid down before God, but the world gets away the heart: though the eyes be closed, the man sees a thousand vanities: the mind, in the mean time, is like a bird got loose out of the cage, skipping from bush to bush; so that, in effect, the man never comes to himself till he be gone from the presence of the Lord. Say not, it is impossible to get the mind fixed. It is hard indeed, but not impossible. Grace from the Lord can do it, Psal. cviii. 1. Agreeable objects will do it. A pleasant

Head I. *Corruption of the Understanding.* 53

speculation will arrest the minds of the inquisitive: the worldly man's mind is in little hazard of wandering, when he is contriving of business, casting up his accounts, or telling his money: if he answers you not at first, he tells you he did not hear you, he was busy; his mind was fixed. Were we admitted into the presence of a king, to petition for our lives, we should be in no hazard of gazing through the chamber of presence. But here lies the case, the carnal mind, employed about any spiritual good, is out of its element, and therefore cannot fix.

Evid. 5. But however hard it is to keep the mind on good thoughts, it sticks as glue to what is evil and corrupt, like itself, 2 Pet. ii. 14. *Having eyes full of adultery, and that cannot cease from sin.* Their eyes cannot cease from sin (so the words are constructed) that is, their hearts and minds, venting by the eyes what is within, like a furious beast, which cannot be held in when once it has got out its head. Let the corrupt imagination once be let loose on its proper object; it will be found hard work to call it back again, though both reason and will are for its retreat. For then it is in its own element; and to draw it off from its impurities, is as the drawing of a fish out of the water, or the renting of a limb from a man. It runs like fire set to a train of powder, that resteth not till it can get no farther.

Evid. 6. Consider how the carnal imagination supplies the want of real objects to the corrupt heart; that it may make sinners happy, at least, in the imaginary enjoyment of their lusts. Thus the corrupt heart feeds itself with imagination-sins; the unclean person is filled with speculative impurities, having eyes full of adultery, the covetous man fills his heart with the world, though he cannot get his hands full of it: the malicious person, with delight, acts his revenge within his own breast; the envious man, within his own narrow soul, beholds, with satisfaction, his neighbour laid low; and every lust finds the corrupt imagination a friend to it in time of need. This it doth, not only when people are awake, but sometimes even when they are asleep; whereby it comes to pass, that those sins are acted in dreams, which their hearts are carried out after while they are awake. I know that some question the sinfulness of these things: but can it be thought they are consistent with that holy nature and frame of spirit which was in innocent Adam, and in Jesus Christ, and should be in every man? It is the corruption of nature, then, that makes filthy dreamers condemned, Jude 8. Solomon had experience of the exercise of grace in sleep: in a dream he prayed, in a dream he made the best choice; both were accepted of God, 1 Kings iii. 5. 15. And if a man may, in his sleep, do what is good and acceptable to God, why may he not also, when asleep, do that which is evil and displeasing to God? The same Solomon would have men aware of this; and prescribes the best remedy against it, namely, *The law upon the heart*, Prov. vi. 20, 21. *When thou sleepest* (says he, ver. 22.) *it shall keep thee*, to wit, from sinning in thy sleep; that is, from sinful dreams: for a man's being kept from sin (not his being kept from affliction) is the immediate proper effect of the law of God impressed upon the heart, Psal. cxix. 11. And thus the whole verse is to be understood, as appears from ver. 23. *For the commandment is a lamp, and the law is light, and reproofs of instruction are the way of life.* Now the law is a lamp and light, as it guides in the way of duty; and instructing reproofs from the law, are the way of life, as they keep from sin: they do not guide into the way of peace, but as they lead into the way of duty; nor do they keep a man out of trouble, but as they keep him from sin. Remarkable is the particular in which Solomom instanceth, namely, the sin of uncleanness, *to keep thee from the evil woman*, &c. verse 24. which is to be joined to verse 22. inclosing the 23d in a parenthesis, as some versions have it. These things may suffice to convince us of the natural bias of the mind to evil.

Fourthly, There is in the carnal mind an opposition to spiritual truths, and an aversion to the receiving them. It is as little a friend to divine truths, as it is to holiness. The truths of natural religion, which do, as it were, force their entry into the minds of natural men, they hold prisoners in unrighteousness, Rom. i. 18. As for the truths of revealed religion, there is an evil heart of unbelief in them, which opposeth their entry; and there is an armed force necessary to captivate the mind to the belief of them, 2 Cor. x. 4, 5. God has made a revelation of his mind and will to sinners, touching the way of salvation; he has given us the doctrine of his holy word: but do natural men believe it indeed? No, they do not; for he that believeth not on the Son of God, believeth not God, as is plain from 1 John v. 10. They believe not the promises of the word: they look on them, in effect, only as fair words; for those that receive them are thereby made partakers of the divine nature, 2 Pet. i. 4. The promises are as silver cords let down from heaven, to draw sinners unto God, and to waft them over into the promised land; but they cast them from them. They believe not the threatenings of the word. As men travelling in desarts carry fire about with them, to fright away wild beasts: so God has made his law a *fiery law*, Deut. xxxiii. 2. hedging it about with threats of wrath: but men naturally are more brutish than beasts themselves; and will needs touch the fiery smoaking mountain, though they should be thrust through with a dart. I doubt not but most, if not all of you, who are yet in the black state of nature, will here plead, *Not guilty*: But remember, the carnal Jews in Christ's time were as confident as you are, that they believed Moses, John ix. 28, 29. But he confutes their confidence, roundly telling them, John v. 46. *Had ye believed Moses, ye would have believed me.* If you believed the truths of God, you durst not reject, as ye do, him who is truth itself. The very difficulty you find in assenting to this truth, discovers that unbelief which I am charging you with. Has it not proceeded so far with some at this day, that it has steeled their fore-heads with the impudence and impiety, openly to reject all revealed religion? Surely it is out of the abundance of the heart their mouth speaketh. But, though ye set not your mouths against the heavens, as they do, the same bitter root of unbelief is in all men by nature, and reigns in you, and will reign till overcoming grace brings our minds to the belief of the truth. To convince you in this point, confider thefe three things.

Evidence 1. How few are there who have been bleffed with an inward illumination, by the fpecial operation of the Spirit of Chrift, leading them into a view of divine truths in their fpiritual and heavenly luftre! How have you learned the truths of religion which you pretend to believe? You have them merely by the benefit of external revelation, and by education; fo that you are Chriftians, becaufe you were not born and bred in a Pagan, but in a Chriftian country. You are ftrangers to the inward work of the Holy Spirit, bearing witnefs by and with the word in your hearts; and fo you cannot have the affurance of faith, with refpect to the outward divine revelation made in the word, 1 Cor. ii. 10, 11, 12. Therefore ye are ftill unbelievers. *It is written in the Prophets, They fhall be all taught of God—Every man, therefore, that hath heard, and hath learned of the Father, cometh unto me,* fays our Lord, John vi. 45. Now you have not come to Chrift, therefore you have not been taught of God: you have not been fo taught, and therefore ye have not come; ye believe not. Behold the revelation from which the faith, even of the fundamental principles in religion doth fpring, Mat. xvi. 17, 18. *Thou art Chrift, the Son of the living God—Bleffed art thou Simon Barjonas: for flefh and blood hath not revealed it unto thee, but my Father which is in heaven.* If ever the Spirit of the Lord take thee in hand, to work in thee that faith which is of the operation of God, it may be as much time will be fpent in razing the old foundation, as will make thee find the neceffity of the working of his mighty power, to enable thee to believe the very foundation-principles, which now thou thinkeft thou makeft no doubt of, Eph. i. 19.

Evid. 2. How many profeffors have made fhip-wreck of their faith (fuch as it was) in time of temptation and trial! See how they fall, like ftars from heaven, when antichrift prevails! 2 Theff. ii. 11, 12. *God fhall fend them ftrong delufions, that they fhould believe a lie: that they all might be damned who believed not the truth.* They fall into damning delufions; becaufe they never

Head I. *Corruption of the Understanding.* 57

really believed the truth, though they themselves, and others too, thought they did believe it. That house is built upon the sand, and that faith is but ill-founded, that cannot stand, but is quite overthrown, when the storm comes.

Evid. 3. Consider the utter inconsistency of most men's lives, with the principles of religion which they profess: you may as soon bring East and West together, as their principles and practice. Men believe that fire will burn them, and therefore they will not throw themselves into it: but the truth is, most men live as if they thought the gospel a mere fable, and the wrath of God, revealed in his word against their unrighteousness and ungodliness, a mere scare-crow. If you believe the doctrines of the word, how is it that you are so unconcerned about the state of your souls before the Lord? How is it that you are so little concerned with this weighty point, Whether you be born again or not? Many live as they were born, and are likely to die as they live, and yet live in peace. Do such believe the sinfulness and misery of a natural state? Do they believe that they are children of wrath? Do they believe that there is no salvation without regeneration? and no regeneration but what makes man a new creature? If you believe the promises of the word, why do you not embrace them, and seek to enter into the promised rest? What sluggard would not dig for a hid treasure, if he really believed that he might so obtain it? Men will work and sweat for a maintainance, because they believe that by so doing they shall get it: yet they will be at no tolerable pains for the eternal weight of glory; why, but because they do not believe the word of promise? Heb. iv. 1, 2. If ye believe the threatenings, how is it that ye live in your sins, live out of Christ, and yet hope for mercy? Do such believe God to be the holy and just One, who will by no means clear the guilty? No, no; none believe, none (or next to none) believe what a just God the LORD is, and how severely he punisheth.

Fifthly, There is in the mind of man a natural proneness to lies and falshood, which make for the

I

safety of lusts. *They go aftray as foon as they be born, fpeaking lies*, Pfal. lvii. 3. We have this with the reft of the corruption of our nature, from our firft parents. God revealed the truth to them; but through the follicitation of the tempter, they firft doubted, then difbelieved it, and embraced a lie inftead of it. For an inconteftible evidence hereof, we may fee the firft article of the devil's creed, *Ye fhall not furely die*, Gen. iii. 4. which was obtruded by him on our firft parents, and by them received; naturally embraced by their pofterity, and held faft, till light from heaven oblige them to quit it. It fpreads itfelf through the lives of natural men; who, till their confciences be awakened, walk after their own lufts; ftill retaining the principle, *That they fhall not furely die*. And this is often improved to fuch perfection, that the man can fay, in the face of the denounced curfe, *I fhall have peace, though I walk in the imaginations of mine heart, to add drunkennefs to thirft*, Deut. xxix. 19. Whatever advantage the truths of God have over error, by means of education, or otherwife, error has always, with the natural man, this advantage againft truth, namely, that there is fomething within him which fays, *O that it were true*; fo that the mind lies fair for affenting to it. And here is the reafon of it. The true doctrine is *the doctrine that is according to godlinefs*, 1 Tim. vi. 3. *and the truth which is after godlinefs*, Tit. i. 1. error is the doctrine which is according to ungodlinefs; for there is never an error in the mind, nor an untruth vented in the world (in matters of religion), but what has an affinity with one corruption of the heart or another: according to that of the apoftle, 2 Theff. ii. 12. *They believed not the truth, but had pleafure in unrighteoufnefs*. So that truth and error being otherwife attended with equal advantages for their reception, error, by this means, has moft ready accefs into the minds of men in their natural ftate. Wherefore, it is nothing ftrange that men reject the fimplicity of gofpel truths and inftitutions, and greedily embrace error and external pomp in religion; as they are fo agreeable to the lufts of the heart, and the vanity of the mind of the natural man. From hence also it is, that so many embrace atheistical principles; for not any do it but in compliance with their irregular passions: not any but those whose advantage it would be that there were no God.

Lastly, Man naturally is high-minded; for when the gospel comes in power to him, it is employed in *casting down imaginations, and every high thing that exalteth itself against the knowledge of God,* 2 Cor. x. 5. Lowliness of mind is not a flower that grows in the field of nature, but is planted by the finger of God in a renewed heart, and learned of the lowly Jesus. It is natural to man to think highly of himself, and what is his own. For the stroke which he got by his fall in Adam, has produced a false light, whereby mole-hills about him appear like mountains; and a thousand airy beauties present themselves to his deluded fancy. *Vain man would be wise,* (so he accounts himself, and so he would be accounted by others) *though man be born like a wild ass's colt,* Job xi. 12. His way is right, because it is his own: for *every way of a man is right in his own eyes,* Prov. xxi. 7. His state is good, because he knows not any better, he his alive without the law, Rom. vii. 9. and therefore his hope is strong, and his confidence firm. It is another tower of Babel reared up against heaven; and it will not fall while the power of darkness can hold it up. The word batters it, yet it stands: one while breaches are made in it, but they are quickly repaired; at another time, it is all made to shake, but still it is kept up, till either God himself by his Spirit raise an heart-quake within the man, which tumbles it down, and leaves not one stone upon another, (2 Cor. x. 4, 5,) or death batter it down, and raze the foundations of it, Luke xvi. 23. And as the natural man thinks highly of himself, so he thinks meanly of God, whatever he pretends, Psal. l. 21. *Thou thoughtest that I was altogether such an one as thyself.* The doctrine of the gospel, and the mystery of Christ, are foolishness to him; and in his practice he treats them as such, 1 Cor. i. 18. and ii. 14. He brings the word and the works of God, in the government of the world, before the bar of his carnal reason; and there they are presumptuously censured and condemned, Hof. xiv. 9. Sometimes the ordinary reſtraint of providence is taken off, and Satan is permitted to ſtir up the carnal mind; and in that caſe it is like an ant's neſt, uncovered and diſturbed; doubts, denials, and helliſh reaſonings crowd in it, and cannot be laid by all the arguments brought againſt them, till power from on high ſubdue the mind, and ſtill the mutiny of the corrupt principles.

Thus much of the corruption of the underſtanding; which, although the half be not told, may diſcover to you the abſolute neceſſity of regenerating grace. Call the underſtanding now Ichabod; for the glory is departed from it. Conſider this, you that are yet in the ſtate of nature, and groan out your caſe before the Lord, that the Sun of Righteouſneſs may ariſe upon you, before you be ſhut up in everlaſting darkneſs. What avails your worldly wiſdom? What do your attainments in religion avail, while your underſtanding lies wrapt up in its natural darkneſs and confuſion, utterly void of the light of life? Whatever be the natural man's gifts or attainments, we muſt (as in the caſe of the leper, Lev. xiii. 41.) *pronounce him utterly unclean, his plague is in his head.* But that is not all; it is in his heart too, his will is corrupted, as I ſhall ſoon ſhew.

Of the Corruption of the Will.

II. The will, that commanding faculty, (which ſometime was faithful, and ruled with God) is now turned traitor, and rules with and for the devil. God planted it in man wholly a right ſeed; but now it is *turned into the degenerate plant of a ſtrange vine.* It was originally placed in due ſubordination to the will of God, as was ſhewn before; but now it is gone wholly aſide. However ſome magnify the power of free will, a view of the ſpirituality of the law, to which acts of moral diſcipline in no ways anſwer, and a deep inſight into the corruption of nature, given by the inward operation of the Spirit, convincing of ſin, righteouſneſs, and judgement, would make men find an abſolute need of the power of free-grace, to remove the bands of wickedneſs from off their free-will. To open up this plague of the heart, I offer thefe following things to be confidered,

Firſt, There is, in the unrenewed will, utter inability for what is truly good and acceptable in the fight of God. The natural man's will is in Satan's fetters, hemmed in within the circle of evil, and cannot move beyond it, any more than a dead man can raife himfelf out of his grave, Eph. ii. 1. We deny him not a power to chufe, purfue, and act, what, as to the matter, is good: but though he can will what is good and right, he can will nothing aright and well, John xv. 5. *Without me*, i. e. feparate from me, as a branch from the ftock, (as both the word and context will bear) *ye can do nothing*; to wit, nothing truly and fpiritually good. His very choice and defire of fpiritual things is carnal and felfifh, John vi. 26. *Ye feek me—becaufe ye did eat of the loaves and were filled.* He not only comes not to Chrift, but *he cannot come*, John vi. 44. and what can he do acceptable to God, who believeth not on him whom the Father hath fent? To evidence this inability for good in the unregenerate, confider thefe two things.

Evidence 1. How often does the light fo fhine before men's eyes, that they cannot but fee the good which they fhould chufe, and the evil which they fhould refufe; and yet their hearts have no more power to comply with that light, than if they were arrefted by fome invifible hand? They fee what is right; yet they follow, and cannot but follow, what is wrong. Their confciences tell them the right way, and approves of it too, yet their will cannot be brought up to it: their corruption fo chains them, that they cannot embrace it; fo that they figh and go backward, notwithftanding their light. If it be not thus, how is it that the word, and way of holinefs meet with fuch entertainment in the world? How is it that clear arguments and reafon on the fide of piety and a holy life, which feem to have weight even with the carnal mind, do not bring men over to that fide? Although the being of a heaven and a hell were but a may-be, it were fufficient to determine the will to the choice of holinefs, were it capable to be determined thereto by mere reason: but men *knowing the judgement of God, (that they who commit such things are worthy of death) not only do the same, but have pleasure in them that do them,* Rom. i. 32. And how is it that those who magnify the power of free-will, do not confirm their opinion before the world, by an ocular demonstration, in a practice as far above others in holiness, as the opinion of their natural ability is above that of others? Or is it maintained only for protection of lusts, which men may hold fast as long as they please; and when they have no more use for them, throw them off in a moment, and leap out of Delilah's lap into Abraham's bosom? Whatever use some make of that principle; it does of itself, and in its own nature, cast a broad shadow for a shelter to wickedness of heart and life. It may be observed, that the generality of the hearers of the gospel, of all denominations, are plagued with it: for it is a root of bitterness natural to all men; from whence spring so many fearlesness about the soul's eternal state; so many delays and put-offs in that weighty matter, whereby much work is laid up for a death-bed by some; while others are ruined by a legal walk, and unacquaintedness with the life of faith, and the making use of Christ for sanctification; all flowing from the persuasion of sufficient natural abilities. So agreeable is it to corrupt nature.

Evid. 2. Let those who, by the power of the spirit of bondage, have had the law opened before them, in its spirituality, for their conviction, speak and tell, if they found themselves able to incline their hearts toward it, in that case; nay, whether the more that light shone into their souls, they did not find their hearts more and more unable to comply with it! There are some, who have been brought unto the place of the breaking forth, who are yet in the devil's camp, who from their experience can tell, that light let into the mind cannot give life to the will, to enable it to comply therewith; and could give their testimony here, if they would. But take Paul's testimony concerning it, who, in his unconverted state, was far from believing his utter inability for good, but learned it by experience, Rom. vii. 8—13. I own the natural man may have a kind of love to the letter of the law : but here lies the ſtreſs of the matter, he looks on the holy law in a carnal dreſs; and ſo, while he hugs a creature of his own fancy, he thinks that he has the law ; but in very deed he is without the law : for as yet he ſees it not in its ſpirituality; if he did, he would find it the very reverſe of his own nature, and what his will could not fall in with, till changed by the power of grace.

Secondly, There is in the unrenewed will an averſeneſs to good. Sin is the natural man's element ; he is as unwilling to part with it, as fiſh are to come out of the water into dry land. He not only cannot come to Chriſt, but he *will not come,* John v. 40. He is polluted, and hates to be waſhed, Jer. xiii. 27. *Wilt thou not be made clean ? When ſhall it once be ?* He is ſick, yet utterly averſe to the remedy : he loves his diſeaſe ſo, that he loathes the Phyſician. He is a captive, a priſoner, and a ſlave ; but he loves his conqueror, his jailor, and maſter :·he is fond of his fetters, priſon, and drudgery ; and has no liking to his liberty. For evidence of this averſeneſs to good in the will of man, I will inſtance in ſome particulars.

Evidence 1. The untowardneſs of children. Do we not ſee them, naturally, lovers of ſinful liberty? How unwilling are they to be hedged in ? How averſe to reſtraint ? The world can bear witneſs, that they are as bullocks unaccuſtomed to the yoke : and more, that it is far eaſier to bring young bullocks tamely to bear the yoke, than to bring young children under diſcipline, and make them tamely ſubmit to be reſtrained in ſinful liberty. Every body may ſee in this, as in a glaſs, that man is naturally wild and wilful, according to Zophar's obſervation, (Job. xi. 12.) that *man is born like a wild aſs's colt.* What can be ſaid more ? He is like a colt, the colt of an aſs, the colt of a wild aſs. Comp. Jer. ii. 24. *A wild aſs uſed to the wilderneſs, that ſnuffeth up the wind at her pleaſure, in her occaſion who can turn her away ?*

Evid. 2. What pain and difficulty men often find in bringing their hearts to religious duties ! And what a taſk is it to the carnal heart to abide at them ! It is a pain to it, to leave the world but a little, to come before God. It is not eafy to borrow time from the many things, to fpend it upon the one thing needful. Men often go to God in duties, with their faces towards the world; and when their bodies are on the mount of ordinances, their hearts will be found at the foot of the hill, going after their covetoufnefs, Ezek. xxxiii. 31. They are foon wearied of well-doing; for holy duties are not agreeable to their corrupt nature. Take notice of them at their worldly bufinefs, fet them down with their carnal company, or let them be fucking the breafts of a luft; time feems to them to fly, and drive furioufly, fo that it is gone ere they are aware. But how heavily does it pafs while a prayer, a fermon, or a Sabbath lafts? The Lord's day is the longeft day of all the week with many; therefore they muft fleep longer that morning, and go fooner to bed that night, than ordinarily they do; that the day may be made of a tolerable length: for their hearts fay within them, *When will the Sabbath be gone?* Amos viii. 5. The hours of worfhip are the longeft hours of that day: hence, when duty is over, they are like men eafed of a burden: and when fermon is ended, many have neither the grace nor the good manners to ftay till the bleffing be pronounced, but like the beafts, their head is away as foon as a man puts his hand to loofe them; and why? becaufe while they are at ordinances, they are as Doeg, detained before the Lord, 1 Sam. xxii. 7.

Evid. 3. Confider how the will of the natural man rebels againft the light, Job xxiv. 13. Light fometimes entereth in, becaufe he is not able to keep it out: but he loveth darknefs rather than light. Sometimes, by the force of truth, the outer-door of the underftanding is broke open; but the inner-door of the will remains faft bolted. Then lufts rife againft light; corruption and confcience encounter, and fight as in the field of battle; till corruption getting the upper-hand, confcience is forced to turn the back; convictions are murdered; and truth is made and held prifoner, fo that it can create no more difturbance. While the word is preached or read, or the rod of God is upon

Head I.   *Corruption of the Will.*   65

the natural man, sometimes convictions are darted in on him, and his spirit is wounded, in greater or lesser measure: but those convictions not being able to make him fall, he runs away with the arrows sticking in his conscience, and at length, one way or other, gets them out, and makes himself whole again. Thus, while the light shines, men, naturally averse to it, wilfully shut their eyes; till God is provoked to blind them judicially, and they become proof against his word and providences too; so go where they will, they can sit at ease: there is never a word from heaven to them, that goeth deeper than into their ears, Hof. iv. 17. *Ephraim is joined to idols, let him alone.*

Evid. 4. Let us observe the resistance made by elect souls, when the Spirit of the Lord is at work, to bring them from the power of Satan unto God. Zion's King gets no subjects but by stroke of sword, in the day of his power, Psal. cx. 2, 3. None come to him, but such as are drawn by the divine hand, John vi. 44. When the Lord comes to the soul, he finds the strong man keeping the house, and a deep peace and security there, while the soul is fast asleep in the devil's arms. But *the prey must be taken from the mighty,* and *the captive delivered.* Therefore the Lord awakens the sinner, opens his eyes, and strikes him with terror, while the clouds are black above his head, and the sword of vengeance is held to his breast. Now he is at no small pains to put a fair face on a black heart; to shake off his fears, to make head against them, and to divert himself from thinking on the unpleasant and ungrateful subject of his soul's case. If he cannot so rid himself from them, carnal reason is called in to help, and urgeth that there is no ground for so great fear; all may be well enough yet; and if it be be ill with him, it will be ill with many. When the sinner is beat from this, and sees no advantage in going to hell with company, he resolves to leave his sins, but cannot think of breaking off so soon; there is time enough, and he will do it afterwards. Conscience says, *To-day, if ye will hear his voice, harden not your hearts:* but he cries, To-morrow, Lord; to-morrow, Lord; and just now, Lord; till that now is

K

never like to come. Thus, many times
his prayers and confeſſions, with nothin
full of ſharper convictions; for the heart c
caſt up the ſweet morſel, as ſoon as con
with the mouth, Judges x. 10—16. A
ſcience obligeth them to part with ſom
are kept as right eyes and right hands;
rueful looks after thoſe that are put a
with the Iſraelites, who, with bitter heart
the fiſh they did eat in Egypt freely,
Nay, when he is ſo preſſed, that he muſ
fore the Lord, that he is content to pa
idols, the heart will be giving the tongu
word, the ſoul, in this caſe, will ſhift f
to another; like a fiſh with the hook in
can do no more, and power come to m
the wild aſs in her mouth, Jer. ii. 24.

Thirdly, There is in the will of man a
ſity to evil, a woeful bent toward ſin.
are bent to backſliding from God, Ho
hang (as the word is) towards backſlidi
hanging wall, whoſe breaking cometh
inſtant. Set holineſs and life upon the
and death upon the other, and leave t
will to itſelf, and it will chooſe ſin, and
This is no more to be doubted, than tha
on the ſide of a hill, will run downwar
ward, or that a flame will aſcend, and r

Evid. 1. Is not the way of evil the j
the children of men go? Do not the
plainly appear on the wrong ſide, while
no cunning to hide them? In the firſt (
eyes in the world, we look a-ſquint,
heaven-ward. As ſoon as it appears th
tional creatures, it appears that we are ſi
Pſal. lviii. 3. *The wicked are eſtranged j
they go aſtray as ſoon as they be born*,]
*Fooliſhneſs is bound in the heart of a child:
correction ſhall drive it far from him.* Fol
the heart, it is woven in our very
knot will not unlooſe, it muſt be brok

Head I.   *Corruption of the Will.*   67

ſtrokes. Words will not do it, the rod muſt be taken to drive it away: and if it be not driven far away, the heart and it will meet and knit again. Not that the rod of itſelf will do this: the ſad experience of many parents teſtifies the contrary; and Solomon himſelf tells you, Prov. xxvii. 22. *Though thou ſhouldſt bray a fool in a mortar, among wheat, with a peſtle, yet will not his fooliſhneſs depart from him.* It is ſo bound in his heart. But the rod is an ordinance of God, appointed for that end; which, like the word, is made effectual, by the Spirit's accompanying his own ordinance. This, by the way, ſhews that parents, in adminiſtering correction to their children, have need, firſt of all, to correct their own irregular paſſions; and look upon it as a matter of awful ſolemnity, ſetting about it with much dependence on the Lord, and following it with prayer for a bleſſing, if they would have it effectual.

Evid. 2. How eaſily are men led aſide to ſin! The children who are not perſuaded to good, are otherwiſe ſimple ones, eaſily wrought upon; thoſe whom the word cannot draw to holineſs, are *led by Satan at his pleaſure.* Profane Eſau, that cunning man, (Gen. xxv. 27.) was as eaſily cheated of the bleſſing, as if he had been a fool or an idiot. The more natural a thing is, the more eaſy it is: ſo Chriſt's yoke is eaſy to the ſaints, ſo far as they are partakers of the divine nature: and ſin is eaſy to the unrenewed man; but to learn to do good, is as difficult as for the Ethiopian to change his ſkin; becauſe the will naturally hangs towards evil, and is averſe to good. A child can cauſe a round thing to run, when he cannot move a ſquare thing of the ſame weight; for the roundneſs makes it fit for motion, ſo that it goes with a touch. Even ſo, men find the heart eaſily carried towards ſin, while it is as a dead weight in the way of holineſs; we muſt ſeek for the reaſon of this from the natural ſet and diſpoſition of the heart, whereby it is prone and bent to evil. Were man's will, naturally, but in equal balance to good and evil, the one might be embraced with as little difficulty as the other; but experience teſtifies it is not ſo. In the ſacred hiſtory of the Iſraelites, eſpecially in the

K 2

book of Judges, how often do we find them forsaking Jehovah, the mighty God, and doting upon the idols of the nations about them! But did ever any one of these nations grow fond of Israel's God, and forsake their own idols? No, no; though man is naturally given to changes, it is but from evil to evil, not from evil to good, Jer. ii. 10, 11. *Hath a nation changed their gods, which yet are no gods? But my people have changed their glory for that which doth not profit.* Surely the will of man stands not in equal balance, but has a cast to the wrong side.

Evid. 3. Consider how men go on still in the way of sin, till they meet with a stop, and that from another hand than their own, Isa. lvii. 17. *I hid me, and he went on frowardly in the way of his heart.* If God withdraw his restraining hand, and lay the reins on the sinner's neck, he is under no doubt what way to choose; for (observe it) the way of sin is *the way of his heart*; his heart naturally lies that way; it hath a natural propensity to sin. As long as God suffereth them, they walk in their own way, Acts xiv. 16. The natural man is so fixed in his woeful choice, that there needs no more to shew he is off from God's way, than to say he is upon his own.

Evid. 4. Whatever good impressions are made upon him, they do not last. Though his heart be firm as a stone, yea, harder than the nether-millstone, in point of receiving of them; it is otherwise unstable as water, and cannot keep them. It works against the receiving of them; and, when they are made, it works them off, and returns to its natural bias, Hos. vi. 4. *Your goodness is as a morning cloud, and as the early dew, it goeth away.* The morning cloud promiseth a hearty shower, but, when the sun ariseth, it vanisheth : the sun beats upon the early dew, and it evaporates; the husbandman's expectation is disappointed. Such is the goodness of the natural man. Some sharp affliction, or piercing conviction, obligeth him, in some sort, to turn from his evil course: but his will not being renewed, religion is still against the grain with him, therefore this goes off again, Psal. lxxviii. 34. 36, 37. Though a stone thrown up into the air, may abide there a little while: yet its natural heaviness will bring it down to the earth again: so do unrenewed men return to the wallowing in the mire; because, although they washed themselves, yet their swinish nature was not changed. It is hard to cause wet wood to take fire, hard to make it keep fire; but it is harder than either of these, to make the unrenewed will retain attained goodness; which is a plain evidence of the natural bent of the will to evil.

Evid. 5. Do the saints serve the Lord now, as they were wont to serve sin, in their unconverted state? Very far from it, Rom. vi. 20. *When ye were the servants of sin, ye were free from righteousness.* Sin got all, and admitted no partner: but now, when they are the servants of Christ, are they free from sin? Nay, there are still with them some deeds of the old man, shewing that he is but dying in them, and hence their hearts often misgive them, and slip aside into evil, when they would do good, Rom. vii. 21. They need to watch, and keep their hearts with all diligence; and their sad experience teacheth them, *That he that trusteth in his own heart is a fool,* Prov. xxviii. 26. If it be thus in the green tree, how must it be in the dry?

Fourthly, There is a natural contrariety, direct opposition and enmity, in the will of man, to God himself, and his holy will, Rom. viii. 7. *The carnal mind is enmity against God; for it is not subject to the law of God, neither indeed can be.* The will was once God's deputy in the soul, set to command there for him; but now it is set up against him. If you would have the picture of it in its natural state, the very reverse of the will of God represents it. If the fruit hanging before one's eyes be but forbidden, that is sufficient to draw the heart after it. Let me instance in the sin of profane swearing and cursing, to which some are so abandoned, that they take a pride in them; belching out horrid oaths and curses, as if hell opened with the opening of their mouths; or larding their speeches with minced oaths; and all this without any manner of provocation, though even that would not excuse them. Pray tell me, (1.) What profit is there here in this? A thief gets something in his hand for his pains; a drunkard gets a belly-full; but what do you get? Others serve the devil for pay; but you are volunteers, that expect no reward, but your work itself in affronting of Heaven; and if you repent not, you will get your reward in full tale: when you go to hell, your work will follow you. The drunkard shall not have a drop of water to cool his tongue there. Nor will the covetous man's wealth follow him into the other world: you may drive on your old trade there: eternity will be long enough to give you your heart's fill of it. (2.) What pleasure is there here, but what flows from your trampling upon the holy law? Which of your senses doth swearing and cursing gratify? If it gratify your ears, it can only be by the noise it makes against the heavens. Though you had a mind to give up yourselves to all manner of profanity and sensuality, there is so little pleasure can be strained out of these sins, that we must needs conclude, your love to them, in this case, is a love to them for themselves; a devilish unhired love, without any prospect of profit or pleasure from them. If any shall say, These are monsters of men: be it so; yet, alas! the world is fruitful of such monsters, that they are to be found almost every where. Allow me to say, they must be admitted as the mouth of the whole unregenerate world against Heaven, Rom. iii. 14. 19. *Whose mouth is full of cursing and bitterness. Now we know that what things soever the law saith, it saith to them who are under the law, that every mouth may be stopped, and all the world may become guilty before God.*

I have a charge against every unregenerate man and woman, young and old, to be verified by the testimonies of the Scriptures of truth, and the testimony of their own consciences; namely, that whether they be professors or profane, seeing they are not born again, they are heart-enemies to God, to the Son of God, to the Spirit of God, and to the law of God. Hear this, ye careless souls, that live at ease in your natural state.

First, You are enemies to God in your mind, Col. i. 21. You are not as yet reconciled to him; the natural enmity is not as yet slain, though perhaps it lies hid, and you do not perceive it. (1.) You are enemies to the very being of God, Pfal. xiv. 1. *The fool hath faid in his heart, There is no God.* The proud man would that none were above himfelf; the rebel, that there were no king; and the unrenewed man, who is a mafs of pride and rebellion, that there were no God. He faith in his heart, I wifh it were fo; though he is afhamed and afraid to fpeak it out. That all natural men are fuch fools, appears from the apoftle's quoting a part of this Pfalm, *That every mouth may be flopped*, Rom. iii. 10, 11, 12. 19. I own, indeed, that while the natural man looks on God as the Creator and Preferver of the world, becaufe he loves his own felf, therefore his heart rifeth not againft the being of his Benefactor: but this enmity will quickly appear, when he looks on God as the Rector and Judge of the world, binding him, under the pain of the curfe, to exact holinefs, and girding him with the cords of death, becaufe of his fin. Liften, in this cafe, to the voice of the heart, and thou wilt find it to be, *No God.* (2.) You are enemies to the nature of God, Job xxi. 14. *They fay unto God, Depart from us: for we defire not the knowledge of thy ways.* Men fet up to themfelves an idol of their own fancy, inftead of God, and then fall down and worfhip it. They love him no other way than Jacob loved Leah, while he took her for Rachel. Every natural man is an enemy to God, as he is revealed in his word. The infinitely holy, juft, powerful, and true being, is not the God whom he loves, but the God whom he loathes. In fact, men naturally are haters of God, Rom. i. 30. If they could, they certainly would make him otherwife than what he is. For confider, it is a certain truth, that whatfoever is in God, is God; therefore his attributes or perfections are not any thing really diftinct from himfelf. If God's attributes be not God himfelf, he is a compound being, and fo not the firft being; (which to fay is blafphemous) for the parts compounding are before the compound itfelf; but he is Alpha and Omega, the Firft and the Laft.

Now upon this I would, for your conviction, propofe to your confciences a few queries. (1.) How ftand your hearts affected towards the infinite purity and holiness of God? Conscience will give an answer to this, which the tongue will not speak out. If you be not partakers of his holiness, you cannot be reconciled to it. The Pagans finding that they could not be like God in holiness, make their gods like themselves in filthiness; and thereby discover what sort of a God the natural man would have. God is holy; can an unholy creature love his unspotted holiness? Nay, it is the righteous only, that can give thanks at the remembrance of his holiness, Psal. xcvii. 12. God is light; can creatures of darkness rejoice therein? Nay; *Every one that doth evil, hateth the light*, John iii. 20. *For what communion hath light with darkness?* 2 Cor. vi. 14. (2.) How stand your hearts affected to the justice of God? There is not a man, who is wedded to his lusts, as all the unregenerate are, but would be content, with the blood of his body, to blot that letter out of the name of God. Can the malefactor love his condemning judge? or an unjustified sinner, a just God? No, he cannot, Luke vii. 47. *To whom little is forgiven, the same loveth little.* Hence, as men cannot get the doctrine of his justice blotted out of the Bible, it is such an eye-sore to them, that they strive to blot it out of their minds. They ruin themselves by presuming on his mercy; while they are not careful to get a righteousness, wherein they may stand before his justice; but, *say in their heart, The Lord will not do good, neither will he do evil*, Zeph. i. 12. (3.) How stand you affected to the omniscience and omnipresence of God? Men naturally would rather have a blind idol, than the all-seeing God, therefore they do what they can, as Adam did, to hide themselves from the presence of the Lord. They no more love the all-seeing, every-where present God, than the thief loves to have the judge witness to his evil deeds. If it could be carried by votes, God would be voted out of the world, and closed up in heaven: for the language of the carnal heart is, *The Lord seeth us not; the Lord hath forsaken the earth*, Ezek. viii. 12. (4.) How stand you affected to the truth and veracity of God? There are but few in the world who can heartily subscribe to this sentence of the apostle, Rom. iii. 4. *Let God be true, but every man a liar.* Nay, truly, there are many, who, in effect, hope that God will not be true to his word. There are thousands who hear the gospel, that hope to be saved, and think all safe with them for eternity, who never had any experience of the new birth, nor at all concern themselves in the question, Whether they are born again, or not? A question that is like to wear out from among us this day. Our Lord's words are plain and peremptory, *Except a man be born again, he cannot see the kingdom of God.* What are such hopes, then, but real hopes that God (with profoundest reverence be it spoken) will recall his word, and that Christ will prove a false prophet? What else means the sinner, who when he heareth the words of the curse, blesseth himself in his heart, saying, *I shall have peace, though I walk in the imagination of mine heart?* Deut. xxix. 19. *Lastly,* How stand you affected to the power of God? None but new creatures will love him for it, on a fair view thereof; though others may slavishly fear him, upon the account of it. There is not a natural man but would contribute, to the utmost of his power, to the building of another tower of Babel, to hem it in. On these grounds, I declare every unrenewed man an enemy to God.

Secondly, You are enemies to the Son of God. That enmity to Christ is in your hearts, which would have made you join the husbandmen, who killed the heir, and cast him out of the vineyard; if you had been beset with their temptations, and no more restrained than they were. *Am I a dog*, you will say, that I should so treat my sweet Saviour? So did Hazael ask, in another case; but when he had the temptation, he was a dog to do it. Many call Christ their sweet Saviour, whose consciences can bear witness that they never sucked so much sweetness from him as from their sweet lusts, which are ten times sweeter to them than the Saviour. He is no other way sweet to them, than as they abuse his death and sufferings, for the peaceable enjoyment of their lusts, that they may live as they please in the world;

and when they die, be kept out of hell. Alas! it is but a miſtaken Chriſt that is-ſweet to you, whoſe ſouls loath that Chriſt who is the *brightneſs of the Father's glory, and the expreſs image of his perſon.* It is with you as it was with the carnal Jews, who delighted in him, while they miſtook his errand into the world, fancying that he would be a temporal deliverer to them, Mal. iii. 1. But when he *ſat as a refiner and purifier of ſilver*, ver. 2, 3. and rejected them as reprobate ſilver, who thought to have had no ſmall honour in the kingdom of the Meſſiah, his doctrine galled their conſciences, and they had no reſt till they imbrued their hands in his blood. To open your eyes in this point, which you are ſo averſe to believe, I will lay before you the enmity of your hearts againſt Chriſt in all his offices.

Firſt, Every unregenerate man is an enemy to Chriſt in his prophetical office. He is appointed of the Father the great Prophet and Teacher; but not upon the call of the world, who, in their natural ſtate, would have unanimouſly voted againſt him: therefore, when he came, he was condemned as a ſeducer and blaſphemer. For evidence of this enmity, I will inſtance in two things.

Evidence 1. Conſider the entertainment which he meets with when he comes to teach ſouls inwardly by his Spirit. Men do what they can to ſtop their ears, like the deaf adder, that they may not hear his voice. They always reſiſt the Holy Ghoſt. They deſire not the knowledge of his ways; and therefore bid him depart from them. The old calumny is often raiſed upon him on that occaſion, John x. 20. *He is mad, why hear ye him?* Soul-exerciſe, raiſed by the ſpirit of bondage, is accounted, by many, nothing elſe but diſtraction, and melancholy fits; men thus blaſpheming the Lord's work, becauſe they themſelves are beſide themſelves, and cannot judge of theſe matters.

Evid. 2. Conſider the entertainment which he meets with, when he comes to teach men outwardly by his word.

1. His written word, the Bible, is ſlighted: Chriſt hath left it to us, as the book of our inſtruction, to ſhew us what way we muſt ſteer our courſe, if we go to

Head I.   *Corruption of the Will.*   75

Immanuel's land. It is a lamp to light us through a dark world, to eternal light: and he hath enjoined us to search it with that diligence wherewith men dig into mines for silver and gold, John v. 39. But, ah! how is this sacred treasure profaned by many! They ridicule that holy word, by which they must be judged at the last day; and will rather lose their souls than their jest, dressing up the conceits of their wanton wits in Scripture phrases: in which they act as mad a part, as one who would dig into a mine, to procure metal, to melt and pour down his own and his neighbour's throat. Many exhaust their spirits in reading romances, and their minds pursue them, as the flame doth the dry stubble; while they have no heart for, nor relish to the holy word, and therefore seldom take a Bible in their hands. What is agreeable to the vanity of their minds, is pleasant and taking: but what recommends holiness, to their unholy hearts, makes their spirits dull and flat. What pleasure they find, in reading a profane ballad or story book, to whom the Bible is tasteless, as the white of an egg! Many lay by their Bibles with their Sabbath-days cloaths, and whatever use they have for their cloaths, they have none for their Bibles, till the return of the Sabbath. Alas! the dust or the finery about your Bibles, is a witness now, and will, at the last day, be a witness of the enmity of your hearts against Christ, as a Prophet. Besides all this, among those who usually read the Scripture, how few are there that read it as the word of the Lord to their souls, and keep up communion with him in it! They do not make his statutes their counsellors, nor doth their particular case send them to their Bibles. They are strangers to the solid comfort of the Scriptures. And when they are dejected, it is something else than the word that revives them; as Ahab was cured of his sullen fit, by the securing of Naboth's vineyard for him.

2. Christ's word preached is despised. The entertainment which most of the world, to whom it is come, have always given it, is that which is mentioned, Mat. xxii. 5. *They made light of it.* And for his sake they are despised whom he employs to preach it; what-

L 2

ever other face men put upon their contempt of the miniſtry, John xv. 20, 21. *The ſervant is not greater than the Lord: if they have perſecuted me, they will alſo perſecute you: if they have kept my ſaying, they will keep your's alſo. But all theſe things will they do unto you for my name's ſake.* That Levi was the ſon of *the hated*, ſeems not to have been without a myſtery, which the world, in all ages, hath unriddled. But though the earthen veſſels, wherein God has put the treaſure, be turned, with many, into veſſels wherein there is no pleaſure; yet why is the treaſure itſelf ſlighted? But ſlighted it is, and that with a witneſs, this day. *Lord, who hath believed our report? To whom ſhall we ſpeak?* Men can, without remorſe, make to themſelves ſilent Sabbaths, one after another. And alas! when they come to ordinances, for the moſt part, it is but *to appear* (or, as the word is, *to be ſeen*) before the Lord; and to *tread his courts*; namely, as a company of beaſts would do, if they were driven into them, Iſa. i. 12. So little reverence and awe of God appear on their ſpirits. Many ſtand like brazen walls before the word, in whoſe corrupt converſation the preaching of the word makes no breach. Nay, not a few are growing worſe and worſe, under precept upon precept; and the reſult of all is, *They go and fall backward, and are broken, and ſnared, and taken,* Iſa. xxviii. 13. What tears of blood are ſufficient to lament that (the goſpel) the grace of God is thus received in vain! We are but the voice of one crying; the Speaker is in heaven, and ſpeaks to you from heaven by men: why do you refuſe him that ſpeaketh? Heb. xii. 25. God has made our Maſter heir of all things, and we are ſent to court a ſpouſe for him. There is none ſo worthy as he; none more unworthy than they to whom this match is propoſed: but the prince of darkneſs is preferred before the Prince of Peace. A diſmal darkneſs overclouded the world by Adam's fall, more terrible than if the ſun, moon, and ſtars, had been for ever wrapped up in blackneſs of darkneſs; and there we ſhould have eternally lain, had not this grace of the goſpel, as a ſhining ſun, appeared to diſpel it, Tit. ii. 11. Yet we fly like night-owls from it; and like

Head I. Corruption of the Will.

the wild beasts, lay ourselves down in our dens, when the sun ariseth. We are struck blind with the light thereof; and as creatures of darkness, love darkness rather than light. Such is the enmity of the hearts of men against Christ, in his prophetical office.

Secondly, The natural man is an enemy to Christ in his priestly office. He is appointed of the Father a Priest for ever; that by his alone sacrifice and intercession, sinners may have peace with, and access to, God: but Christ crucified is a stumbling-block, and foolishness, to the unrenewed part of mankind, to whom he is preached, 1 Cor. i. 23. They are not for him, as the new and living way. Nor is he, by the voice of the world, an High-priest over the house of God. Corrupt nature goes quite another way to work.

Evidence 1. Not any of Adam's children naturally incline to receive the blessing in borrowed robes; but would always, according to the spider's motto, *owe all to themselves*; and so climb up to heaven on a thread spun out of their own bowels: for they desire to be under the law, Gal. iv. 21. and go about to establish their own righteousness, Rom. x. 3. Man naturally looks on God as a great Master, and himself as his servant, that must work, and win heaven as his wages. Hence, when conscience is awakened, he thinks, that to the end he may be saved, he must answer the demands of the law; serve God as well as he can, and pray for mercy wherein he comes short. Thus many come to duties, that never come out of them to Jesus Christ.

Evid. 2. As men naturally think highly of their duties, which seem to them to be well done; so they look for acceptance with God, according as their work is done, not according to the share they have in the blood of Christ. *Wherefore have we fasted, say they, and thou seest not?* They value themselves on their performances and attainments; yea, their very opinions in religion, (Phil. iii. 4, 5, 6, 7.) taking to themselves what they rob from Christ, the great High-priest.

Evid. 3. The natural man, going to God in duties, will always be found either to go without a Mediator, or with more than the one only Mediator, Jesus Christ.

Nature is blind, and therefore venturesome: it sets men a-going immediately to God without Christ; to rush into his presence, and put their petitions in his hand, without being introduced by the Secretary of heaven, or putting their requests into his hand. So fixed is this disposition in the unrenewed heart, that when many hearers of the gospel are conversed with, upon the point of their hopes of salvation, the name of Christ will scarcely be heard from their mouths. Ask them how they think to obtain the pardon of sin; they will tell you, they beg and look for mercy, because God is a merciful God; and that is all they have to confide in. Others look for mercy for Christ's sake: but how do they know that Christ will take their plea in hand? Why, as the Papists have their mediators with the Mediator, so have they. They know he cannot but do it; for they pray, confess, mourn, and have great desires, and the like: and so have something of their own to commend them unto him: they were never made poor in spirit, and brought empty handed to Christ, to lay the stress of all on his atoning blood.

Thirdly, The natural man is an enemy to Christ in his kingly office. The Father hath appointed the Mediator King in Zion, Psal. ii. 6. All to whom the gospel comes are commanded, on their highest peril, to kiss the Son, and submit themselves unto him, ver. 12. But the natural voice of mankind is, *Away with him*, as you may see, ver. 2, 3. They will not have him to reign over them, Luke xix. 14.

Evidence 1. The workings of corrupt nature, to wrest the government out of his hands. No sooner was he born, but, being born a king, Herod persecuted him, Mat. ii. And when he was crucified, they *set up over his head his accusation written, This is Jesus, the King of the Jews*, Mat. xxvii. 37. Though his kingdom be a spiritual kingdom, and not of this world, yet they cannot allow him a kingdom within a kingdom, which acknowledgeth no other head or supreme, but the royal Mediator. They make bold with his royal prerogatives, changing his laws, institutions, and ordinances; modelling his worship according to the devices of their

Corruption of the Will.

own hearts; introducing new offices and officers into his kingdom, not to be found in the book of the manner of his kingdom; difpofing of the external government thereof as may beft fuit their carnal defigns. Such is the enmity of the hearts of men againft Zion's King.

Evid. 2. How unwilling are men naturally to fubmit unto, and be hedged in, by the laws and difcipline of his kingdom! As a King, he is a law-giver, (Ifa. xxxiii 22.) and has appointed an external government, difcipline and cenfures, to controul the unruly, and to keep his profeffed fubjects in order, to be exercifed by officers of his own appointment, Matt. xviii. 17, 18. 1 Cor. xx. 28. 1 Tim. v. 17. Heb. xiii. 17. But thefe are the great eye-fores of the carnal world, who love finful liberty, and therefore cry out, *Let us break their bands afunder, and caft their cords away from us,* Pfal. ii. 3. Hence this work is found to be, in a fpecial manner, a ftriving againft the ftream of corrupt nature; which, for the moft part, puts fuch a face on the church, as if there were no king in Ifrael, every one doing that which is right in his own eyes.

Evid. 3. However natural men may be brought to feign fubmiffion to the King of faints, yet lufts always retain the throne and dominion in their hearts, and they are ferving divers lufts and pleafures, Tit. iii. 3. None but thofe in whom Chrift is formed, really put the crown on his head, and receive the kingdom of Chrift within them. His crown is the crown wherewith his mother crowned him in the day of his efpoufals. Who are they, whom the power of grace has not fubdued, that will allow him to fet up and to put down in their fouls as he will? Nay, as for others, any lord fhall fooner get the rule over them, than the lord of glory: they kindly entertain his enemies, but will never abfolutely refign themfelves to his government, till conquered in a day of power. Thus you may fee, that the natural man is an enemy to Jefus Chrift, in all his offices.

But O how hard it is to convince men in this point! They are very loath to take it up. And, in a fpecial manner, the enmity of the heart againft Chrift, in his prieftly office, feems to be hid from the view of moft of the hearers of the gospel. There appears to be a peculiar malignity in corrupt nature against that office of his. It may be observed, that the Socinians, those enemies of our blessed Lord, allow him to be properly a Prophet and a King, but deny him to be properly a Priest. And this is agreeable enough to the corruption of our nature; for, under the covenant of works, the Lord was known as a Prophet or Teacher, and also as a King or Ruler; but not at all as a Priest: so man knows nothing of the mystery of Christ, as the way to the Father, till it be revealed to him. And when it is revealed, the will riseth up against it; for corrupt nature lies cross to the mystery of Christ, and the great contrivance of salvation through the crucified Saviour, revealed in the gospel. For clearing of which weighty truths, let these four things be considered.

First, The soul's falling in with the grand scheme of salvation by Jesus Christ, and setting the matters of salvation on that footing before the Lord, is declared by the Scriptures of truth to be an undoubted mark of a real saint, who is happy here, and shall be happy hereafter, Mat. xi. 6. *Blessed is he whosoever shall not be offended in me.* 1 Cor. i. 23, 24. *But we preach Christ crucified, unto the Jews a stumbling-block, and unto the Greeks foolishness: but unto them which are called, both Jews and Greeks, Christ the power of God, and the wisdom of God.* Phil. iii. 3. *For we are the circumcision, which worship God in the Spirit, and rejoice in Jesus Christ, and have no confidence in the flesh.* Now how could this be, if nature could comply with that grand scheme?

Secondly, Corrupt nature is the very reverse of the gospel plan. In the gospel, God proposeth Jesus Christ as the great means of re-uniting man to himself: he has named him as the Mediator, one in whom he is well-pleased, and will have none but him, Mat. xvii. 5. But nature will have none of him, Psal. lxxi. 11. God appointed the place of meeting for the reconciliation, namely, the flesh of Christ; accordingly, God was in Christ, (2 Cor. v. 12.) as the tabernacle of meeting, to make up the peace with sinners: but natural men, though they should die for ever, will not come to Christ,

Head I.   *Corruption of the Will.*

John v. 40. *Ye will not come to me, that ye may have life.* In the way of the gospel, the sinner must stand before the Lord in imputed righteousness; therefore, so far as natural men follow after righteousness, they follow after *the law of righteousness,* Rom. xi. 31, 32. and not after *the Lord our righteousness.* Nature is always for building up itself, and to have some ground for boasting: but the great design of the gospel is to exalt grace, to depress nature, and exclude boasting, Rom. iii. 17. The sum of our natural religion is, to do good from and for ourselves, John v. 44. The sum of gospel religion is, to deny ourselves, and to do good from and for Christ, Phil. i. 21.

Thirdly, Every thing in nature is against believing in Jesus Christ. What beauty can the blind man discern in the crucified Saviour, for which he is to be desired? How can the will, naturally impotent, yea, and averse to good, make choice of him? Well may the soul then say to him, in the day of the spiritual siege, as the Jebusites said to David in another case, *Except thou take away the blind and the lame, thou shalt not come in hither,* 2 Sam. v. 6. The way of nature is to go into one's self for all; according to the fundamental maxim of unsanctified morality, that a man should trust in himself; which, according to the doctrine of faith, is mere foolishness: for so it is determined, Prov. xviii. 26. *He that trusteth in his own heart is a fool.* Now faith is the soul's going out of itself for all: and this nature, on the other hand, determines to be foolishness, 1 Cor. i. 18. 23. Wherefore, there is need of the working of mighty power, to cause sinners to believe, Eph. i. 19. Isa. liii. 1. We see the promises of welcome to sinners, in the gospel covenant, are ample, large, and free, clogged with no conditions, Isa. lv. 1. Rev. xxii. 17. If they cannot believe his bare word, he has given them his oath upon it, Ezek. xxxiii. 11. and, for their greater assurance, he has annexed seals to his sworn covenant, namely the holy sacraments. So that no more could be demanded of the most faithless person in the world, to make us believe him, than the Lord hath condescended to give us, to make us believe himself. This plainly speaks nature to be against believing, and those who flee to Christ for a refuge, to have need of strong consolation, (Heb. vi. 18.) to balance their strong doubts, and propensity to unbelief. Farther, also, it may be observed, how, in the word sent to a secure graceless generation, their objections are answered before-hand: and words of grace are heaped, one upon another, as you may read, Isa. lv. 7, 8, 9. Joel ii. 13. Why? Because the Lord knows, that when these secure sinners are throughly awakened, doubts, fears, and carnal reasonings against believing, will be getting into their breasts, as thick as dust in the house, raised by sweeping a dry floor.

Lastly, Corrupt nature is bent towards the way of the law, or covenant of works; and every natural man, so far as he sets himself to seek after salvation, is engaged in that way, and will not quit it, till beat from it by divine power. Now the way of salvation by works, and that of free grace in Jesus Christ, are contrary, Rom. xi. 6. *And if by grace, then it is no more of works; otherwise grace is no more grace. But if it be of works, then it is no more grace; otherwise work is no more work*, Gal. iii 12. *And the law is not of* faith; *but the man that doth them shall live in them.* Wherefore, if the will of man naturally incline to the way of salvation by the law, it lies cross to the gospel plan. And that such is the natural bent of our hearts will appear, if these following things be considered,

1. The law was Adam's covenant; and he knew no other, as he was the head and representative of all mankind, that were brought into it with him, and left under it by him, though without strength to perform the condition thereof. Hence, this covenant is interwoven with our nature; and though we have lost our father's strength, yet we still incline to the way he was set upon, as our head and representative in that covenant; that is, by doing, to live. This is our natural religion, and the principle which men naturally take for granted. Mat. xix. 16. *What good thing shall I* do, *that I may have eternal life.*

2. Consider the opposition that has always been made in the world, against the doctrine of free grace in Jesus

Chrift, by men fetting up for the way of works; thereby difcovering the natural tendency of the heart. It is manifeft, that the great defign of the gofpel plan is to exalt the free grace of God in Jefus Chrift, Rom. iv. 16. *Therefore it is of faith, that it might be by grace.* See Eph. i. 6. and chap. ii. 7. All gofpel-truths centre in Chrift: fo that to learn the truth, is to learn Chrift, Eph. iv. 20. And to be truly taught it, is to be taught. as *the truth is in Jefus,* ver. 21. All difpenfations of grace and favour from heaven, whether to nations or particular perfons, have ftill had fomething about them proclaiming the freedom of grace; as in the very firft feparation made by the divine favour, Cain, the elder brother, is rejected, and Abel, the younger, accepted. This fhines through the whole hiftory of the Bible: but, as true it is, this has been the point principally oppofed by corrupt nature. One may well fay, that, of all errors in religion, fince Chrift the feed of the woman was preached, this of works, in oppofition to free grace in him, was the firft that lived, and, it is likely, will be the laft that dies. There have been vaft numbers of errors, which fprung up one after another, whereof, at length, the world became afhamed and weary; fo that they died away. But this has continued from Cain, the firft author of this herefy, unto this day; and never wanted fome that clave to it, even in the times of greateft light. I do not, without ground, call Cain the author of it, who when Abel brought a facrifice of atonement, a bloody offering of the firftlings of his flock (like the Publican, fmiting on his breaft, and faying, *God be merciful to me a finner),* advanced with his thank-offering of the fruit of the ground, (Gen. iv. 3, 4.) like the proud Pharifee, with his *God, I thank thee.* For what was the caufe of Cain's wrath, and of his murdering Abel? Was it not, that he was not accepted of God for his work? Gen. iv. 4, 5. *And wherefore flew he him? becaufe his own works were evil, and his brother's righteous,* (1 John iii. 12.) that is, done in faith, and accepted, when his were done without faith, and therefore rejected, as the apoftle teacheth, Heb. xi. 4 So he wrote his indignation againft juftification and acceptance with God, through faith, in oppofition to works, in the blood of his brother, to convey it down to pofterity. And fince that time, the unbloody facrifice has often fwimmed in the blood of thofe that rejected it. The promife made to Abraham, of the feed in which all nations fhould be bleffed, was fo over-clouded among his pofterity in Egypt, that the generality of them faw no need of that way of obtaining the bleffing, till God himfelf confuted their error, by a fiery law from mount Sinai; which *was added becaufe of tranfgreffions, till the feed fhould come*, Gal. iii. 19. I need not infift in telling you, how Mofes and the Prophets had ftill much to do, to lead the people off the conceit of their own righteoufnefs. The ninth chapter of Deuteronomy is intirely fpent on that purpofe. They were very grofs in that point in our Saviour's time: in the time of the apoftles, when the doctrine of free grace was moft clearly preached, that error lifted up its head in the face of the cleareft light; witnefs the epiftles to the Romans and Galatians. And fince that time it has not been wanting; Popery being the common fink of former herefies, and the heart and life of that delufion. And, finally, it may be obferved, that always as the church declined from her purity otherwife, the doctrine of free grace was obfcured proportionably.

3. Such is the natural propenfity of man's heart to the way of the law, in oppofition to Chrift; that, as the tainted veffel turns the tafte of the pureft liquor put into it, fo the natural man turns the very gofpel into law, and transforms the covenant of grace into a covenant of works. The ceremonial law was to the Jews a real gofpel; which held blood, death, and tranflation of guilt, before their eyes continually, as the only way of falvation; yet their very table, (*i. e.* their altar, with the feveral ordinances pertaining thereto, Mal. i. 12.) was a fnare unto them, Rom. ii. 9. while they ufed it to make up the defects in their obedience to the moral law; and clave to it fo, as to reject him whom the altar and facrifices pointed them to, as the fubftance of all: even as Hagar, whofe duty was only to ferve, was by their father brought into her miftrefs's bed; not

without a myſtery in the purpoſe of God, for theſe are the two covenants, Gal. iv. 24. Thus is the doctrine of the goſpel corrupted by Papiſts, and other enemies to the doctrine of free grace. And, indeed, however natural men's heads may be ſet right in this point, as ſurely as they are out of Chriſt, their faith, repentance, and obedience (ſuch as they are), are placed by them in the room of Chriſt and his righteouſneſs, and ſo truſted to, as if by theſe they fulfilled a new law.

4. Great is the difficulty, in Adam's ſons, of their parting with the law as a covenant of works. None part with it, in that reſpect, but thoſe whom the power of the Spirit of grace ſeparates from it. The law is our firſt huſband, and gets every one's virgin love. When Chriſt comes to the ſoul, he finds it married to the law; ſo as it neither can nor will be married to another, till it be obliged to part with the firſt huſband, as the apoſtle teacheth, Rom. vii. 1—4. That you may ſee what ſort of a parting this is, conſider,

(1.) It is a death, Rom. vii. 4. Gal. ii. 19. Intreaties will not prevail with the ſoul here; it ſaith to the firſt huſband, as Ruth to Naomi, *The Lord do ſo to me, and more alſo, if ought but death part thee and me.* Here ſinners are true to their word; they die to the law, ere they be married to Chriſt. Death is hard to every body: but what difficulty do you imagine muſt a loving wife, on her death-bed, find in parting with her huſband, the huſband of her youth, and with the dear children ſhe has brought forth to him? The law is that huſband; all the duties performed by the natural man are theſe children. What a ſtruggle, as for life, will be in the heart before they be parted? I may have occaſion to touch upon this afterwards. In the mean time, take the apoſtle's ſhort but pithy deſcription of it, Rom. x. 3. *For they being ignorant of God's righteouſneſs, and going about to eſtabliſh their own righteouſneſs, have not ſubmitted themſelves to the righteouſneſs of God.* They go about to eſtabliſh their own righteouſneſs, like an eager diſputant in ſchools, ſeeking to eſtabliſh the point in queſtion; or like a tormentor, extorting a confeſſion from one upon the rack. They go about to eſtabliſh it, to make it stand: their righteousness is like a house built upon the sand, it cannot stand; but they would have it stand: it falls, they set it up again; but still it tumbles down on them; yet they cease not to go about to make it stand. But wherefore all this pains about a tottering righteousness? Because, such as it is, it is their own. What sets them against Christ's righteousness? Why, that would make them free grace's debtors for all: and that is what the proud heart can by no means submit to. Here lies the stress of the matter, Psal. x. 4. *The wicked, through the pride of his countenance, will not seek* (to read it without the supplement); that is, in other terms, *He cannot dig,* and *to beg he is ashamed.* Such is the struggle ere the soul die to the law. But, what speaks yet more of this woful disposition of the heart, nature oft-times gets the mastery of the disease; in-so-much that the soul, which was like to have died to the law, while convictions were sharp and piercing, fatally recovers of the happy and promising sickness; and (what is natural) cleaves more closely than ever to the law, even as a wife, brought back from the gates of death, would cleave to her husband. This is the issue of the exercises of many about their soul's case: they are indeed brought to follow duties more closely; but they are as far from Christ as ever, if not farther.

(2.) It is a violent death, Rom. vii. 4. *Ye are become dead to the law,* being killed, slain, or put to death, as the word bears. The law itself has a great hand in this; the husband gives the wound, Gal. ii. 19. *I, through the law, am dead to the law.* The soul that dies this death, is like a loving wife matched with a rigorous husband. She does what she can to please him, yet he is never pleased, but tosseth, harasseth, and beats her, till she breaks her heart, and death sets her free; as will afterwards more fully appear. Thus it is made evident, that men's hearts are naturally bent to the way of the law, and lie cross to the gospel method: and the second article of the charge, against you that are unregenerate, is verified, namely, that you are enemies to the Son of God.

Thirdly, You are enemies to the Spirit of God. He is the Spirit of holiness: the natural man is unholy,

Head I.   *Corruption of the Will.*   87

and loves to be fo, and therefore refifts the Holy Ghoft, Acts vii. 51. The work of the Spirit is to convince the world of fin, and of righteoufnefs, and of judgment, John xvi. 8. But O how do men ftrive to ward off thefe convictions, as much as they would ward off a blow threatening the lofs of a right eye, or a right hand! If the Spirit of the Lord dart them in, fo that they cannot avoid them, the heart fays, in effect, as Ahab to Elijah, whom he both hated and feared, *Haft thou found me, O mine enemy!* And, indeed, they treat him as an enemy, doing their utmoft to ftifle convictions, and to murder thefe harbingers, that come to prepare the Lord's way into the foul. Some fill their hands with bufinefs, to put their convictions out of their heads; as Cain, who fet about building a city: fome put them off with delays and fair promifes, as Felix did: fome will fport them away in company, and fome fleep them away. The Holy Spirit is the Spirit of fanctification; whofe work is to fubdue lufts, and burn up corruption: how then can the natural man, whofe lufts are to him as his limbs, yea, as his life, fail of being an enemy to him?

Laftly, You are enemies to the law of God. Though the natural man defires to be under the law, as a covenant of works; choofing that way of falvation, in oppofition to the myftery of Chrift: yet, as it is a rule of life to him, requiring univerfal holinefs, and forbidding all manner of impurity, he is an enemy to it; *is not fubject to the law of God, neither indeed can be*, Rom. viii. 7. for, (1.) There is no unrenewed man who is not wedded to fome one luft or another, which his heart can by no means part with. Now that he cannot bring up his inclinations to the holy law, he would fain have the law brought down to his inclinations: a plain evidence of the enmity of the heart againft it. Therefore to delight in the law of God, after the inward man, is propofed in the word as a mark of a gracious foul, Rom. vii. 22. Pfal. i. 2. It is from this natural enmity of the heart againft the law, that all the Pharifaical gloffes upon it have arifen; whereby the commandment, which is in itfelf exceeding broad, has been made very narrow, to the intent it might be the more agreeable to the natural difpofition of the heart. (2.) The law laid home on the natural confcience, in its fpirituality, irritates corruption. The nearer it comes, nature rifeth the higher againft it. In that cafe, it is as oil to the fire, which, inftead of quenching it, makes it flame the more : *when the commandment came, fin revived*, fays the apoftle, Rom. vii. 9. What reafon can be affigned for this, but the natural enmity of the heart againft the holy law? Unmortified corruption, the more it is oppofed, the more it rageth. Let us conclude, then, that the unregenerate are heart-enemies to God, his Son, his Spirit, and his law; that there is a natural contrariety, oppofition, and enmity, in the will of man, to God himfelf, and his holy will.

Fifthly, There is, in the will of man, contumacy againft the Lord. Man's will is naturally wilful in an evil courfe : he will have his will, though it fhould ruin him. It is with him as with the Leviathan, (Job. xli. 29. *Darts are counted as ftubble, he laugheth at the fhaking of a fpear*. The Lord calls to him by his word; fays to him, (as Paul to the jailor, when he was about to kill himfelf) *Do thyfelf no harm*; finner, *why will you die?* Ezek. xvii. 31. But they will not hearken; *Every one turneth to his courfe, as the horfe rufheth into the battle*, Jer. viii. 6. We have a promife of life, in the form of a command, Prov. iv. 4. *Keep my commandments, and live :* it fpeaks impenitent finners to be felf-deftroyers, wilful felf-murderers. They tranfgrefs the command of living; as though a man's fervant fhould wilfully ftarve himfelf to death, or greedily drink a cup of poifon, which his mafter commands him to forbear : even fo do they ; they will not live, they will die, Prov. viii. 36. *All they that hate me love death.* O what a heart is this ! It is a ftony heart, (Ezek. xxxvi. 26.) hard and inflexible as a ftone : mercies melt it not, judgments break it not ; yet it will break ere it bow. It is an infenfible heart : though there be upon the finner a weight of fin, which makes the earth to ftagger; although there is a weight of that wrath on him, which makes the devils tremble, yet he goes lightly under the burden, he feels not the weight, any more than a stone would, till the Spirit of the Lord quickens him so far as to feel it.

Lastly, The unrenewed will is wholly perverse, in reference to man's chief and highest end. The natural man's chief end is not God, but himself. The being of man is merely relative, dependent, and derived. He has neither being nor goodness originally from himself; but all he hath is from God, as the first cause and spring of all perfection, natural or moral: dependence is woven into his very nature; so that, if God were totally to withdraw from him, he would dwindle into nothing. Seeing, then, whatever man is, he is of him; surely, in whatever he is, he should be to him; as the waters which come from the sea, do of course return thither again. Thus man was created, directly looking to God as his chief end. But, falling into sin, he fell off from God, and turned into himself; and, like a traitor usurping the throne, he gathers in the rents of the crown to himself. This infers a total apostasy, and universal corruption in man; for where the chief and last end is changed, there can be no goodness there. This is the case of all men in their natural state, Psal. xiv. 2, 3. *The Lord looked down—to see if there were any that did—seek God. They are all gone aside,* to wit, from God; they seek not God, but themselves. Though many fair shreds of morality are to be found amongst them, yet *there is none that doth good, no, not one;* for though some of them, in appearance, run well, yet they are still off the way; they never aim at the right mark: they are *lovers of their own selves more than God,* 2 Tim. iii. 2. 4. Wherefore, Jesus Christ having come into the world to bring men back to God again, came to bring them out of themselves in the first place, Mat. xvi. 24. The godly groan under this woful disposition of the heart: they acknowledge it, and set themselves against it in its subtile and dangerous insinuations. The unregenerate, though most insensible of it, are under the power thereof; and whithersoever they turn themselves, they cannot move beyond the circle of self:

they feek themfelves, they act for themfelves; their natural, civil, and religious actions, from whatever fprings they come, all run into, and meet in, the dead fea of felf. Moft men are fo far from making God their chief end, in their natural and civil actions, that, in thefe matters, God is not in all their thoughts. Their eating and drinking, and fuch like natural actions, are for themfelves, their own pleafure or neceffity, without any higher end, Zech. vii. 6. *Did ye not eat for yourfelves?* They have no eye to the glory of God in thefe things, as they ought to have, 1 Cor. x. 31. They do not eat and drink, to keep up their bodies for the Lord's fervice; they do them not becaufe God has faid, *Thou fhalt not kill:* neither do thofe drops of fweetnefs, which God has put into the creature, raife up their fouls towards that ocean of delights that are in the Creator; though they are a fign, hung out at heaven's door, to tell men of the fulnefs of goodnefs that is in God himfelf, Acts xiv. 17. But it is felf, and not God, that is fought in them by natural men. And what are the unrenewed man's civil actions, fuch as buying, felling, working, &c. but fruit to himfelf? Hof. x. 1. So, marrying, and giving in marriage, are reckoned amongft the fins of the old world, (Mat. xxiv. 38.) for they had no eye to God therein, to pleafe him; but all they had in view was, to pleafe themfelves, Gen. vi. 3. Finally, felf is natural men's higheft end in their religious actions. They perform duties for a name, Mat. vi. 1, 2. or fome other worldly intereft, John vi. 26. Or, if they be more refined, it is their peace, and, at moft, their falvation from hell and wrath, or their own eternal happinefs, that is their chief and higheft end, Mat. xix. 16—22. Their eyes are held, that they fee not the glory of God. They feek God, indeed, but not for himfelf, but for themfelves: they feek him not at all, but for their own welfare: fo their whole life is woven into one web of practical blafphemy; making God the means, and felf their end, yea, their chief end.

Thus I have given you fome rude draught of man's will, and his natural ftate, drawn by Scripture, and men's own experience. Call it no more Naomi, but

Marah; for bitter it is, and a root of bitterness. Call it no more free-will, but flavish luft; free to evil, but free from good, till regenerating grace unloofe the bands of wickedness. Now, since all muft be wrong, and nothing can be right, where the underftanding and will are fo corrupt, I fhall briefly difpatch what remains, as following of courfe, on the corruption of the prime faculties of the foul; viz.

The Corruption of the Affections, the Confcience, and the Memory. The Body Partaker of this Corruption.

III. The *affections* are corrupted. The unrenewed man's affections are wholly difordered and diftempered: they are as the unruly horfe, that either will not receive, or violently runs away with the rider. So man's heart naturally is a mother of abominations, Mark vii. 21, 22. *For from within, out of the heart of man proceed evil thoughts, adulteries, fornications, murders, thefts, covetoufnefs,* &c. The natural man's affections are wretchedly mifplaced; he is a fpiritual monfter. His heart is where his feet fhould be, fixed on the earth; his heels are lifted up againft heaven, which his heart fhould be fet on, Acts ix. 5 His face is towards hell, his back towards heaven; and therefore God calls to him to turn. He loves what he fhould hate, and hates what he fhould love; joys in what he ought to mourn for, and mourns for what he fhould rejoice in; glorieth in his fhame, and is afhamed of his glory; abhors what he fhould defire, and defires what he fhould abhor, Prov. ii. 13, 14, 15. They hit the point, indeed (as Caiphas did in another cafe), who cried out againft the apoftles, as men that turned the world upfide down; for that is the work which the gofpel has to do in the world, wherein has put all things fo out of order, that heaven lies under, and earth a-top. If the unrenewed affections be fet on lawful objects, then they are either exceffive, or defective. Lawful enjoyments of the world have fometimes too little, but moftly too much of them: Either they get not their due, or, if they do, it is meafure preffed down, and running over. Spiritual things have always too little of them. In a word, they are never right; *only evil*.

Now here is a three-fold cord, againſt heaven and holineſs, not eaſily broken; a blind mind, a perverſe will, and diſorderly diſtempered affections. The mind, ſwelled with ſelf-conceit, ſays, the man ſhould not ſtoop; the will, oppoſite to the will of God, ſays, he will not; and the corrupt affections, riſing againſt the Lord, in defence of the corrupt will, ſay, he ſhall not. Thus the poor creature ſtands out againſt God and goodneſs, till a day of power come, in which he is made a new creature.

Fourthly, The conſcience is corrupt and defiled, Tit. i. 15. It is an evil eye, that fills one's converſation with much darkneſs and confuſion; being naturally unable to do its office; till the Lord, by letting in new light to the ſoul, awaken the conſcience, it remains ſleepy and inactive. Conſcience can never do its work, but according to the light it hath to work by. Wherefore, ſeeing the natural man cannot ſpiritually diſcern ſpiritual things, (1 Cor. ii. 14.) the conſcience naturally is quite uſeleſs in that point; being caſt into ſuch a deep ſleep, that nothing but ſaving illumination from the Lord can ſet it on work in that matter. The light of the natural conſcience, in good and evil, ſin and duty, is very defective: therefore, though it may check for groſſer ſins, yet, as to the more ſubtile workings of ſin, it cannot check for them, becauſe it diſcerns them not. Thus, conſcience will fly in the face of many, if at any time they be drunk, ſwear, neglect prayer, or be guilty of any groſs ſin; who otherwiſe have a profound peace, though they live in the ſin of unbelief, and are ſtrangers to ſpiritual worſhip, and the life of faith. Natural light, being but faint and languiſhing, in many things which it doth reach, conſcience, in that caſe, ſhoots like a ſtitch in one's ſide, which quickly goes off; its incitements to duty, and checks for, and ſtruggles againſt ſin, are very remiſs, which the natural man eaſily gets over. But becauſe there is a falſe light in the dark mind, the natural conſcience following the ſame, will call evil good, and good evil,

Isa. v. 20. So it is often found like a furious and blind horse, which violently runs down himself, his rider, and all that come in his way, John xvi. 2. *Whosoever killeth you, will think that he doth God service.* When the natural conscience is awakened by the Spirit of conviction, it will indeed rage and roar, and put the whole man in a dreadful consternation; awfully summon all the powers of the soul to help in a strait; make the stiff heart to tremble, and the knees to bow; set the eyes a weeping, the tongue a confessing, and oblige the man to cast out the goods into the sea, which it apprehends are likely to sink the ship of the soul, though the heart still goes after them: yet it is an evil conscience, which naturally leads to despair, and will do it effectually, as in Judas's case; unless either lusts prevail over it, to lull it asleep, as in the case of Felix, Acts xxiv. 25. or the blood of Christ prevail over it, sprinkling and purging it from dead works, as in the case of all true converts, Heb. ix. 14. and x. 22.

Lastly, Even the memory bears evident marks of this corruption. What is good and worthy to be remembered, as it makes but slender impression, so that im pression easily wears off; the memory, as a leaking vessel, lets it slip, Heb. ii. 1. As a sieve that is full when in the water, lets all go when it is taken out, so is the memory with respect to spiritual things. But how does it retain what ought to be forgotten ! Naughty things so bear in themselves upon it, that though men would fain have them out of mind, yet they stick there like glew However forgetful men are in other things, it is hard to forget an injury. So the memory often furnishes new fewel to old lusts; makes men in old age re-act the sins of their youth, while it presents them again to the mind with delight, which thereupon licks up the former vomit. Thus it is like a riddle, that lets through the pure grain, and keeps the refuse. Thus far of the corruption of the soul.

The body itself also is partaker of this corruption and defilement, so far as it is capable thereof. Wherefore the Scripture calls it *sinful flesh,* Rom. viii. 3. We may take this up in two things: (1.) The natural temper, or rather diftemper, of the bodies of Adam's children, as it in an effect of original fin, fo it hath a natural tendency to fin, incites to fin, leads the foul into fnares, yea, is itfelf a fnare to the foul. The body is a furious beaft, of fuch metal, that if it be not beat down, kept under, and brought into fubjection, it will caft the foul into much fin and mifery, 1 Cor. ix. 27. There is a vilenefs in the body, (Phil. iii. 21.) which, as to the faints, will never be removed, until it be melted down in the grave, and caft into a new mould, at the refurrection, to come forth a fpiritual body: and will never be carried off from the bodies of thofe who are not partakers of the refurrection to life. (2.) It ferves the foul in many fins. Its members are inftruments or weapons of unrighteoufnefs, whereby men fight againft God, Rom. vi. 13. The eyes and ears are open doors, by which impure motions and finful defires enter the foul: the tongue is *a world of iniquity*, James iii. 6. 8. *an unruly evil, full of deadly poifon.* By it the impure heart vents a great deal of its filthinefs. *The throat is an open fepulchre,* Rom. iii. 13. The feet run the devil's errands, ver. 15. The belly is made a God, Phil. iii. 19. not only by drunkards and riotous livers, but by every natural man, Zech. vii. 6. So the body naturally is an agent for the devil, and a magazine of armour againft the Lord.

To conclude; Man by nature is wholly corrupted: from the fole of the foot, even unto the head, there is no foundnefs in him. As in a dunghill, every part contributes to the corruption of the whole: fo the natural man, while in that ftate, grows ftill worfe and worfe. The foul is made worfe by the body, and the body by the foul: and every faculty of the foul ferves to corrupt another more and more. Thus much for the fecond general head.

How Man's Nature was corrupted.

THIRDLY, I fhall fhew how man's nature comes to be thus corrupted. The heathens perceived that man's nature was corrupted; but how fin entered, they could not tell. But the Scripture is very plain in that point,

Head I. *How man's Nature was corrupted.* 95

Rom. vi. 12. 19. *By one man sin entered into the world. By one man's disobedience many were made sinners.* Adam's sin corrupted man's nature, and leavened the whole lump of mankind. We putrified in Adam, as our root. The root was poisoned, and so the branches were invenomed; the vine turned into the vine of Sodom, and so the grapes became grapes of gall. Adam, by his sin, became not only guilty, but corrupt; and so transmits guilt and corruption to his posterity, Gen. v. 3. Job xiv. 4. By his sin he stripped himself of his original righteousness, and corrupted himself: we were in him representatively, being represented by him, as our moral head, in the covenant of works; we were in him seminally, as our natural head; hence we fell in him, and by his disobedience were made sinners, as Levi, in the loins of Abraham, paid tithes, Heb. vii. 9, 10. His first sin is imputed to us; therefore justly are we left under the want of his original righteousness, which being given to him as a common person, he cast off by his sin: and this necessarily followed, in him and us, by the corruption of the whole nature; righteousness and corruption being two contraries, one of which must needs always be in man, as a subject capable thereof. And Adam, our common father, being corrupt, we are so too; for *who can bring a clean thing out of an unclean?*

Although it is sufficient to prove the righteousness of this dispensation, that it was from the Lord, who doth all things well; yet to silence the murmurings of proud nature, let these few things further be considered: (1.) In the covenant, wherein Adam represented us, eternal happiness was promised to him and his posterity, upon condition of his, that is Adam's, perfect obedience, as the representative of all mankind: whereas, if there had been no covenant, they could not have pleaded eternal life upon their most perfect obedience, but might have been, after all, reduced to nothing; notwithstanding, by natural justice, they would have been liable to God's eternal wrath, in case of sin. Who, in that case, would not have consented to that representation? (2.) Adam had a power given him to stand. Being made upright, he was as capable of standing for himfelf, and all his pofterity, as any after him could be for themfelves. This trial of mankind in their head, would foon have been over, and the crown won for them all, had he ftood; whereas, had his pofterity been independent of him, and every one left to act for himfelf, the trial would have been continually carrying on, as men came into the world. (3.) He had the ftrongeft natural affection to engage him, being our common father. (4.) His own ftock was in the fhip, his all lay at ftake, as well as ours. He had no feparate intereft from ours; but if he forgot ours, he muft necefſarily forget his own. (5.) If he had ftood, we fhould have had the light of his mind, the righteoufnefs of his will, and the holinefs of his affections, with entire purity, tranfmitted unto us: we could not have fallen; the crown of glory, by his obedience, would have been for ever fecured to him and his. This is evident from the nature of a federal reprefentation; and no reafon can be given why, feeing we are loft by Adam's fin, we fhould not have been faved by his obedience. On the other hand, it is reafonable, that he falling, we fhould with him bear the lofs. *Laftly,* Such as quarrel with this difpenfation, muft renounce their part in Chrift; for we are no otherwife made finners by Adam, than we are made righteous by Chrift; from whom we have both imputed and inherent righteoufnefs. We no more made choice of the fecond Adam, for our head and reprefentative in the fecond covenant, than we did of the firft Adam in the firft covenant.

Let none wonder that fuch an horrible change could be brought on, by one fin of our firft parents; for thereby they turned away from God, as their chief end, which necefſarily infers an univerfal depravation. Their fin was a complication of evils, a total apoftafy from God, a violation of the whole law. By it they broke all the ten commands at once. (1.) They chofe new gods. They made their belly their god, by their fenfuality; felf their god, by their ambition; yea, and the devil their god, by believing him, and difbelieving their

Head I. *How Man's Nature was corrupted.*

Maker. (2.) Though they received, yet they obferved not, that ordinance of God about the forbidden fruit. They contemned that ordinance, fo plainly enjoined them, and would needs carve out to themfelves how to ferve the Lord. (3.) They took the name of the Lord their God in vain; defpifing his attributes, his juftice, truth, power, &c. They grofly profaned the facramental tree; abufed his word, by not giving credit to it; abufed that creature of his, which they fhould not have touched; and violently mifconftrued his providence, as if God, by forbidding them that tree, had been ftanding in the way of their happinefs: therefore he fuffered them not to efcape his righteous judgement. (4.) They remembered not the Sabbath to keep it holy, but put themfelves out of a condition to ferve God aright on his own day: neither kept they that ftate of holy reft wherein God had put them. (5.) They caft off their relative duties: Eve forgets herfelf, and acts without advice of her hufband, to the ruin of both: Adam, inftead of admonifhing her to repent, yields to the temptation, and confirms her in her wickednefs. They forgot all duty to their pofterity. They honoured not their Father in heaven; and therefore their days were not long in the land which the Lord their God gave them. (6.) They ruined themfelves and all their pofterity. (7.) Gave up themfelves to luxury and fenfuality. (8.) Took away what was not their own, againft the exprefs will of the great Owner. (9.) They bore falfe witnefs, and lied againft the Lord, before angels, devils, and one another; in effect giving out that they were hardly dealt by, and that Heaven grudged their happinefs. (10.) They were difcontent with their lot, and coveted an evil covetoufnefs to their houfe; which ruined both them and theirs. Thus was the image of God on man defaced all at once.

The Doctrine of the Corruption of Nature applied.

Use I. For information. Is man's nature wholly corrupted? Then,

1. No wonder that the grave opens its devouring mouth for us, as foon as the womb hath caft us forth:

and that the cradle be turned into a coffin, to receive the corrupt lump: for we are all, in a spiritual sense, dead-born; yea, and filthy, (Psal. xiv. 3.) noisome, rank, and stinking as a corrupt thing, as the word imports. Then let us not complain of the miseries which we are exposed to, at our entrance into, nor of the continuance of them, while we are in the world. Here is the venom that has poisoned all the springs of earthly enjoyments which we have to drink of. It is the corruption of man's nature that brings forth all the miseries of human life in churches, states, and families; and in men's souls and bodies.

2. Behold here, as in a glass, the spring of all the wickedness, profanity, and formality, which is in the world; the source of all the disorders in thy own heart and life. Every thing acts like itself, agreeable to its own nature; and so corrupt man acts corruptly. You need not wonder at the sinfulness of your own heart and life, nor at the sinfulness and perverseness of others: if a man be crooked, he cannot but halt; and if the clock be set wrong, how can it point the hour aright.

3. See here why sin is so pleasant, and religion such a burden to carnal spirits: sin is natural, holiness not so. Oxen cannot feed in the sea, nor fishes in the fruitful fields: a swine, brought into a palace, would soon get away again, to wallow in the mire: and corrupt nature tends ever to impurity.

1. Learn from this the nature and necessity of regeneration. *First*, This discovers the nature of regeneration in these two things; (1.) It is not a partial, but a total change, though imperfect in this life. Thy whole nature is corrupted, and therefore the cure must go through every part. Regeneration makes not only a new head for knowledge, but a new heart, and new affections for holiness. All things become new, 2 Cor. v. 17. If one having received many wounds, should be cured of them all, save one only, he might bleed to death by that one, as well as a thousand. So if the change go not through the whole man, it is naught. (2.) It is not a change made by human industry, but by the mighty power of the Spirit of God. A man must be born of

the Spirit, John iii. 5. Accidental difeafes may be cured by men, but thofe which are natural, not without a miracle, John ix. 32. The change brought upon men by good education, or forced upon them by a natural confcience, though it may pafs among men for a faving change, yet it is not fo; for our nature is corrupt, and none but the God of nature can change it. Though a gardener, ingrafting a pear-branch into an apple-tree, may make the apple tree bear pears; yet the art of man cannot change the nature of the apple-tree: fo a man may pin a new life to his old heart, but he can never change the heart. *Secondly*, This alfo fhews the neceffity of regeneration. It is abfolutely neceffary in order to falvation, John iii. 3. *Except a man be born again, he cannot fee the kingdom of God.* No unclean thing can enter the new Jerufalem: but thou art wholly unclean, while in thy natural ftate. If every member of thy body were disjointed, each joint muft be loofened, before the members can be fet right again. This is the cafe of thy foul, as thou haft heard: therefore thou muft be born again, otherwife thou fhalt never fee heaven, unlefs it be afar off, as the rich man in hell did. Deceive not thyfelf: no mercy of God, no blood of Chrift, will bring thee to heaven, in thy unregenerate ftate: for God will never open a fountain of mercy to wafh away his own holinefs and truth; nor did Chrift fhed his precious blood to blot out the truths of God, or to overturn God's meafures about the falvation of finners. Heaven! what would you do there, who are not born again? you who are no ways fitted for Chrift the Head? That would be a ftrange fight, a holy Head, and members wholly corrupt! a Head full of treafures of grace! members wherein are nothing but treafures of wickednefs! a Head obedient to the death, and heels kicking againft heaven! You are no better adapted for the fociety above, than beafts for converfe with men. Thou art a hater of true holinefs; and, at the firft fight of a faint there, wouldft cry out, *Haft thou found me, O mine enemy!* Nay, the unrenewed man, if it were poffible he could go to heaven in that ftate, he would no otherwife go to it, than now he comes to the duties of holiness, that is, leaving his heart behind him.

USE II. For lamentation. Well may we lament thy case, O natural man, for it is the saddest case one can be in, out of hell. It is time to lament for thee; for thou art dead already, dead while thou livest; thou carriest about with thee a dead soul in a living body; and because thou art dead thou canst not lamen' thy own case. Thou art loathsome in the sight of God; for thou art altogether corrupt; thou hast no good in thee. Thy soul is a mass of darkness, rebellion, and vileness before the Lord. Thou thinkest, perhaps, that thou hast a good heart to God, good inclinations, and good desires: but God knows there is nothing good in thee; every imagination of thine heart is only evil continually. Thou canst do no good; thou canst do nothing but sin. For,

First, Thou art the servant of sin, Rom. vi. 17. and therefore free from righteousness, verse 20. Whatever righteousness be, poor soul, thou art free from it; thou dost not, thou canst not meddle with it. Thou art under the dominion of sin; a dominion where righteousness can have no place. Thou art a child and servant of the devil, though thou be neither wizzard nor witch; seeing thou art yet in a state of nature, John viii. 44. *Ye are of your Father the devil.* And, to prevent any mistake, consider, that sin and Satan have two sorts of servants: (1.) There are some employed, as it were, in coarser work: those bear the devil's mark in their foreheads, having no form of godliness; but are profane, grossly ignorant, mere moralists, not so much as performing the external duties of religion, but living in the view of the world as sons of earth, only minding earthly things, Phil. iii. 19. (2.) There are some employed in a more refined sort of service to sin, who carry the devil's mark in their right hand; which they can and do hide from the view of the world. These are close hypocrites, who sacrifice as much to the corrupt mind, as the others to the flesh, Eph. ii. 3. These are ruined by a more undiscernible trade of sin: pride, unbelief, self-seeking, and the like, swarm in, and prey upon their corrupted, wholly corrupted souls. Both are servants of the same house; the latter as far as the former from righteousness.

Head I. *Doctrine of Natural Corruption applied.* 101

Secondly, How is it possible that thou shouldst be able to do any good, thou whose nature is wholly corrupt? Can fruit grow where there is no root? or can there be an effect without a cause? *Can the fig-tree bear olive-berries, either a vine figs?* If thy nature be wholly corrupt, as indeed it is, all thou dost is certainly so too; for no effect can exceed the virtue of its cause. *Can a corrupt tree bring forth good fruit?* Matth. vii. 18.

Ah! what a miserable spectacle is he that can do nothing but sin! Thou art the man, whoever thou art, that art yet in thy natural state. Hear, O sinner, what is thy case.

First, Innumerable sins compass thee about; mountains of guilt are lying upon thee; floods of impurities overwhelm thee. Living lusts, of all sorts, roll up and down in the dead sea of thy soul; where no good can breath, because of the corruption there. Thy lips are unclean: the opening of thy mouth is as the opening of an unripe grave, full of stench and rottenness, Rom. iii. 13. *Their throat is an open sepulchre.* Thy natural actions are sin; for *when ye did eat, and when ye did drink, did not ye eat for yourselves, and drink for yourselves?* Zech. vii. 9. Thy civil actions are sin, Prov. xxi. 4. *The ploughing of the wicked is sin.* Thy religious actions are sin, Prov. xv. 8. *The sacrifice of the wicked is an abomination to the Lord.* The thoughts and imaginations of thy heart are only evil continually. A deed may be soon done, a word soon spoken, a thought swiftly pass through the heart; but each of these is an *item* in thy accounts. O sad reckoning! As many thoughts, words, and actions, so many sins. The longer thou livest, thy accounts swell the more. Should a tear be dropt for every sin, thine head must be waters, and thine eyes a fountain of tears: for nothing but sin comes from thee. Thy heart frames nothing but evil imaginations: there is nothing in thy life but what is framed by thine heart; and therefore there is nothing in thy heart or life, but evil.

Secondly, All thy religion, if thou hast any, is lost labour, as to acceptance with God, or any saving effect on thyself. Art thou yet in thy natural state? Truly, then, thy duties are sins, as was just now hinted. Would not the best wine be loathsome, in a vessel wherein there is no pleasure? So is the religion of an unregenerate man. Under the law, the garment which the flesh of the sacrifice was carried in, though it touched other things, did not make them holy: but he that was unclean, touching any thing, whether common or sacred, made it unclean. Even so thy duties cannot make thy corrupt soul holy, though they in themselves be good; but thy corrupt heart defiles them, and makes them unclean, Hag. ii. 12, 13, 14. Thou wast wont to divide thy works into two sorts, some good, some evil: but thou must count again, and put them all under one head; for God writes on them all, Only evil. This is lamentable. It will be no wonder to see those beg in harvest, who fold their hands, and sleep, in feed-time: but to be labouring with others in the spring, and yet have nothing to reap when the harvest comes, is a very sad case; and will be the case of all professors, living and dying in their natural state.

Lastly, Thou canst not help thyself. What canst thou do to take away thy sin, who art wholly corrupt? Nothing, truly, but sin. If a natural man begin to relent, drop a tear for his sin, and reform, presently the corrupt nature apprehends at least a merit of congruity: he has done much himself (he thinks), and God cannot but do more for him on that account. In the mean time he does nothing but sin: so that the fitness of the merit is, that the leper be put out of the camp; the dead soul buried out of sight; and the corrupt lump cast into the pit. How canst thou think to recover thyself, by any thing which thou canst do? Will mud and filth wash out filthiness? and wilt thou purge out sin by sinning? Job took a potsherd to scrape himself, because his hands were as full of boils as his body. This is the case of thy corrupt soul; not to be recovered, but by Jesus Christ, whose strength was dried up like a potsherd, Psal. xxii. 15. Thou art poor indeed, extremely *miserable and poor*, Rev. iii. 17. Thou hast no shelter but a refuge of lies; no garment for thy soul, but filthy rags; nothing to nourish it but husks, that cannot satisfy. And more than this, thou didst

Head I. *Doctrine of Natural Corruption applied.* 103

get such a bruise in the loins of Adam, as is not yet cured. Thou art *without strength*, Rom. v. 6. unable to do or work for thyself: nay more than all this, thou canst not so much as think aright, but art lying helpless, as an infant exposed in the open field, Ezek. xvi. 5.

Use III. I exhort you to believe this sad truth. Alas! it is evident, that it is very little believed in the world. Few are concerned to get their corrupt conversation changed: but fewer, by far, to get their nature changed. Most men know not what they are, nor what spirits they are of: they are as the eye, which seeing many things, never sees itself. But until you know every one the plague of his own heart, there is no hope of your recovery. Why will you not believe it? You have plain scripture testimony for it; but you are loath to entertain such an ill opinion of yourselves: alas! this is the nature of your disease, Rev. iii. 17. *Thou—knowest not that thou art wretched, and miserable, and poor, and blind, and naked.* Lord, open their eyes to see it, before they die of it; and in hell lift up their eyes, and see what they will not see now.

I shall shut up this weighty point, of the corruption of man's nature, with a few words as to another doctrine from the text.

Doctrine, God takes special notice of our natural corruption, or the sin of our nature. This he testifies two ways; (1.) By his word, as in the text, *God saw that every imagination of the thoughts of man's heart was only evil continually.* See Psal. xiv. 2, 3. (2.) By his works. God marks his particular notice of it, and displeasure with it, as in many of his works, so especially in these two,

(1.) In the death of the infant children of men. Many miseries they have been exposed to: they were drowned in the deluge, consumed in Sodom by fire and brimstone; they have been slain with the sword, dashed against the stones, and are still dying ordinary deaths. What is the true cause of this? On what ground doth the holy God thus pursue them? Is it the sin of their parents? That may be the occasion of the Lord's raising the procefs againft them; but it muft be their own fin that is the ground of the fentence paffing on them : for *the foul that finneth, it fhall die*, faith God, Ezek. xviii. 4. Is it their own actual fin? They have none. But as men do with toads and ferpents, which they kill at firft fight, before they have done any hurt; becaufe of their venomous nature : fo it is in this cafe.

(2.) In the birth of the elect children of God. When the Lord is about to change their nature, he makes the fin of their nature lie heavy upon their fpirits. When he means to let out the corruption, the lance goes deep into their fouls, reaching to the root of fin, Rom. vii. 7, 8, 9. The flefh, or corruption of nature, is pierced, being crucified, as well as the affections and lufts, Gal. v. 24.

USE. Let us then have a fpecial eye upon the corruption and fin of our nature. God fees it: O that we faw it too, and that fin were ever before us! What avails it to notice other fins, while this mo.her-fin is not noticed! Turn your eyes inward to the fin of your nature. It is to be feared, that many have this work to begin yet; that they have fhut the door, while the grand thief is yet in the houfe undifcovered. This is a weighty point; and in handling of it,

I. I fhall, for conviction, point at fome evidences of men's overlooking the fin of their nature; which yet the Lord takes particular notice of. (1.) Men's looking on themfelves with fuch confidence, as if they were in no hazard of grofs fins. Many would take it very hainoufly to get fuch a caution as Chrift gave his apoftles, Luke xxi. 3 4. *Take heed of furfeiting and drunkennefs*. If any fhould fuppofe them to break out in grofs abominations, each would be ready to fay, Am I a dog? It would raife the pride of their hearts, but not their fear and trembling; becaufe they know not the corruption of their nature. (2.) Want of tendernefs towards thofe that fall. Many, in that cafe, caft off all bowels of Chriftian compaffion; for they do not confider themfelves, left they alfo be tempted, Gal. vi. 1. Men's paffions are often higheft againft the faults of others, when fin fleeps foundly in their own breafts. Even good Da-

Head I. *Men's overlooking their Natural Sin.*

vid, when he was at his worst, was most violent against the faults of others. While his conscience was asleep under his guilt, in the matter of Uriah, the Spirit of the Lord takes notice, that his anger was greatly kindled against the man in the parable, 2 Sam. xii. 5. And on good grounds it is thought, it was at the same time that he treated the Ammonites so cruelly, as is related ver. 31. *Putting them under saws, and under harrows of iron, and under axes of iron, and making them pass through the brick-kiln.* Grace makes men zealous against sin in others, as well as in themselves: but eyes turned inward to the corruption of nature, cloathe them with pity and compassion; and fill them with thankfulness to the Lord, that they themselves were not the persons left to be such spectacles of human frailty. (3.) There are not a few, who, if they be kept from afflictions in worldly things, and from gross out-breakings in their conversation, know not what it is to have a sad heart. If they meet with a cross, which their proud hearts cannot stoop to bear, they are ready to say, O to be gone! But the corruption of their nature never makes them long for heaven. Lusts, scandalously breaking out at a time, will mar their peace: but the sin of their nature never makes them a heavy heart. (4.) Delaying of repentance, in hopes to set about it afterwards. Many have their own appointed time for repentance and reformation: as if they were such complete masters over their lusts, that they can allow them to gather more strength, and yet overcome them. They take up resolutions to amend, without an eye to Jesus Christ, union with him, and strength from him; a plain evidence that they are strangers to themselves: so they are left to themselves, and their flourishing resolutions wither; for, as they see not the necessity, so they get not the benefit, of the dew from heaven, to water them. (5.) Men's venturing freely on temptations, and promising liberally in their own strength. They cast themselves fearlesly into temptation, in confidence of their coming off fairly: but, were they sensible of the corruption of their nature, they would beware of entering on the devil's ground: as one girt about with bags of gun-powder, would be unwilling to walk where sparks of fire are flying, left he should be blown up. Self-jealousy well becomes Christians. *Lord, is it I?* They that know the deceit of their bow, will not be very confident that they shall hit the mark. (6.) Unacquaintedness with heart plagues. The knowledge of the plagues of the heart is a rare qualification. There are indeed some of them written in such great characters, that he who runs may read them: but there are others more subtile, which few discern. How few are there, to whom the bias of the heart to unbelief is a burden? Nay, they perceive it not. Many have had sharp convictions of other sins, that were never to this day convinced of their unbelief; though that is the sin especially aimed at in a thorough conviction, John xvi. 8, 9. *He will reprove the world of sin,—because they believe not on me.* A disposition to establish our own righteousness, is a weed that naturally grows in every man's heart; but few sweat at the plucking of it up: it lurks undiscovered. The bias of the heart, to the way of the covenant of works, is a hidden plague of the heart to many. All the difficulty which they find is, in getting up their hearts to duties: they find no difficulty in getting their hearts off them, and over them to Jesus Christ. How hard is it to bring men off from their own righteousness? Yea, it is very hard to convince them of their leaning to it at all. *Lastly*, Pride and self-conceit. A view of the corruption of nature would be very humbling, and oblige him that has it to reckon himself the chief of sinners. Under the greatest attainments and enlargements, it would be ballast to his heart, and hide pride from his eyes. The want of thorough humiliation, piercing to the sin of one's nature, is the ruin of many professors: for digging deep makes great difference between wise and foolish builders, Luke vi. 48, 49.

II. I will lay before you a few things, in which you should have a special eye to original sin. (1.) Have a special eye to it, in your application to Jesus Christ. Do you find any need of Christ, which sends you to him as the Physician of souls? O forget not your di-

Head I.   *Original Sin specially noticed.*   107

seafe, when you are with the Physician. They never yet knew well their errand to Christ, that went not to him for the sin of their nature: for his blood to take away the guilt of it, and his Spirit to break the power of it. Though in the bitterness of your souls you should lay before him a catalogue of your sins of omission and commission, which might reach from earth to heaven; yet, if original sin were wanting in it, assure yourselves, that you have forgot the best part of the errand which a poor sinner has to the Physician of souls. What would it have availed the people of Jericho, to have set before Elisha all the vessels in their city, full of the water that was naught, if they had not led him forth to the spring, to cast in the salt there? 2 Kings ii. 19, 20, 21. The application is easy. (2.) Have a special eye to it, in your repentance, whether initiative or progressive; in your first repentance, and in the renewing of your repentance afterwards. Though a man be sick, there is no fear of death, if the sickness strike not to his heart: and there is as little fear of the death of sin, as long as the sin of our nature is not touched. But if you would repent indeed, let the streams lead you up to the fountain; and mourn over your corrupt nature, as the cause of all sin, in heart, lip, and life, Psal. li. 4, 5. *Against thee, thee only, have I sinned, and done this evil in thy sight.—Behold, I was shapen in iniquity, and in sin did my mother conceive me.* (3.) Have a special eye upon it in your mortification, Gal. v. 24. *They that are Christ's, have crucified the flesh.* It is the root of bitterness that must be struck at; which the axe of mortification must be laid to, else we labour in vain. In vain do men go about to purge the streams, while they are at no pains about the muddy fountain: it is vain religion to attempt to make the life truly good, while the corruption of nature retains its ancient vigour, and the power of it is not broken. *Lastly*, You are to eye it in your daily walk. He that would walk aright, must have one eye upward to Jesus Christ, and another inward to the corruption of his own nature. It is not enough that we look about us, we must also look within us. There the wall is weakest; there our greatest enemy lies;

Original Sin specially noticed. State II.

and there are grounds for daily watching and mourning.

III. I shall offer some reasons, why we should especially notice the sin of our nature.

1. Because, of all sins, it is the most extensive and diffusive. It goes through the whole man, and spoils all. Other sins mar particular parts of the image of God: but this doth at once deface the whole. A disease, affecting any particular member of the body, is dangerous: but that which affects the whole is worse. The corruption of nature is the poison of the old serpent, cast into the fountain of action; and infects every action, and every breathing of the soul.

2. It is the cause of all particular lusts, and actual sins, in our hearts and lives. It is the spawn which the great leviathan has left in the souls of men, from whence comes all the fry of actual sins and abominations, Mark vii. 21. *Out of the heart of men proceed evil thoughts, adulteries,* &c. It is the bitter fountain: particular lusts are but rivulets running from it, which bring forth into the life a part only, and not the whole of what is within. The fountain is always above the streams: and where the water is good, it is best in the fountain; where it is bad, it is worse there. The corruption of nature being that which defiles all, itself must needs be the most abominable thing.

3. It is virtually all sin: for it is the feed of all sins, which want but the occasion to set up their heads, being, in the corruption of nature, as the effect in the virtue of its cause. Hence it is called *a body of death,* (Rom. vii. 24.) as consisting of the several members belonging to such *a body of sins,* (Col. ii. 11.) whose life lies in spiritual death. It is the cursed ground, fit to bring forth all manner of noxious weeds. As the whole nest of venomous creatures must needs be more dreadful than any few of them that come creeping forth: so the sin of thy nature, that mother of abominations, must be worse than any particular lusts, that appear stirring in thy heart and life. Never did every sin appear, in the conversation of the vilest wretch that ever lived; but look thou into thy corrupt nature, and there thou mayest see all and every sin, in the feed and root there-

Head I. *Why it is to be specially noticed.* 109

of. There is a fulness of all unrighteousness there, Rom. i. 29. There is atheism, idolatry, blasphemy, murder, adultery, and whatsoever is vile. Possibly none of these appear to thee in thy heart : but there is more in that unfathomable depth of wickedness than thou knowest. Thy corrupt heart is like an ant's nest, on which, while the stone lieth, none of them appear; but take off the stone, and stir them up but with the point of a straw, you will see what a swarm is there, and how lively they be. Just such a sight would thy heart afford thee, did the Lord but withdraw the restraint he has upon it, and suffer Satan to stir it up by temptation.

4. The sin of our nature is, of all sins, the most fixing and abiding. Sinful actions, though the guilt and stain of them may remain, yet in themselves they pass away. The drunkard is not always at his cups, nor the unclean person always acting lewdness. But the corruption of nature is abiding sin : it remains with men in its full power, by night and by day ; at all times fixed, as with bands of iron and brass, till their nature be changed by converting grace; and it remains even with the godly, until the death of the body, though not in its reigning power. Pride, envy, covetousness, and the like, are not always stirring in thee. But the proud, envious, carnal nature, is still with thee : even as the clock that is wrong, is not always striking wrong; but the wrong set continues with her without interruption.

5. It is reigning sin, Rom. vi. 12. *Let not sin, therefore, reign in your mortal body, that you should obey it in the lusts thereof.* There are three things which you may observe in the corrupt heart: (1.) There is in the corrupt nature, the corrupt set of the heart, whereby men are unapt for all good, and fitted for all evil. This the apostle here calls *sin*, which reigns. (2.) There are particular lusts, or dispositions of corrupt nature, which the apostle calls *the lusts thereof*; such as pride, covetousness, &c. (3.) There is one among these, which is (like Saul among the people) higher by far than the rest, namely, *the sin which doth so easily beset us*, Heb. xii. 1. This we usually call the *predominant sin*, because it doth,

as it were, reign over other particular lufts; fo that other lufts muft yield to it. Thefe three are like a river, which divides itfelf into many ftreams, whereof one is greater than the reft. The corruption of nature is the river head, which has many particular lufts in which it runs; but it chiefly difburdens itfelf into what is commonly called one's predominant fin. Now all of thefe being fed by the fin of our nature, it is evident, that it is reigning fin, which never lofeth its fuperiority over particular lufts, that live and die with it, and by it. But, as in fome rivers, the main ftreams runs not always in one and the fame channel; fo particular predominants may be changed, as luft in youth may be fucceeded by covetoufnefs in old age. Now what doth it avail to reform in other things, while reigning fin remains in its full power? What though fome particular luft be broken? If fin, the fin of our nature, keep the throne, it will fet up another in its ftead; as when a water courfe is ftopped in one place, if the fountain is not dammed up, it will ftream forth another way. Thus, fome caft off their prodigality, but covetoufnefs comes up in its ftead: fome caft away their profanity, and the corruption of nature fends not its main ftream that way, as before; but it runs in another channel; namely, in that of a legal difpofition, felf-righteoufnefs, or the like. So that people are ruined, by their not eyeing the fin of their nature.

Laftly, It is hereditary evil, Pfal. li. 5. *In fin did my mother conceive me.* Particular lufts are not fo, but in the virtue of their caufe. A prodigal father may have a frugal fon; but this difeafe is neceffarily propagated in nature, and therefore hardeft to cure. Surely, then, the word fhould be given out againft original fin, as againft the king of Ifrael, 1 Kings xxii. 31. *Fight neither with fmall nor great, fave only with this:* For this fin being broke, all other fins are broken with it; and while it ftands entire, there is no victory.

IV. That you may get a view of the corruption of your nature, I would recommend to you three things. (1.) Study to know the fpirituality and extent of the law of God, for that is the glafs wherein you may fee

Head I. *Why it is to be specially noticed.* 111

yourselves. (2.) Observe your hearts at all times, but especially under temptation. Temptation is a fire that brings up the scum of the vile heart: carefully mark the first risings of corruption. *Lastly*, Go to God, through Jesus Christ, for illumination by his Spirit. Lay out your soul before the Lord, as willing to know the vileness of your nature: say to him, That which I know not, teach thou me. And be willing to take light in from the word. Believe, and you shall see. It is by the word that the Spirit teacheth, but without the Spirit's teaching, all other teaching will be to no purpose. Though the gospel were to shine about you, like the sun at noon day, and this great truth ever so plainly preached, you will never see yourselves aright, until the Spirit of the Lord light his candle within your breast: the fulness and glory of Christ, and the corruption and vileness of our nature, are never rightly learned, but where the Spirit of Christ is the teacher.

To shut up this weighty point, let the consideration of what has been said, commend Christ to you all. You that are brought out of your natural state of corruption, unto Christ, be humble; still coming to Christ, and so improve your union with him, to the further weakening of your natural corruption. Is your nature changed? The day was you would not stir: now you are cured; but remember the cure is not yet perfected, you still go halting. Though it were better with you than it is, the remembrance of what you were by nature should keep you low. You that are yet in your natural state, take this with you: believe the corruption of your nature; and let Christ, and his grace, be precious in your eyes. O that you would at length be serious about the state of your souls! What do you intend to do? You must die; you must appear before the judgment-seat of God. Will you lie down and sleep another night at ease in this case? Do it not: for before another day you may be summoned before God's dreadful tribunal, in the grave-cloaths of your corrupt state; and your vile souls cast into the pit of destruction, as a corrupt lump, to be for ever buried out of God's sight. For I testify unto you all, there is no peace with God, no pardon, no heaven for you, in your natural state: there is but a step between you and eternal destruction from the presence of the Lord: if the brittle thread of your life, which may be broke with a touch, ere you are aware, be broken while you are in this state, you are ruined for ever, without remedy: but come speedily to Jesus Christ; he has cleansed as vile souls as yours; and yet he will *cleanse the blood that he hath not cleansed*, Joel iii. 21. Thus far of the *sinfulness of man's natural state*.

H E A D   II.

The MISERY of Man's Natural State.

Ephes. ii. 3. *We were by nature the children of wrath, even as others.*

HAVING shewed you the sinfulness of man's natural state, I come now to lay before you the *misery* of it. A *sinful* state cannot but be a *miserable* state. If sin go before, wrath follows of course. Corruption and destruction are so knit together, that the Holy Ghost calls destruction, even eternal destruction, *corruption*, Gal. vi. 8. *He that soweth to his flesh, shall of the flesh reap corruption*, that is, everlasting destruction; as is clear from its being opposed to life everlasting, in the following clause. The apostle having shewn the Ephesians their real state by nature, to wit, that they were dead in sins and trespasses, altogether corrupt, he tells them, in the words of the text, their relative state, namely, that the pit was digged for them, while in that state of corruption: Being dead in sins, they *were by nature children of wrath, even as others.*

In the words we have four things:

1. The *misery* of a natural state; it is a state of wrath, as well as a state of sin. *We were*, says the apostle, *children of wrath*, bound over and liable to the wrath of God; under wrath in some measure; and, in wrath, bound over to more, even the full measure of

Head II. *The Misery of Man's natural State.* 113

it, in hell, where the floods of it go over the prisoners for ever. Thus Saul, in his wrath, adjudging David to die, (1 Sam. xx. 31.) and David, in his wrath passing sentence of death against the man in the parable, (2 Sam. xii. 5.) says, each of them, of his supposed criminal, *He shall surely die;* or as the words in the first language are, *he is a son of death.* So the natural man is *a child of wrath, a son of death.* He is a malefactor, dead in law, lying in chains of guilt; a criminal, held fast in his fetters till the day of execution; which will not fail to come, unless a pardon be obtained from his God, who is his judge and opponent too. By that means, indeed, children of wrath may become children of the kingdom. The phrase in the text, however common in the holy language, is very significant. As it is evident that the apostle, calling natural men the *children of disobedience*, (ver 2.) means more than that they were disobedient children; for such may the Lord's own children be; so, to be children of wrath, is more than simply to be liable to, or under wrath. Jesus Christ was liable to, and under wrath: but I doubt whether we have any warrant to say he was a *child of wrath.* The phrase seems to intimate, that men are, whatever they are in their natural state, under the wrath of God; that they are wholly under wrath: wrath is, as it were, woven into their very nature, and mixeth itself with the whole of the man, who is (if I may so speak) a very lump of wrath, a child of hell, as the iron in the fire is all fire. For men naturally are children of wrath; come forth, so to speak, out of the womb of wrath; as Jonah's gourd was the *son of a night,* (which we render, *came up in a night,* Jonah iv. 10.) as if it had come out of the womb of the night, (as we read of the *womb of the morning,* Psal. cx. 3.) and so the birth, following the womb whence it came, was soon gone. Thus, sparks of fire are called *sons of the burning coal,* Job v. 7. marg. Isa. xxi. 10. *O my threshing, and the corn (*or *son) of my floor,* threshing in the floor of wrath, and, as it were, brought forth by it. Thus the natural man is a *child of wrath:* it *comes into his bowels like water, and like oil into his bones,* Psalm

Q

cix. 18. For, though Judas was the only son of perdition among the apostles, yet all men, by nature, are of the same family.

2. Here is the rise of this misery; men have it by nature. They owe it to their nature; not to their substance or essence: for that neither is nor was sin, and therefore cannot make them children of wrath; though, for sin, it may be under wrath: not to their nature, as qualified, at man's creation, by his Maker; but to their nature, as vitiated and corrupted by the fall; to the vitious quality, or corruption, of their nature, (whereof before) which is their principle of action, and ceasing from action, the only principle in an unregenerate state. Now, by this nature, men are children of wrath; as, in time of pestilential infection, one draws in death with the disease then raging. Wherefore seeing, from our first being, as children of Adam, we be corrupt children, shapen in iniquity, conceived in sin; we are also from that moment children of wrath.

3. The universality of this misery. All are by nature children of wrath; *We* saith the apostle, *even as others*; Jews as well as Gentiles. Those that are now, by grace, the children of God, were, by nature, in no better case than those that are still in their natural state.

Lastly, Here is a glorious and happy change intimated; we *were* children of wrath, but are not so now; grace has brought us out of that fearful state. This the apostle says of himself, and other believers. And thus, it well becomes the people of God to be often standing on the shore, and looking back to the red-sea of the state of wrath they were weltering in, even as others.

Man's Natural State is a State of Wrath.

DOCTRINE, The state of nature is a state of wrath. Every one, in a natural unregenerate state, is in a state of wrath. We are born children of wrath; and continue so, until we be born again. Nay, as soon as we are children of Adam, we are children of wrath.

I shall usher in what I am to say on this point, with a few observations touching the universality of this state

Head II. *The Misery of Man's natural State.* 115

of wrath, which may serve to prepare the way for the word into your consciences.

Wrath has gone as wide as ever sin went. When angels sinned, the wrath of God broke in upon them as a flood. *God spared not the angels that sinned, but cast them down to hell,* 2 Pet. ii. 4. It was thereby demonstrated, that no natural excellency in the creature can shield it from the wrath of God, if once it become a sinful creature. The finest and nicest piece of the workmanship of heaven, if once the Creator's image upon it be defaced by sin, God can and will dash it in pieces in his wrath, unless satisfaction be made to justice, and that image be restored; neither of which the sinner himself can do. Adam sinned; and the whole lump of mankind was leavened, and bound over to the fiery oven of God's wrath. From the text you may learn, (1.) The ignorance of that state cannot free men from it. The Gentiles, that knew not God, *were by nature children of wrath, even as others.* A man's house may be on fire, his wife and children perishing in the flames, while he knows nothing of it; and therefore is not concerned about it. Such is your case, O you that are ignorant of these things! Wrath is silently sinking into your souls, while you are blessing yourselves, saying, We shall have peace. You need not a more certain token that you are children of wrath, than that you never yet saw yourselves such. You cannot be the children of God, that never yet saw yourselves children of the devil. You cannot be in the way to heaven, that never saw yourselves by nature in the high-road to hell. You are grosly ignorant of your state by nature; and so ignorant of God and of Christ, and your need of him: and though you look on your ignorance as a covert from wrath, yet, take it out of the mouth of God himself, that it will ruin you, if it be not removed, Isa. xxvii. 11 *It is a people of no understanding: therefore he that made them, will not have mercy on them.* See 2 Thess. i. 8. Hos. ix. 6. (2.) No outward privileges can exempt men from this state of wrath; for the Jews, the children of the kingdom, God's peculiar people, were children of wrath, even as others. Though you be

Q 2

church-members, partakers of all church-privileges; though you be defcended of godly parents, of great and honourable families; be what you will, you are by nature heirs of hell, children of wrath. (3.) No profeffion, no attainments in a profeffion of religion, do or can exempt a man from this ftate of wrath. Paul was one of the ftricteft fect of the Jewifh religion, Acts xxvi. 5. yet a child of wrath, even as others, till he was converted. The clofe hypocrite, and the profane, are alike, as to their ftate; however different their converfation be: and they will be alike in their fatal end, Pfal. cxxv. 5. *As for fuch as turn afide unto their crooked ways, the Lord fhall lead them forth with the workers of iniquity.* (4.) Young ones, that are but fetting out into the world, have not that to do to make themfelves children of wrath, by following the gracelefs multitude. They are children of wrath by nature; fo it is done already: they were born heirs of hell; they will indeed make themfelves more fo, if they do not, while they are young, flee from that wrath which they are born to, by fleeing to Jefus Chrift. *Laftly,* Whatever men are now by grace, they are even as others by nature. This may be a fad meditation to them that have been at eafe from their youth, and have had no changes.

Now, thefe things being premifed, I fhall, in the firft place, Shew what this ftate of wrath is; next, Confirm the doctrine; and then apply it.

I. I am to fhew what this ftate of wrath is. But who can fully defcribe the wrath of an angry God? None can do it. Yet fo much of it may be difcovered, as may ferve to convince men of the abfolute neceffity of fleeing to Jefus Chrift, out of that ftate of wrath. Anger, in men, is a paffion and commotion of the fpirit, for an injury received, with a defire to refent the fame: when it comes to a height, and is fixed in one's fpirit, it is called *wrath.* Now there are no paffions in God, properly fpeaking: they are inconfiftent with his abfolute unchangeablenefs and independency: therefore Paul and Barnabas (to remove the miftake of the Lycaonians, who thought that they were gods) tells them, *they were*

Head II. *The Misery of Man's natural State.* 117

men of like passions with themselves, Acts xiv. 15. Wrath, when it is attributed to God, must not be considered in respect of the affection of wrath, but the effects thereof. Wrath is a fire in the bowels of man, tormenting the man himself: but there is no perturbation in God. His wrath does not in the least mar that infinite repose and happiness which he hath in himself. It is a most pure, undisturbed act of his will, producing dreadful effects against the sinner. It is little which we know of the infinite God; but, condescending to our weakness, he is pleased to speak of himself to us after the manner of men. Let us therefore notice man's wrath, but remove every thing, in our consideration of the wrath of God, that implies imperfection; and so we may attain to some view of it, however scanty. By this means we are led to take up the wrath of God against the natural man in these three particulars:

First, There is wrath in the heart of God against him. The Lord approves him not, but is displeased with him. Every natural man lies under the displeasure of God; and that is heavier than mountains of brass. Although he be pleased with himself, and others be pleased with him too, yet God looks down on him displeased. *First,* His person is under God's displeasure; *Thou hatest all workers of iniquity,* Psal. v. 5. A godly man's sin is displeasing to God, yet his person is still *accepted in the beloved,* Eph. i. 6. But *God is angry with the wicked every day,* Psal. vii. 11. There is a fire of wrath burns continually against him in the heart of God. They are as dogs and swine, most abominable creatures, in the sight of God. Though their natural state be gilded over with a shining profession, yet they are abhorred of God; they are to him as smoke in his nose, Isa. lxv. 5. and lukewarm water, to be spewed out of his mouth, Rev. iii. 16. whited sepulchres, Matt. xxiii. 27. a generation of vipers, Mat. xii. 34. and a people of his wrath, Isa. x. 6. *Secondly,* He is displeased with all they do: it is impossible for them to please him, being unbelievers, Heb. xi. 6. He hates their persons; and so hath no pleasure in, but is displeased with, their best works, Isa. lxvi. 6. *He that sacrificeth a lamb, is as if he cut off a dog's neck*, &c. Their duty, as done by them, is an abomination to the Lord, Prov. xv. 8. And as men turn their back on thofe with whom they are angry, fo the Lord refufing communion with the natural man in his duties, is a plain indication of this wrath.

Secondly, There is wrath in the word of God againſt him. When wrath is in the heart, it feeks a vent by the lips; fo God fights againſt the natural man with the fword of his mouth, Rev. ii. 16. The Lord's word never fpeaks good of him, but always curfeth and condemneth him. Hence it is, that when he is awakened, the word read or preached often increafeth his horror. *Firſt*, It condemns all his actions, together with his corrupt nature. There is nothing which he does, but the law declares it to be fin. It is a rule of perfect obedience, from which he always, in all things, declines; and fo it rejects every thing he doth, as finful. *Secondly*, It pronounceth his doom, and denounceth God's curfe againſt him, Gal. iii. 10. *For as many as are of the works of the law, are under the curfe: for it is written, Curfed is every one that continueth not in all things which are written in the book of the law, to do them.* Be he never fo well in the world, it pronounceth a woe from heaven againſt him, Ifa. iii. 11. The Bible is a quiver filled with arrows of wrath againſt him; ready to be poured in on his foul. God's threatnings, in his word, hang over his head as a black cloud, ready to fhower down on him every moment. The word is indeed the faints fecurity againſt wrath: but it binds the natural man's fin and wrath together, as a certain pledge of his ruin, if he continues in that ſtate. So the confcience being awakened, and perceiving this tie made by the law, the man is filled with terrors in his foul.

Thirdly, There is wrath in the hand of God, againſt the natural man. He is under heavy ſtrokes of wrath already, and is liable to more.

Firſt. There is wrath on his body. It is a piece of curfed clay, which wrath is finking into, by virtue of the threatening of the firſt covenant, Gen. ii. 17. *In the day that thou eateſt thereof thou ſhalt furely die.* There is neither a difeafe, gripe, nor ſtitch, that affects him, but it comes on him with the sting of God's indignation in it. They are all cords of death, sent before to bind the prisoner.

Secondly, There is wrath upon his soul. (1.) He can have no communion with God; he is *foolish, and shall not stand in God's sight*, Psal. v. 5. When Adam sinned, God turned him out of paradise: and natural men are, as Adam left them, banished from the gracious presence of the Lord; and can have no access to him in that state. There is war between heaven and them: and so all commerce is cut off. *They are without God in the world*, Eph. ii. 12. The sun is gone down on them, and there is not the least glimpse of favour towards them from heaven. (2.) Hence the soul is left to pine away in its iniquity, The natural darkness of their minds, the averseness to good in their wills, the disorder of their affections, and distemper of their consciences, and all their natural plagues, are left upon them in a penal way; and, being so left, increase daily. God casts a portion of worldly goods to them, more or less, as a bone is thrown to a dog: but, alas! his wrath against them appears, in that they get no grace. The Physician of souls comes by them, and goes by them, and cures others on each side of them, while they are consuming away in their iniquity, and ripening daily for utter destruction. (3.) They lie open to fearful additional plagues on their souls, even in this life. *First*, Sometimes they meet with deadening strokes, silent blows, from the hand of an angry God: arrows of wrath, that enter into their souls without noise, Isa. vi. 10. *Make the heart of this people fat, and make their ears heavy, and shut their eyes; lest they see with their eyes.* God strives with them for a while, and convictions enter their consciences; but they rebel against the light; and, by a secret judgment, they receive a blow on the head; so that, from that time, they do, as it were, live and rot above ground. Their hearts are deadened, their affections withered, their consciences stupified, and their whole souls blasted, *cast forth as a branch, and withered*, John xv. 16. They are plagued with judicial blindness. They shut their eyes against the light, and they are given over to the devil, the god of this world, to be blinded more, 2 Cor. iv. 4. Yea, *God sends them strong delusions, that they should believe a lie.* 2 Theff. ii. 11. Even confcience, like a falfe light on the fhore, leads them upon rocks: by which they are broken in pieces. They harden themfelves againft God and he leaves them to Satan and their own hearts, whereby they are hardened more and more. They are often given up to vile affections, Rom. i. 26. The reins are laid on their necks; and they are left to run into all excefs, as their furious lufts draw them. *Secondly,* Sometimes they meet with fharp fiery ftrokes, whereby their fouls become like mount Sinai, where nothing is feen but fire and fmoke; nothing heard but the thunder of God's wrath, and the voice of the trumpet of a broken law, waxing louder and louder: which makes them like Pafhur, (Jer. xx. 4.) *A terror to themfelves.* God takes the filthy garments of their fin, which they were wont to fleep in fecurely, overlays them with brimftone, and fets them on fire about their ears: fo they have a hell within them.

Thirdly, There is wrath on the natural man's enjoyments. Whatever be wanting in his houfe, there is one thing that is never wanting there, Prov. iii. 33. *The curfe of the Lord is in the houfe of the wicked.* Wrath is on all that he has; on the bread that he eats, the liquor he drinks, the cloaths which he wears. His bafket and ftore are curfed, Deut. xxvi. 17. Some things fall wrong with him; and that comes to pafs by virtue of this wrath: other things go according to his wifh, and there is wrath in that too; for it is a fnare to his foul, Prov. i. 32. *The profperity of fools fhall deftroy them.* This wrath turns his bleffings into curfes, Mal. ii. 2. *I will curfe your bleffings; yea, I have curfed them already.* The holy law is *a killing letter to him,* 2 Cor. iii. 6. The miniftry of the gofpel *a favour of death unto death,* chap. ii. 16. In the facrament of the Lord's Supper, *he eatheth and drinketh damnation to himfelf,* 1 Cor. xi. 29. Nay, more than all that, Chrift himfelf is to him *a ftone of ftumbling, and a rock of offence,* 1 Pet. iii. 8. Thus wrath follows the natural man, as his fhadow doth his body.

Head II. *The Misery of Man's natural State.*

Fourthly, He is under the power of Satan, Acts xxvi. 18. The devil has overcome him, so he is his by conquest, his lawful captive, Isa. xlix. 24. The natural man is condemned already, John iii. 18. and therefore under the heavy hand of him that hath the power of death, that is the devil. He keeps his prisoners in the prison of a natural state, bound hand and foot, Isa. lxi. 1. laden with divers lusts, as chains wherewithal he holds them fast. Thou needest not, as many do, call on the devil to take thee; for he has a fast hold of thee already, as a child of wrath.

Lastly, The natural man hath no security for a moment's safety, from the wrath of God coming on him to the uttermost. The curse of the law, denounced against him, has already tied him to the stake: so that the arrows of justice may pierce his soul; and, in him may meet all the miseries and plagues that flow from the avenging wrath of God. See how he is set as a mark to the arrows of wrath, Psal. vii. 11, 12, 13. *God is angry with the wicked every day. If he turn not, he will whet his sword: he hath bent his bow, and made it ready; he hath also prepared for him the instruments of death.* Doth he lie down to sleep? There is not a promise that he knows of, or can know, to secure him that he shall not be in hell ere he awake. Justice pursues and cries for vengeance on the sinner: the law casts the fire-balls of its curses continually upon him: wasted and long tired patience is that which keeps in his life. He walks amidst enemies armed against him: his name may be Magor-Missabib, *i. e. Terror round about*, Jer. xx. 3. Angels, devils, men, beasts, stones, heaven, and earth, are in readiness, on a word of command from the Lord, to ruin him.

Thus the natural man lives, but he must die too; and death is a dreadful messenger to him. It comes upon him armed with wrath, and puts three sad charges in his hand. (1.) Death chargeth him to bid an eternal farewell to all things in this world; to leave it, and haste away to another world. Ah! what a dreadful charge must this be to a child of wrath! He can have no comfort from heaven, for God is his enemy: as for the things of the world, and the enjoyment of his lusts, which were the only springs of his comfort; these are in a moment dried up to him for ever. He is not ready for another world: He was not thinking of removing so soon; or, if he was, yet he has no portion secured to him in the other world, but that which he was born to, and was increasing all his days, namely, a treasure of wrath. But go he must; his clay-god, the world, must be parted with, and what has he more? There was never a glimmering of light, or favour from heaven to his soul: the wrath which hung in the threatening, as a cloud like a man's hand, is darkening the whole heaven above him: if he *look unto the earth* (from whence all his light was wont to come), *behold, trouble and darkness, dimness of anguish; and he shall be driven to darkness,* Isa. viii. 22. (2.) Death charges soul and body to part, till the great day. His soul is required of him, Luke xii. 20. O what a miserable parting must this be to a child of wrath! Care was indeed taken to provide for the body things necessary for this life: but, alas! there is nothing laid up for another life, nothing to be a seed of a glorious resurrection: as it lived, so it must die, and rise again, sinful flesh, fuel for the fire of God's wrath. As for the soul, he was never solicitous to provide for it. It lay in the body, dead to God, and all things truly good; and so must be carried out into the pit, in the grave-cloaths of its natural state: for, now death comes, the companions in sin must part. (3.) Death chargeth the soul to appear before the tribunal of God, while the body lies to be carried to the grave, Eccl. xii. 7. *The spirit shall return unto God who gave it*, Heb. ix. 27. *It is appointed unto all men once to die, but after this the judgment.* Well were it for the sinful soul, if it might be buried together with the body. But that cannot be; It must go and receive its sentence; and shall be shut up in the prison of hell, while the cursed body lies imprisoned in the grave, till the day of the general judgment.

When the end of the world, appointed of God, is come, the trumpet shall sound, and the dead arise.

Then shall the weary earth, at the command of the Judge, cast forth the bodies, the cursed bodies, of those that lived and died in their natural state; *The sea, death, and hell, shall deliver up their dead*, Rev. xx. 13. Their miserable bodies and souls shall be re-united, and they summoned before the tribunal of Christ. Then shall they receive that awful sentence, *Depart from me, ye cursed, into everlasting fire, prepared for the devil and his angels*, Mat. xxv. 41. *Whereupon they shall go away into everlasting punishment*, ver. 49. They shall be eternally shut up in hell, never to get the least drop of comfort, nor the least ease of their torment. There they will be punished with the punishment of loss, being excommunicated for ever from the presence of God, his angels and saints. All means of grace, all hopes of a delivery, will be for ever cut-off from their eyes. They will not have a drop of water to cool their tongues, Luke xiv. 24, 25. They will be punished with the punishment of sense. They must not only depart from God, but depart into fire, into everlasting fire. There the worm, that shall gnaw them, will never die; the fire, that will scorch them, shall never be quenched. God will, through eternity, hold them up with the one hand, and pour the full vials of wrath into them with the other.

This is that state of wrath which natural men live in; being under much of the wrath of God, and liable to more. But, for a further view of it, let us consider the qualities of that wrath. (1.) It is irresistible, there is no standing before it; *Who may stand in thy sight, when once thou art angry!* Psal. lxxxvi. 7. Can the worm or moth defend themselves against him that designs to crush them? Much less can the worm man stand before an angry God. Foolish man, indeed, practically bids defiance to Heaven. But the Lord often, even in this world, opens such sluices of wrath upon them, as all their might cannot stop; and they are carried away thereby, as with a flood. How much more will it be so in hell! (2.) It is insupportable. What a man cannot resist, he will try to endure: but, who shall dwell in devouring fire? who shall dwell with everlasting burnings? God's wrath is a weight that will sink men into the lowest hell. It is a burden which no man is able to stand under. *A wounded spirit who can bear?* Prov. xviii. 14. (3.) It is unavoidable to such as go on impenitently, and die in their sinful course. *He that being often reproved, hardeneth his neck, shall suddenly be destroyed, and that without remedy,* Prov. xxix. 1. We may now flee from it indeed, by fleeing to Jesus Christ: but such as flee from Christ will never be able to avoid it. Whither can men flee from the avenging God? where will they find a shelter? The hills will not hear them. The mountains will be deaf to their loudest cries: when they cry to them, to hide them from the wrath of the Lamb. (4.) It is powerful and fierce wrath, Psal. xc. 11. *Who knoweth the power of thine anger? Even according to thy fear, so is thy wrath.* We are apt to fear the wrath of man more than we ought: but no man can apprehend the wrath of God to be more dreadful than it really is: the power of it can never be known to the utmost; for it is infinite, and (properly speaking) has no utmost. How fierce soever it be, either on earth, or in hell, God can still carry it further. Every thing in God is most perfect in its kind; and therefore no wrath so fierce as his. O sinner! how wilt thou be able to endure that wrath, which will tear thee in pieces! Psal. l. 22. and grind thee to powder! Luke xx. 18. The history of the two she-bears, that tare the children of Bethel, is an awful one, 2 Kings ii. 23, 24. but the united force of the rage of the lions, leopards, and she-bears, bereaved of their whelps, is not sufficient to give us even a faint idea of the power of the wrath of God, Hos. xiii. 7, 8. *Therefore I will be unto them as a lion; as a leopard by the way will I observe them. I will meet them as a bear that is bereaved of her whelps, and will rend the caul of their heart,* &c. (5.) It is penetrating and piercing wrath. It is burning wrath, and fiery indignation. There is no pain more exquisite than that which is caused by fire; and no fire so piercing as the fire of God's indignation, that burns unto the lowest hell, Deut. xxxii. 22. The arrows of men's wrath can pierce flesh, blood, and bones; but cannot reach the soul: but the wrath of God will sink into the soul, and so pierce a man in the most tender part: like as, when a person is thunder-struck, oft-times there is not a wound to be seen in the skin; yet life is gone, and the bones are, as it were, melted: so God's wrath can penetrate into, and melt a man's soul within him, when his earthly comforts stand about him entire, and untouched; as in Belshazzar's case, Dan. v. 6. (6.) It is constant wrath, running parallel with the man's continuance in an unregenerate state; constantly attending him, from the womb to the grave. There are few days so dark, but the sun sometimes looks out from under the clouds: but the wrath of God is an abiding cloud on the objects of it, John iii. 36. The wrath of God abideth on him that believes not. (7.) It is eternal. O, miserable soul! If thou flee not from this wrath, unto Jesus Christ, though thy misery had a beginning, yet it will never have an end. Should devouring death wholly swallow thee up, and for ever hold thee fast in a grave, it would be kind: but thy body must be re-united to thy immortal soul, and live again, and never die; that thou mayest be ever dying, in the hands of the living God. Cold death will quench the flame of men's wrath against us, if nothing else do: but God's wrath, when it has come on the sinner millions of ages, will still be the wrath to come, Mat. iii. 7. 1 Thess. i. 10. as the water of a river is still coming, how much soever of it has passed. While God is, he will pursue the quarrel. *Lastly*, However dreadful it is, and though it be eternal, yet it is most just wrath. It is a clear fire, without the least smoke of injustice. The sea of wrath, raging with greatest fury against the sinner, is clear as chrystal. The Judge of all the earth can do no wrong: he knows no transports of passion, for they are inconsistent with the perfection of his nature. *Is God unrighteous, who taketh vengeance? (I speak as a man) God forbid; for then, how shall God judge the world?* Rom. iii. 5. 6.

The Doctrine of the State of Wrath confirmed and vindicated.

II. I shall confirm the doctrine. Consider, (1) How peremptory the threatening of the first covenant is: In the day thou eateſt thereof thou ſhalt ſurely die, Gen. iii. 17. Hereby ſin and puniſhment being connected, the veracity of God aſcertains the execution of the threatening. Now, all men being by nature under this covenant, the breach of it lays them under the curſe. (2.) The juſtice of God requires, that a child of ſin be a child of wrath; that the law being broken, the ſanction thereof ſhould take place. God cannot but do right, Gen. xviii. 25. Now it is a righteous thing with God to recompence ſin with wrath, 1 Theſſ. i. 6. He *is of purer eyes than to behold evil*, Hab. i. 13. And *he hates all the workers of iniquity*, Pſal. v. 6. (3.) The horrors of a natural conſcience prove this. Conſcience, in the breaſts of men, tells them that they are ſinners, and therefore liable to the wrath of God. Let men, at any time, ſoberly commune with themſelves, and they will find that they have the witneſs in themſelelves, *knowing the judgment of God, that they that commit ſuch things are worthy of death*, Rom. i. 32. (4.) The pangs of the new birth, the work of the Spirit on elect ſouls, in order to their converſion, demonſtrate this. Hereby their natural ſinfulneſs and miſery, as liable to the wrath of God, are plainly taught them, filling their hearts with fear of that wrath. As it is the Spirit's work to convince of ſin, righteouſneſs, and judgment, (John xvi. 8.) this teſtimony muſt needs be true; for the Spirit of truth cannot witneſs an untruth. But true believers, being freed from the ſtate of wrath, *receive not the Spirit of bondage again to fear, but receive the Spirit of adoption*, Rom. viii. 15. Therefore, if fears of that nature ariſe, after the ſoul's union with Chriſt, they come from the ſaint's own ſpirit, or from a worſe. *Laſtly*, The ſufferings of Chriſt plainly prove this doctrine. Wherefore was the Son of God a Son under wrath, but becauſe the children of men were children of wrath? He ſuffered the wrath of God; not for himſelf, but for thoſe that were liable to it in their own perſons. Nay, this not only ſhews us to have been liable to wrath; but alſo that wrath muſt have a vent, in the puniſhing of ſin. If this was done in the green tree, what will become of the dry? What a miſerable caſe muſt a ſin-

Head II. *The Misery of Man's natural State.* 127

ner be in, that is out of Christ; that is not vitally united to Christ, and partakes not of his Spirit? God, who spared not his own Son, surely will not spare such an one.

But the unregenerate man, who has no great value for the honour of God, will be apt to rise up against his Judge, and in his own heart condemn his procedure. Nevertheless, the Judge being infinitely just, the sentence must be righteous. Therefore, to stop thy mouth, O proud sinner! and to still thy clamour against thy righteous Judge, consider, *First*, Thou art a sinner by nature; and it is highly reasonable, that guilt and wrath be as old as sin. Why should not God begin to vindicate his honour, as soon as vile worms attempt to impair it? Why shall not a serpent bite a thief, as soon as he leaps over the hedge? Why should not the threatening take hold of the sinner, as soon as he casts away the command? The poisonous nature of the serpent affords a man sufficient ground to kill it, as soon as ever he can reach it: and by this time thou mayest be convinced, that thy nature is a very compound of enmity against God. *Secondly*, Thou hast not only enmity against God in thy nature, but hast discovered it by actual sins, which are in his eye acts of hostility. Thou hast brought forth thy lusts into the field of battle against thy sovereign Lord. And because thou art such a criminal, thy condemnation is just: for, besides the sin of thy nature, thou hast done that against Heaven, which if thou hadst done against men, thy life must have gone for it; and shall not wrath from heaven overtake thee? (1.) Thou art guilty of high treason and rebellion against the King of heaven. The thought and wish of thy heart, which he knows as well as the language of thy mouth, has been, *No God*, Psal. xiv. 1. Thou hast rejected his government, blown the trumpet, and set up the standard of rebellion against him, being one of those that say, *We will not have this man to reign over us*, Luke xix. 14. Thou hast striven against, and quenched his Spirit; practically disowned his laws, proclaimed by his messengers; stopped thine ears at their voice, and sent them away mourning for thy pride.

Thou haſt confpired with his grand enemy, the devil. Although thou art a fervant of the King of glory, daily receiving of his favours, and living on his bounty, thou art holding a correfpondence, and haſt contracted a friendſhip, with his greateſt enemy, and art acting for him againſt thy Lord; for *the luſts of the devil you will do*, John viii. 44. (2.) Thou art a murderer before the Lord. Thou haſt laid the ſtumbling-block of thine iniquity before the blind world; and haſt ruined the fouls of others, by thy finful courfe. Though thou doſt not fee now, the time may come, when thou ſhalt fee the blood of thy relations, neighbours, acquaintances, and others, upon thy head, Mat. xviii. 7. *Wo unto the world becauſe of offences—Wo to that man by whom the offence cometh.* Yea, thou art a felf-murderer before God, Prov. viii. 36. *He that finneth againſt me, wrongeth his own foul: all they that hate me, love death.* Ezek. viii. 31. *Why will ye die?* The laws of men go as far as they can againſt the felf-murderer, denying his body a burial-place with others, and confifcating his goods: what wonder is it, that the law of God is fo fevere againſt foul-murderers? Is it ſtrange, that they who will needs depart from God now, coſt what it will, ſhould be forced to depart from him at laſt, into everlaſting fire? But, what is yet more criminal, thou art guilty of the murder of the Son of God; for the Lord will reckon thee amongſt thofe that pierced him, Rev. i. 7. Thou haſt rejected him, as the Jews did; and by thy rejecting him thou haſt juſtified their deed. They indeed did not acknowledge him to be the Son of God, but thou doſt. What they did againſt him, was in his ſtate of humiliation; but thou haſt acted againſt him in his ſtate of exaltation. Thefe things will aggravate thy condemnation. What wonder, then, if the voice of the Lamb change to the roaring of the lion, againſt the traitor and murderer?

Object. But fome will fay, Is there not a vaſt difproportion between our fin, and that wrath you talk of? I anfwer, No; God puniſheth no more than the finner deferves. To rectify your miſtake, in this matter, confider, (1.) The vaſt rewards which God has annexed to obedience. His word is no more full of fiery wrath againſt ſin, than it is of gracious rewards to the obedience it requires. If heaven be in the promiſes, it is altogether equal that hell ſhould be in the threatenings. If death were not in the balance with life, eternal miſery with eternal happineſs, where were the proportion? Moreover, ſin deſerves the miſery, but our beſt works do not deſerve the happineſs: yet both are ſet before us; ſin and miſery, holineſs and happineſs. What reaſon is there then to complain? (2.) How ſevere ſoever the threatenings be, yet all have enough to do to reach the end of the law. *Fear him,* ſays our Lord, *which, after he hath killed, hath power to caſt into hell: yea, I ſay unto you, fear him,* Luke xii. 5. This beſpeaks our dread of divine power and majeſty; yet how few fear him indeed! The Lord knows the hearts of ſinners to be exceedingly intent upon fulfilling their luſts: they cleave ſo fondly to theſe fulſome breaſts, that a ſmall force does not ſuffice to draw them away from them. They that travel through deſarts, where they are in hazard from wild beaſts, have need to carry fire along with them; and they have need of a hard wedge that have knotty timber to cleave: ſo a holy law muſt be fenced with dreadful wrath, in a world lying in wickedneſs. But who are they that complain of that wrath as too great, but thoſe to whom it is too little to draw them off from their ſinful courſes? It was the man who pretended to fear his lord, becauſe he was an auſtere man, that kept his pound laid up in a napkin: and ſo he was condemned out of his own mouth, Luke xix. 20, 21, 22. Thou art that man, even thou whoſe objection I am anſwering. How can the wrath which thou art under, and liable to, be too great, when, as yet, is is not ſufficient to awaken thee to flee from it? Is it time to relax the penalties of the law, when men are trampling the commands of it under foot? (3.) Conſider how God dealt with his own Son, whom he ſpared not, Rom. viii. 32. The wrath of God ſeized on his ſoul and body both, and brought him into the duſt of death. That his ſufferings were not eternal, flowed from the quality of the Sufferer, who was infinite; and therefore able to bear, at once, the whole load of wrath: and, upon that account, his fufferings were infinite in value. But as the fufferings of a mere creature cannot be infinite in value, they muft be protracted to eternity. And what confidence can a rebel fubject have to quarrel with his part of a punifhment executed on the king's fon? (4.) The finner doth againft God what he can. *Behold, thou haft done evil things as thou couldft,* Jer. iii. 5. That thou haft not done more, and worfe, thanks to him who reftrained thee; to the chain which the wolf was kept in by, not to thyfelf. No wonder that God fhews his power on the finner, who puts forth his power againft God, as far as it will reach. The unregenerate man puts no period to his finful courfe; and would put no bounds to it neither, if he were not reftrained by divine power, for wife ends: therefore it is juft that he be for ever under wrath. (5.) It is infinite majefty which fin ftrikes againft; and fo it is, in fome fort, an infinite evil. Sin rifeth in its demerit, according to the quality of the party offended. If a man wound his neighbour, his goods muft go for it; but if he wound his prince, his life muft go for that. The infinity of God makes infinite wrath the juft demerit of fin. God is infinitely difpleafed with fin: and when he acts, he muft act like himfelf, and fhew his difpleafure, by proportionable means. *Laftly,* Thofe that fhall lie for ever under his wrath, will be eternally finning; and therefore muft eternally fuffer: not only in refpect of divine judicial procedure; but becaufe fin is its own punifhment, in the fame manner as holy obedience is its own reward.

The Doctrine of the Mifery of Man's natural State applied.

USE (1.) Of information. Is our ftate by nature a ftate of wrath? Then,

1. Surely we are not born innocent. Thofe chains of wrath, which by nature are upon us, fhew us to be born criminals. The fwadling-bands, wherewith infants are bound hand and foot, as foon as they are born, may put us in mind of the cords of wrath, with which they are held prifoners, as children of wrath.

2. What defperate madnefs is it, for finners to go on in their finful courfe! What is it but to heap coals of

Head II. *The Misery of Man's natural State.* 131
fire on thine own head! to lay more and more fuel to the fire of wrath! to *treasure up unto thyself wrath against the day of wrath,* Rom. ii. 5. Thou mayest perish, *when his wrath is kindled but a little,* Psal. ii. 12. Why wilt thou increase it yet more? Thou art already bound with such cords of death, as cannot easily be loosed: What need is there of more? Stand, careless sinner, and consider this.

3. Thou hast no reason to complain, as long as thou art out of hell. *Wherefore doth a living man complain?* Lam. iii. 39. If one, who has forfeited his life, be banished his native country, and exposed to many hardships; he may well bear all patiently, seeing his life is spared. Do you murmur, because you are under pain and sickness? Nay, bless God you are not there where the worm never dieth. Dost thou grudge, that thou art not in so good a condition in the world as some of thy neighbours are? Be thankful, rather, that you are not in the case of the damned. Is thy substance gone from thee? wonder that the fire of God's wrath hath not consumed thy self. Kiss the rod, O sinner! and acknowledge mercy; for God punisheth us less than our iniquities deserve, Ezra ix. 13.

4. Here is a memorandum, both for poor and rich. (1.) The poorest that go from door to door, and had not one penny left them by their parents, were born to an inheritance. Their first father Adam left them children of wrath: and, continuing in their natural state, they cannot miss of it: for *this is the portion of a wicked man from God, and the heritage appointed to him by God,* Job xx. 29. An heritage that will furnish them with a habitation, who have not where to lay their head; they shall be *cast into utter darkness,* Mat. xxv. 30. for to them *is reserved the blackness of darkness for ever,* Jude 13. where their bed shall be sorrow; *they shall lie down in sorrow,* Isa. l. 11. their food shall be judgment; for God will feed them with judgment, Ez. xxxiv. 16. and their drink shall be the red wine of God's wrath, *the dregs whereof all the wicked of the earth shall wring out, and drink them,* Psal. lxxv. 8. I know that those who are destitute of worldly goods, and withal void of the
know-

knowledge and grace of God, who therefore may be called the devil's poor, will be apt to say here, "We hope God will make us suffer all our misery in this world, and that we shall be happy in the next:" as if their miserable outward condition, in time, would secure their happiness in eternity. A gross and fatal mistake! There is another inheritance which they have, *viz. Lies, vanity, and things wherein there is no profit*, Jer. xvi. 19. but *the hail shall sweep away the refuge of lies*, Isa. xxviii. 17. Dost thou think, O sinner! that God, who commands judges on earth *not to respect the person of the poor in judgment*, Lev. xix. 15. will pervert judgment for thee? Nay, know for certain, that however miserable thou art here, thou shalt be eternally miserable hereafter, if thou livest and diest in thy natural state. (2.) Many that have enough in the world, have far more than they know of. Thou hast (it may be), O unregenerate man! an estate, a good portion, a large stock left thee by thy father; thou hast improved it, and the sun of prosperity shines upon thee; so that thou canst say with Esau, Gen. xxxiii. 9. *I have enough*. But know, thou hast more than all that, an inheritance thou dost not think of: thou art a child of wrath, an heir of hell. That is an heritage which will abide with thee, amidst all the changes in the world, as long as thou continuest in an unregenerate state. When thou shalt leave thy substance to others, this shall go along with thee into another world. It is no wonder that a slaughter-ox is fed to the full, and is not toiled as others are; Job xxi. 30. *The wicked is reserved to the day of destruction; they shall be brought forth to the day of wrath.* Well then, *Rejoice, let thine heart cheer thee, walk in the ways of thine heart, and in the sight of thine eyes.* Live above reproofs and warnings from the word of God; shew thyself a man of a fine spirit, by casting off all fear of God; mock at seriousness, live like thyself, a child of wrath, an heir of hell: *But know thou, that for all these things God shall bring thee in to judgment*, Eccl. xi. 9. Assure thyself, *thy breaking shall come suddenly at an instant*, Isa. xxx. 13. For, *as the crackling of thorns under a pot, so is the laughter of a fool,*

Head II. *The Misery of Man's natural State.* 133

Eccl. vii. 6. The fair blaze, and the great noise which they make, is quickly gone: so shall thy mirth be. Then that wrath, that is now silently sinking into thy soul, shall make a fearful hissing.

5. Wo to him that, like Moab, *hath been at ease from his youth*, Jer. xlviii. 11. and never saw the black cloud of wrath hanging over his head. There are many who *have no changes, therefore they fear not God*, Psal. lv. 19. They have lived in a good belief (as they call it) all their days; that is, they never had power to believe an ill report of their soul's state. Many have come by their religion too easily: and as it came lightly to them, so it will go from them, when the trial comes. Do you think men flee from wrath in a morning dream? Or will they flee from the wrath they never saw pursuing them?

6. Think it not strange, if you see one in great distress about his soul's condition, who was wont to be as jovial, and as little concerned for salvation as any of his neighbours. Can one get a right view of himself, as in a state of wrath, and not be pierced with sorrows, terrors, and anxiety? When a weight, quite above a man's strength lies on him, and he is alone, he can neither stir hand nor foot; but, when one comes to lift it off him, he will struggle in getting from under it. Thunder-claps of wrath from the word of God, conveyed to the soul by the Spirit of the Lord, will surely keep a man awake.

Lastly, It is no wonder that wrath come upon churches and nations, and upon us in this land, and that infants and children yet unborn smart under it. Most of the society are yet children of wrath; few are fleeing from it, or taking the way to prevent it; but people of all ranks are helping it on. The Jews rejected Christ; and their children have been smarting under wrath these sixteen hundred years. God grant that the bad entertainment given to Christ and his gospel, by this generation, be not pursued with wrath on the succeeding one,

Use 2. Of exhortation. Here, (1.) I shall drop a word to those who are yet in an unregenerate state.

(2.) To those who are brought out of it. (3.) To all indifferently.

I. To you that are yet in an unregenerate state, I would sound the alarm, and warn you to flee to yourselves, while there is yet hope. O you children of wrath, take no rest in this dismal state; but flee to Christ, the only refuge: haste, and make your escape thither. The state of wrath is too hot a climate for you to live in, Micah ii. 10. *Arise ye, and depart, for this is not your rest.* O sinner, knowest thou where thou art? Dost thou not see thy danger? The curse has entred into thy soul. Wrath is thy covering: the heavens are growing blacker and blacker above thy head: the earth is weary of thee, the pit is opening her mouth for thee; and should the thread of thy life be cut this moment, thou art thenceforth past all hope for ever. Sirs, if we saw you putting a cup of poison to your mouth, we should flee to you, and snatch it out of your hands. If we saw the house on fire about you, while you were fast asleep in it, we would run to you and drag you out of it. But alas! you are in ten thousand times greater hazard: yet we can do no more, than tell you your danger; invite, exhort, and beseech you, to look to yourselves; and lament your stupidity and obstinancy, when we cannot prevail with you to take warning. If there were no hope of your recovery, we should be silent, and would not torment you before the time: but though you be lost and undone, there is hope in Israel concerning this thing. Wherefore, I cry unto you, in the name of the Lord, and in the words of the prophet, Zech. ix. 12. *Turn ye to the strong hold, ye prisoners of hope.* Flee to Jesus Christ, out of this your natural state.

Motive 1. While you are in this state, you must stand or fall according to the law, or covenant of works. If you understood this aright, it would strike through your hearts as a thousand darts. One had better be a slave to the Turks, condemned to the gallies, or under Egyptian bondage, than be under the covenant of works now. All mankind were brought under it in Adam, as we heard before; and thou, in thy unregenerate state, art still where Adam left thee. It is true, there is

Head II. *The Misery of Man's natural State.* 135

another covenant brought in : but what is that to thee, who art not brought into it? Thou must needs be under one of the two covenants; either under the law, or under grace. That thou art not under grace, the dominion of sin over thee manifestly evinceth; therefore thou art under the law, Rom. vi. 14. Do not think God has laid aside the first covenant, Mat. v. 17, 18. Gal. iii. 10. No, he will *magnify the law, and make it honourable.* It is broken, indeed, on thy part; but it is absurd to think, that therefore your obligation is dissolved. Nay, thou must stand and fall by it, till thou canst produce thy discharge from God himself,. who is the party in that covenant; and this thou canst not pretend to, seeing thou art not in Christ.

Now, to give you a view of your misery, in this respect, consider these following things : (1.) Hereby you are bound over to death, in virtue of the threatening of death in the covenant, Gen. ii. 17. the condition being broken, you fall under the penalty. So it concludes you under wrath. (2.) There is no salvation for you under this covenant, but on a condition impossible to be performed by you. The justice of God must be satisfied for the wrong which you have done already. God has written this truth in characters of the blood of his own Son. Yea, and you must perfectly obey the law for the time to come. So faith the law, Gal. iii. 12. *The man that doth them, shall live in them.* Come, then, O sinner! see if thou canst make a ladder, whereby thou mayest reach the throne of God : stretch forth thine arms, and try if thou canst flee on the wings of the wind, catch hold of the clouds, and pierce through these visible heavens; and then either climb over, or break through, the jasper walls of the city above. These things thou mayest do, as well as be able to reach heaven, in thy natural state, or under this covenant. (3.) There is no pardon under this covenant. Pardon is the benefit of another covenant, with which thou hast nothing to do, Acts xiii. 39. *By him all that believe are justified from all things, from which ye could not be justified by the law of Moses.* As for thee, thou art in the hand of a merciless creditor, who will take thee by the throat, faying, *Pay what thou owest*; and caft thee into prifon, there to remain till thou haft paid the utmoft farthing: unlefs thou be fo wife as to get a furety in time, who is able to anfwer for all thy debt, and get up thy difcharge. This Jefus Chrift alone can do. Thou abideft under this covenant, and pleadeft mercy: but what is thy plea founded on? There is not one promife of mercy or pardon in that covenant. Doft thou plead mercy for mercy's fake? Juftice will ftep in between it and thee; and plead God's covenant-threatening, which he cannot deny. (4.) There is no place for repentance in this covenant, fo as the finner can be helped by it. For as foon as ever thou finneft, the law lays its curfe on thee, which is a dead weight that thou canft by no means throw off; no, not though thine head were waters, and thine eyes a fountain of tears, to weep day and night for thy fin. That is what the law cannot do, in that it is weak through the flefh, Rom. viii. 3. Thou art another profane Efau, that haft fold the bleffing; and there is no place for repentance, though you feek it carefully with tears, while under that covenant. (5.) There is no acceptance of the will for the deed under this covenant, which was not made for good will, but good works. The miftake in this point ruins many. They are not in Chrift, but ftand under the firft covenant; yet they will plead this privilege. This is juft like a man's having made a feaft for thofe of his own family; and when they fit down at table, another man's fervant, that has run away from his mafter, prefumptuoufly comes forward, and fits down among them: would not the mafter of the feaft give fuch a ftranger that check, *Friend, how cameft thou in hither?* And, fince he is none of his family, command him to be gone quickly? Though a mafter accept the good will of his own child for the deed, can a hired fervant expect that privilege? (6.) You have nothing to do with Chrift, while under that covenant. By the law of God, a woman cannot be married to two hufbands at once: either death or divorce muft diffolve the firft marriage, ere fhe can marry another. So we muft firft be dead to the law, ere we can be married to Christ, Rom. vii. 4. The law is the first husband; Jesus Christ, who raiseth the dead, marries the widow, that was heart-broken, and slain by the first husband. But while the soul is in the house with the first husband, it cannot plead a marriage-relation to Christ; nor the benefits of a marriage-covenant, which is not yet entered into, Gal. v. 4. *Christ is become of no effect to you; whosoever of you are justified by the law, ye are fallen from grace.* Peace, pardon, and such like benefits, are all benefits of the covenant of grace. You must not think to stand off from Christ, and the marriage-covenant with him, and yet plead these benefits; more than one man's wife can plead the benefit of a contract of marriage past between another man and his wife. *Lastly,* See the bill of exclusion, passed in the court of heaven, against all under the covenant of works, Gal. iv. 30. *The son of the bond-woman shall not be heir.* Compare ver. 24. Heirs of wrath must not be heirs of glory. Whom the first covenant has power to exclude out of heaven, the second covenant cannot bring in to it.

Objection. Then it is impossible for us to be saved: *Answer.* It is so, while you are in that state. But if you would be out of that dreadful condition, hasten out of that state. If a murderer be under sentence of death, so long as he lives within the kingdom, the laws will reach his life: but if he can make his escape, and go over the sea, into the dominions of another prince our laws cannot reach him there. This is what we would have you to do: flee out of the kingdom of darkness into the kingdom of God's dear Son; out of the dominion of the law, into the dominion of grace: then all the curses of the law, or covenant of works, shall never be able to reach you.

Motive 2. O ye children of wrath, your state is wretched, for you have lost God, and that is an unspeakable loss. You are without God in the world, Eph. ii. 12. Whatever you may call yours, you cannot call God yours. If we look to the earth, perhaps you can tell us, that land, that house, or that herd of cattle, is yours. But let us look upward to heaven; is that

God, that grace, that glory, yours? Truly, you have neither part nor lot in this matter. When Nebuchadnezzar talks of cities and kingdoms, O how big does he speak; *Great Babylon that I have built—my power— my majesty:* but he tells a poor tale, when he comes to speak of God, saying, Your God, Dan. ii. 47. and iv. 30. Alas, sinner, whatever thou hast, God is gone from thee. O the misery of a godless soul! Hast thou lost God? Then, (1.) The sap and substance of all thou hast in the world is gone. The godless man, have what he will, is one that hath not, Mat. xxv. 29. I defy the unregenerate man to attain to soul-satisfaction whatever he possesseth; since God is not his God. All his days he eateth in darkness: in every condition there is a secret dissatisfaction haunts his heart, like a ghost: the soul wants something, though perhaps it knoweth not what it is; and so it will be always, till the soul return to God, the fountain of satisfaction. (2.) Thou canst do nothing to purpose for thyself; for God is gone, his soul is departed from thee, Jer. vi. 8. like a leg out of joint, hanging by, whereof a man has no use, as the word there used doth bear. Losing God, thou hast lost the fountain of good; and so all grace, all goodness, all the saving influences of his Spirit. What canst thou do then? What fruit canst thou bring forth, more than a branch cut off from the stock? John xv. 5. Thou art become unprofitable, Rom. iii. 12. as a filthy rotten thing, fit only for the dunghill. (3.) Death has come up into thy windows, yea, and has settled on thy face; for God, in whose favour is life, Psal. xxx. 5. is gone from thee, and so the soul of thy soul is departed. What a loathsome lump is the body, when the soul is gone! Far more loathsome is thy soul in this case. Thou art dead while thou livest. Do not deny it, seeing thy speech is laid, thine eyes closed, and all spiritual motion in thee ceaseth. Thy true friends, who see thy case, lament; because thou art gone into the land of silence. (4.) Thou hast not a steady friend among all the creatures of God; for now thou hast lost the master's favour, all the family is set against thee. Conscience is thine enemy: the word never speaks good of thee : God's people loath thee, so far as they see what thou art, Psal. xv. 4. The beasts and stones of the field are banded together against thee, Job v. 23. Hof. ii. 18. Thy meat, drink, and cloaths, grudge to be serviceable to the wretch that has lost God, and abuseth them to his dishonour. The earth groaneth under thee ; yea, the *whole creation groaneth, and travelleth in pain together,* because of thee, and such as thou art, Lam. viii. 22. Heaven will have nothing to do with thee ; for *there shall in no wise enter into it any thing that defileth*, Rev. xxi. 27. Only *hell from beneath is moved for thee, to meet thee at thy coming*, Isa. xiv. 9. *Lastly*, Thy hell is begun already. What makes hell, but exclusion from the presence of God ? *Depart from me, ye cursed.* You are gone from God already, with the curse upon you. That which is now your choice, shall be your punishment at length, if you turn not. As a gracious state is a state of glory in the bud ; so a graceless state is hell in the bud, which, if it continue, will come at length to perfection.

Motive 3. Consider the dreadful instances of the wrath of God ; and let them serve to awaken thee, to flee out of this state. Consider, (1.) How it has fallen on men. Even in this world, many have been set up as monuments of divine vengeance, that others might fear. Wrath has swept away multitudes, who have fallen together by the hand of an angry God. Consider how the Lord *spared not the old world, bringing in the flood upon the world of the ungodly. And turning the cities of Sodom and Gomorrah into ashes, condemned them with an overthrow, making them an example unto those that after should live ungodly,* 2 Pet. ii. 5, 6. But it is yet more dreadful to think of that weeping, wailing, and gnashing of teeth, among those who in hell lift up their eyes, but cannot get a drop of water to cool their tongues. Believe these things, and be warned by them, lest destruction come upon thee, for a warning to others. (2.) Consider how wrath fell upon the fallen angels, whose case is absolutely hopeless. They were the first that ventured to break the hedge of the divine law ; and God set them up for monuments of his wrath againſt ſin. They once left their own habitation, and were never allowed to look in again at the hole of the door ; but they are *reſerved in everlaſting chains, under darkneſs, unto the judgment of the great day*, Jude, ver. 6. *Laſtly*, Behold how an angry God dealt with his own Son, ſtanding in the room of elect ſinners, Rom. viii. 32. *God ſpared not his own Son*. Sparing mercy might have been expected, if any at all. If any perſon could have obtained it, ſurely his own Son would have got it : but he ſpared him not. The Father's delight is made a man of ſorrows : he who is the wiſdom of God, becomes ſore amazed, ready to faint away in a fit of horror. The weight of this wrath makes him ſweat great drops of blood. By the fierceneſs of this fire, his heart was like wax melted in the midſt of his bowels. Behold, here, how ſevere God is againſt ſin ! The ſun was ſtruck blind with this terrible ſight, rocks were rent, graves opened. death, as it were, in the exceſs of aſtoniſhment, letting its priſoners ſlip away. What is a deluge, a ſhower of fire and brimſtone on Sodomites, the terrible noiſe of a diſſolving world, the whole fabric of heaven and earth falling down at once, and angels caſt down from heaven into the bottomleſs pit ! What are all theſe, I ſay, in compariſon with this, God ſuffering ! groaning ! dying on a croſs ! Infinite holineſs did it, to make ſin look like itſelf, *viz.* infinitely odious. And will men live at eaſe, while expoſed to this wrath ?

Laſtly, Conſider what a God he is, with whom thou haſt to do, and whoſe wrath thou art liable unto. He is the God of infinite knowledge and wiſdom : ſo that none of thy ſins, however ſecret, can be hid from him. He infalliibly finds out all means, whereby wrath may be executed, toward the ſatisfying of juſtice. He is of infinite power, and ſo can do what he will againſt the ſinner. How heavy muſt the ſtrokes of wrath be, which are laid on by the omnipotent hand ! Infinite power can make the ſinner priſoner, even when he is in his greateſt rage againſt heaven. It can bring again the ſeveral parcels of duſt, out of the grave, put them together again, re-unite the ſoul and body, ſummon them before the tribunal, hurry them away to the pit, and hold them

Head II. *The Misery of Man's natural State.*

up with the one hand, through eternity, while they are lashed with the other. He is infinitely just, and therefore must punish; it were acting contrary to his nature to suffer the sinner to escape wrath. Hence the executing of this wrath is pleasing to him: for though the Lord hath no delight in the death of a sinner, as it is the destruction of his own creature; yet he delights in it, as it is the execution of justice. *Upon the wicked he shall rain snares, fire and brimstone, and an horrible tempest.* Mark the reason; *For the righteous Lord loveth righteousness*, Psal. xi. 6, 7. *I will cause my fury to rest upon them, and I will be comforted*, Ezek. v. 13. *I also will laugh at your calamity*, Prov. i. 26. Finally, he lives for ever, to pursue the quarrel. Let us therefore conclude, *It is a fearful thing to fall into the hands of the living God.*

Be awakened, then, O young sinner! be awakened, O old sinner! who art yet in the state thou wast born in! Your security is none of God's allowance; it is the sleep of death: rise out of it, ere the pit close its mouth upon you. It is true, you may put on a breastplate of iron, make your brow brass, and your heart as an adamant: and who can help it? But God will break that brazen brow, and make that adamantine heart, at last, to fly into a thousand pieces. You may, if you will, labour to put these things out of your heads, that you may yet sleep in a found skin, though in a state of wrath. You may run away, with the arrows sticking in your consciences, to your work, to work them away; or to your beds, to sleep them out; or to company, to sport and laugh them away: but convictions, so stifled, will have a fearful resurrection; and the day is coming, when the arrows of wrath shall so stick in thy soul, as thou shalt never be able to pluck them out through the ages of eternity, unless thou take warning in time.

But, if any desire to flee from the wrath to come; and, for that end, to know what course to take, I offer them these few advices; and implore and beseech them, as they love their own souls, to fall in with them. (1.) Retire in some secret place, and there meditate on this your misery. Believe it, and fix your thoughts on it. Let each put the question to himself, How can I live in this state? How can I die in it? How shall I rise again, and stand before the tribunal of God in it? (2.) Consider seriously the sin of your nature, heart, and life. A proper sight of wrath flows from a deep sense of sin. They who see themselves exceeding sinful, will find no great difficulty to perceive themselves to be heirs of wrath. (3.) Labour to justify God in this matter. To quarrel with God about it, and to rage like a wild bull in a net, will but fix you the more in it. Humiliation of soul, before the Lord, is necessary for an escape. God will not sell deliverance, but freely gives it to those who see themselves altogether unworthy of his favour. *Lastly,* Turn your eyes, O prisoners of hope, towards the Lord Jesus Christ; and embrace him, as he offereth himself in the gospel. *There is no salvation in any other,* Acts iv. 12. God is a consuming fire; you are children of wrath: if the Mediator interpose not between him and you, you are undone for ever. If you would be safe, come under his shadow: one drop of that wrath cannot fall there, for he delivereth us from the wrath to come, 1 Thess. i. 10. Accept of him in his covenant, wherein he offereth himself to thee: so thou shalt, as the captive woman, redeem thy life, by marrying the Conqueror. His blood will quench that fire of wrath which burns against thee: in the white raiment of his righteousness thou wilt be safe; for no storm of wrath can pierce it.

II. I shall drop a few words to the saints.

First, *Remember—that at that time* (namely, when you were in your natural state) *ye were without Christ— having no hope, and without God in the world.* Call to mind that state you were in formerly; and review the misery of it. There are five memorandums which I may thence give in to the whole assembly of the saints, who are no more children of wrath; but heirs, and joint-heirs with Christ, though as yet in their minority: (1.) Remember, that in the day that our Lord took you by the hand, you were in no better a condition than others. O! what moved him to take you, when

Head II. *The Misery of Man's natural State.* 145

he passed by your neighbours! He found you children of wrath, even as others; but he did not leave you so. He came into the common prison, where you lay in your fetters, even as others: from amongst the multitude of condemned malefactors he picked you out, commanded your fetters to be taken off, put a pardon in your hand, and brought you into the glorious liberty of the children of God, while he left others in the devil's fetters. (2.) Remember, there was nothing in you to engage him to love you, in the day that he first appeared for your deliverance. Ye were children of wrath, even as others; fit for hell, and altogether unfit for heaven: yet the King brought you into the palace; the King's Son made love to you, a condemned criminal, and espoused you to himself, on the day in which you might have been led forth to execution. *Even so, Father, for so it seemeth good in thy sight*, Mat. ix. 26. (3.) Remember, ye were fitter to be loathed than loved in that day. Wonder, that when he saw you in your blood, he looked not at you with abhorrence, and passed by you. Wonder, that ever such a time could be a time of love, Ezek. xvi. 8. (4.) Remember, you are decked with borrowed feathers. It is his comeliness which is upon you, ver. 14. It was he that took off your prison garments, and cloathed you with robes of righteousness, garments of salvation; garments wherewith you are arrayed as the lilies, which toil not, neither do they spin. He took the chains from off your arms, the rope from about your neck; put you in such a dress, as you might be fit for the court of heaven, even to eat at the King's table. (5.) Remember your faults this day, as Pharaoh's butler, who had forgotten Joseph. Mind how you have forgotten, and how unkindly you have treated him, who remembered you in your low estate. Is this your kindness to your Friend? In the day of your deliverance, did you think you could have thus requited him, your Lord.

Secondly, Pity the children of wrath, the world that lies in wickedness. Can you be unconcerned for them, you who were once in the same condition? You have got a-shore, indeed, but your fellows are yet in hazard of perishing; and will not you give them all possible help for their deliverance? What they are, you sometimes were. This may draw pity from you, and engage you to use all means for their recovery. See Tit. iii. 1, 2, 3.

Thirdly, Admire that matchless love which brought you out of the state of wrath. Christ's love was active love; he brought thy soul from the pit of corruption. It was no easy work to purchase the life of the condemned sinner; but he gave his life for thy life. He gave his precious blood to quench that flame of wrath, which otherwise would have burnt thee up. Men get the best view of the stars from the bottom of a deep pit: from this pit of misery, into which thou wast cast by the first Adam, thou mayest get the best view of the Sun of Righteousness, in all his dimensions. He is the Second Adam, who took thee out of the horrible pit, and out of the miry clay. How broad were the skirts of that love, which covered such a multitude of sins! Behold the length of it, reaching from everlasting to everlasting, Psal. ciii. 17. The depth of it, going so low as to deliver thee from the lowest hell, Psal. lxxxvi. 13. The height of it, raising thee up to sit in heavenly places, Eph. ii. 6.

Fourthly, Be humble, carry low sails, walk softly all your years. Be not proud of your gifts, graces, privileges, or attainments: but remember you were children of wrath, even as others. The peacock walks slowly, hangs down his starry feathers, while he looks to his black feet. Look ye to the hole of the pit whence ye are digged, and walk humbly, as it becomes free grace's debtors.

Lastly, Be wholly for your Lord. Every wife is obliged to be dutiful to her husband; but double ties lie upon her who was taken from a prison, or a dunghill. If your Lord has delivered you from wrath, you ought, on that very account, to be wholly his; to act for him, to suffer for him, and to do whatever he calls you to. The saints have no reason to complain of their lot in the world, whatever it be. Well may they bear the cross for him, by whom the curse was borne away from them. Well may they bear the wrath of men in his cause, who has freed them from the wrath of God; and chearfully go to a fire for him, by whom hell fire is quenched as to them. Soul and body, and all thou hadst in the world, were sometimes under wrath: he has removed that wrath, shall not all these be at his service? That thy soul is not overwhelmed with the wrath of God, is owing purely to Jesus Christ: and shall it not then be a temple for his Spirit? That thy heart is not filled with horror and despair, is owing to him only; to whom then should it be devoted, but to him alone? That thine eyes are not blinded with the smoke of the pit, thy hands are not fettered with chains of darkness, thy tongue is not broiling in the fire of hell, and thy feet are not standing in the lake that burns with fire and brimstone, is owing purely to Jesus Christ: and shall not these eyes be employed for him, these hands act for him, this tongue speak for him, and these feet speedily run his errands? To him who believes that he was a child of wrath, even as others, but is now delivered by the blessed Jesus, nothing will appear too much, to do or suffer for his Deliverer, when he has a fair call to it.

III. To conclude with a word to all. Let no man think lightly of sin, which lays the sinner open to the wrath of God. Let not the sin of our nature, which wreaths the yoke of God's wrath so early about our necks, seem a small thing in our eyes. Fear the Lord, because of his dreadful wrath. Tremble at the thoughts of sin, against which God has such fiery indignation. Look on his wrath, and stand in awe and sin not. Do you think this is to press you to slavish fear? if it were so, one had better be a slave to God with a trembling heart, than a free man to the devil, with a seared conscience, and a heart of adamant. But it is not so; you may love him, and thus fear him too; yea, you ought to do it, though you were saints of the first magnitude. See Psal. cxix. 120. Matth. x. 28. Luke xii. 5. Heb. xii. 28, 29. Although you have past the gulph of wrath, being in Jesus Christ, yet it is but reasonable that your hearts should shiver when you look back to it. Your sin still deserves wrath, even as the sins of others: and it would be terrible to be in a fiery furnace, although, by a miracle, we were so fenced against it, as that it could not harm us.

HEAD III.

Man's utter Inability to recover himself.

Rom. v. 6. *For when ye were yet without strength, in due time Christ died for the ungodly.*
John vi. 44. *No man can come unto me, except the Father which hath sent me draw him.*

WE have now had a view of the total corruption of man's nature, and that load of wrath which lies on him, that gulph of misery which he is plunged into in his natural state. But there is one part of his misery that deserves particular consideration; namely, his *utter inability to recover himself,* the knowledge of which is necessary for the due humiliation of a sinner. What I design here is, only to propose a few things, whereby to convince the unregenerate man of this his inability; that he may see an absolute need of Christ; and of the power of his grace.

As a man that has fallen into a pit, cannot be supposed to help himself out of it, but by one of two ways; either by doing all himself alone, or taking hold of, and improving the help offered him by others: so an unconverted man cannot be supposed to help himself out of his natural state, but either in the way of the law, or covenant of works, by doing all himself without Christ; or else in the way of the gospel, or covenant of grace, by exerting his own strength to lay hold upon, and to make use of the help offered him by a Saviour. But alas! the unconverted man is dead in the pit, and cannot help himself either of these ways: not the first way; for the first text tells us, that when our Lord came to help us, *we were without strength,* unable to recover ourſelves. We were *ungodly*; therefore under a burden of guilt and wrath; yet *without ſtrength*, unable to ſtand under it; and unable to throw it off, or get from under it: ſo that all mankind had undoubtedly periſhed, had not *Chriſt died for the ungodly*, and brought help to them, who could never have recovered themſelves. But when Chriſt comes and offereth help to ſinners, cannot they take it? Cannot they improve help, when it comes to their hands? No; the ſecond text tells us, they cannot; *No man can come unto me*, (*i. e.* believe in me, John vii. 35.) *except the Father draw him*. This is a drawing which enables them to come, who, till then, *could not* come; and therefore could not help themſelves, by improving the help offered. It is a drawing, which is always effectual: for it can be no leſs than *hearing and learning of the Father*, which whoever partakes of cometh to Chriſt, ver. 25. Therefore it is not drawing in the way of mere moral perſuaſion, which may be, yea, and always is, ineffectual. But it is drawing by mighty power, Eph. i. 19. abſolutely neceſſary for them that have no power in themſelves to come and take hold of the offered help.

Hearken then, O unregenerate man, and be convinced, that as thou art in a moſt miſerable ſtate by nature; ſo thou art utterly unable to recover thyſelf in any way. Thou art ruined: and what way wilt thou go to work, to recover thyſelf? Which of the two ways wilt thou chooſe? Wilt thou try it alone? Or wilt thou make uſe of help? Wilt thou fall on the way of works, or on the way of the goſpel? I know very well, that thou wilt not ſo much as try the way of the goſpel, till once thou haſt found thy recovery impracticable in the way of the law. Therefore we ſhall begin where corrupt nature teaches men to begin, *viz.* at the way of the law of works.

I. Sinner, I would have thee believe that thy working will never effect it. Work, and do thy beſt; thou wilt never be able to work thyſelf out of this ſtate of corruption and wrath. Thou muſt have Chriſt, otherwiſe thou wilt periſh eternally. It is only Chriſt in you can be the hope of glory. But if thou wilt needs try it; then I muſt lay before thee, from the unalterable word of the living God, two things which thou muſt do for thyſelf. If thou canſt do them, it muſt be yielded, that thou art able to recover thyſelf: but if not, then thou canſt do nothing this way for thy recovery.

FIRST, *If thou wilt enter into life, keep the commandments,* Mat. xix. 17. That is, if thou wilt by doing enter into life, then perfectly keep the ten commands; for the drift of theſe words is to beat down the pride of the man's heart, and to let him ſee an abſolute need of a Saviour, from the impoſſibility of keeping the law. The anſwer is given ſuitable to the addreſs. Our Lord checks him for his compliment, *Good Maſter,* ver. 16. telling him, *There is none good but one, that is God,* ver. 17. As if he had ſaid, you think yourſelf a good man, and me another; but where goodneſs is ſpoken of, men and angels may vail their faces before the good God. As to his queſtion, wherein he diſcovered his legal diſpoſition, Chriſt does not anſwer him, ſaying, *Believe and thou ſhalt be ſaved;* that would not have been ſo ſeaſonable in the caſe of one who thought he could do well enough for himſelf, if he but knew what *thing he ſhould do;* but ſuitable to the humour the man was in, he bids him *keep the commandments;* keep them nicely and accurately, as thoſe that watch malefactors in priſon, leſt any of them eſcape, and their life go for theirs. See, then, O unregenerate man! what thou canſt do in this matter; for if thou wilt recover thyſelf in this way, thou muſt perfectly keep the commandments of God.

(1.) Thy obedience muſt be perfect, in reſpect of the principle of it; that is, thy ſoul, the principle of action, muſt be perfectly pure, and altogether without ſin; for the law requires all moral perfection; not only actual, but habitual: and ſo condemns original ſin; impurity of nature, as well as of actions. Now, if thou canſt bring this to paſs, thou ſhalt be able to anſwer that queſtion of Solomon, ſo as never one of Adam's poſterity could yet anſwer it, Prov. xx. 9. *Who can ſay I have made my heart clean?* But if thou canſt not, the very want of this perfection is fin; and fo lays thee open to the curfe, and cuts thee off from life. Yea, it makes all thine actions, even thy beft actions, finful: *For who can bring a clean thing out of an unclean?* Job xiv. 4. And doft thou think by fin to help thyfelf out of fin and mifery? (2.) Thy obedience muft alfo be perfect in parts. It muft be as broad as the whole law of God: if thou lackeft one thing, thou art undone; for the law denounceth the curfe on him that continueth not in every thing written therein, Gal. iii. 10. Thou muft give internal and external obedience to the whole law; keep all the commands in heart and life. If thou breakeft any one of them, that will infure thy ruin. A vain thought, or idle word, will ftill fhut thee up under the curfe. (3.) It muft be perfect in refpect of degrees; as was the obedience of Adam, while he ftood in his innocence. This the law requires, and will accept of no lefs, Mat. xxii. 37. *Thou fhalt love the Lord thy God, with all thine heart, and with all thy foul, and with all thy mind.* If one degree of that love, required by the law, be wanting; if each part of thy obedience be not brought up to the greateft height commanded, that want is a breach of the law, and fo leaves thee ftill under the curfe. A man may bring as many buckets of water to a houfe that is on fire as he is able to carry; and yet it may be confumed, and will be fo, if he bring not as many as will quench the fire. Even fo, although thou fhouldft do what thou art able, in keeping the commands, yet if thou fail in the leaft degree of obedience, which the law enjoins, thou art certainly ruined for ever; unlefs thou take hold of Chrift, renouncing all thy righteoufnefs, as filthy rags. See Rom. x. 5. Gal. iii. 10. *Laftly,* It muft be perpetual, as the man Chrift's obedience was, who always did the things that pleafed the Father; for the tenor of the law is, *Curfed is he that continueth not in all things written in the law, to do them.* Hence, though Adam's obedience was, for a while, abfolutely perfect; yet becaufe at length he tripped in one point, *viz.* in eating the forbidden fruit, he fell under the curfe of the law. If a man were to live a dutiful fubject to his prince, till the close of his days, and then conspire against him, he must die for his treason. Even so, though thou shouldst all the time of thy life, live in perfect obedience to the law of God, and yet at the hour of death only entertain a vain thought, or pronounce an ill word; that idle word, or vain thought, would blot out all thy former righteousness, and ruin thee; namely, in this way in which thou art seeking to recover thyself.

Now, such is the obedience which thou must perform, if thou wouldst recover thyself in the way of the law. But though thou shouldst thus obey, the law stakes thee down in the state of wrath, till another demand of it be satisfied, *viz.*

SECONDLY, Thou must pay what thou owest. It is undeniable that thou art a sinner: and whatever thou mayest be in time to come, justice must be satisfied for thy sin already committed. The honour of the law must be maintained, by thy suffering the denounced wrath. It may be thou hast changed thy course of life, or art now resolved to do it, and to set about keeping the commands of God: but what hast thou done, or what wilt thou do with the old debt? Your obedience to God, though it were perfect, is a debt due to him, for the time wherein it is performed; and can no more satisfy for former sins, than a tenant's paying the current year's rent, can satisfy the landlord for all arrears. Can the paying of new debts acquit a man from old accounts? Nay, deceive not yourselves, you will find these laid up in store with God, and sealed up among his treasures, Deut. xxxii. 34. It remains, then, that either thou must bear that wrath, to which for thy sin thou art liable according to the law; or else thou must acknowledge that thou canst not bear it, and thereupon have recourse to the Surety, the Lord Jesus Christ. Let me now ask thee, Art thou able to satisfy the justice of God? Canst thou pay thy own debt? surely not: for, as he is the infinite God, whom thou hast offended; the punishment, being suited to the quality of the offence, must be infinite. But thy punishment, or sufferings for sin, cannot be infinite in value, for thou art a finite creature: therefore they must be infinite in duration or continuance; that is, they muſt be eternal. And ſo all thy ſufferings in this world are but an earneſt of what thou muſt ſuffer in the world to come.

Now, ſinner, if thou canſt anſwer theſe demands, thou mayeſt recover thyſelf in the way of the law. But art thou not conſcious of thy inability to do any of theſe things; much more to do them all ? yet if thou do not all, thou doſt nothing. Turn, then, to what courſe of life thou wilt, thou art ſtill in a ſtate of wrath. Screw up thy obedience to the greateſt height thou canſt; ſuffer what God lays upon thee, yea, add, if thou wilt, to the burden, and walk under all, without the leaſt impatience : yet all this will not ſatisfy the demands of the law ; therefore thou art ſtill a ruined creature. Alas! ſinner, what art thou doing, while thou ſtriveſt to help thyſelf, but doſt not receive, and unite with Jeſus Chriſt ? Thou art labouring in the fire, wearying thyſelf for very vanity; labouring to enter into heaven, by the door which Adam's ſin ſo bolted, as neither he, nor any of his loſt poſterity, can ever enter in by it. Doſt thou not ſee the flaming ſword of juſtice, keeping thee off from the tree of life ? Doſt thou not hear the law denouncing a curſe on thee, for all thou art doing; even for thy obedience, thy prayers, thy tears, thy reformation of life, and ſo on ; becauſe being under the law's dominion, thy beſt works are not ſo good as it requires them to be ? Believe it, ſirs, if you live and die out of Chriſt, without being actually united to him as the ſecond Adam, the life-giving Spirit, and without coming under the covert of his atoning blood; though you ſhould do the utmoſt that any man on earth can do, in keeping the commands of God, you can never ſee the face of God in peace. If you ſhould, from this moment, bid an eternal farewell to this world's joys, and all the affairs thereof; and henceforth buſy yourſelves with nothing but the ſalvation of your ſouls ; if you ſhould go into ſome wilderneſs, live upon the graſs of the field, and be companions to dragons and owls ; if you ſhould retire to ſome dark cavern of the earth, and weep there for your ſins, until you have wept yourſelves blind, yea, weep out all the moisture of your body; if you should confess with your tongue, until it cleave to the roof of your mouth; pray till your knees grow hard as horns; fast till your body become like a skeleton; and after all this, give it to be burnt; the word is gone out of the Lord's mouth in righteousness, and cannot return; that you shall perish for ever, notwithstanding all this, as not being in Christ, John xiv. 6. *No man cometh unto the Father, but by me.* Acts iv. 12. *Neither is there salvation in any other.* Mark xvi. 16. *He that believeth not, shall be damned.*

Object. But God is a merciful God, and he knows that we are not able to answer these demands: we hope therefore to be saved, if we do as well as we can, and keep the commands as well as we are able. *Answer.* (1.) Though thou art able to do many things, thou art not able to do one thing right: thou canst do nothing acceptable to God, being out of Christ. John xv. 5. *Without me ye can do nothing.* An unrenewed man, as thou art, can do nothing but sin; as we have already proved. Thy best actions are sin, and so they increase thy debt to justice: how then can it be expected they should lessen it? (2.) Though God should offer to save men, upon condition that they did all they could do in obedience to his commands, yet we have reason to think, that those who should attempt it, would never be saved: for where is the man that does as well as he can? Who sees not many false steps that he has made, which he might have avoided? There are so many things to be done, so many temptations to carry us out of the road of duty, and our nature is so very apt to be set on fire of hell, that we surely must fail, even in some point that it within the compass of our natural abilities. But, (3.) Though thou shouldst do all thou art able to do, in vain dost thou hope to be saved in that way. What word of God is this hope of thine founded on? It is neither founded on law nor gospel; therefore is but a delusion. It is not founded on the gospel; for the gospel leads the soul out of itself, to Jesus Christ for all; and it establisheth the law, Rom. iii. 31. Whereas this hope of yours cannot be established, but on the ruins of the law, which God will magnify and make honourable. Hence it appears, that it is not founded on the law neither. When God set Adam a-working for happiness for himself and his posterity, perfect obedience was the condition required of him; and the curse was denounced in case of disobedience. The law being broken by him, he and his posterity was subjected to the penalty, for sin committed; and withal still bound to perfect obedience: for it is absurd to think, that man's sinning, and suffering for his sin, should free him from his duty of obedience to his Creator. When Christ came in the room of the elect, to purchase their salvation, the terms were the same. Justice had the elect under arrest: if he is desirous to deliver them, the terms are known. He must satisfy for their sin, by suffering the punishment due to it: he must do what they cannot do, to wit, obey the law perfectly; and so fulfil all righteousness. Accordingly all this he did, and so became *the end of the law for righteousness, to every one that believeth*, Rom. x. 4. And dost thou think that God will abate of these terms as to thee, when his own Son got no abatement of them? Expect it not, though thou shouldst beg it with tears of blood; for if they prevailed, they must prevail against the truth, justice, and honour of God, Gal. iii. 10. *Cursed is every one that continueth not in all things, which are written in the book of the law, to do them.* Verse 22. *The law is not of faith, but the man that doth them shall live in them.* It is true, that God is merciful: but cannot he be merciful, unless he saves you in a way that is neither consistent with his law, nor his gospel? Hath not his goodness and mercy sufficiently appeared, in sending the Son of his love, to do *what the law could not do, in that it was weak through the flesh?* He has provided help for them that cannot help themselves: but thou, insensible of thine own weakness, wilt needs think to recover thyself by thine own works, while thou art no more able to do it, than to remove mountains of brass out of their place.

Wherefore I conclude, that thou art utterly unable to recover thyself in the way of works, or by the law.

O that thou wouldst conclude the same concerning thyself.

II. Let us try next, what the sinner can do to recover himself, in the way of the gospel. It may be thou thinkest, that though thou canst not do all by thyself alone, yet Jesus Christ offering thee help, thou canst of thyself embrace it, and use it for thy recovery. But, O sinner, be convinced of thine absolute need of the grace of Christ: for truly, there is help offered, but thou canst not accept it: there is a rope cast out to draw ship-wrecked sinners to land: but alas! they have no hands to catch hold of it. They are like infants exposed in the open field, that must starve, though their food be lying by them, unless one put it in their mouths. To convince natural men of this, let it be considered,

First, That although Christ is offered in the gospel, yet they cannot believe in him. Saving faith is the faith of God's elect; the special gift of God to them, wrought in them by his Spirit. Salvation is offered to them that will believe in Christ, but how can you believe? John v. 44. It is offered to those that will come to Christ, but *no man can come unto him, except the Father draw him*. It is offered to them that will look to him, as lifted up on the pole of the gospel, Isa. xlv. 22. but the natural man is spiritually blind, Rev. iii. 17. and as to the things of the Spirit of God, he cannot know them, for they are spiritually discerned, 1 Cor. ii. 14. Nay, whosoever will, he is welcome; let him come, Rev. xxii. 17. But there must be a day of power on the sinner, before he can be willing, Psal. cx. 3.

Secondly, Man naturally has nothing wherewith to improve, for his recovery, the help brought in by the gospel. He is cast away in a state of wrath; and is bound hand and foot, so that he cannot lay hold on the cords of love thrown out to him in the gospel. The most cunning artificer cannot work without instruments; neither can the most skilful musician play well on an instrument that is out of tune. How can one believe, how can he repent, whose understanding is darkness, Eph. v. 8. whose heart is a stony heart, inflexible, insensible, Ezek. xxxvi. 26. whose affections are wholly disordered and distempered; who is averse to good, and bent to evil? The arms of natural abilities are too short to reach supernatural help: hence those who most excel in them, are oft-times most estranged from spiritual things, Mat. xi. 25. *Thou hast hid these things from the wise and prudent.*

Thirdly, Man cannot work a saving change on himself: but so changed he must be, else he can neither believe nor repent, nor ever see heaven. No action can be without a suitable principle. Believing, repenting, and the like, are the product of the new nature; and can never be produced by the old corrupt nature. Now, what can the natural man do in this matter? He must be regenerate; begotten again unto a lively hope: but as the child cannot be active in his own generation, so a man cannot be active, but passive only, in his own regeneration. The heart is shut against Christ: man cannot open it, only God can do it by his grace, Acts xvi. 14. He is dead in sins: he must be quickened, raised out of his grave; who can do this but God himself? Eph. ii. 5. Nay, he must be created in Christ Jesus, unto good works, Eph. ii. 10. These are works of omnipotency, and can be done by no less power.

Fourthly, Man, in his depraved state, is under an utter inability to do any thing truly good, as was cleared before at large: how then can he obey the gospel? His nature is the very reverse of the gospel: how can he, of himself, fall in with the plan of salvation, and accept the offered remedy? The corruption of man's nature infallibly includes his utter inability to recover himself in any way: and whoso is convinced of the one, must needs admit the other; for they stand and fall together. Were all the purchase of Christ offered to the unregenerate man, for one good thought, he cannot command it, 2 Cor. iii. 5. *Not that we are sufficient of ourselves, to think any thing as of ourselves.* Were it offered on condition of a good word, yet *how can ye, being evil, speak good things?* Matt. xii. 35. Nay, were it left to yourselves, to choose what is easiest, Christ himself tells you, John xv. 5. *Without me ye can do nothing.*

Lastly, The natural man cannot but resist the Lord's offering to help him; yet that resistance is infallibly overcome in the elect, by converting grace. Can the stony heart choose but resist the stroke? There is not only an inability, but an enmity and obstinacy in man's will by nature. God knows, O natural man (whether thou knoweft it or not), that *thou art obstinate, and thy neck an iron sinew, and thy brow brass,* Isa. xlviii. 4. and cannot be overcome, but by him who hath *broken the gates of brass, and cut the bars of iron in sunder.* Hence, commonly speaking, there is such hard work in converting a sinner. Sometimes he seems to be caught in the net of the gospel; yet quickly he slips away again. The hook catcheth hold of him; but he struggles, till getting free of it, he goes away with a bleeding wound. When good hopes are conceived of him, by those that travel in birth for the forming of Christ in him, there is oft-times nothing brought forth but wind. The deceitful heart makes many a shift to avoid the Saviour, and cheat the man of eternal happiness. Thus the natural man lies sunk in a state of sin and wrath, utterly unable to recover himself.

Object. (1.) If we be under utter inability to do any good, how can God require us to do it? *Answ.* God making man upright, Eccl. vii. 29. gave him a power to do every thing that he should require of him: this power man lost by his own fault. We were bound to serve God, and do whatever he commanded us, as being his creatures; and also, we were under the superadded tie of a covenant, for that purpose. Now, we having, by our own fault, disabled ourselves, shall God lose his right of requiring our task, because we have thrown away the strength he gave us, whereby to perform it? Has the creditor no right to require payment of his money, because the debtor has squandered it away, and is not able to pay him? Truly, if God can require no more of us than we are able to do, we need no more to save us from wrath, but to make ourselves unable for every duty, and to incapacitate ourselves for serving God any manner of way, as profane men frequently do: and so the deeper a man is plunged in sin, he will be the more secure from wrath; for where God can require no duty of us, we do not sin in omitting it;

and where there is no sin, there can be no wrath. (As to what may be urged by the unhumbled soul, against the putting our stock into Adam's hand, the righteousness of that dispensation was cleared before.) But, moreover, the unrenewed man is daily throwing away the very remains of natural abilities; that rational light and strength which are to be found amongst the ruins of mankind. Nay, further, he will not believe his own utter inability to help himself; so that out of his own mouth he must be condemned. Even those who make their natural impotency to good a covert to their sloth, do, with others, delay the work of turning to God from time to time, and, under convictions, make large promises of reformation, which afterwards they never regard, and delay their repentance to a death-bed, as if they could help themselves in a moment; which shews them to be far from a due sense of their natural inability, whatever they pretend.

Now if God can require of men the duty they are not able to do, he can in justice punish them for their not doing it, notwithstanding their inability. If he has power to exact the debt of obedience, he has also power to cast the insolvent debtor into prison for his not paying it. Further, though unregenerate men have no gracious abilities, yet they want not natural abilities, which, nevertheless, they will not improve. There are many things they can do, which they do not, they will not do them; and therefore their damnation will be just. Nay, all their inability to good is voluntary; they will not come to Christ, John v. 40. They will not repent, they will die, Ezek. xviii. 51. So they will be justly condemned; because they will neither turn to God, nor come to Christ; but love their chains better than their liberty, and darkness rather than light, John iii. 19.

Object. (2.) Why do you then preach Christ to us; call us to come to him, to believe, repent, and use the means of salvation? *Answ.* Because it is your duty so to do. It is your duty to accept of Christ, as he is offered in the gospel; to repent of your sins, and to be holy in all manner of conversation: these things are commanded you of God; and his command, not your ability, is the meafure of your duty. Moreover, thefe calls and exhortations are the means that God is pleafed to make ufe of for converting his elect, and working grace in their hearts: to them, *faith cometh by hearing*, Rom. x. 17. while they are as unable to help themfelves as the reft of mankind are. Upon very good grounds may we, at the command of God, who raifeth the dead, go to their graves, and cry in his name, *Awake, thou that fleepeft, and arife from the dead, and Chrift fhall give thee light*, Eph. v. 14. And feeing the elect are not to be known and diftinguifhed from others before converfion; as the fun fhines on the blind man's face, and the rain falls on the rocks, as well as on the fruitful plains; fo we preach Chrift to all, and fhoot the arrow at a venture, which God himfelf directs as he fees meet. Moreover, thefe calls and exhortations are not altogether in vain, even to thofe that are not converted by them. Such perfons may be convinced, though they be not converted: although they be not fanctified by thefe means, yet they may be reftrained by them, from running into that excefs of wickednefs which otherwife they would arrive at. The means of grace ferve, as it were, to embalm many dead fouls, which are never quickened by them: though they do not reftore them to life, yet they keep them from fmelling fo rank as otherwife they would do. *Finally*, Though you cannot recover yourfelves, nor take hold of the faving help offered to you in the gofpel, yet, even by the power of nature, you may ufe the outward and ordinary means, whereby Chrift communicates the benefits of redemption to ruined finners, who are utterly unable to recover themfelves out of the ftate of fin and wrath. You may and can, if you pleafe, do many things that would fet you in a fair way for help from the Lord Jefus Chrift. You may go fo far on, as to be not far from the kingdom of God, as the difcreet fcribe had done, Mark xii. 34. though (it fhould feem) he was deftitute of fupernatural abilities. Though you cannot cure yourfelves, yet you may come to the pool, where many fuch di-

Head III. *Man's Inability to recover himself.*

seased persons, as you are, have been cured: though you have none to put you into it, yet you may lie at the side of it: who knows but the Lord may return, and leave a blessing behind him? as in the case of the impotent man, recorded John v. 5—8. I hope Satan does not chain you to your houses, nor stake you down in your fields on the Lord's day; but you are at liberty, and can wait at the posts of wisdom's doors, if you will. When you come thither, he doth not beat drums at your ears, that you cannot hear what is said: there is no force upon you, obliging you to apply all you hear to others; you may apply to yourselves what belongs to your state and condition. When you go home, you are not fettered in your houses, where perhaps no religious discourse is to be heard; but you may retire to some separate place, where you can meditate, and put pertinent questions to your consciences upon what you have heard. You are not possessed with a dumb devil, that you cannot get your mouths opened in prayer to God. You are not so driven out of your beds to your worldly business, and from your worldly business to your beds again, but you might, if you would, make some prayer to God upon the case of your perishing souls. You may examine yourselves as to the state of your souls, in a solemn manner, as in the presence of God; you may discern that you have no grace, and that you are lost and undone without it; and you may cry unto God for it. These things are within the compass of natural abilities, and may be practised where there is no grace. It must aggravate your guilt, that you will not be at so much pains, about the state and case of your precious souls. If you do not what you can, you will be condemned, not only for your want of grace, but for your despising it.

Object. (3.) But all this is needless, seeing we are utterly unable to help ourselves out of the state of sin and wrath. *Answ.* Give not place to that delusion, which puts asunder what God hath joined; namely, the use of means, and a sense of our own impotency. If ever the Spirit of God graciously influence your souls, you will become thoroughly sensible of your absolute inability, and yet enter upon a vigorous use of means. You will do for yourselves, as if you were to do all; and yet overlook all you do, as if you had done nothing. Will you do nothing for yourselves, because you cannot do all? Lay down no such impious conclusion against your own souls. Do what you can; and, it may be, while you are doing what you can for yourselves, God will do for you what you cannot. *Understandest thou what thou readest?* said Philip to the Eunuch: *How can I*, saith he, *except some man should guide me?* Acts viii. 30, 31. He could not understand the Scripture he read; yet he could read it: he did what he could, he read; and while he was reading, God sent him an interpreter. The Israelites were in a great strait at the Red Sea: and how could they help themselves, when on the one hand were mountains, and on the other the enemy's garrison; when Pharaoh and his host were behind them, and the Red Sea before them? What could they do? *Speak unto the children of Israel*, saith the Lord to Moses, *that they go forward*, Exod. xiv. 15. For what end should they go forward? Can they make a passage to themselves through the sea? No; but let them go forward, saith the Lord; though they cannot turn sea to dry land, yet they can go forward to the shore: so they did; and when they did what they could, God did for them what they could not do.

Quest. Has God promised to convert and save them who, in the use of means, do what they can towards their own relief? *Answ.* We may not speak wickedly for God: natural men being strangers to the covenant of promise, Eph. ii. 12. have no such promise made to them. Nevertheless they do not act rationally, unless they exert the powers they have, and do what they can. For, (1.) It is possible this course may succeed with them. If you do what you can, it may be, God will do for you what you cannot do for yourselves. This is sufficient to determine a man, in a matter of the utmost importance, such as this is, Acts viii. 22. *Pray God, if perhaps the thoughts of thy heart may be forgiven thee.* Joel ii. 14. *Who knoweth if he will return?* If success may be, the trial should be. If, in a wreck at sea, all the sailors

Head III. *Man's Inability to recover himself.*

and paſſengers betake themſelves each to a broken board for ſafety; and one of them ſhould ſee all the reſt periſh, notwithſtanding their utmoſt endeavour to ſave themſelves: yet the very poſſibility of eſcaping by that means, would determine that one ſtill to do his beſt with his board. Why then do not you reaſon with yourſelves, as the four lepers did, who ſat at the gate of Samaria, 2 Kings vii. 3, 4. Why do you not lay, *If we ſit ſtill*, not doing what we can, *we die*; let us put it to a trial; if we be ſaved, *we ſhall live*; if not, *we ſhall but die?* (2.) It is propable this courſe may ſucceed. God is good and merciful: he loves to ſurpriſe men with his grace, and is often *found of them that ſought him not*, Iſa. lxv. 1. If you do this, you are ſo far in the road of your duty; and you are uſing the means, which the Lord is wont to bleſs, for men's ſpiritual recovery: you lay yourſelves in the way of the great Phyſician; and ſo it is propable you may be healed. Lydia went, with others, to the place where prayer was wont to be made; and the Lord opened her heart, Acts xvi. 13, 14. You plough and ſow, though no body can tell you for certain that you will get ſo much as your ſeed again: you uſe means for the recovery of your health, though you are not ſure they will ſucceed. In theſe caſes probability determines you; and why not in this alſo? Importunity, we ſee, does very much with men: therefore pray, meditate, deſire help of God; be much at the throne of grace, ſupplicating for grace; and do not faint. Though God regard you not, who in your preſent ſtate are but one maſs of ſin, univerſally depraved, and vitiated in all the powers of your ſoul; yet he may regard prayer, mediation, and the like means of his own appointment, and he may bleſs them to you. Wherefore, if you will not do what you can; you are not only dead, but you declare yourſelves unworthy of eternal life.

To conclude, let the ſaints admire the freedom and power of grace, which came to them in their helpleſs condition, made their chains fall off, the iron gate to open to them, raiſed the fallen creatures; and brought them out of the ſtate of ſin and wrath, wherein they

Y

would have lain and perished, had not they been mercifully visited. Let the natural man be sensible of his utter inability to recover himself. Know, thou art without strength; and canst not come to Christ, till thou be drawn. Thou art lost, and canst not help thyself. This may shake the foundation of thy hopes, who never saw thy absolute need of Christ and his grace; but thinkest to shift for thyself by thy civility, morality, drowsy wishes and duties; and by a faith and repentance which have sprung out of thy natural powers, without the power and efficacy of the grace of Christ. O be convinced of thy absolute need of Christ, and his overcoming grace: believe thy utter inability to recover thyself: that so thou mayst be humbled, shaken out of thy self-confidence, and lie down in dust and ashes, groaning out thy miserable case before the Lord. A proper sense of thy natural impotency, the impotency of depraved human nature, would be a step towards a delivery.

Thus far of man's *natural state*, the state of entire depravation.

STATE III.

NAMELY,

The STATE of GRACE; or BEGUN RECOVERY.

HEAD I.
REGENERATION.

1 PETER i. 23. *Being born again, not of corruptible seed, but of incorruptible, by the word of God, which liveth and abideth for ever.*

WE proceed now to the *state of grace*, the state of *begun recovery* of human nature, into which all that shall partake of eternal happiness are translated, sooner or later, while in this world. It is the result of a gracious change, made upon those who shall inherit eternal life; which change may be taken up in these two particulars: (1.) In opposition to their natural real state, the state of corruption, there is a change made upon them in regeneration; whereby their nature is changed. (2.) In opposition to their natural relative state, the state of wrath, there is a change made upon them, in their union with the Lord Jesus Christ; by which they are placed beyond the reach of condemnation. These, therefore; namely, regeneration and union with Christ, I design to handle, as the great and comprehensive changes on a sinner, bringing him into the state of grace.

The first of these we have in the text; together with the outward and ordinary means by which it is brought about. The apostle here, to excite the saints to the study of holiness, and particularly of brotherly love, puts them in mind of their spiritual origin. He tells them that they were born again; and that of incorruptible

Y 2

164   *Of Regeneration.*   State III.

seed, the word of God. This shews them to be brethren, partakers of the same new nature; which is the root from which holiness, and particularly brotherly-love, spring. We are once born sinners; we must be born again, that we may be saints. The simple word signifies *to be begotten*; and so it may be read, Mat. xi. 11. *to be conceived*, Mat. i. 20. and *to be born*, Mat. ii. 1. Accordingly, the compound word, used in the text, may be taken in its full latitude, the last idea presupposing the two former: so regeneration is a supernatural real change on the whole man, fitly compared to natural or corporal generation, as will afterward appear. The ordinary means of regeneration, called the *seed*, whereof the new creature is formed, is not corruptible seed. Of such, indeed, our bodies are generated: but the spiritual seed, of which the new creature is generated, is incorruptible; namely, *the word of God, which liveth and abideth for ever*. The sound of the word of God, passeth, even as other sounds do: but the word lasteth, liveth, and abideth, in respect of its everlasting effects on all upon whom it operates. This *word, which by the gospel is preached unto you*, (ver. 25.) impregnated by the Spirit of God, is the means of regeneration: and by it are dead sinners raised to life.

DOCTRINE. All men, in the state of grace, are born again. All gracious persons, namely, such as are in a state of favour with God, and endowed with gracious qualities and dispositions, are regenerate persons. In discoursing on this subject, I shall shew what regeneration is; next, why it is so called; and then apply the doctrine.

Of the Nature of Regeneration.

II. For the better understanding of the nature of regeneration, take this along with you in the first place, that as there are false conceptions in nature, so there are also in grace: by these many are deluded, mistaking some partial changes made upon them, for this great and thorough change. To remove such mistakes, let these few things be considered; (1.) Many call the church their mother, whom God will not own to be

Head I. *Of Regeneration.* 165

his children, Cant. i. 6. *My mother's children (i. e.* falſe brethren) *were angry with me.* All that are baptized are not born again. Simon was baptized, yet ſtill in the gall of bitterneſs, and in the bond of iniquity, Acts viii. 13. 23. Where Chriſtianity is the religion of the country, many are called by the name of Chriſt, who have no more of him than the name: and no wonder, for the devil had his goats among Chriſt's ſheep, in thoſe places where but few profeſſed the Chriſtian religion, 1 John ii. 19. *They went out from us, but they were not of us.* (2.) Good education is not regeneration. Education may chain up men's luſts, but cannot change their hearts. A wolf is ſtill a ravenous beaſt, though it be in chains. Joaſh was very devout during the life of his good tutor Jehoiada; but afterwards he quickly ſhewed what ſpirit he was of, by his ſudden apoſtaſy, 2 Chron. xxiv. 2. 17, 18. Good example is of mighty influence to change the outward man: but that change often goes off, when a man changes his company; of which the world affords many ſad inſtances. (3.) A turning from open profanity, to civility and ſobriety, falls ſhort of this ſaving change. Some are for a while very looſe, eſpecially in their younger years: but at length they reform, and leave their profane courſes. Here is a change, yet only ſuch as may be found in men utterly void of the grace of God, and whoſe righteouſneſs is ſo far from exceeding, that it doth not come up to the righteouſneſs of the Scribes and Phariſees (4.) One may engage in all the outward duties of religion, and yet not be born again. Though lead be caſt into various ſhapes, it remains ſtill but a baſe metal. Men may eſcape the pollutions of the world, and yet be but dogs and ſwine, 2 Pet. ii. 20. 22. All the external acts of religion are within the compaſs of natural abilities. Yea, hypocrites may have the counterfeit of all the graces of the Spirit: for we read of *true holineſs,* Eph. iv. 23. and *faith unfeigned,* 1 Tim. i. 5. which ſhews us that there is a counterfeit holineſs, and a feigned faith. (5.) Men may advance to a great deal of ſtrictneſs in their own way of religion, and yet be ſtrangers to the new-birth, Acts xxvi. 5. *After the ſtrict-*

eſt ſect of our religion I lived a Phariſee. Nature has its own unſanctified ſtrictneſs in religion. The Phariſees had ſo much of it, that they looked on Chriſt as little better than a mere Libertine. A man whoſe conſcience hath been awakened, and who lives under the felt influence of the covenant of works, what will he not do that is within the compaſs of natural abilities! It is a truth, though it came out of a helliſh mouth, that *ſkin for ſkin, all that a man hath will he give for his life,* Job ii. 4. (6.) A perſon may have ſharp ſoul exerciſes and pangs, and yet die in the birth. Many have been in pain, that have but, as it were, brought forth wind. There may be ſore pangs and throws of conſcience, which turn to nothing at laſt. Pharaoh and Simon Magus had ſuch convictions, as made them deſire the prayers of others for them. Judas repented himſelf, and, under terrors of conſcience, gave back his ill-gotten pieces of ſilver. All is not gold that glitters. Trees may bloſſom fairly in the ſpring, on which no fruit is to be found in the harveſt: and ſome have ſharp ſoul-exerciſes, which are nothing but foretaſtes of hell.

The new-birth, however in appearance hopefully begun, may be marred two ways. *Firſt,* Some, like Zarah, Gen. xxxviii. 28, 29. are brought to the birth, but go back again. They have ſharp convictions for a while; but theſe go off, and they turn as careleſs about their ſalvation, and as profane as ever; and uſually worſe than ever; *their laſt ſtate is worſe than their firſt,* Mat. xii. 45. They get awakening grace, but not converting grace; and that goes off by degrees, as the light of the declining day, till it iſſue in midnight darkneſs. *Secondly,* Some, like Iſhmael, come forth too ſoon; they are born before the time of the promiſe, Gen. xvi. 2. compare Gal. iv. 22. They take up with a mere law-work, and ſtay not till the time of the promiſe of the goſpel. They ſnatch at conſolation, not waiting till it be given them; and fooliſhly draw their. comfort from the law that wounded them. They apply the healing plaſter to themſelves, before their wound be ſufficiently ſearched. The law, that rigorous huſ-band, ſeverely beats them, and throws in curſes and

Head I. *Of Regeneration.* 167

vengeance upon their fouls; then they fall to reforming, praying, mourning, promifing, and vowing, till this ghoft be laid: which done, they fall afleep again in the arms of the law: but they are never fhaken out of themfelves and their own righteoufnefs, nor brought forward to Jefus Chrift.

Laftly, There may be a wonderful moving of the affections, in fouls that are not at all touched with regenerating grace. Where there is no grace, there may, notwithftanding, be a flood of tears, as in Efau, who found no place of repentance, though he fought it carefully with tears, Heb. xii. 17. There may be great flafhes of joy; as in the hearers of the word reprefented in the parable of the ftony ground, who anon with joy receive it, Matt. xiii 20. There may alfo be great defires after good things, and great delight in them too; as in thefe hypocrites defcribed, Ifa. lviii. 2. *They feek me daily, and delight to know my ways.—They take delight in approaching to God.* See how high they may fometimes ftand, who yet fall away, Heb. vi. 4, 5, 6. They may be *enlightened, tafte of the heavenly gift, be partakers of the Holy Ghoft, tafte the good word of God, and the powers of the world to come.* Common operations of the divine Spirit, like a land flood, make a ftrange turning of things upfide down: but when they are over, all runs again in the ordinary channel. All thefe things may be, where the fanctifying Spirit of Chrift never refts upon the foul, but the ftony heart ftill remains; and in that cafe thefe affections cannot but wither, becaufe they have no root.

But regeneration is a real thorough change, whereby the man is made a new creature, 2 Cor. v. 17. The Lord God makes the creature a new creature, as the gold-fmith melts down the veffel of difhonour, and makes it a veffel of honour. Man is, in refpect of his fpiritual ftate, altogether disjointed by the fall; every faculty of the foul is, as it were, diflocated. In regeneration the Lord loofeth every joint, and fets it right again. Now this change made in regeneration is,

1. A change of qualities or difpofitions: it is not a change of the fubftance, but of the qualities of the

soul. Vitious qualities are removed, and the contrary dispositions are brought in their room. The old man is put off, Eph. ix. 22. the new man put on, verse 24. Man lost none of the rational faculties of his soul by sin: he had an understanding still, but it was darkened; he had still a will, but it was contrary to the will of God. So in regeneration, there is not a new substance created, but new qualities are infused; light instead of darkness, righteousness instead of unrighteousness.

2. It is a supernatural change; he that is born again, is born of the Spirit, John iii. 5. Great changes may be made, by the power of nature, especially when assisted by external revelation. Nature may be so elevated by the common influences of the Spirit, that a person may thereby be turned into another man, (as Saul was, 1 Sam. x. 6.) who yet never becomes a new man. But in regeneration, nature itself is changed, and we become partakers of the divine nature; and this must needs be a supernatural change. How can we, that are dead in trespasses and sins, renew ourselves, any more than a dead man can raise himself out of his grave? Who but the sanctifying Spirit of Christ can form Christ in a soul, changing it into the same image? Who but the Spirit of sanctification can give the new heart? Well may we say, when we see a man thus changed, This is the finger of God.

3. It is a change into the likeness of God, 2 Cor. iii. 18. *We—beholding, as in a glass, the glory of the Lord, are changed into the same image.* Every thing that generates, generates its like: the child bears the image of the parent; and they that are born of God, bear God's image. Man aspiring to be as God, made himself like the devil. In his natural state he resembles the devil, as a child doth his father, John viii. 44. *Ye are of your father the devil.* But when this happy change comes, the image of Satan is defaced, and the image of God is restored. Christ himself, who is the brightness of his Father's glory, is the pattern after which the new creature is made, Rom. viii. 29. *For whom he did foreknow, he also did predestinate to be conformed to the*

image of his Son. Hence he is said to be formed in the regenerate, Gal. iv. 19.

4. It is an universal change; all things become new, 2 Cor. v. 17. It is a blessed leaven, that leavens the whole lump, the whole spirit, and soul, and body. Original sin infects the whole man; and regenerating grace, which is the salve, goes as far as the sore. This fruit of the Spirit is in all goodness; goodness of the mind, goodness of the will, goodness of the affections, goodness of the whole man. He gets not only a new head, to know religion, or a new tongue, to talk of it; but a new heart, to love and embrace it in the whole of his conversation. When the Lord opens the sluice of grace, on the soul's new-birth-day, the waters run through the whole man, to purify and make him fruitful. In those natural changes, spoken of before, there are, as it were, pieces of new cloth put into an old garment; as new life sewed to an old heart: but the gracious change is a thorough change; a change both of heart and life.

Yet though every part of the man is renewed, there is no part of him perfectly renewed. As an infant has all the parts of a man, but none of them come to a perfect growth; so regeneration brings a perfection of parts, to be brought forward in the gradual advances of sanctification, 1 Pet. ii. 2. *As new born babes, desire the sincere milk of the word, that ye may grow thereby.* Although in regeneration there is heavenly light let into the mind; yet there is still some darkness there: though the will is renewed, it is not perfectly renewed; there is still some of the old inclination to sin remaining: and thus it will be, till that which is in part be done away, and the light of glory come. Adam was created at his full stature; but they that are born, must have their time to grow up: so those that are born again, come forth into the new world of grace, as new born babes: Adam being created upright, was at the same time perfectly righteous, without the least mixture of sinful imperfection.

Lastly, Nevertheless, it is a lasting change, which never goes off. The seed is incorruptible, saith the text; and so is the creature that is formed of it. The life given in regeneration, whatever decays it may fall under, can never be utterly loft. His feed remaineth in him, who is born of God, 1 John iii. 9. Though the branches fhould be cut down, the root fhall abide in the earth; and being watered with the dew of heaven, fhall fprout again: for *the root of the righteous fhall not be moved*, Prov. xii. 3.

But to come to particulars:

Firft, In regeneration the mind is favingly enlightened. There is a light let into the underftanding; fo that they who were fometimes darknefs, are now light in the Lord, Eph. v. 8. The beams of the light of life make their way into the dark dungeon of the heart: then the night is over, and the morning light is come, which will fhine more and more unto the perfect day. The man is illuminated,

1. In the knowledge of God. He has far other thoughts of God than ever he had before, Hof. ii. 20. *I will even betrothe thee unto me in faithfulnefs, and thou fhalt know the Lord.* The Spirit of the Lord brings him back to this queftion, What is God? and catechifeth him anew upon that grand point, fo that he is made to fay, *I have heard of thee by the hearing of the ear; but now mine eye feeth thee*, Job xiii. 5. The fpotlefs purity of God, his exact juftice, his all-fufficiency, and other glorious perfections, revealed in his word, are by this new light difcovered to the foul, with a plainnefs and certainty, that doth as far exceed the knowledge which it had of thefe things before, as ocular demonftration exceeds common report. For now he fees what he only heard of before.

2. He is enlightened in the knowledge of fin. He hath different thoughts of it than he was wont to have. Formerly his fight could not pierce through the cover Satan laid over it: but now the Spirit of God removes it, and wipes off the paint and varnifh; fo that he fees it in its natural colours, as the worft of evils, exceeding finful, Rom. vii. 13. O what deformed monfters do formerly beloved lufts appear! Were they right eyes, he would pluck them out. Were they right hands, he would confent to their cutting off. He fees

how offensive sin is to God, how destructive it is to the soul; and calls himself a fool, for fighting so long against the Lord, and harbouring that destroyer as a bosom friend.

3. He is instructed in the knowledge of himself. Regenerating grace bringeth the prodigal to himself, Luke xv. 17. and makes men full of eyes within, knowing every one the plague of his own heart. The mind being savingly enlightened, the man sees how desperately corrupt his nature is; what enmity against God, and his holy law, has long lodged there: so that his soul loaths itself. No open sepulchre, no puddle so vile and loathsome, in his eyes, as himself, Ezek. xxxvi. 31. *Then shall ye remember your evil ways, and your doings that were not good, and shall loathe yourselves in your own sight.* He is no worse than he was before: but the sun is shining; and so those pollutions are seen, which he could not discern, when there was no dawning in him: as the word is, Isa. viii. 20. while as yet there was no breaking of the day of grace with him.

4. He is enlightened in the knowledge of Jesus Christ, 1 Cor. i. 23. *But we preach Christ crucified, unto the Jews a stumbling-block, and unto the Greeks foolishness: but unto them which are called, both Jews and Greeks, Christ the power of God, and the wisdom of God* The truth is, unregenerate men, though capable of preaching Christ, have not (properly speaking) the knowledge of him, but only an opinion, a good opinion of him, as a man has of many controverted points of doctrine, wherein he is far from certainty. As when you meet with a stranger on the road, who behaves himself discreetly, you conceive a good opinion of him; and therefore willingly converse with him: but yet you will not commit your money to him; because, though you have a good opinion of the man, he is a stranger to you, you do not know him: so may they think well of Christ; but they will never commit themselves to him, seeing they know him not. But saving illumination carries the soul beyond opinion, to the certain knowledge of Christ and his excellency, 1 Thess. i. 5. *For our gospel came not unto you in word only, but also in power, and in*

the Holy Ghost, and in much assurance. The light of grace thus discovers the suitableness of the mystery of Christ to the divine perfections, and to the sinner's case. Hence the regenerate admire the glorious plan of salvation, through Christ crucified, lay their whole weight upon it, and heartily acquiesce therein; for whatever he be to others he is to them, *Christ the power of God, and the wisdom of God.* But unrenewed men, not seeing this, are offended in him; they will not venture their souls in that bottom, but betake themselves to the broken boards of their own righteousness. The same light convincingly discovers a superlative worth, a transcendant glory and excellency in Christ, which darken all created excellency; as the rising sun makes the stars hide their heads: it engages the merchant-man to sell all that he hath, to buy the one pearl of great price, Matt. xiii. 45, 46. makes the soul heartily content to take Christ for all, and instead of all. An unskilful merchant, to whom one offereth a pearl of great price, for all his petty ware, dares not venture on the bargain; for though he thinks that one pearl may be worth more than all he has, yet he is not sure of it: but when a jeweller comes to him, and assures him it is worth double all his wares; he then greedily embraces the bargain, and cheerfully parts with all he has for that pearl. *Finally,* This illumination, in the knowledge of Christ, convincingly discover to men a fulness in him, sufficient for the supply of all their wants, enough to satisfy the boundless desires of an immortal soul. And they are persuaded that such fulness is in him, in order to be communicated. They depend upon it, as a certain truth; and therefore their souls take up their eternal rest in him.

5. The man is instructed in the knowledge of the vanity of the world, Psal. cxix. 96. *I have seen an end of all perfection.* Regenerating grace elevates the soul, translates it into the spiritual world, from whence this earth cannot but appear a little, yea, a very little thing; even as heaven appeared before, while the soul was grovelling in the earth, Grace brings a man into a new world; where this world is reputed but a stage of

Head I. *Of Regeneration.*

vanity, an howling wilderneſs, a valley of tears. God hath hung the ſign of vanity at the door of all created enjoyments: yet how do men throng into the houſe, calling and looking for ſomewhat that is ſatisfying; even after it has been a thouſand times told them, that there is no ſuch thing in it, it is not to be got there! Iſa. lvii. 10.. *Thou art wearied in the greatneſs of thy ways; yet ſaidſt thou not, There is no hope.* The truth of the matter lies here, they do not ſee by the light of grace, they do not ſpiritually diſcern that ſight of vanity. They have often indeed made a rational diſcovery of it: but can that truly wean the heart from the world? Nay, no more than painted fire can burn off the priſoner's bands. But the light of grace is the light of life, powerful and efficacious.

Laſtly, (To ſum up all in one word) in regeneration the mind is enlightened in the knowledge of ſpiritual things, 1 John ii. 20. Ye have an unction from the holy One, (that is from Jeſus Chriſt, Rev. iii. 18. It is an alluſion to the ſanctuary, whence the holy oil was brought to anoint the prieſts) and ye know all things, *viz.* neceſſary to ſalvation. Though men be not book-learned, if they are born again, they are Spirit-learned; for all ſuch are taught of God, John vi. 45. The Spirit of regeneration teacheth them what they knew not before; and what they knew by the ear only, he teacheth them over again as by the eye. The light of grace is an overcoming light, determining men to aſſent to divine truths, on the mere teſtimony of God. It is no eaſy thing for the mind of man to acquieſce in divine revelation. Many pretend great reſpect to the Scriptures, whom, nevertheleſs, the clear Scripture-teſtimony will not divorce from their pre-conceived opinions. But this illumination will make men's minds run, as willing captives, after Chriſt's chariot-wheels, which they are ready to allow to drive over, and *caſt down* their *imaginations, and every thing high that exalteth itſelf againſt the knowledge of God*, 2 Cor. x. 5. It will bring them to receive the kingdom of God as a little child, Mark x. 15. who thinks he has ſufficient ground to believe any thing, if his father do but ſay it is ſo.

Secondly, The will is renewed. The Lord takes away the stony heart, and gives a heart of flesh, Ezek. xxxvi. 26. and so of stones raiseth up children to Abraham. Regenerating grace is powerful and efficacious, and gives the will a new turn. It does not indeed force it; but sweetly, yet powerfully draws it, so that his people are willing in the day of his power, Psal. cx. 3. There is heavenly oratory in the Mediator's lips, to perfuade finners, Pf. xlv. 2. *Grace is poured into thy lips.* There are cords of a man; and bands of love in his hands, to draw them after him, Hos. xi. 4. Love makes a net for elect souls, which will infallibly catch them, and bring them to land. The cords of Christ's love are strong cords: and they need to be so, for every sinner is heavier than a mountain of brass: and Satan, together with the heart itself, draws the contrary way. But love is strong as death: and the Lord's love to the soul he died for, is the strongest love; which acts so powerfully, that it must come off victorious.

1. The will is cured of its utter inability to will what is good. While the opening of the prison, to them that are bound, is proclaimed in the gospel, the Spirit of God comes and opens the prison door, goes to the prisoner, and by the power of his grace makes his chains fall off; breaks the bonds of iniquity, wherewith he was held in sin, so as he could neither will nor do any thing truly good; brings him forth into a large place, *working in him both to will and to do of his good pleasure*, Phil. ii. 13. Then it is that the soul, that was fixed to the earth, can move heavenward; the withered hand is restored, and can be stretched out.

2. There is wrought in the will a fixed aversion to evil. In regeneration, a man gets a new spirit put within him, Ezek. xxxvi. 26. and that spirit lusteth against the flesh, Gal. v. 17. The sweet morsel of sin, so greedily swallowed down, he now loaths, and would fain be rid of it; even as willingly as one that had drunk a cup of poison would throw it up again. When the spring is stopped, the mud lies in the well unmoved: but when once the spring is cleared, the

Head I. *Of Regeneration.* 175

waters springing up will work away the mud by degrees. Even so, while a man continues in an unregenerate state, sin lies at ease in the heart: but as soon as the Lord strikes the rocky heart with the rod of his strength, in the day of conversion, grace is *in him a well of water, springing up into everlasting life,* John iv. 14. working away natural corruption, and gradually purifying the heart, Acts xv. 9. The renewed will riseth up against sin, strikes at the root thereof, and the branches too. Lusts are now grievous, and the soul endeavours to starve them; the corrupt nature is the source of all evil; and therefore the soul will be often laying it before the great Physician. O what sorrow, shame, and self-loathing fills the heart, in the day that grace makes its triumphant entrance into it! For now the mad-man is come to himself, and the remembrance of his follies cannot but cut him to the heart.

Lastly, The will is renewed with an inclination, bent, and propensity to good. In its depraved state, it lay quite another way, being prone and bent to evil only; But now, by the drawing of the omnipotent, all-conquering arm, it is drawn from evil to good; and gets another turn. As the former was natural, so this is natural too, in respect of the new nature given in regeneration, which has its own holy lustings, as well as the corrupt nature hath its sinful lustings, Gal. v. 17. The will, as renewed, inclines and points towards God and godliness. When God made man, his will, in respect of its intention, was directed towards God, as his chief end; in respect of its choice, it pointed towards that which God willed. When man unmade himself, his will was framed to the very reverse hereof: he made himself his chief end, and his own will his law. But when man is new made, in regeneration, grace rectifies this disorder in some measure, though not perfectly; because we are but renewed in part, while in this world. It brings back the sinner, out of himself, to God as his chief end, Psal. lxxiii. 25. *Whom have I in heaven but thee? and there is none upon earth that I desire besides thee.* Phil. i. 21. *For to me to live is Christ.* It makes him to deny himself, and whatever way he turns, to point habitually towards God, who is the centre of the gracious soul, his home, his *dwelling place in all generations*, Psal. xc. 1. By regenerating grace, the will is brought into conformity to the will of God. It is conformed to his preceptive will, being indowed with holy inclinations, agreeably to every one of his commands. The whole law is impressed on the gracious soul: every part of it is written on the renewed heart. Although remaining corruption makes such blots in the writing, that oft-times the man himself cannot read it, yet he that wrote it can read it at all times; it is never quite blotted out, neither can it be. What he has written, he has written, and it shall stand; *For this is the covenant—I will put my laws into their mind, and write them in their hearts*, Heb. viii. 10. It is a covenant of salt, a perpetual covenant. It is also conformed to his providential will; so that the man would no more be master of his own process, nor carve out his lot for himself. He learns to say, from his heart, *The will of the Lord be done; he shall choose our inheritance for us*, Psal. xlvii. 4. Thus the will is disposed to fall in with those things, which in its depraved state it could never be reconciled to.

Particularly, (1.) The soul is reconciled to the covenant of peace. The Lord God proposeth a covenant of peace to sinners; a covenant which he himself hath framed, and registered in the Bible: but they are not pleased with it. Nay, an unregenerate heart cannot be pleased with it. Were it put into their hands, to frame it according to their mind, they would blot many things out of it, which God has put in, and put in many things which God has kept out. But the renewed heart is intirely satisfied with the covenant, 2 Sam. xxiii. 5. *He hath made with me an everlasting covenant, ordered in all things and sure; this is all my salvation, and all my desire.* Though the covenant could not be brought down to their depraved will, their will is by grace brought up to the covenant: they are well pleased with it: there is nothing in it which they would have out; nor is any thing left out of it, which they would have in. (2.) The will is difpofed to receive Chrift Jefus the Lord. The foul is content to fubmit to him. Regenerating grace undermines, and brings down the towering imaginations of the heart, raifed up againft its rightful Lord: it breaks the iron finew, which kept the finner from bowing to him; and difpofes him to be no more ftiff necked, but to yield. He is willing to have on the yoke of Chrift's commands, to take up the crofs, and to follow him. He is content to take Chrift, on any terms, Pfal. cx. 3. *Thy people fhall be willing in the day of thy power.*

The mind being favingly enlightened, and the will renewed, the finner is thereby determined and enabled to anfwer the gofpel-call. So the main work in regeneration is done; the fort of the heart is taken; there is room made for the Lord Jefus Chrift, in the inmoft parts of the foul; the inner-door of the will being now opened to him, as well as the outer-door of the underftanding. In one word, Chrift is paffively received into the heart; he is come into the foul, by his quickening Spirit, whereby fpiritual life is given to the man, who in himfelf was dead in fin. His firft vital act we may conceive to be an active receiving of Jefus Chrift, difcerned in his glorious excellencies; that is, a believing on him, a clofing with him, as difcerned, offered, and exhibited in the word of his grace, the glorious gofpel: the immediate effect of which is union with him, John i. 12, 13. *To as many as received him, to them gave he power* (or privilege) *to become the fons of God, even to them that believe on his name: which were born, not of blood, nor of the will of the flefh, nor of the will of man, but of God.* Eph. iii. 17. *That Chrift may dwell in your hearts by faith.* Chrift having taken the heart by ftorm, and triumphantly entered into it, in regeneration, the foul by faith, yields itfelf to him, as it is expreffed, 2 Chron. xxx. 8. Thus, this glorious King, who came into the heart, by his Spirit, dwells in it by faith. The foul being drawn, runs; and being effectually called, comes.

Thirdly, In regeneration there is a happy change made on the affections; they are both rectified and regulated.

1. The change rectifies the affections, placing them on suitable objects, 2 Theff. iii. 5. *The Lord direct your hearts into the love of God.* The regenerate man's defires are rectified; they are fet on God himfelf, and the things above. He, who before cried with the world, *Who will fhew us any good?* has changed his note, and fays, Lord, *lift up the light of thy countenance upon us*, Pf. iv. 6. Before, he faw no beauty in Chrift, for which he was to be defired; but now he is all defires, he is altogether lovely, Cant. v. 16. The main ftream of his defires is turned to run towards God; for there is the one thing he defireth, Pfal. xxvii. 4. He defires to be holy, as well as to be happy; and rather to be gracious than great. His hopes, which before were low, and ftaked down to things on earth, are now raifed, and fet on the glory which is to be revealed. He entertains the hope of eternal life, founded on the word of promife, Tit. i. 2. Which hope he has, as an anchor of the foul, fixing the heart under trials, Heb. vi. 16. It puts him upon purifying himfelf, even as God is pure, John iii. 3. For he is begotten again unto a lively hope, 1 Pet. i. 3. His love is raifed, and fet on God himfelf, Pfal. xviii. 1. on his holy law, Pfal. cxix. 97. Though it ftrike againft his moft beloved luft, he fays, *The law is holy, and the commandment holy, and juft, and good,* Rom. vii. ver. 12. He loves the ordinances of God, Pfal. lxxxiv. 1. *How amiable are thy tabernacles, O Lord of Hofts!* Being paffed from death unto life, he loves the brethren, (1 John iii. 14.) the people of God, as they are called, 1 Pet. iii 10. He loves God for himfelf; and what is God's, for his fake. Yea, as being a child of God, he loves his own enemies. His heavenly Father is compaffionate and benevolent: *He maketh his fun to rife on the evil, and on the good; and fendeth rain on the juft, and on the unjuft*; therefore he is in like manner difpofed, Mat. v. 44, 45. His hatred is turned againft fin, in himfelf and others, Pfal. ci. 3. *I hate the work of them that turn afide, it fhall not cleave to me.* He groans under the body of it, and longs for deliverance, Rom. vii. 24. *O wretched man that I am, who fhall deliver me from the body of this death!* His

Head I. *Of Regeneration.* 179

joys and delights are in God the Lord, in the light of his countenance, in the law, and in his people, becaufe they are like him. Sin is what he chiefly fears: it is a fountain of forrow to him now, though formerly a fpring of pleafure.

2. It regulates the affections placed on fuitable objects. Our affections, when placed on the creature, are naturally exorbitant. When we joy in it, we are apt to overjoy; and when we forrow, we are ready to forrow overmuch: but grace bridles thefe affections, clips their wings, and keeps them within bounds, that they overflow not their banks. It makes a man *hate his father, and mother, and wife, and children; yea, and his own life alfo*, comparatively; that is, to love them lefs than he loves God, Luke xiv. 26. It alfo rectifies lawful affections; bringing them forth from right principles, and directing them to right ends. There may be unholy defires after Chrift and his grace; as when men defire Chrift, not from any love to him, but merely out of love to themfelves. *Give us of your oil,* faid the foolifh virgins, *for our lamps are gone out,* Mat. xxv. 8. There may be an unfanctified forrow for fin; as when one forroweth for it, not becaufe it is difpleafing to God, but only becaufe of the wrath annexed to it; as did Pharaoh, Judas, and others. So a man may love his father and mother, from mere natural principles, without any refpect to the command of God, binding him thereto. But grace fanctifies the affections, in fuch cafes, making them to run in a new channel of love to God, refpect to his commands, and regard to his glory. Again, grace raifes the affections, where they are too low. It gives the chief feat in them to God, and pulls down all other rivals, whether perfons or things, making them lie at his feet, Pfal. lxxiii. 25. *Whom have I in heaven but thee? and there is none upon earth that I defire befides thee.* He is loved for himfelf, and other perfons or things for his fake. What is lovely in them, to the renewed heart, is fome ray of the divine goodnefs appearing in them: for unto gracious fouls they fhine only by borrowed light. This accounts for the faints loving all men; and yet hating thofe that hate

A a 2

God, and contemning the wicked, as vile perfons. They hate and contemn them for their wickednefs; there is nothing of God in that, and therefore nothing lovely nor honourable in it: but they love them for their commendable qualities or perfections, whether natural or moral; becaufe, in whoever thefe are, they are from God, and can be traced to him as their fountain. *Finally*, Regenerating grace fets the affections fo firmly on God, that the man is difpofed, at God's command, to quit his hold of every thing elfe, in order to keep his hold of Chrift; to hate father and mother, in comparifon with Chrift, Luke xiv. 26. It makes even lawful enjoyments, like Jofeph's mantle, to hang loofe about a man, that he may quit them, when he is in hazard to be enfnared by holding them.

If the ftream of our affections were never thus turned, we are, doubtlefs, going down the ftream into the pit. If the luft of the eye, the luft of the flefh, and the pride of life, have the throne in your hearts, which fhould be poffeffed by the Father, Son, and Holy Ghoft; if we never had fo much love to God as to ourfelves; if fin has been fomewhat bitter to us, but never fo bitter as fuffering, never fo bitter as the pain of being weaned from it; truly we are ftrangers to this faving change. For grace turns the affections upfide down, whenever it comes into the heart.

Fourthly, The confcience is renewed. As a new light is fet up in the foul, in regeneration, confcience is enlightened, inftructed, and informed. That candle of the Lord, (Prov. xx. 27.) is now fnuffed and brightened; fo as it fhines, and fends forth its light into the moft retired corners of the heart; difcovering fins which the foul was not aware of before; and in a fpecial manner difcovering the corruption and depravity of nature, that feed and fpawn whence all actual fins proceed. This produces the new complaint, Rom. vii. 24. *O wretched man that I am, who fhall deliver me from the body of this death!* Confcience, which lay fleeping in the man's bofom before, is now awakened, and makes its voice to be heard through the whole foul: therefore there is no more reft for him in the fluggard's bed; he

Head I. *Of Regeneration.* 181

must get up and be doing, arise, haste, and escape for his life. It powerfully incites to obedience, even in the most spiritual acts, which lay not within the view of the natural conscience; and powerfully restrains from sin, even from those sins which do not lie open to the observation of the world. It urgeth the sovereign authority of God, to which the heart is now reconciled, and which it willingly acknowledges: and so it engageth the man in duty, whatever be the hazard from the world; for it fills the heart so with the fear of God, that the force of the fear of man is broken. This hath engaged many to put their life in their hand, and follow the cause of religion, which they once contemned, and resolutely walk in the path they formerly abhorred, Gal. i. 23. *He which persecuted us in times past, now preacheth the faith which once he destroyed.* Guilt now makes the conscience smart. It hath bitter remorse for sins past, which fills the soul with anxiety, sorrow, and self-loathing. And every new reflection on these sins is apt to affect, and make its wounds bleed afresh with regret. It is made tender, in point of sin and duty, for the time to come: being once burnt, it dreads the fire, and fears to break the hedge where it was formerly bit by the serpent. Finally, the renewed conscience drives the sinner to Jesus Christ, as the only Physician that can draw out the sting of guilt; and whose blood alone can purge the conscience from dead works, Heb. ix. 14. refusing all ease offered to it from any other hand. This is an evidence that the conscience is not only fired, as it may be in an unregenerate state, but oiled also with regenerating grace.

Fifthly, As the memory wanted not its share of depravity, it is also bettered by regenerating grace. The memory is weakened, with respect to those things that are not worth their room therein; and men are taught to forget injuries, and drop their resentments, Matt. v. 44, 45. *Do good to them that hate you, and pray for them which despitefully use you*—*That ye may be (i. e.* appear to be*) the children of your Father which is in heaven.* It is strengthened for spiritual things. We have Solomon's receipt for an ill memory, Prov. iii. 1. *My son,* saith he, *forget not my law.* But how shall it be kept in mind ? *Let thine heart keep my commandments.* Grace makes a heart-memory, even, where there is no good head-memory, Psal. cxix. 11. *Thy word have I hid in mine heart.* The heart, truly touched with the powerful sweetness of truth, will help the memory to retain what is so relished. If divine truths made deeper impressions on our hearts, they would imprefs themselves with more force on our memories, Psal. cxix. 93. *I will never forget thy precepts, for with them thou hast quickened me.* Grace sanctifies the memory. Many have large but unsanctified memories, which serve only to gather knowledge, whereby to aggravate their condemnation : but the renewed memory serves to remember his commandments, to do them, Psal. ciii. 18. It is a sacred store-house, from whence a Christian is furnished in his way to Zion ; for faith and hope are often supplied out of it, in a dark hour. It is the store-house of former experiences, and these are the believer's way-marks, by noticing of which he comes to know where he is, even in a dark time, Psal. xlvii. 6. *O my God, my soul is cast down within me : therefore will I remember thee from the land of Jordan,* &c. It also helps the soul to godly sorrow and self-loathing, presenting old guilt anew before the conscience, and making it bleed afresh, though the sin be already pardoned, Psal. xxv. 7. *Remember not the sins of my youth.* Where unpardoned guilt is lying on the sleeping conscience, it is often employed to bring in a word, which, in a moment, sets the whole soul on the stir : as, when Peter *remembered the words of Jesus—he went out and wept bitterly*, Matt. xxvi. 75. The word of God, laid up in a sanctified memory, serves a man to resist temptations, puts the sword in his hand against his spiritual enemies, and is a light to direct his steps in the way of religion and righteousness.

Sixthly, There is a change made on the body, and the members thereof, in respect of their use : they are consecrated to the Lord. Even the body is for the Lord, 1 Cor. vi. 13. It is the temple of the Holy Ghost, ver. 19. The members thereof, that were formerly instruments of unrighteousness unto sin, become

Head I.   *Of Regeneration.*   183

instruments of righteousness unto God, Rom. vi. 13. servants to righteousness unto holiness, ver. 19. The eye, that conveyed sinful imaginations into the heart, is under a covenant, Job xxxi. 1. to do so no more; but to serve the soul, in viewing the works, and reading the word, of God. The ear, that had often been death's porter, to let in sin, is turned to be the gate of life, by which the word of life enters the soul. The tongue, that set on fire the whole course of nature, is restored to the office it was designed for by the Creator; namely, to be an instrument of glorifying him, and setting forth his praise. In a word, the whole man is for God, in soul and body, which by this blessed change are made his.

Lastly, This gracious change shines forth in the conversation. Even the outward man is renewed. A new heart makes newness of life. When *the King's daughter is all glorious within, her cloathing is of wrought gold,* Psal. xlv. 13. The single eye makes the whole body full of light, Mat. vi. 22. This change will appear in every part of a man's conversation; particularly in the following things:

1. In the change of his company. He before despised the company of the saints, but now they are the *excellent, in whom is all his delight:* Psal. xvi. 3. *I am a companion to all that fear thee,* faith the royal Psalmist, Psal. cxix. 63. A renewed man joins himself with the saints: for he and they are like minded, in that which is their main work and business: they have all one new nature; they are travelling to Immanuel's land, and can converse together in the language of Canaan. In vain do men pretend to religion, while ungodly company is their choice; for *a companion of fools shall be destroyed,* Prov. xiii. 20. Religion will make a man shy of throwing himself into an ungodly family, or any unnecessary familiarity with wicked men; as one that is clean will beware of going into an infected house.

2. In his relative capacity, he will be a new man. Grace makes men gracious in their several relations, and naturally leads them to the conscientious performance of relative duties: It does not only make good

men, and good women, but makes good subjects, good husbands, good wives, children, servants, and, in a word, good relatives in the church, common-wealth, and family. It is a just exception made against the religion of many, namely, that they are bad relatives, they are ill husbands, wives, masters, servants, &c. How can we prove ourselves to be new creatures, if we be just such as we were before, in our several relations? 2 Cor. v. 17. *Therefore, if any man be in Christ, he is a new creature: old things are passed away; behold, all things are become new.* Real godliness will gain a testimony to a man, from the conscience of his nearest relations; though they know more of his sinful infirmities than others do, as we see in the case, 2 Kings iv. 2. *Thy servant, my husband, is dead, and thou knowest that thy servant did fear the Lord.*

3. In the way of his following his worldly business, there is a great change. It appears to be no more his all, as it was before. Though saints apply themselves to worldly business, as well as others, yet their hearts are not swallowed up in it. It is evident that they are carrying on a trade with heaven, as well as a trade with earth, Philip. iii. 20. *For our conversation is in heaven.* They go about their employment in the world, as a duty laid upon them by the Lord of all, doing their lawful business as the will of God, Eph. vi. 7. working, because he has said, *Thou shalt not steal.*

4. They have a special concern for the advancement of the kingdom of Christ in the world: they espouse the interests of religion, and prefer Jerusalem above their chief joy, Psal. cxxxviii. 6. How privately soever they live, grace gives them a public spirit, which will concern itself in the ark and work of God, in the gospel of God, and in the people of God, those even of them whom they never saw. As children of God they naturally care for these things. They have a new concern for the spiritual good of others: no sooner do they taste of the power of grace themselves, but they are inclined to set up to be agents for Christ and holiness in the world; as appears in the case of the woman of Samaria, who when Christ had manifested him-

Head I. *Of Regeneration* 185

felf to her, *went her way into the city, and faith unto the men, Come, fee a man which told me all things that ever I did; Is not this the Chrift?* John iv. 28, 29. They have feen and felt the evil of fin, and therefore pity the world lying in wickednefs. They would fain pluck the brands out of the fire, remembering that they themfelves were plucked out of it. They labour to commend religion to others, both by word and example; and rather deny themfelves their liberty in indifferent things, than by the uncharitable ufe of them deftroy others, 1 Cor. viii. 13. *Wherefore, if meat make my brother to offend, I will eat no flefh while the world ftandeth, left I make my brother to offend.*

In their ufe of lawful comforts, there is a great change. They reft not in them, as their end; but ufe them as means to help them in their way. They draw their fatisfaction from the higher fprings, even while the lower fprings are running. Thus Hannah, having obtained a fon, rejoiced not fo much in the gift, as in the Giver, 1 Sam. ii. 1. *And Hannah prayed, and faid, My heart rejoiceth in the Lord.* Yea, when the comforts of life are gone, they can fubfift without them, and rejoice in the Lord, although the fig-tree doth not bloffom, Hab. iii. 17, 18. Grace teacheth to ufe the conveniencies of the prefent life paffingly; and to fhew a holy moderation in all things. The heart, which formerly revelled in thefe things without fear, is now fhy of being over-much pleafed with them. Being apprehenfive of danger, it ufes them warily; as the dogs of Egypt run, while they lap their water out of the river Nile, for fear of the crocodiles that are in it.

Laftly, This change fhines forth in the man's performance of religious duties. He who lived in the neglect of them, will do fo no more, if once the grace of God enter into his heart. If a man be new-born, he will defire the fincere milk of the word, 1 Pet. ii. 2, 3. Whenever the prayerlefs perfon gets the Spirit of grace, he will be in him a Spirit of fupplication, Zech. xii. 10. It is as natural for one that is born again to pray, as for the new-born babe to cry, Acts ix. 11. *Behold he pray-*

B b

eth. His heart will be a temple for God, and his houſe a church. His devotion, which before was ſuperficial and formal, is now ſpiritual and lively; foraſmuch as heart and tongue are touched with a live-coal from heaven: and he reſts not in the mere performance of duties, as careful only to get his taſk done, but in every duty ſeeks communion with God in Chriſt; juſtly conſidering them as means appointed of God for that end, and reckoning himſelf diſappointed if he miſs of it. Thus far of the nature of regeneration.

The Reſemblance between Natural and Spiritual Generation.

II. I come to ſhew why this change is called *regeneration*, a being *born again*. It is ſo called, becauſe of the reſemblance between natural and ſpiritual generation, which lies in the following particulars.

Firſt, Natural generation is a myſterious thing: and ſo is ſpiritual generation, John iii. 8. *The wind bloweth where it liſteth, and thou heareſt the ſound thereof, but canſt not tell whence it cometh, and whither it goeth: ſo is every one that is born of the Spirit.* The work of the Spirit is felt; but his way of working is a myſtery we cannot apprehend. New light is let into the mind, and the will is renewed; but how that light is conveyed thither, how the will is fettered with cords of love, and how the rebel is made a willing captive, we can no more tell, than we can tell *how the bones do grow in the womb of her that is with child,* Eccl. xi. 5. As a man hears the ſound of the wind, and finds it ſtirring, but knows not where it begins, and where it ends; *ſo is every one that is born of the Spirit:* he finds the change that is made upon him; but how it is produced, he knows not. One thing he may know, that whereas he was blind, now he ſeeth: the ſeed of grace doth *ſpring and grow up, he knoweth not how,* Mark iv. 26, 27.

Secondly, In both, the creature comes to a being it had not before. The child is not, till it be generate; and a man has no gracious being, no being in grace, till he be regenerate. Regeneration is not ſo much the curing of a ſick man, as the quickening of a dead man, Eph. ii. 1. 5. Man, in his depraved ſtate, is a mere nonentity in grace, and is brought into a new being by the power of him *who calleth things that be not as though they were*; being *created in Jesus Christ unto good works*, Eph. ii. 10. Therefore our Lord Jesus, to give ground of hope to the Laodiceans, in their wretched and miserable state, proposed himself as the *beginning of the creation of God*, Rev. iii. 14. namely, the active beginning of it; for all things were made by him at first, John i. 3. From whence they might gather, that as he made them when they were nothing, he could make them over again, when worse than nothing; the same hand that made them his creatures, could make them new creatures.

Thirdly, As the child is passive in generation, so is the child of God in regeneration. The one contributes nothing to its own generation; neither does the other contribute any thing, by way of efficiency, to its own regeneration: for though a man may lay himself down at the pool, yet he hath no hand in moving the water, no power in performing the cure. One is born the child of a king, another the child of a beggar: the child has no hand at all in this difference. God leaves some in their depraved state; others he brings into a state of grace, or regeneracy. If thou be thus honoured, no thanks to thee; for *who maketh thee to differ from another?* 1 Cor. iv. 17.

Fourthly, There is a wonderful contexture of parts in both births. Admirable is the structure of man's body, in which there is such a variety of organs; nothing wanting, nothing superfluous. The Psalmist, considering his own body, looks on it as a piece of marvellous work; *I am fearfully and wonderfully made*, saith he, Psal. cxxxix. 14, 15. *and curiously wrought in the lower parts of the earth*, that is, in the womb, where I know not how the bones grow, more than I know what is doing in the lowest parts of the earth. In natural generation we are curiously wrought, as a piece of needle-work; as the word imports: even so it is in regeneration, Psal. xlv. 14. *She shall be brought unto the King in raiment of needle work*, raiment curiously wrought. It is the same word in both texts. What that raiment is, the apostle tells us, Eph. iv. 20. it is the *new man*, which after God is created in righteousness and true holiness. This is the raiment which he saith, in the same place, we must put on; not excluding the imputed righteousness of Christ. Both are curiously wrought, as masterpieces of the manifold wisdom of God. O the wonderful contexture of graces in the new creature! O glorious creature, new-made after the image of God! It is grace for grace in Christ, which makes up this new man, John i. 16. Even as in bodily generation, the child has member for member in the parent; has every member which the parent has, in a certain proportion.

Fifthly All this, in both cases, hath its rise from that which in itself is very small and inconsiderable. O the power of God, in making such a creature of the corruptible seed, and much more in bringing forth the new creature from so small beginnings! It is as the little cloud, like a man's hand, which spread, till *heaven was black with clouds and wind, and there was a great rain*, 1 Kings xviii. 44, 45. A man gets a word at a sermon, which hundreds besides him hear, and let slip: but it remains with him, works in him, and never leaves him, till the little world be turned upside down by it; that is, till he become a new man. It is like the vapour that got up into Ahasuerus's head, and cut off sleep from his eyes, Esther vi. 1. which proved a spring of such motions, as never ceased, until Mordecai, in royal pomp, was brought on horseback through the streets, proud Haman trudging at his foot; the same Haman afterwards hanged, Mordecai advanced, and the church delivered from Haman's hellish plot. *The grain of mustard seed—becometh a tree*, Mat. xiii. 31, 32. God loves to bring great things out of small beginnings.

Sixthly, Natural generation is carried on by degrees, Job x. 10. *Hast thou not poured me out as milk, and curdled me like cheese?* So is regeneration. It is with the foul ordinarily, in regeneration, as with the blind man, cured by our Lord, who first saw men as trees walking, afterwards saw very clearly, Mat. viii. 23, 24, 25. It

Head I. *Of Regeneration.* 189

is true, regeneration being, strictly speaking, a passing from death to life, the soul is quickened in a moment; like as when the embryo is brought to perfection in the womb, the soul is infused into the lifeless lump. Neverthelefs, we may imagine fomewhat like conception in spiritual regeneration, whereby the soul is prepared for quickening; and the new creature is capable of growth, 1 Pet. ii. 2. and of life more abundantly, John x. 10.

Seventhly, In both there are new relations. The regenerate may call God, *Father*; for they are his children, John i. 12, 13. *begotten of him*, 1 Pet. i. 3. the bride the Lamb's wife (that is, the church) is their mother, Gal. iv. 26. They are related, as brethren and sisters, to angels and glorified saints; *the family of heaven*, They are of the heavenly stock: the meanest of them, *the base things of the world*, 2 Cor. i. 28. the kinless things (as the word imports) who cannot boast of the blood that runs in their veins, are yet, by their new-birth, near of kin with the excellent in the earth.

Eighlly, There is a likenefs between the parent and the child. Every thing that generates, generates its like; and the regenerate are *partakers of the divine nature*, 2 Pet. i. 4. The moral perfections of the divine nature are, in meafure and degree, communicated to the renewed foul: thus the divine image is retrieved; fo that, as the child resembles the father, the new creature resembles God himself, being holy as he is holy.

Laftly, As there is no birth without pain, both to the mother and to the child; fo there is great pain in bringing forth the new creature. The children have more or less of thefe birth-pains, whereby they are *pricked in their heart*, Acts ii. 37. The foul hath fore pains, when under conviction and humiliation. *A wounded fpirit who can bear?* The mother is pained; *Zion travels*, Isa. xlvi. 8. She sighs, groans, crieth, and hath hard labour, in her ministers and members, to bring forth children to her Lord, Gal. iv. 19. *My little children, of whom I travail in birth again, until Chrift be formed in you.* Never was a mother more feelingly touched with joy, *that a man child was born into the world*, than she is upon the new birth of her children. But what is more remarkable than all this, we read not only of our Lord Jesus Christ's *travail* (or *toil*) *of soul*, Isa. liii. 11. but (what is more directly to our purpose) of his *pains*, or *pangs*, as of one travailing in child-birth; so the word used, Acts ii. 24. properly signifies. Well may he call the new creature, as Rachel called her dear bought son, Benoni, *i. e.* the son of my sorrow; and as she called another Naphtali, *i. e.* my wrestling: for the pangs of that travail put him to *strong crying and tears*, Heb. v. 7. yea, into an *agony and bloody sweat*, Luke xxii. 44. and in the end he died of these pangs; they became to him *the pains of death*, Acts ii. 24.

The Doctrine of Regeneration applied.

USE I. By what is said, you may try whether you are in the state of grace, or not. If you be brought out of the state of wrath and ruin, into the state of grace, or salvation, you are new creatures, you are born again. But you will say, How shall we know whether we be born again, or not? *Answ.* Were you to ask me if the sun were risen, and how you should know whether it were risen or not; I would bid you look up to the heavens, and see it with your eyes. And, would you know if the light be risen in your heart? Look in, and see. Grace is light, and discovers itself. Look into thy mind; see if it hath been illuminated in the knowledge of God. Hast thou been inwardly taught what God is? Were thine eyes ever turned inward, to see thyself, the sinfulness of thy depraved state; the corruption of thy nature, the sins of thy heart and life? Wast thou ever led into a view of the exceeding sinfulness of sin? Have thine eyes seen King Jesus in his beauty; the manifold wisdom of God in him, his transcendent excellency, and absolute fulness and sufficiency, with the vanity and emptiness of all things else? Next, what change is there on thy will? Are the fetters taken off, wherewith it was sometimes bound up from moving heaven-ward? Has thy will got a new turn? Dost thou find an aversion to sin, and a proneness to good, wrought in thy heart? Is thy soul turned

Head I. *Of Regeneration.* 191

towards God, as thy chief end? Is thy will new moulded, into some measure of conformity to the preceptive and providential will of God? Art thou heartily reconciled to the covenant of peace, and fixedly disposed to the receiving of Christ, as he is offered in the gospel? And as to a change on your affections, are they rectified, and placed on right objects? Are your desires going out after God? are they to his name, and the remembrance of him? Isa. xxvi. 8. Are your hopes in him? Is your love set upon him, and your hatred set against sin? Does your offending a good God affect your heart with sorrow? and do you fear sin more than suffering? Are your affections regulated? are they, with respect to created comforts, brought down, as being too high; and, with respect to God in Christ, raised up, as being too low? Has he the chief seat in your heart? and are all your lawful worldly comforts and enjoyments laid at his feet? Has thy conscience been enlightened and awakened, refusing all ease, but from the application of the blood of the Redeemer? Is thy memory sanctified, thy body consecrated to the service of God? and art thou now walking in newness of life? Thus you may discover whether you are born again, or not.

But, for your further help in this matter, I will discourse a little of another sign of regeneration, namely, *the love of the brethren*; an evidence whereby the weakest and most timorous saints have often had comfort, when they could have little or no consolation from other marks proposed to them. This the apostle lays down, 1 John iii. 14. *We know that we have passed from death unto life, because we love the brethren.* It is not to be thought that the apostle, by the *brethren*, in this place, means brethren by a common relation to the first Adam, but to the Second Adam, Christ Jesus: because, however true it is, that universal benevolence, a good-will to the whole race of mankind, takes place in the renewed soul, as being a lively lineament of the divine image; yet the whole context speaks of those that are *the sons of God*, ver. 1, 2. *children of God*, ver. 10. *born of God*, ver. 9. distinguishing between *the children of*

God, and *the children of the devil*, ver. 10. between those that are *of the devil*, ver. 8. 12. and those that are *of God*, ver. 10. The text itself comes in as a reason why we should not marvel that the world hates the brethren, the children of God, ver. 13. How can we marvel at it, seeing the love of the brethren is an evidence of one's having passed from death to life ? Therefore it were absurd to look for that love amongst the men of the world, who are dead in trespasses and sins. They cannot love the brethren; no wonder, then, that they hate them. Wherefore it is plain, that by brethren here, are meant brethren by regeneration.

Now, in order to set this mark of regeneration in a true light, consider these three things : (1.) This love to the brethren is a love to them as such. Then do we love them in the sense of the text, when the grace, or image of God in them, is the chief motive of our love to them. When we love the godly for their godliness, the saints for their sanctity or holiness, then we love God in them, and so may conclude we are born of God ; *for every one that loveth him that begat, loveth him also that is begotten of him*, 1 John v. 1. Hypocrites may love saints, on account of civil relations to them; because of their obliging conversation; for their being of the same opinion with themselves in religious matters; and on many other such accounts, whereby wicked men may be induced to love the godly. But happy they who love them for naked grace in them ; for their heaven-born temper and disposition ; who can pick this pearl out of a dunghill of infirmities in and about them ; lay hold on it, and love them for it. ' (2.) It is a love that will be given to all in whom the grace of God appears. They that love one saint, because he is a saint, will have love to all the saints, Eph. i. 5. They will love all who, to their discerning, bear the image of God. They that cannot love a gracious person in rags, but confine their love to those of them who wear gay cloathing, have not this love to the brethren in them. Those who confine their love to a party, to whom God has not confined his grace, are souls too narrow to put among the children. In what points fo-

Head I. *Of Regeneration.* 193

ever men differ from us, in their judgment or way, yet if they appear to agree with us, in love to God, and our Saviour Jefus Chrift, and in bearing his image, we fhall love them as brethren, if we are of the heavenly family. (3.) If this love be in us, the more grace any perfon appears to be poffeffed of, he will be the more beloved by us. The more vehemently the holy fire of grace doth flame in any, the hearts of true Chriftians will be the more warmed in love to them. It is not with the faints as with many other men, who make themfelves the ftandards for others ; and love them fo far as they think they are like themfelves But if they feem to out-fhine, and darken them, their love is turned to hatred and envy ; and they endeavour to detract from the due praife of their examplary piety ; becaufe nothing relifheth with them, in the practice of religion, that goes beyond their own meafure ; what of the life and power of religion appears in others, ferves only to raife the ferpentine grudge in their Pharifaical hearts. But as for them that are born again, their love and affection to the brethren bears proportion to the degrees of the divne image which they difcern in them.

Now, if you would improve thefe things to the knowledge of your ftate, I would advife you, (1.) To fet apart fome time, when you are at home, for a review of your cafe ; and try your ftate by what has been faid. Many have comfort and clearnefs as to their ftate, at a fermon, who in a little time lofe it again : becaufe, while they hear the word preached, they make application of it ; but do not confider thefe things more deliberately and leifurely when alone. The action is too fudden and fhort, to give lafting comfort. It is often fo indeliberate, that it has bad confequences. Therefore fet about this work at home, after earneft and ferious prayer to God for his help in it. Complain not of your want of time, while the night follows the bufy day; nor of place, while fields and out-houfes are to be got. (2.) Renew your repentance before the Lord. Guilt lying on the confcience, unrepented of, may darken all your evidences of grace. It provokes the Spirit of grace to withdraw; and when he goes, our light ceases. It is not fit time for a saint to read his evidences, when the candle is blown out by some conscience-wounding guilt. *Lastly*, Exert the powers of the new nature; let the graces of the divine Spirit in you, discover themselves by action. If you would know whether there is sacred fire in your breast, or not, you must blow the coal; for although it be, and be a live-coal; yet if it be under the ashes, it will give you no light. Settle in your hearts a firm purpose, through the grace that is in Christ Jesus, to comply with every known duty, and watch against every known sin; having readiness of mind to be instructed in what you know not. If gracious souls would thus manage their enquiries into their state, it is likely that they would have a comfortable issue. And if others would take such a solemn review, and make trial of their state, impartially examining themselves before the tribunal of their consciences, they might have a timely discovery of their own naughtiness; but the neglect of self-examination leaves most men under sad delusions as to there state; and deprives many saints of the comfortable sight of the grace of God in them.

But that I may afford some further help to true Christians in their enquiries into their state; I shall propose and briefly answer some cases or doubts, which may possibly hinder some persons from the comfortable view of their happy state. The children's bread must not be with-held; though while it is held forth to them, the dogs should snatch at it.

CASE I. I doubt if I be regenerate, because, I know not the precise time of my conversion; nor can I trace the particular steps in the way in which it was brought to pass. *Answ.* Though it is very desirable, to be able to give an account of the beginning, and the gradual advances of the Lord's work upon our souls, as some saints can distinctly do, (howbeit the manner of the Spirit's working is still a mystery) yet this is not necessary to evidence the truth of grace. Happy he that can say, in this case, as the blind man in the gospel, *One thing I know, that whereas I was blind, now I see.* As, when we see flame, we know there is fire; though we know

Head I. *Of Regeneration.* 155

not how nor when it began: so the truth of grace in us may be discerned, though we know not how, nor when it was dropped into our hearts. If thou canst perceive the happy change which is wrought on thy soul; if thou findest thy mind is enlightened, thy will inclined to comply with the will of God in all things; especially to fall in with the divine plan of salvation, through the crucified Redeemer; in vain dost thou trouble thyself, and refuse comfort, because thou knowest not how and what way it was brought about.

CASE 2. If I were a new creature, sin could not prevail against me as it doth. *Answ.* Though we must not lay pillows, for hypocrites to rest their heads upon; who indulge themselves in their sins, and make the doctrine of God's grace subservient to their lusts, lying down contentedly in the bond of iniquity, like men that are fond of golden chains; yet it must be owned, *the just man falleth seven times a day*; and iniquity may prevail against the children of God. But if thou art groaning under the weight of the body of death, the corruption of thy nature; loathing thyself for the sins of thy heart and life; striving to mortify thy lusts; fleeing daily to the blood of Christ for pardon; and looking to his Spirit for sanctification; though thou mayest be obliged to say with the Psalmist, *Iniquities prevail against me:* yet thou mayest add with him, *As for our transgressions, thou shalt purge them away,* Psal. lxv. 3. the new creature doth not yet possess the house alone: it dwells by the side of an ill neighbour, namely, remaining corruption, the reliques of depraved nature. These struggle together for the mastery: *The flesh lusteth against the spirit, and the spirit against the flesh,* Gal. v. 17. And sometimes corruption prevails, bringing the child of God into captivity to the law of sin, Rom. vii. 23. Let not, therefore, the prevailing of corruption make thee, in this case, conclude thou art none of God's children: but let it humble thee, to be the more watchful, and to thirst the more intensely after Jesus Christ, his blood and Spirit; and that very disposition will evidence a principle of grace in thee, which seeks the destruction of sin, that prevails so often against thee.

CASE 3. I find the motions of sin in my heart more violent since the Lord began his work on my soul, than they were before that time. Can this consist with a change of my nature? *Answ.* Dreadful is the case of many, who, after God has had a remarkable dealing with their souls, tending to their reformation, have thrown off all bonds, and have become grosly and openly immoral and profane; as if the devil had returned into their hearts with seven spirits worse than himself. All I shall say to such persons is, that their state is exceeding dangerous; they are in danger of sinning against the Holy Ghost: therefore let them repent, before it be too late. But if it be not thus with you; though corruption is stirring more violently than formerly, as if all the forces of hell were raised, to hold fast, or bring back a fugitive; yet these stirrings may consist with a change of your nature. When the restraint of grace is newly laid upon corruption, it is no wonder if it acts more vigorously than before, *warring against the law of the mind*, Rom. vii. 23. The motions of sin may really be most violent, when the new principle is brought in to cast it out. The sun, sending its beams through the window, discovers the motes in the house, and their motions, which were not seen before: so the light of grace may discover the risings and actings of corruption, in another manner than ever the man saw them before, though they really do not rise nor act more vigorously. Sin is not quite dead in the regenerate soul; it is but dying, and dying a lingering death, being crucified: no wonder there be great fightings, when it is sick at the heart, and death is at the door. Besides, temptations may be more in number, and stronger, while Satan is striving to bring you back, who are escaped, than while he only endeavoured to retain you: *After ye were illuminated, ye endured a great fight of affliction*, says the apostle to the Hebrews, chap. x. 32. But *cast not away your confidence*, ver. 34. Remember, his *grace is sufficient for you; and the God of peace will bruise Satan under your feet shortly*. Pharaoh and his Egyptians never made such a formidable appearance against the Israelites as at the Red Sea, after they were

Head I. *Of Regeneration.* 197
brought out of Egypt: but then were the purfuers neareft to a total overthrow, Exod. xiv. Let not this cafe, therefore, make you raze your foundations: but be ye emptied of yourfelves, and ftrong in the Lord, and in the power of his might, and you fhall come off victorious.

CASE 4. But when I compare my love to God, with my love to fome created enjoyments, I find the pulfe of my affections beat ftronger to the creature than the Creator. How then can I call him Father? Nay, alas! thefe turnings of heart within me, and glowings of affection to him, which I had, are gone; fo that I fear all the love which I ever had to the Lord, has been but a fit and flafh of affection, fuch as hypocrites often have. *Anfw.* It cannot be denied, that the predominant love of the world is a certain mark of an unregenerate ftate, 1 John iii. 15. *If any man love the world, the love of the Father is not in him.* Neverthelefs, thofe are not always the ftrongeft affections which are moft violent. A man's affections may be more moved, on fome occafions, by an object that is little regarded, than by another that is exceedingly beloved: even as a little brook fometimes makes a greater noife than a great river. The ftrength of our affections is to be meafured by the firmnefs and fixednefs of the root; not by the violence of their actings. Suppofe a perfon meeting with a friend, who has been long abroad, finds his affections more vehemently acting towards his friend on that occafion, than towards his own wife and children; will he therefore fay, that he loves his friend more than them? Surely no. Even fo, although the Chriftian may find himfelf more moved in his love to the creature, than in his love to God, yet it is not therefore to be faid, that he loves the creature more than God; feeing love to God is always more firmly rooted in a gracious heart, than love to any created enjoyment whatever; as appears when competition arifes in fuch a manner, that the one or the other is to be foregone. Would you then know your cafe? Retire into your own hearts, and there lay the two in the balance, and try which of them weighs down the other. Afk thyfelf, as in the fight of God, whether thou wouldft part with

Chrift for the creature, or part with the creature for Chrift, if thou wert left to thy choice in the matter? If you find your heart difpofed to part with what is deareft to you in the world for Chrift, at his call, you have no reafon to conclude you love the creature more than God; but on the contrary, that you love God more than the creature, although you do not feel fuch violent motions in the love of God, as in the love of fome created thing, Mat. x. 37. *He that loveth father or mother more than me, is not worthy of me.* Luke xvi. 26. *If any man come to me, and hate not his father and mother, he cannot be my difciple.* From which texts compared we may infer, that he who hates, *i. e.* is ready to part with, father and mother for Chrift, is, in our account, one that loves them lefs than him; and not one who loves father and mother more than him. Moreover, you are to confider, that there is a two-fold love to Chrift. (1.) There is a *fenfible* love to him, which is felt as a dart in the heart, and makes a holy love-ficknefs in the foul, arifing either from want of enjoyment, as in the cafe of the fpoufe, Cant. v. 8. *I charge you, O daughters of Jerufalem, if ye find my beloved, that ye tell him that I am fick of love;* or elfe from the fulnefs of it, as in Cant. ii. 5. *Stay me with flaggons, comfort me with apples, for I am fick of love.* Thefe glowings of affections are ufually wrought in young converts, who are ordinarily made to fing in the days of their youth, Hof. ii. 14. While the fire-edge is upon the young convert, he looks upon others, reputed to be godly, and not finding them in fuch a temper or difpofition as himfelf, he is ready to cenfure them; and to think there is far lefs religion in the world than indeed there is. But when his own cup comes to fettle below the brim, and he finds that in himfelf which made him queftion the ftate of others, he is more humbled, and feels more and more the neceflity of daily recourfe to the blood of Chrift for pardon, and to the Spirit of Chrift for fanctification; and thus grows downwards in humiliation, felf-loathing, and felf-denial. (3.) There is a *rational* love to Chrift, which, without thefe fenfible emotions felt in the former cafe, evidences itfelf by a dutiful re-

Head I.   Of Regeneration.   199

gard to the divine authority and command, When a perfon bears fuch a love to Chrift; though the vehement ftirrings of affection be wanting, yet he is truly tender of offending a gracious God; endeavours to walk before him unto all pleafing; and is grieved at the heart for what is difpleafing unto him, 1 John v. 3. *For this is the love of God, that we keep his commandments.* Now,' although that fenfible love doth not always continue with you, you have no reafon to deem it a hypocritical fit, while the rational love remains with you, more than a loving and faithful wife needs queftion her love to her hufband, when her fondnefs is abated.

CASE 5. The attainments of hypocrites and apoftates are a terror to me, and come like a fhaking ftorm on me, when I am about to conclude, from the marks of grace which I feem to find in myfelf, that I am in the ftate of grace. *Anfw.* Thefe things fhould indeed ftir us up to a moft ferious and impartial examination of ourfelves; but ought not to keep us in continued fufpence as to our ftate. Sirs, you fee the outfide of hypocrites, their duties, their gifts, their tears, and fo on, but you fee not their infide; you do not difcern their hearts, the bias of their fpirits. Upon what you fee of them, you found a judgment of charity as to their ftate; and you do well to judge charitably in fuch a cafe, becaufe you cannot know the fecret fprings of their actings. But you are fpeaking of, and ought to have a judgment of certainty as to your own ftate; and therefore are to look into that part of religion which none in the world but yourfelves can difcern in you; and which you can as little fee in others. In hypocrites, religion may appear far greater than in that of a fincere foul: but that which makes the greateft figure in the eyes of men, is often of leaft worth before God. I would rather utter one of thofe groans which the apoftle fpeaks of, Rom. viii. 26. than fhed Efau's tears, have Balaam's prophetic fpirit, or the joy of the ftony ground hearer. The fire that fhall try every man's work, will try not of what bulk it is, but of what fort it is, 1 Cor. iii. 13. Though you may know what bulk of religion another has; and that it be more bulky than your own, yet God doth not regard that; why then do you make fuch a matter of it? It is impoffible for you, without divine revelation, certainly to know of what fort another man's religion is: but you may certainly know what fort your own is of, without extraordinary revelation; otherwife the apoftle would not exhort the faints to *give diligence to make their calling and election fure*, 2 Pet. i. 10. Therefore the attainments of hypocrites and apoftates fhould not difturb you, in your ferious inquiry into your own ftate. I will tell you two things, wherein the meaneft faints go beyond the moft refined hypocrites. (1.) In denying themfelves; renouncing all confidence in themfelves, and their own works, acquiefcing in, being well-pleafed with, and venturing their fouls upon, God's plan of falvation through Jefus Chrift, Matt. v. 3. *Bleffed are the poor in fpirit, for theirs is the kingdom of heaven.* And chap. ix. 6. *Bleffed is he whofoever fhall not be offended in me.* Phil. iii. 3. *We are the circumcifion, which worfhip God in the fpirit, and rejoice in Chrift Jefus, and have no confidence in the flefh.* (2.) In a real hatred of all fin; being willing to part with every luft, without exception, and to comply with every duty which the Lord makes, or fhall make known to them, Pfal. cxix. 6. *Then fhall 1 not be afhamed, when I have refpect unto all thy commandments.* Try yourfelves by thefe.

CASE 6. I fee myfelf fall fo far fhort of the faints mentioned in the Scriptures, and of feveral excellent perfons of my own acquaintance, that when I look on them, I can hardly look on myfelf as one of the fame family with them. *Anfw.* It is indeed matter of humiliation, that we do not get forward to that meafure of grace and holinefs which we fee is attainable in this life. This fhould make us more vigoroufly prefs towards the mark: but furely it is from the devil, that weak Chriftians make a rack for themfelves, of the attainments of the ftrong. To yield to this temptation, is as unreafonable as for a child to difpute away his relation to his father, becaufe he is not of the fame ftature with his elder brethren. There are faints of feveral fizes in Chrift's family; fome fathers, fome young men, and fome little children, 1 John iii. 13, 14.

Head I. *Of Regeneration.* 201

CASE 7. I never read in the word of God, nor did I ever know, of a child of God fo tempted, and fo left of God, as I am; and therefore no faint's cafe being like mine, I cannot but conclude that I am none of their number. *Anfw.* This objection arifes to fome from their unacquaintednefs with the Scriptures, and with experienced Chriftians. It is profitable, in this cafe, to impart the matter to fome experienced Chrif- tian friend, or to fome godly minifter. This has been a bleffed means of peace to fome perfons; while their cafe, whch appeared to them to be fingular, has been proved to have been the cafe of other faints. The Scriptures give inftances of very horrid temptations, wherewith the faints have been affaulted. Job was tempted to blafpheme: this was the great thing the de- vil aimed at, in the cafe of that great faint, Job i. 11. *He will curfe thee to thy face.* Chap. ii. 9. *Curfe God and die.* Afaph was tempted to think it was in vain to be religious, which was in effect to throw off all religion. Pfal. lxviii. 13. *Verily I have cleanfed my heart in vain.* Yea, Chrift himfelf was tempted to *caft himfelf down from a pinnacle of the temple,* and to *worfhip the devil,* Matt. iv. 6. 9. And many of the children of God have not only been attacked with, but have actually yielded to, very grofs temptations for a time. Peter denied Chrift, and curfed and fwore that he knew him not, Mark xiv. 71. Paul, when a perfecutor, com- pelled even faints to blafpheme, Acts xxvi. 10, 11. Many of the faints can, from their fad experience, bear witnefs to very grofs temptations, which have aftonifhed their fpirits, made their very flefh to tremble, and fick- ened their bodies. Satan's fiery darts make terrible work; and will coft pains to quench them, by a vigor- ous managing of the fhield of faith, Eph. vi. 16. Some- times he makes fuch defperate attacks, that never was one more put to it, in running to and fro, without in- termiffion, to quench the fire-balls inceffantly thrown into his houfe by an enemy, defigning to burn the houfe about him, than the poor tempted faint is, to repel fatanical injections. But thefe injections, thefe horrid temptations, though they are a dreadful affliction, they are not the sins of the tempted, unless they make them theirs, by consenting to them. They will be charged upon the tempter alone, if they be not consented to; and will no more be laid to the charge of the tempted party, than a bastard's being laid down at a chaste man's door, will fix guilt upon him.

But suppose neither minister nor private Christian, to whom you go, can tell you of any who has been in your case; yet you ought not thence to infer, that your case certainly is singular, far less to give up hope: for it is not to be thought, that every godly minister, or private Christian, has had experience of all the cases which a child of God may be in. We need not doubt but some have had distresses known only to God, and their own consciences; and so to others these distresses are as if they had never been. Yea, and though the Scriptures contain suitable directions for every case which a child of God can be in, and these illustrated with a sufficient number of examples; yet it is not to be imagined, that there are in the Scriptures perfect instances of every particular case incident to the saints. Therefore, though you cannot find an instance of your case in the Scripture, yet bring your case to it, and you shall find suitable remedies prescribed there for it. Study rather to make use of Christ for your case, who has salve for all sores, than to know if ever any was in your case. Though one should shew you an instance of your case, an undoubted saint, yet none could promise that it would certainly give you ease: for a scrupulous conscience would readily find out some difference. And if nothing but a perfect conformity of another case to yours will satisfy, it will be hard, if not impossible, to satisfy you. For it is with people's cases, as with their natural faces. Though the faces of all men are of one make; and some are so very like others, that at first view we are ready to take them for the same; yet, if you view them more accurately, you will see something in every face, distinguishing it from all others; though possibly you cannot tell what it is. Wherefore I conclude, that if you can find in yourselves the marks of regeneration, proposed to you from the word; you ought to conclude you are in the state of grace, though your case were singular, which is indeed unlikely.

CASE 8. The afflictions I meet with are strange and unusual. I doubt if ever a child of God was tried with such dispensations of providence as I am. *Answ.* Much of what was said on the preceding case, may be helpful in this. Holy Job was assaulted with this temptation, Job v. 1. *To which of the saints wilt thou turn?* But he rejected it, and held fast his integrity. The apostle supposes that Christians may be tempted to *think strange concerning the fiery trial*, 1 Pet. iv. 12. But they have need of larger experience than Solomon's, who will venture to say, *See this is new*, Eccl. i. 10. What though, in respect of the outward dispensations of providence, *it happen to you according to the work of the wicked?* yet you may be just notwithstanding; according to Solomon's observation, Eccles. viii. 14. Sometimes we travel in ways where we can neither perceive the prints of the foot of man nor beast; yet we cannot from thence conclude that there was never any there before us: so though thou canst not perceive the footsteps of the flock, in the way of thine affliction, thou must not therefore conclude that thou art the first who ever travelled that road. But what if it were so? Some one saint or other must be first, in drinking of each bitter cup the rest have drunk of. What warrant have you or I to limit the holy One of Israel to a trodden path, in his dispensations towards us? *Thy way is in the sea, and thy path in the great waters: and thy footsteps are not known*, Psal. lxxvii. 19. If the Lord should carry you to heaven by some retired road, (so to speak) you would have no ground to complain. Learn to allow sovereignty a latitude; be at your duty: and let no affliction cast a vail over any evidences you otherwise have for your being in the state of grace: for *no man knoweth either love or hatred by all that is before them*, Eccles. ix. 1.

USE II. You that are strangers to this new-birth, be convinced of the absolute necessity of it. Are all who are in the state of grace born again? Then you have neither part nor lot in it, who are not born again. I must tell you, in the words of our Lord and Saviour, (and O that he would speak them to your hearts) *you must be born again*, John iii. 7. For your conviction, consider these few things:

First, Regeneration is absolutely necessary to qualify you to do any thing really good and acceptable to God. While you are not born again, your best works are but glittering sins; for though the matter of them is good, they are quite marred in the making. Consider, (1.) That without regeneration there is no faith, and without faith it is impossible to please God, Heb. ix 6. Faith is a vital act of the new-born soul. The evangelist, shewing the different entertainment which our Lord Jesus had from different persons, some receiving him, some rejecting him, points at regenerating grace as the true rise of that difference, without which never any one would have received him. He tells us, that *as many as received him*, were those *which were born—of God*, John i. 11, 12, 13. Unregenerate men may presume; but true faith they cannot have. Faith is a flower that grows not in the field of nature. As the tree cannot grow without a root, neither can a man believe without the new nature, whereof the principle of believing is a part. (2.) Without regeneration, a man's works are dead works. As is the principle, so must the effects be: if the lungs be rotten, the breath will be unsavoury; and he who at best is dead in sin, his works at best will be but dead works. *Unto them that are defiled and unbelieving, is nothing pure—being abominable, and disobedient, and unto every good work reprobate*, Tit. i. 15, 16. Could we say of a man, that he is more blameless in his life than any other in the world; that he macerates his body with fasting; and has made his knees as horns with continual praying; but he is not born again: that exception would marr all. As if one should say, There is a well-proportioned body, but the soul is gone; it is but a dead lump. This is a melting consideration. Thou dost many things materially good: but God saith, All these things avail not, as long as I see the old nature reigning in the man,

Head I. · *Of Regeneration.*

Gal. vi. 15. *For in Jesus Christ neither circumcision availeth any thing, nor uncircumcision, but a new creature.*

If thou art not born again, (1.) All thy reformation is naught in the fight of God. Thou haſt ſhut the door, but the thief is ſtill in the houſe. It may be thou art not what once thou waſt: yet thou art not what thou muſt be, if ever thou ſee heaven; for *except a man be born again, he cannot ſee the kingdom of God,* John iii. 3. (2.) Thy prayers are an abomination to the Lord, Prov. xv. 8. It may be others admire thy ſeriouſneſs, thou crieſt as for thy life; but God accounts for the opening of thy mouth, as one would account of the opening of a grave full of rottenneſs, Rom. iii. 13. *Their throat is an open ſepulchre.* Others are affected with thy prayers; which ſeem to them, as if they would rend the heavens; but God accounts them but as the howling of a dog: *They have not cried unto me with their hearts, when they howled upon their beds,* Hoſ. vii. 14. Others take thee for a wreſtler and prevailer with God; but he can take no delight in thee, nor thy prayers, Iſa. lxvi. 13. *He that killeth an ox, is as if he ſlew a man: he that ſacrificeth a lamb, as if he cut off a dog's neck.—He that burneth incenſe, as if he bleſſed an idol.* Why? becauſe thou art yet *in the gall of bitterneſs, and bond of iniquity!* (3.) All thou haſt done for God, and in his cauſe in the world, though it may be followed with temporal rewards, yet is loſt as to divine acceptance. This is clear from the caſe of Jehu, who was indeed rewarded with a kingdom, for his executing due vengeance upon the houſe of Ahab; as being a work good for the matter of it, becauſe it was commanded of God, as you may ſee, 2 Kings x. 13. yet was he puniſhed for it in his poſterity, becauſe he did it not in a right manner, Hoſ. i. 4. *I will avenge the blood of Jezreel upon the houſe of Jehu.* God looks mainly to the heart: and if ſo, truly, though thy outward appearance be fairer than that of many others, yet the hidden man of thy heart is loathſome; you look well before men, but are not as Moſes was, fair to God, as the margin hath it, Acts vii. 20. O what a difference is there between the characters of Aſa and Amaziah! *The high places were not removed: neverthelefs, Afa his heart was perfect with the Lord all his days,* 1 Kings x. 14. *Amaziah did that which was right in the fight of the Lord, but not with a perfect heart,* 2 Chron. xxv. 2. It may be thou art zealous againſt ſin in others, and doſt admoniſh them of their duty, and reprove them for their ſin; and they hate thee, becauſe thou doſt thy duty: but I muſt tell thee, God hates thee too, becauſe thou doſt it not in a right manner; and that thou canſt never do, whilſt thou art not born again. *Laſtly,* All thy ſtruggles againſt ſin, in thine own heart and life are naught. The proud Phariſee, afflicted his body with faſting, and God ſtruck his foul, in the mean time, with a ſentence of condemnation. Luke xviii. Balaam ſtruggled with his covetous temper, to that degree, that though he loved the wages of unrighteouſneſs, yet he would not win them by curſing Iſrael: but he died the death of the wicked, Numb. xxxi. 8. All thou doſt, while in an unregenerate ſtate, is for thyſelf: therefore it will fare with thee as with a ſubject, who having reduced the rebels, puts the crown on his own head, and loſeth all his good ſervice, and his head too.

Object. If it be thus with us, then we need never perform any religious duty at all. *Anſw.* The concluſion is not juſt. No inability of thine can excuſe thee from the duty which God's law lays on thee: and there is leſs evil in thy doing thy duty, than there is in the omitting of it. But there is a difference between omitting of duty, and the doing of it as thou doſt it. A man orders the maſons to build him a houſe. If they quite neglect the work, that will not be accepted; if they build on the old rotten foundation, that will not pleaſe neither: but they muſt raze the foundation, and build on firm ground. *Go thou and do likewiſe.* In the mean time, it is not in vain for thee, even for thee, to ſeek the Lord: for though he regards thee not, yet he may have reſpect to his own ordinances, and do thee good thereby, as was ſaid before.

Secondly, Without regeneration there is no communion with God. There is a ſociety on earth, whoſe

Head I. *Of Regeneration.*

fellowſhip *is with the Father, and with his Son Jeſus Chriſt,* 1 John i. 3. But out of that ſociety, all the unregenerate are excluded; for they are all enemies to God, as you heard before at large. Now, *can two walk together, except they be agreed?* Amos iii. 3. They are all unholy: and *what communion hath light with darkneſs— Chriſt with Belial?* 2 Cor. vi. 14, 15. They may have a ſhew and ſemblance of holineſs; but they are ſtrangers to true holineſs, and therefore *without God in the world.* How ſad is it, to be employed in religious duties, yet to have no fellowſhip with God in them! You would not be content with your meat, unleſs it nouriſhed you; nor with your cloaths, unleſs they kept you warm: and how can you ſatisfy yourſelves with your duties, while you have no communion with God in them?

Thirdly, Regeneration is abſolutely neceſſary to qualify you for heaven. None go to heaven but they that are made meet for it, Col. i. 12. As it was with Solomon's temple, 1 Kings vi. 7. ſo it is with the temple above. It is built of ſtone, made ready before it is brought thither; namely, of *lively ſtones,* 1 Pet. ii. 5. *wrought for the ſelf ſame thing,* 2 Cor. v. 5. for they cannot be laid in that glorious building, juſt as they came out of the quarry of depraved nature. Jewels of gold are not meet for ſwine, and far leſs jewels of glory for unrenewed ſinners. Beggars, in their rags, are not meet for king's houſes; nor ſinners to enter into the King's palace, without the raiment of needle-work, Pſ. xlvi. 14, 15. What wiſe man would bring fiſh out of the water, to feed in his meadows? Or ſend his oxen to feed in the ſea? Even as little are the unregenerate meet for heaven; or heaven meet for them. It would never be liked by them.

The unregenerate would find fault with heaven on ſeveral accounts. As, (1.) That it is a ſtrange country. Heaven is the renewed man's native country: his Father is in heaven; his mother is Jeruſalem, which is above, Gal. iv. 26. He is born from above, John iii. 3. heaven is his home, 1 Cor. v. 1. therefore he looks on himſelf as a ſtranger on this earth, and his head is homeward, Heb. xi. 16. *They deſire a better country, that is an heavenly country.* But the unregenerate man is the man of the earth, Pſal. x. 18. written in the earth, Jer. xvii. 13. Now, home is home, be it never ſo homely: therefore he minds earthly things, Phil. iii. 19. There is a peculiar ſweetneſs in our native ſoil; and hardly are men drawn to leave it, and dwell in a ſtrange country. In no caſe does that prevail more than in this; for unrenewed men would quit their pretenſions to heaven, were it not that they ſee they cannot make a better bargain. (2.) There is nothing in heaven that they delight in, as agreeable to the carnal heart, Rev. xxi. 27. *for there ſhall in no wiſe enter into it any thing that defileth.* When Mahomet gave out paradiſe to be a place of ſenſual delights, his religion was greedily embraced; for that is the heaven men naturally chooſe. If the covetous man could get bags full of gold there, and the voluptuous man could promiſe himſelf his ſenſual delights, they might be reconciled to heaven, and meet for it too: but ſince is is not ſo, though they may utter fair words about it, truly it has little of their hearts. (3.) Every corner there is filled with that which of all things they have the leaſt liking for; and that is holineſs, true holineſs, perfect holineſs. Were one that abhors ſwine's fleſh, bidden to a feaſt, where all the diſhes were of that ſort of meat, but variouſly prepared, he would find fault with every diſh at the table, notwithſtanding all the art uſed to make them palatable. It is true, there is joy in heaven, but it is holy joy; there are pleaſures in heaven, but they are holy pleaſures; there are places in heaven, but it is holy ground. That holineſs that is in every place, and in every thing there, would marr all to the unregenerate. (4.) Were they carried thither, they would not only change their place, which would be a great heart-break to them; but they would change their company too. Truly, they would never like the company there, who care not for communion with God here; nor value the fellowſhip of his people, at leaſt in the vitals of practical godlineſs. Many, indeed, mix themſelves with the godly on earth, to procure a name to themſelves, and to cover the naughti-

Head I. *Of Regeneration.*

ness of their hearts; but that trade cannot be managed there. (5.) They would never like the employment of heaven, they care so little for it now. The business of the saints there, would be an intolerable burden to them, seeing it is not agreeable to their nature. To be taken up in beholding, admiring, and praising of him that sitteth on the throne, and of the Lamb, would be work unsuitable, and therefore unsavoury, to an unrenewed soul. *Lastly*, They would find this fault with it, that the whole is of everlasting continuance. This would be a killing ingredient in it to them. How would such, as now account the Sabbath-day a burden, brook the celebrating of an everlasting Sabbath in the heavens?

Lastly, Regeneration is absolutely necessary to your being admitted into heaven, John iii. 3. No heaven without it. Though carnal men could digest all those things which make heaven unsuitable for them, yet God will never bring them hither. Therefore born again you must be, else you shall never see heaven; *Except a man be born again, he cannot see the kingdom of God*, John iii. 3. Here is a bar before you, that men and angels cannot remove. To hope for heaven, in the face of this peremptory sentence, is to hope that God will recall his word, and sacrifice his truth and faithfulness to your safety; which is infinitely more than to hope that the earth shall be forsaken for you, and the rock removed out of his place. (2.) There is no holiness without regeneration. It is the new man which is created in true holiness, Eph. iv. 24. And no heaven without holiness; for *without holiness no man shall see the Lord*, Heb. xii. 14. Will the gates of pearl be opened to let in dogs and swine? No; their place is without, Rev. xxii. 15. God will not admit such into the holy place of communion with him here; and will he admit them into the holiest of all hereafter? Will he take the children of the devil, and give them to sit with him in his throne? Or will he bring the unclean into the city, whose street is pure gold? Be not deceived; grace and glory are but two links of one chain, which God hath joined, and no man shall put asunder.

None is tranfplanted into the paradife above, but out of the nurfery of grace below. If you be unholy while in this world, you will be for ever miferable in the world to come. (3.) All the unregenerate are without Chrift, and therefore having no hope while in that cafe, Eph. ii. 12. Will Chrift prepare manfions of glory for them that refufe to receive him into their hearts? Nay, rather, will he not laugh at their calamity, who now fet at nought all his counfel? Prov. i. 25, 26. *Laftly*, There is an infallible connection between a finally unregenerate ftate and damnation, arifing from the nature of the things themfelves, and from the decree of heaven, which is fixed and immoveable as mountains of brafs, John iii. 3. Rom. viii. 6. *To be carnally minded is death.* An unregenerate ftate is hell in the bud. It is eternal deftruction in embryo, growing daily, though thou doft not difcern it. Death is painted on many a fair face in this life. Depraved nature makes men meet to be partakers of the inheritance of the damned, in utter darknefs. (1.) The heart of ftone within thee is a finking weight. As a ftone naturally goes downward; fo the hard ftony-heart tends downward to the bottomlefs pit. You are hardened againft reproof: though you are told your danger, yet you will not fee it, you will not believe it. But remember that the confcience, being now feared with a hot iron, is a fad prefage of everlafting burnings. (2.) Your unfruitfulnefs under the means of grace, fits you for the ax of God's judgments. Mat. iii. 10. *Every tree that bringeth not forth good fruit, is hewn down, and caft into the fire.* The withered branch is fewel for the fire, John xv. 16. Tremble at this, you defpifers of the gofpel: if you be not thereby made meet for heaven, you will be like the barren ground, bearing briars and thorns, *nigh unto curfing, whofe end is to be burned*, Heb. vi. 8. (3.) The hellifh difpofitions of mind, which difcover themfelves in profanity of life, fit the guilty for the regions of horror. A profane life will have a miferable end. *They which do fuch things fhall not inherit the kingdom of God*, Gal. v. 19, 20, 21. Think on this, ye prayerlefs perfons,

Head 1.   *Of Regeneration.*   211

ye mockers of religion, ye curfers and fwearers, ye unclean and unjuft perfons, who have not fo much as moral honefty to keep you from lying, cheating, and ftealing. What fort of a tree think you it to be, upon which thefe fruits grow? Is it a tree of righteoufnefs which the Lord hath planted? Or is it not fuch an one as cumbers the ground, which God will pluck up for fewel to the fire of his wrath? (4.) Your being dead in fin, makes you meet to be wrapped in flames of brimftone, as a winding-fheet; and to be buried in the bottomlefs pit, as in a grave. Great was the cry in Egypt, when the firft-born in each family was dead; but are there not many families, where all are dead together? Nay, many there are who are twice dead, plucked up by the roots. Sometimes in their life they have been rouzed by apprehenfions of death, and its confequences; but now they are fo far on their way to the land of darknefs, that they hardly ever have the leaft glimmering of light from heaven. (5.) The darknefs of your minds prefages eternal darknefs. O the horrid ignorance which fome are plagued with; while others, who have got fome rays of the light of reafon in their heads, are utterly void of fpiritual light in their hearts! If you knew your cafe, you would cry out, Oh! darknefs! darknefs! darknefs, making way for the blacknefs of darknefs forever! The face-covering is upon you already, as condemned perfons; fo near are you to everlafting darknefs. It is only Jefus Chrift who can ftop the execution, pull the napkin off the face of the condemned malefactor, and put a pardon into his hand, Ifa. xxx. 7. *He will deftroy, in this mountain, the face of the covering caft over all people,* i. e. The face-covering caft over the condemned, as in Haman's cafe, Efther vii. 8. *As the word went out of the king's mouth, they covered Haman's face.* Laftly, The chains of darknefs you are bound with in the prifon of your depraved ftate, Ifa. lxi. 1. fits you to be caft into the burning fiery furnace. Ah miferable men! Sometimes their confciences ftir within them, and they begin to think of amending their ways. But alas! they are in chains; they cannot do it. They are chained by the heart?

their lufts cleave fo faft to them, that they eannot, nay, they will not, fhake them off. Thus you fee what affinity there is between an unregenerate ftate, and the ftate of the damned, the ftate of abfolute and irretrievable mifery. Be convinced, then, that you muft be born again; put a high value on the new birth, and eagerly defire it.

The text tells you, that the word is the feed, whereof the new creature is formed : therefore take heed to it, and entertain it, for it is your life. Apply yourfelves to the reading of the Scripture. You that cannot read, get others to read it to you. Wait diligently on the preaching of the word, as by divine appointment the fpecial mean of converfion; *for it pleafeth God, by the foolifhnefs of preaching, to fave them that believe,* 1 Cor. i. 21. Wherefore caft not yourfelves out of Chrift's way; reject not the means of grace, left you be found to judge yourfelves unworthy of eternal life. Attend carefully to the word preached. Hear every fermon, as if you were hearing for eternity : take heed that the fowls of the air pick not up the feed from you, as it is fown. *Give thyfelf wholly to it,* 1 Tim. iv. 15. *Receive it not as the word of men, but as it is in truth, the word of God,* 1 Theff. ii. 13. Hear it with application, looking on it as a meffage fent from heaven, to you in particular; though not to you only, Rev. iii. 22. *He that hath an ear to hear, let him hear what the Spirit faith unto the churches.* Lay it up in your hearts; meditate upon it; and be not as the unclean beafts, that chew not the cud. But by earneft prayer beg that the dew of heaven may fall on thy heart, that the feed may fpring up there.

More particularly, (1.) Receive the teftimony of the word of God, concerning the mifery of an unregenerate ftate, the finfulnefs thereof, and the abfolute neceffity of regeneration. (2.) Receive its teftimony concerning God, what a holy and juft one he is. (3.) Examine thy ways by it; namely, the thoughts of thy heart, the expreffions of thy lips, and the tenor of thy life. Look back through the feveral periods of thy life, and fee thy fins from the precepts of the word;

and learn, from its threatenings, what thou art liable to on the account of thefe fins. (4.) View the corruption of thy nature, by the help of the fame word of God; as in a glafs, which reprefents our ugly face in a lively manner. Were thefe things deeply rooted in the heart, they might be the feed of that fear and forrow, on account of thy foul's ftate, which are neceffary to prepare and ftir thee up to look after a Saviour. Fix your thoughts upon him offered to thee in the gofpel, as fully fuited to thy cafe; having, by his obedience to the death, perfectly fatisfied the juftice of God, and brought in everlafting righteoufnefs. This may prove the feed of humiliation, defire, hope, and faith; and move thee to ftretch out the withered hand unto him, at his own command.

Let thefe things fink deeply into your hearts, and improve them diligently. Remember, whatever you be, you *muft* be born again; elfe it had been better for you that you had never been born. Wherefore, if any of you fhall live and die in an unregenerate ftate, you will be inexcufable, having been fairly warned of your danger.

HEAD II.

The MYSTICAL UNION between CHRIST and BELIEVERS.

JOHN xv. 5. *I am the Vine, ye are the Branches.*

HAVING fpoken of the change made by regeneration, on all thofe who will inherit eternal life, in oppofition to their natural real ftate, the ftate of degeneracy; I proceed to fpeak of the change made on them, in their union with the Lord Jefus Chrift, in oppofition to their natural relative ftate of mifery. The doctrine of the faint's union with Chrift, is very plainly and fully infifted on, from the beginning to the 12th verfe of this chapter; which is a part of our

Lord's farewell-sermon to his disciples. Sorrow had now filled their hearts: they were apt to say, Alas!. what will become of us, when our Master is taken from our head? who will then instruct us? who will solve our doubts? how shall we be supported, under our difficulties and discouragements? how shall we be able to live, without our wonted communication with him? Therefore, our Lord Jesus Christ seasonably teaches them the mystery of their union with him, comparing himself to the vine, and them to the branches.

He compares, (1.) Himself to a vine. *I am the vine.* He had been celebrating, with his disciples, the sacrament of his supper, that sign and seal of his people's union with him; and had told them, *That he would drink no more of the fruit of the vine, till he should drink it new with them in his Father's kingdom:* and now he shews himself to be the vine, from whence the wine of their consolation should come. The vine hath less beauty than many other trees; but is exceeding fruitful; fitly representing the low condition which our Lord was then in, yet bringing many sons to glory. But that which is chiefly aimed at, in his comparing himself to a vine, is to represent himself as the supporter and nourisher of his people, in whom they live, and bring forth fruit. (2.) He compares them to branches; ye are the branches of that vine. Ye are the branches knit to, and growing on this stock, drawing all your life and sap from it. It is a beautiful comparison; as if he had said, I am as a vine, you are as the branches of that vine. Now there are two sorts of branches; (1.) Natural branches, which at first spring out of the stock. These are the branches that are in the tree, and were never out of it. (2.) There are ingrafted branches, which are branches cut off from the tree that first gave them life, and put into another, to grow upon it. Thus branches come to be on a tree, which originally were not on it. The branches mentioned in the text are of the latter sort; Branches broken off (as the word in the original language denotes), namely, from the tree that first gave them life. None of the children of men is a natural

Head II. *Of the Union between Chrift and Belivers.* 215
branch of the fecond Adam, *viz.* Jefus Chrift, the true
vine; they are all the natural branches of the firft Adam,
that degenerate vine: but the elect are all of them,
fooner or later, broken off from their natural ftock, and
ingrafted into Chrift, the true vine.

DOCTRINE. They who are in the ftate of grace,
are ingrafted in, and united to, the Lord Jefus Chrift.
They are taken out of their natural ftock, cut off from
it; and are now ingrafted into Chrift, as the new
ftock. In handling of this, I fhall fpeak to the myftical union. (1.) More generally. (2.) More particularly.

A general View of the Myftical Union.

FIRST, In the general, for underftanding the union
between the Lord Jefus Chrift and his elect, who believe in him, and on him.

1. It is a fpiritual union. Man and wife, by their
marriage union, become one flefh; Chrift and true believers, by this union, become one fpirit, 2 Cor. vi. 17.
As one foul or fpirit actuates both the head and the
members in the natural body; fo the one Spirit of
God dwells in Chrift and the Chriftian; for, *if any man
have not the Spirit of Chrift, he his none of his*, Rom. viii. 9.
Corporal union is made by contact; fo the ftones in a
building are united: but this is an union of another nature. Were it poffible that we could eat the flefh, and
drink the blood of Chrift, in a corporal and carnal manner; it would profit nothing, John vi. 63. It was not
Mary's bearing him in her womb, but her believing
on him, that made her a faint, Luke vii. 27, 28. *A
certain woman faid unto him, Bleffed is the womb that bare
thee, and the paps which thou haft fucked. But he faid,
Yea, rather bleffed are they that hear the word of God, and
keep it.*

2. It is a real union. Such is our weaknefs in our
prefent ftate, fo much are we funk in fin, that we are
prone to form in our fancy an image of every thing
propofed to us: and as to whatever is denied us, we
are apt to fufpect it to be but a fiction, or what has no
reality. But nothing is more real than what is fpiritual;

as approaching neareſt to the nature of him who is the fountain of all reality, namely, God himſelf. We do not ſee with our eyes the union between our own ſoul and body; neither can we repreſent it to ourſelves truly, by imagination, as we do ſenſible things: yet the reality of it is not to be doubted. Faith is no fancy, but the ſubſtance of things hoped for, Heb. xi. Neither is the union thereby made between Chriſt and believers imaginary, but moſt real: *for we are members of his body, of his fleſh, and of his bones,* Eph. v. 30.

3. It is a moſt cloſe and intimate union. Believers, regenerate perſons, who fiducioufly credit him, and rely on him, have put on Chriſt, Gal. iii. 27. If that be not enough, he is in them, John xvii. 23. formed in them, as the child in the womb, Gal. iv. 19. He is the foundation, 1 Cor. iii. 11. they are the lively ſtones built upon him, 1 Pet. ii. 5. he is the Head, and they the body, Eph. i. 22, 23. nay, he liveth in them, as their very ſouls live in their bodies. Gal. ii. 34. And, what is more than all this, they are one in the Father and the Son, as the Father is in Chriſt, and Chriſt in the Father, John xvii. 21. *That they all may be one, as thou the Father art in me, and I in thee, that they alſo may be one in us.*

4. Though it is not a mere legal union, yet it is an union ſupported by law. Chriſt, as the Surety, and Chriſtians as the principal debtors, are one in the eye of the law. When the elect had run themſelves with the reſt of mankind, in debt to the juſtice of God, Chriſt became Surety for them, and paid the debt. When they believe on him, they are united to him in ſpiritual marriage union; which takes effect ſo far, that what he did and ſuffered for them, is reckoned in law as if they had done and ſuffered it themſelves. Hence, they are ſaid to be crucified with Jeſus, Gal. ii. 20. buried with him, Col. ii. 12. yea, raiſed up together, (namely with Chriſt) *and made to ſit together in heavenly places in Chriſt Jeſus,* Eph. ii. 6. In which places, ſaints on earth, of whom the Apoſtle there ſpeaks, cannot be ſaid to be ſitting, but in the way of law reckoning.

Head II. *Of the Union between Chrift and Believers.* 217

5. It is an indiffoluble union. Once in Chrift, ever in him. Having taken up his habitation in the heart, he never removes. None can untie this happy knot. Who will diffolve this union? Will he himfelf? No, he will not; we have his word for it: *I will not turn away from them*, Jer. xxxii. 40. But perhaps the finner will do this mifchief for himfelf; no, he fhall not; *They fhall not depart from me*, faith their God, *ibid*. Can devils do it? No, unlefs they be ftronger than Chrift, and his Father too; *Neither fhall any pluck them out of my hand*, faith our Lord, John x. 28. *And none is able to pluck them out of my Father's hand*, ver. 39. But what fay you of death, which parts hufband and wife; yea, feparates the foul from body? will not death do it? No; the Apoftle, Rom. viii. 39. 59. is perfuaded that neither death, (as terrible as it is) nor life, (as defireable as it is) nor devils, thofe evil angels, nor the devil's perfecuting agents, though they be principalities or powers on earth; nor evil things prefent, already lying on us, nor evil things to come on us; nor the height of worldly felicity; nor the depth of worldly mifery; nor any other creature, good or evil, *fhall be able to feparate us from the love of God, which is in Chrift Jefus our Lord*. As death feparated Chrift's foul from his body, but could not feparate either his foul or body from his divine nature: fo, though the faints fhould be feparated from their neareft relations in the world, and from all their earthly enjoyments; yea, though their fouls fhould be feparated from their bodies, and their bodies feparate in a thoufand pieces, their bones fcattered, as when one cutteth or cleaveth wood: yet foul and body, and every piece of the body, the fmalleft duft of it, fhall remain united to the Lord Chrift: for even in death, *they fleep in Jefus*, 1 Theff. iv. 14. *He keepeth all their bones*, Pfal. xxxiv. 20. Union with Chrift is the grace wherein we ftand, firm and ftable, as mount Zion, which cannot be removed.

Laftly, It is a myfterious union. The gofpel is a doctrine of myfteries. It difcovers to us the fubftantial union of the three perfons in one God-head, 1 John v. 7. *Thefe three are one:* the hypoftatical union, of the divine and human natures, in the person of the Lord Jesus Christ, 1 Tim. iii. 16. *God was manifest in the flesh:* and the mystical union, between Christ and believers; this is a great mystery also, Eph. v. 32. O what mysteries are here! the head in heaven, the members on earth, yet really united! Christ in the believer, living in him, walking in him; and the believer dwelling in God, putting on the Lord Jesus, eating his flesh, and drinking his blood! This makes the saints a mystery to the world; yea, a mystery to themselves.

SECONDLY, We come now more particularly to speak of the union with, and ingrafting into Jesus Christ. (1.) I shall consider the natural stock, which the branches are taken out of. (2.) The supernatural stock they are ingrafted into. (3.) What branches are cut off the old stock, and put into the new. (4.) How it is done. And, lastly, The benefits flowing from this union and ingrafting.

Of the Natural and Supernatural Stocks, and the Branches taken out of the former, and ingrafted into the latter.

I. Let us take a view of the stock, which the branches are taken out of. The two Adams, that is, Adam and Christ, are the two stocks: for the Scripture speaks of these two, as if there had been no more men in the world than they, 1 Cor. xv. 45. *The first man Adam was made a living soul, the last Adam was made a quickening Spirit,* ver. 47. *The first man is of the earth, earthy: the second man is the Lord from heaven.* And the reason is, there were never any that were not branches of one of these two; all men being either in the one stock or in the other; for in these two sorts all mankind stand divided, ver. 48. *As is the earthy, such are they also that are earthy: and as is the heavenly, such are they also that are heavenly.* The first Adam, then is the natural stock: on this stock are the branches found growing at first; which are afterwards cut off, and ingrafted into Christ. As for the fallen angels, as they had no relation to the first Adam, so they have none to the second.

There are four things to be remembered here. (1.) That all mankind (the man Christ excepted) are

Head II. *Of the Union between Christ and Believers.* 219

naturally branches of the first Adam, Rom. v. 12. *By one man sin entered into the world, and death by sin: and so death passed upon all men.* (2.) The bond which knit us unto the natural stock, was the covenant of works. Adam being our natural root, was made the moral root also; bearing all his posterity representatively in the covenant of works. For *by one man's disobedience many were made sinners*, Rom. v. 19. It was necessary that there should be a peculiar relation between that one man and the many, as a foundation for imputing his sin to them. This relation did not arise from the mere natural bond between him and us, as a father to his children; for so we are related to our immediate parents, whose sins are not thereupon imputed to us as Adam's sin is; but arise from a moral bond between Adam and us; the bond of a covenant, which could be no other than the covenant of works, wherein we were united to him as branches to a stock. Hence Jesus Christ, though a son of Adam, Luke iii. 23. 38. was none of these branches; for as he came not of Adam, in virtue of the blessing of marriage, which was given before the fall, (Gen. i. 28. Be fruitful and multiply, &c.) but in virtue of a special promise made after the fall, (Gen. iii. 15. *The seed of the woman shall bruise the serpent's head*) he could not be represented by Adam in a covenant made before his fall. (3.) As it is impossible for a branch to be in two stocks at once; so no man can be, at one and the same time, both in the first and second Adam. (4.) Hence it evidently follows, that all who are not ingrafted in Jesus Christ, are yet branches of the old stock; and so partake of the nature of the same. Now, as to the first Adam, our natural stock, Consider,

First, What a stock he was originally. He was a vine of the Lord's planting, a choice vine, a noble vine, wholly good. There was a consultation of the Trinity, at the planting of this vine, Gen i. 26. *Let us make man in our own image, after our own likeness.* There was no rottenness at the heart of it. There was sap and juice enough in it, to have nourished all the branches, to bring forth fruit unto God. My meaning is, Adam was made able perfectly to keep the commandments of God, which would have procured eternal life to himself, and to all his posterity : for as all die by Adams disobedience; all would have had life by his obedience, if he had stood. Consider,

Secondly, What that stock now is: ah! most unlike to what it was, when planted by the author and fountain of all good. A blast from hell, and a bite with the venomous teeth of the old serpent, have made it a degenerate stock, a dead stock ; nay, a killing stock.

First, It is a degenerate naughty stock. Therefore the Lord God said to Adam, in that dismal day, *Where art thou?* Gen. iii. 9. In what condition art thou now? How art thou turned into the degenerate plant of a strange vine, unto me ? Or, *where wast thou?* Why not in the place of meeting with me ? Why so long in coming ? What meaneth this fearful change; this hiding of thyself from me ? Alas ! the stock is degenerate, quite spoiled, is become altogether naught, and brings forth wild grapes. Converse with the devil is preferred to communion with God. Satan is believed; and God, who is truth itself, disbelieved. He who was the friend of God, is now in conspiracy against him. Darkness is come in the room of light : ignorance prevails in the mind, where divine knowledge shone ; the will, which was righteous and regular, is now turned rebel against its Lord : and the whole man is in dreadful disorder.

Before I go further, let me stop and observe, Here is a mirror both for saints and sinners. Sinners, stand here and consider what you are : and saints, learn you what once you were. You, sinners, are branches of a degenerate stock. Fruit you may bear indeed ; but now your vine is the vine of Sodom, your grapes must of course be grapes of gall, Deut. xxxii. 35. The Scripture speaks of two sorts of fruit, which grow on the branches of the natural stock ; and it is plain that they are of the nature of their degenerate stock ;
(1.) The wild grapes of wickedness, Isa. v. 2. These grow in abundance, by influence from hell. See Gal. v. 19, 20, 21. At its gates are all manner of these

Head II. *Of the Union between Christ and Believers.* 221

fruits, both new and old. Storms come from heaven to check them; but they still grow. They are struck at with the sword of the Spirit, the word of God; conscience gives them many a secret blow: yet they thrive. (2.) Fruit to themselves, Hos. x. 1. What else are all the unrenewed man's acts of obedience, his reformation, sober deportment, his prayers, and good works? They are all done chiefly for himself, not for the glory of God. These fruits are like the apples of Sodom, fair to look at, but fall to ashes when handled and tried. You think you have not only the leaves of a profession, but the fruits of a holy practice too; but if you be not broken off from the old stock, and ingrafted in Christ Jesus, God accepts not, nor regards your fruits.

Here I must take occasion to tell you, that there are five faults which will be found in heaven with your best fruits; (1.) Their bitterness; your clusters are bitter, Deut. xxxii. 32. There is a spirit of bitterness, wherewith some come before the Lord, in religious duties, living in malice and envy; and which some professors entertain against others, because they out-shine them in holiness of life, or because they are not of their opinion. This, wherever it reigns, is a fearful sypmtom of an unregenerate state. But I do not so much mean this, as that which is common to all the branches of the old stock, namely, the leaven of hypocrisy, Luke xii. 1. which sowers and imbitters every duty they perform. The wisdom, that is full of good fruits, is without hypocrisy, James iii. 17. (2.) Their ill favour. Their works are abominable, for themselves are corrupt, Psal. xiv. 1. They all favour of the old stock, not of the new. It is the peculiar privilege of the saints, that they are *unto* God *a sweet favour of Christ*, 2 Cor. ii. 15. The unregenerate man's fruits favour not of love to Christ, nor of the blood of Christ, nor of the incense of his intercession, and therefore will never be accepted in heaven. (3.) Their unripeness. Their grape is an unripe grape, Job xv. 33. There is no influence on them from the Sun of Righteousness, to bring them to perfection. They have the shape of fruit, but no more. The matter of duty is in them, but they want right principles and ends: their works are not wrought in God, John ii. 21. Their prayers drop from their lips, before their hearts be impregnated with the vital sap of the Spirit of supplication: their tears fall from their eyes, ere their hearts be truly softened: their feet turn to new paths, and their way is altered, while yet their nature is not changed. (4.) Their lightness; being weighed in the balances, they are found wanting, Dan. v. 27. For evidence whereof you may observe, that they do not humble the soul, but lift it up in pride. The good fruits of holiness bear down the branches they grow upon, making them to salute the ground. 1 Cor xv. 10. *I laboured more abundantly than they all: yet not I, but the grace of God which was with me.* But the blasted fruits of unrenewed men's performances hang lightly, on branches towering up to heaven, Judges xvii. 13. *Now know I that the Lord will do me good, seeing I have a Levite to my priest.* They look indeed too high for God to behold them; *Wherefore have I fasted, say they, and thou seest not?* Isa. lviii. 3. The more duties they do, and the better they seem to perform them, the less are they humbled, and the more are they lifted up. This disposition of the sinner, is the exact reverse of what is to be found in the saint. To men, who neither are in Christ, nor are solicitous to be found in him, their duties are like windy bladders, wherewith they think to swim ashore to Immanuel's land: but these must needs break, and they consequently sink; because they take not Christ for the lifter up of their head, Psal. iii. 3. *Lastly*, They are not all manner of pleasant fruits, Cant. vii. 13. Christ, as a King, must be served with variety. Where God makes the heart his garden, he plants it as Solomon did his, with trees of all kinds of fruits, Eccles. ii. 5. Accordingly it brings forth the fruits of the Spirit in all goodness, Eph. v. 9. But the ungodly are not so; their obedience is never universal; there is always some one thing or other excepted. In one word, their fruits are fruits of an ill tree, that cannot be accepted in heaven.

Head II. *Of the Union between Christ and Believers.* 223

Secondly, Our natural stock is a dead stock, according to the threatening, Gen. ii. 17. *In the day thou eatest thereof, thou shalt surely die.* Our root now is rottenness, no marvel the blossom go up as dust. The stroke has gone to the heart, the sap is let out, and the tree is withered. The curse of the first covenant, like a hot thunder-bolt from heaven, has lighted on it, and ruined it. It is cursed now as that fig-tree, Matth. xxi. 19. *Let no fruit grow on thee henceforward for ever.* Now it is good for nothing, but to cumber the ground, and furnish fuel for Tophet.

Let me enlarge a little here also. Every unrenewed man is a branch of a dead stock. When thou seest, O sinner, a dead stock of a tree, exhausted of all its sap, having branches on it in the same condition, look on it as a lively representation of thy soul's state. (1.) Where the stock is dead, the branches must needs be barren. Alas! the barrenness of many professors plainly discovers on what stock they are growing. It is easy to pretend to faith, but *shew me thy faith without thy works,* if thou canst, James ii. 18. (2.) A dead stock can convey no sap to the branches, to make them bring forth fruit. The covenant of works was the bond of our union with the natural stock; but now it is become weak through the flesh; that is, through the degeneracy and depravity of human nature, Rom. viii. 13. It is strong enough to command, and to bind heavy burdens on the shoulders of those who are not in Christ, but it affords no strength to bear them. The sap, that was once in the root, is now gone: the law like a merciless creditor, apprehends Adam's heirs, saying to each, *Pay me what thou owest*; when, alas! his effects are riotously spent. (3.) All pains and cost are lost on the tree, whose life is gone. In vain do men labour to get fruit on the branches, when there is no sap in the root. *First,* The gardeners pains are lost: ministers lose their labour on the branches of the old stock, while they continue on it. Many sermons are preached to no purpose, because there is no life to give sensation. Sleeping men may be awakened; but the dead cannot be raised without a miracle: even so, the dead finner muſt remain ſo, if he be not reſtored to life by a miracle of grace. *Secondly,* The influences of heaven are loſt on ſuch a tree: in vain doth the rain fall upon it: in vain is it laid open to the winter-cold and froſts. The Lord of the vineyard digs about many a dead ſoul, but it is not bettered. *Bruiſe the fool in a mortar, his folly will not depart.* Though he meets with many croſſes, yet he retains his luſts: let him be laid on a ſick-bed, he will lay there like a ſick beaſt, groaning under his pain, but not mourning for, nor turning from his ſin. Let death itſelf ſtare him in the face, he will preſumptuouſly maintain his hope, as if he would look the grim meſſenger out of countenance. Sometimes he is under legal convictions, and is ſent home with a trembling heart: but at length he prevails againſt theſe things, and turns as ſecure as ever. *Thirdly,* Summer and winter are alike to the branches on the dead ſtock. When others about them are budding, bloſſoming, and bringing forth fruit, there is no change on them: the dead ſtock has no growing time at all. Perhaps it may be difficult to know, in the winter, what trees are dead, and what are alive; but the ſpring plainly diſcovers it. There are ſome ſeaſons wherein there is little life to be perceived, even amongſt ſaints; yet times of reviving come at length. But even when the vine flouriſheth, and the pomegranates bud forth, (when ſaving grace is diſcovering itſelf by its lively actings, wherever it is) the branches on the old ſtock are ſtill withered. When the dry bones are coming together, bone to bone amongſt ſaints, the ſinner's bones are ſtill lying about the grave's mouth. They are trees that cumber the ground, ready to be cut down; and will be cut down for the fire, if God in mercy prevent it not, by cutting them off from that ſtock, and ingrafting them into another.

Laſtly, Our natural ſtock is a killing ſtock. If the ſtock die, how can the branches live? If the ſap be gone from the root and heart, the branches muſt needs wither. *In Adam all die,* 1 Cor. xv. 22. The root died in paradiſe, and all the branches in it, and with it. The root is poiſoned, and from thence the branches

Head II. *Of the Union between Christ and Believers.* 225

are infected; *Death is in the pot*; and all that taste of the pulse, or pottage, are killed.

Know, then, that every natural man is a branch of a killing stock. Our natural root not only gives us no life, but it has a killing power, reaching to all the branches thereof. There are four things which the first Adam conveys to all his branches, and they are abiding in, and lying on such of them as are not ingrafted in Christ. *First*, A corrupt nature. He sinned, and his nature was thereby corrupted and depraved; and this corruption is conveyed to all his posterity. He was infected, and the contagion spread itself over all his seed. *Secondly*, Guilt, that is, an obligation to punishment, Rom. v. 21. *By one man sin entered into the world, and death by sin; and so death passed upon all men, for that all have sinned.* The threatenings of the law, as cords of death, are twisted about the branches of the old stock, to draw them over the hedge into the fire. And till they be cut off from this stock, by the pruning knife, the sword of vengeance hangs over their heads, to cut them down. *Thirdly*, This killing stock transmits the curse into the branches. The stock, as the stock (for I speak not of Adam, in his personal and private capacity) being cursed, so are the branches, Gal. iii. 10. *For as many as are of the works of the law, are under the curse.* This curse affects the whole man, and all that belongs to him, every thing he possesses, and works three ways; (1.) As poison, infecting; thus their blessings are cursed, Mal. ii. 2. Whatever the man enjoys, it can do him no good, but evil, being thus poisoned by the curse. His prosperity in the world destroys him, Prov. i. 22. The ministry of the gospel is a favour of death unto death to him, 2 Cor. ii. 16. His seeming attainments in religion are cursed to him: his knowledge serves but to puff him up, and his duties to keep him back from Christ. (2.) It worketh as a moth, consuming and wasting by little and little, Hos. v. 12. *Therefore will I be unto Ephraim as a moth.* There is a worm at the root, consuming them by degrees. Thus the curse pursued Saul, till it wormed him out of all his enjoyments, and out of the

G g

very shew he had of religion. Sometimes they decay like the fat of lambs, and melt away as the snow in a sun-shine. (3.) It acteth as a lion rampant, Hof. v. 14. *I will be unto Ephraim as a lion.* The Lord *rains on them snares, fire, and brimstone, and an horrible tempest,* in such a manner, that they are hurried away with the stream. He teareth their enjoyments from them in his wrath, pursueth them with terrors, rends their souls from their bodies, and throws the dead branch into the fire. Thus the curse devours like fire, which none can quench. *Lastly,* This killing stock transmits death to the branches upon it. Adam took the poisonous cup, and drunk it off: this occasioned death to himself and us. We came into the world spiritually dead, and thereby obnoxious to eternal death, and absolutely liable to temporal death. This root is to us like the Scythian river, which, they say, brings forth little bladders every day, out of which come certain small flies, which are bred in the morning, winged at noon, and dead at night: a very lively emblem of our mortal state.

Now, sirs, is it not absolutely necessary to be broken off from this our natural stock? what will our fair leaves of a profession, or our fruits of duties avail, if we be still branches of the degenerate, dead, and killing stock? But, alas! of the many questions among us, few are taken up about these, Am I broken off from the old stock, or not? Am I ingrafted in Christ, or not? Ah! wherefore all this waste of time? Why is there so much noise about religion amongst many, who can give no good account of their having laid a good foundation, being mere strangers to experimental religion? I fear, if God does not in mercy undermine the religion of many of us, and let us see that we have none at all, our fruit will be found rottenness, and our blossom go up as dust, in a dying hour. Therefore let us look to our state, that we be not found fools in our latter end.

II. Let us now view the supernatural stock, in which the branches, cut off from the natural stock, are ingrafted. Jesus Christ is sometimes called the *Branch,* Zech. iii. 8. So he is in respect of his human nature,

Head II. *Of the Union between Christ and Believers.* 227

being a branch, and the top-branch of the houfe of David. Sometimes he is called a *Root*, Ifa. xi. 10. we have both together, Rev. xxii. 16. *I am the root, and the offspring of David*; David's root as God, and his offspring as man. The text tells us, that he is the vine, *i. e.* he, as Mediator, is the vine-ftock, whereof believers are the branches. As the fap comes from the earth into the root and ftock, and from thence is diffufed into the branches; fo by Chrift, as Mediator, divine life is conveyed from the fountain, unto thofe who are united to him by faith, John vi. 57. *As the living Father hath fent me, and I live by the Father: fo he that eateth me, even he fhall live by me.* By Chrift as Mediator, not as God only, as fome have afferted; nor yet as man only, as the Papifts generally hold: but as Mediator, God and man, Acts xx. 28. *The church of God, which he hath purchafed with his blood.* Heb. ix. 14. *Chrift, who through the eternal Spirit offered himfelf without fpot to God.* The divine and human natures have their diftinct actings, yet a joint operation, in his difcharging the office of Mediator. This is illuftrated by the fimilitude of a fiery fword, which at once cuts and burns: cutting it burneth, and burning it cutteth; the fteel cuts, and the fire burns. Wherefore Chrift, God-man, is the ftock, whereof believers are the branches: and they are united to whole Chrift. They are united to him in his human nature, as being *members of his body, of his flefh, and of his bones*, Eph. v. 30. And they are united to him in his divine nature; for fo the apoftle fpeaks of this union, Col. i. 27. *Chrift in you the hope of glory.* Thofe who are Chrift's have the Spirit of Chrift, Rom. viii. 9. and by him they are united to the Father, and to the Holy Ghoft, 1 John iv. 15. *Whofoever fhall confefs that Jefus is the Son of God, God dwelleth in him, and he in God.* Faith, the bond of this union, receives whole Chrift, God-man, and fo unites us to him as fuch.

Behold here, O believers, your high privilege. You were once branches of a degenerate ftock, even as others: but you are, by grace, become branches of the true vine, John xv. 1. You are cut out of a dead and killing stock; and ingrafted in the last Adam, who was made a quickening Spirit, 1 Cor. xv. 45. Your loss by the first Adam is made up, with great advantage, by your union with the second. Adam, at his best estate, was but a shrub, in comparison with Christ the tree of life. He was but a servant, Christ is the Son, the Heir, and Lord of all things; *the Lord from heaven.* It cannot be denied, that grace was shewn in the first covenant: but it is as far exceeded, by the grace of the second covenant, as the twilight is by the light of the mid-day.

III. What branches are taken out of the natural stock, and grafted into this vine? *Answ.* These are the elect, and none other. They, and they only, are grafted into Christ; and consequently none but they are cut off from the killing stock. For them alone he interceeds, *That they may be one in him and his Father*, John xvii. 9. 23. Faith, the bond of this union, is given to none else: it is the faith of God's elect, Titus i. 1. The Lord passeth by many branches growing on the natural stock, and cuts off only here one, and there one, and grafts them into the true vine, according as free love hath determined. Oft does he pitch upon the most unlikely branch, leaving the top-boughs; passing by the mighty, and the noble, and calling the weak, base, and despised, 1 Cor. i. 26, 27. Yea, he often leaves the fair and smooth, and takes the rugged and knotty, *and such were some of you, but ye are washed*, &c. 1 Cor. vi. 11. If we enquire why so? We find no other reason, but because they were chosen in him, Eph. i. 4. *Predestinated to the adoption of children by Jesus Christ*, verse 5. Thus are they gathered together in Christ, while the rest are left growing on their natural stock, to be afterwards bound up in bundles for the fire. Therefore, to whoever the gospel may come in vain, it will have a blessed effect on God's elect, Acts xiii. 48. *As many as were ordained to eternal life believed.* Where the Lord has much people, the gospel will have much success, sooner or later. Such as are to be saved, will be added to the mystical body of Christ.

How the Branches are taken out of the Natural Stock, and ingrafted into the Supernatural Stock.

IV. I am to shew how the branches are cut off from the natural stock, the first Adam, and grafted into the true vine, the Lord Jesus Christ. Thanks to the husbandman, not to the branch, that it is cut off from its natural stock, and grafted into a new one. The sinner, in his coming off from the first stock, is passive, and neither can nor will come off from it of his own accord, but clings to it, till almighty power makes him fall off, John vi. 44. *No man can come unto me, except the Father which hath sent me draw him.* And chap. v. 40. *Ye will not come to me, that ye might have life.* The ingrafted branches are *God's husbandry*, 1 Cor. iii. 9. *The planting of the Lord*, Isa. lxi. 3. The ordinary means which he makes use of, in this work, is the ministry of the word, 1 Cor. iii. 9. *We are labourers together with God*; but the efficacy thereof is wholly from him. Whatever the minister's parts or piety be, ver. 7. *Neither is he that planteth any thing, neither he that watereth, but God that giveth the increase.* The apostles preached to the Jews, yet the body of that people remained in infidelity, Rom. x. 16. *Who hath believed our report?* Yea, Christ himself, who spoke as never man spake, saith concerning the success of his own ministry, *I have laboured in vain, I have spent my strength for nought*, Isa. xlix. 4. The branches may be hacked by the preaching of the word; but the stroke will never go through, till it be carried home by the omnipotent arm. However, God's ordinary way is, *by the foolishness of preaching to save them that believe*, 1 Cor. i. 21.

The cutting off the branch from the natural stock, is performed by the pruning knife of the law, in the hand of the Spirit of God, Gal. ii. 19. *For I through the law am dead to the law.* It is by the bond of the covenant of works, as I said before, that we are knit to our natural stock: therefore, as a wife, unwilling to be put away, pleads and hangs by the marriage-tie; so do men by the covenant of works. They hold by it, like the man who held the ship with his hands; and when one hand was cut off, held it with the other; and when both were cut off, held with his teeth. This will appear from a diftinct view of the Lord's work on men, in bringing them off from the old ftock; which now I offer in the following particulars.

Firft, When the Spirit of the Lord comes to deal with a perfon, to bring him to Chrift, he finds him in Laodicea's cafe, in a found fleep of fecurity, dreaming of heaven, and the favour of God, though full of fin againft the holy One of Ifrael, Rev. iii. 17. *Thou knoweft not that thou art wretched, and miferable, and poor, and blind, and naked.* Therefore he darts in fome beams of light into the dark foul; and lets the man fee that he is a loft man, if he turn not over a new leaf, and betake himfelf to a new courfe of life. Thus, by the Spirit of the Lord acting as a Spirit of bondage, there is a criminal court erected in the man's breaft; where he is arraigned, accufed, and condemned, for breaking the law of God, *convinced of fin and judgment*, John xvi. 8. And now he can no longer fleep fecurely in his former courfe of life. This is the firft ftroke which the branch gets, in order to cutting off.

Secondly, Hereupon the man forfakes his former profane courfes, his lying, fwearing, fabbath-breaking, ftealing, and fuch like practices; though they be dear to him as right eyes, he will rather quit them than ruin his foul. The fhip is like to fink, and therefore he throweth his goods overboard, that he himfelf may not perifh. Now he begins to blefs himfelf in his heart, and look joyfully on his evidences for heaven; thinking himfelf a better fervant to God than many others, Luke xviii. 11. *God, I thank thee, I am not as other men are, extortioners, unjuft, adulterers,* &c. But he foon gets another ftroke with the ax of the law, fhewing him that it is only he who doth what is written in the law, that can be faved by it, and that his negative holinefs is too fcanty a covering from the ftorm of God's wrath. Thus, although his fins of commiffion only were heavy on him before, his fins of omiffion now crowd into his thoughts, attended with a train of law-curfes and vengeance. And each of the ten commands difcharges

Head II. *Of the Union between Christ and Believers.* 231
thunder-claps of wrath against him, for his omitting required duties.

Thirdly, Upon this he turns to a positively holy course of life. He not only is not profane, but he performs religious duties : he prays, seeks the knowledge of the principles of religion, strictly observes the Lord's day, and, like Herod, does many things, and hears sermons gladly. In one word, there is a great conformity, in his outward conversation, to the letter of both tables of the law. There is a mighty change upon the man, which his neighbours cannot miss taking notice of. Hence he is chearfully admitted by the godly into their society, as a praying person; and can confer with them about religious matters, yea, and about soul-exercise, which some are not acquainted with; and their good opinion of him confirms his good opinion of himself. This step in religion is fatal to many, who never get beyond it. But here the Lord gives the elect branch a further stroke. Conscience flies in the man's face, for some wrong steps in his conversation, the neglect of some duty, or commission of some sin, which is a blot in his conversation : and then the flaming sword of the law appears again over his head; and the curse rings in his ears; for not continuing in *all* things written in the law, to do them, Gal. iii. 10.

Fourthly, On this account he is obliged to seek another salve for his sore. He goes to God, confesseth his sin, seeks the pardon of it, promising to watch against it for the time to come; and so finds ease, and thinks he may very well take it, seeing the Scripture saith, *If we confess our sins, he is faithful and just to forgive us our sins,* 1 John i. 9. not considering that he grasps at a privilege, which is theirs only who are graffed into Christ, and under the covenant of grace, and which the branches yet growing on the old stock cannot plead. And here sometimes there are formal and express vows made against such and such sins, and binding to such and such duties. Thus many go on all their days, knowing no other religion than to perform duties, and confess and pray for pardon of that wherein they fail, promising themselves eternal happiness, though they are ut-

232 *Of the Union between Christ and Believers.* State III.

ter strangers to Christ. Here many elect ones have been cast down wounded, and many reprobates have been slain, while the wounds of neither of them have been deep enough to cut them off from their natural stock. But the Spirit of the Lord gives yet a deeper stroke to the branch which is to be cut off, shewing him, that as yet he is but an out-side saint, and discovering to him the filthy lusts lodged in his heart, which he took no notice of before, Rom. vii. 9. *When the commandment came, sin revived, and I died.* Then he sees his heart a dunghill of hellish lusts, filled with covetousness, pride, malice, filthiness, and the like. Now, as soon as the door of the chambers of his imagery is thus opened to him, and he sees what they do there in the dark, his out-side religion is blown up as insufficient; and he learns a new lesson in religion, namely, *That he is not a Jew which is one outwardly,* Rom. ii. 28.

Fifthly, Upon this he goes further, even to inside religion; sets to work more vigorously than ever, mourns over the evils of his heart, and strives to bear down the weeds which he finds growing in that neglected garden. He labours to curb his pride and passion, and to banish speculative impurities; prays more fervently, hears attentively, and strives to get his heart affected in every religious duty he performs: thus he comes to think himself not only an out-side, but an in-side Christian. Wonder not at this, for there is nothing in it beyond the power of nature, or what one may attain to under a vigorous influence of the covenant of works; therefore another yet deeper stroke is given. The law chargeth home on the man's conscience, that he was a transgressor from the womb; that he came into the world a guilty creature; and that in the time of his ignorance, and even since his eyes were opened, he has been guilty of many actual sins, either altogether overlooked by him, or not sufficiently mourned over (for spiritual sores, not healed by the blood of Christ, but skinned over some other way, are easily irritated, and soon break out again); therefore the law takes him by the throat, saying, *Pay what thou owest*.

Sixthly, Then the sinner says in his heart, *Have patience with me, and I will pay thee all*; and so falls to

Head II. *Of the Union between Christ and Believers.* 233
work to pacify an offended God, and to atone for those sins. He renews his repentance, such as it is; bears patiently the afflictions laid upon him; yea, he afflicts himself, denies himself the use of his lawful comforts, sighs deeply, mourns bitterly, cries with tears for a pardon, till he hath wrought up his heart to a conceit of having obtained it, as he has thus done penance for what is past, and resolves to be a good servant to God, and to hold on in outward and inward obedience for the time to come. But the stroke must go nearer the heart yet, ere the branch fall off. The Lord discovers to him, in the glass of the law, how he sinneth in all he does, even when he does the best he can; and therefore the dreadful sound returns to his ears, Gal. iii. 10. *Cursed is every one that continueth not in all things*, &c. *When ye fasted and mourned*, saith the Lord, *did you at all fast unto me, even to me?* Will muddy water make clean cloaths? Will you satisfy for one sin with another? Did not your thoughts wander in such a duty? Were not your affections flat in another? Did not your heart give a whorish look to such an idol? And did it not rise in a fit of impatience, under such an affliction? *Should I accept this of your hands? Cursed be the deceiver, which sacrificeth to the Lord a corrupt thing*, Mal. i. 13, 14. And thus he becomes so far broke off, that he sees he is able to satisfy the demands of the law.

Seventhly, Hence, like a broken man, who finds that he is not able to pay all his debt, he goes about to compound with his creditor. And, being in pursuit of ease and comfort, he does what he can to fulfil the law; and wherein he fails, he looks that God will accept the will for the deed. Thus doing his duty, and having a will to be better, he cheats himself into a persuasion of the goodness of his state: and hereby thousands are ruined. But the elect get another stroke, which looseth their hold in this case. The doctrine of the law is borne in on their consciences, demonstrating to them, that exact and perfect obedience is required by it, under pain of the curse; and that it is doing, and not wishing to do, which will avail. Wishing to do better will not answer the law's demands; and therefore the curse sounds again, *Curfed is every one that continueth not—to do them;* that is, actually to do them. In vain is wishing then.

Eighthly, Being broken off from all hopes of compounding with the law, he falls a borrowing. He sees that all he can do to obey the law, and all his defires to be and to do better, will not save his soul: therefore he goes to Christ, intreating that his righteousness may make up what is wanting in his own, and cover all the defects of his doings and sufferings, that so God, for Christ's sake, may accept them, and thereupon be reconciled. Thus doing what he can to fulfil the law, and looking to Christ to make up all his defects, he comes at length again to sleep in a sound skin. Many persons are ruined this way. This was the error of the Galatians, which Paul, in his epistle to them, disputes against. But the Spirit of God breaks off the sinner from this hold also; by bringing home to his conscience that great truth, Gal. iii. 12. *The law is not of* faith, *but the man that* doth *them shall live in them.* There is no mixing of the law and faith in this business: the sinner must hold by one of them, and let the other go. The way of the law, and the way of faith, are so far different, that it is not possible for a sinner to walk in the one, without coming off from the other: and if he be for doing, he must do all alone; Christ will not do a part for him, if he doth not all. A garment pieced up of sundry sorts of righteousness, is not a garment meet for the court of heaven. Thus the man is like one in a dream, who thought he was eating, but being awakened by a stroke, behold his soul is faint: his heart finks in him like a stone, while he finds that he can neither bear his burden himself alone, nor can he get help under it.

Ninthly, What can he do, who must needs pay, and yet has not enough of his own to bring him out of debt, nor can borrow so much, and to beg he is ashamed? What can such a one do, I say, but sell himself, as the man under the law, that was waxen poor? Lev. xxv. 47. Therefore the sinner, beat off from so many holds, attempts to make a bargain with Christ, and to sell himself to the Son of God, (if I may so

Head II. *Of the Union between Christ and Believers.* 235
speak) solemnly promising and vowing, that he will be a servant to Christ, as long as he lives, if he will save his soul. And here, oft-times, the sinner makes a personal covenant with Christ, resigning himself to him on these terms; yea, and takes the sacrament to make the bargain sure. Hereupon the man's great care is, how to obey Christ, keep his commands, and so fulfil his bargain. In this the soul finds a false unsound peace for a while; till the Spirit of the Lord gives another stroke, to cut off the man from this refuge of lies likewise. And that happens in this manner. When he fails of the duties he engaged to perform, and falls again into the sin he covenanted against, it is powerfully carried home on his conscience, that his covenant is broken: so all his comfort goes, and terrors afresh seize on his soul, as one that has broken covenant with Christ. Commonly the man, to help himself, renews his covenant, but breaks it again as before. And how is it possible it should be otherwise, seeing he is still upon the old stock? Thus the work of many, all their days, as to their souls, is nothing but a making and breaking such covenants, over and over again.

Object. Some perhaps will say, Who liveth and sinneth not? Who is there that faileth not of the duties he has engaged to? If you reject this way as unsound, who then can be saved? *Answ.* True believers will be saved; namely, all who do by faith take hold of God's covenant. But this kind of covenant is men's own covenant, devised of their own heart; not God's covenant, revealed in the gospel of his grace: and the making of it is nothing else but the making of a covenant of works with Christ, confounding the law and the gospel; a covenant he will never subscribe to, though we should sign it with our heart's blood, Rom. iv. 14. 16. *For if they which are of the law be heirs, faith is made void, and the promise made of none effect. Therefore it is of faith, that it might be by grace, to the end the promise might be sure to all the seed.* Chap. xi. 6. *And if by grace, then it is no more of works, otherwise grace is no more grace. But if it be of works, then it is no more grace, otherwise work is no more work.* God's covenant is everlasting;

once in, never out of it again; and the mercies of it are sure mercies, Isa. lv. 3. But that covenant of yours is a tottering covenant, never sure, but broken every day. It is a mere servile covenant, giving Christ service for salvation : but God's covenant is a filial covenant, in which the sinner takes Christ and his salvation freely offered, and so becomes a son, John i. 12. *But as many as received him, to them gave he power to become the sons of God:* and being become a son, he serves his Father, not that the inheritance may become his, but because it is his, through Jesus Christ. See Gal. iv. 24. and downward. To enter into that spurious covenant, is to buy from Christ with money; but to take hold of God's covenant, is to buy of him without money and without price, Isa. lv. 1. that is to say, to beg of him. In that covenant men work for life; in God's covenant they come to Christ for life, and work from life. When a person under that covenant fails in his duty, all is gone; the covenant must be made over again. But under God's covenant, although the man fail in his duty, and for his failure falls under the discipline of the covenant, and lies under the weight of it, till such time as he has recourse a-new to the blood of Christ for pardon, and renew his repentance; yet all that he trusted to, for life and salvation, namely, the righteousness of Christ, still stands intire, and the covenant remains firm. See Rom. vii. 24, 25. and viii. 1.

Now, though some men spend their lives in making and breaking such covenants of their own, the terror upon the breaking of them wearing weaker and weaker by degrees, till at last it creates them little or no uneasiness; yet the man, in whom the good work is carried on, till it be accomplished in cutting him off from the old stock, finds these covenants to be as rotten cords, broke at every touch; and the terror of God being thereupon redoubled on his spirit, and the waters at every turn getting in unto his very soul, he is obliged to cease from catching hold of such covenants, and to seek help some other way.

Tenthly, Therefore the man comes at length to beg at Christ's door for mercy : but yet he is a proud beg-

Head II. *Of the Union between Christ and Believers.* 237

gar, standing on his personal worth. For, as the Papists have mediators to plead for them with the only Mediator, so the branches of the old stock have always something to produce, which they think may commend them to Christ, and engage him to take their cause in hand. They cannot think of coming to the spiritual market without money in their hand. They are like persons who have once had an estate of their own, but are reduced to extream poverty, and forced to beg. When they come to beg, they still remember their former character; and though they have lost their substance, yet they retain much of their former spirit: therefore they cannot think they ought to be treated as ordinary beggars, but deserve a particular regard, and, if that be not given them, their spirits rise against him to whom they address themselves for supply. Thus God gives the unhumbled sinner many common mercies, and shuts him not up into the pit according to his deserving: but all this is nothing in his eyes. He must be set down at the children's table, otherwise he reckons himself hardly dealt with and wronged: for he is not yet brought so low, as to think God may be justified when he speaketh (against him), and clear from all iniquity, when he judgeth him according to his real demerit, Psal. li. 4. He thinks, perhaps, that, even before he was enlightened, he was better than many others: he considers his reformation of life, his repentance, the grief and tears which his sin has cost him, his earnest desires after Christ, his prayers and wrestlings for mercy; and useth all these now as bribes for mercy, laying no small weight upon them in his addresses to the throne of grace. But here the Spirit of the Lord shoots a sheaf of arrows into the man's heart, whereby his confidence in these things is sunk and destroyed; and, instead of thinking himself better than many, he is made to see himself worse than any. The naughtiness of his reformation of life is discovered; his repentance appears to him no better than the repentance of Judas; his tears like Esau's, and his desires after Christ to be selfish and loathsome, like those who sought Christ because of the loaves, John vi. 26. His an-

238 *Of the Union between Christ and Believers.* State III.
swer from God seems now to be, Away proud beggar; how shall I put thee among the children? He seems to look sternly on him for his slighting of Jesus Christ by unbelief, which is a sin he scarce discerned before. But now, at length, he beholds it in its crimson colours, and is pierced to the heart, as with a thousand darts, while he sees how he has been going on blindly, sinning against the remedy of sin, and int he whole course of his life trampling on the blood of the Son of God. And now he is, in his own eyes, the miserable object of law-vengeance, yea, and gospel-vengeance too.

Eleventhly, The man being thus far humbled, will no more plead he is worthy for whom Christ should do this thing; but, on the contrary, looks on himself as unworthy of Christ, and unworthy of the favour of God. We may compare him, in this case, to the young man who followed Christ, having a linen cloth cast about his naked body; who when the young men laid hold, left the linen cloth, and fled from them naked, Mark xiv. 51, 52. Even so the man had been following Christ in the thin and cold garment of his personal worthiness; but by it, even by it, which he so much trusted to, the law catched hold of him, to make him prisoner; and then he is fain to leave it, and flees away naked: yet not to Christ, but from him. If you now tell him he is welcome to Christ, if he will come to him; he is apt to say, Can such a vile and unworthy wretch as I be welcome to the holy Jesus? If a plaster be applied to his wounded soul, it will not stick. He says, *Depart from me, for I am a sinful man,* O Lord, Luke v. 8. No man needs speak to him of his repentance for his comfort; he can quickly espy such faults in it as makes it naught: nor of his tears; for he is assured they have never come into the Lord's bottle. He disputes himself away from Christ; and concludes, now that he has been such a slighter of Christ, and is such an unholy and vile creature, that he cannot, he will not, he ought not to come to Christ; and that he must either be in better case, or else he will never believe. Hence he now makes his strongest efforts to amend what was amiss in his way before: he prays more earnestly than ever, mourns more bitterly, strives against sin, in heart and life, more vigorously, and watcheth more diligently, if by any means he may at length be fit to come to Christ. One would think the man is well humbled now: but ah! develtish pride lurks under the veil of all this seeming humility; like a kindly branch of the old stock, he adheres still, and will not submit to the righteousness of God, Rom. x. 3. He will not come to the market of free grace without money. He is bidden to the marriage of the King's Son, where the bridegroom himself furnisheth all the guests with wedding-garments, stripping them of their own: but he will not come, because he wants a wedding-garment: howbeit he is very busy in making one ready. This is sad work; and therefore he must have a deeper stroke yet, else he is ruined. This stroke is given him with the ax of the law, in its irritating power. Thus the law, girding the soul with cords of death, and holding it in with the rigorous commands of obedience, under the pain of the curse; and God, in his holy and wise conduct, with-drawing his restraining grace, corruption is irritated, lusts become violent; and the more they are striven against, the more they rage, like a furious horse checked with the bit. Then corruptions set up their heads, which he never saw in himself before. Here oft-times' atheism, blasphemy, and, in one word, horrible things concerning God, terrible thoughts concerning the faith, arise in his breast; so that his heart is a very hell within him. Thus, while he is sweeping the house of his heart, not yet watered with gospel grace, those corruptions which lay quiet before, in neglected corners, fly up and down in it like dust. He is as one who is mending a dam, and while he is repairing breaches in it, and strengthening every part of it, a mighty flood comes down, overturns his works, and drives all away before it, as well what was newly laid, as what was laid before. Read Rom. vii. 8, 9, 10. 13. This is a stroke which goes to the heart: and by it his hope, of getting himself more fit to come to Christ, is cut off.

Lastly, Now the time is come, when the man, between hope and despair, resolves to go to Christ as he is; and therefore, like a dying man, stretching himself just before his breath goes out, he rallies the broken forces of his soul, tries to believe, and in some sort lays hold on Jesus Christ. And now the branch hangs on the old stock by one single tack of a natural faith, produced by the natural vigour of one's own spirit, under a most pressing necessity, Psal. lxxviii. 34, 35. *When he slew them, then they sought him, and they returned and enquired early after God. And they remembered that God was their Rock, and the high God their Redeemer.* Hos. viii. 1. *Israel shall cry unto me, My God, we know thee.* But the Lord, minding to perfect his work, fetches yet another stroke, whereby the branch falls quite off. The Spirit of God convincingly discovers to the sinner his utter inability to do any thing that is good, and so he dieth, Rom. vii. 9. That voice powerfully strikes through his soul, *How can ye believe?* John vii. 44. Thou canst no more believe than thou canst reach up thine hand to heaven, and bring Christ down from thence. Thus at length he sees, that he can neither help himself by working, nor by believing: and having no more to hang by on the old stock, he falls off. While he is distressed thus, seeing himself like to be swept away with the flood of God's wrath; and yet unable so much as to stretch forth a hand to lay hold of a twig of the tree of life growing on the bank of the river, he is taken up, and ingrafted in the true Vine, the Lord Jesus Christ giving him the spirit of faith.

By what has been said upon this head, I design not to rack or distress tender consciences; for though there are but few such, at this day, yet God forbid I should offend any of Christ's little ones. But, alas! a dead sleep is fallen upon this generation, they will not be awakened, let us go ever so near to the quick: therefore I fear that there is another sort of awakening abiding this sermon-proof generation, which shall make the ears of them that hear it tingle. However, I would not have this to be looked upon as the Sovereign God's stinted method of breaking off sinners from the old stock. But this I assert as a certain truth, that all who are in Christ have been broken off from all these several con-

Head II. *Of the Union between Christ and Believers.*

fidences; and that they who were never broken off from them, are yet in their natural stock. Neverthelefs, if the houfe be pulled down, and the old foundation razed, it is much the fame, whether it was taken down stone by stone, or whether it was undermined, and all fell down together.

Now it is that the branch is ingrafted into Jefus Christ. And as the law, in the hand of the Spirit of God, was the instrument to cut off the branch from the natural stock; fo the gofpel, in the hand of the fame Spirit, is the instrument used for engrafting it in the fupernatural stock, 1 John i. 3. *That which we have seen and heard, declare we unto you, that ye alſo may have fellowſhip with us; and truly our fellowſhip is with the Father, and with his Son Jeſus Chriſt.* See Ifa. lxi. 1, 2, 3. The gofpel is the filver cord let down from heaven, to draw perifhing finners to land. And though the preaching of the law prepares the way of the Lord; yet it is in the word of the gofpel that Christ and the finner meet. Now, as in the natural grafting, the branch being taken up is put into the stock, and, being put into it, becomes one with it, fo that they are united; even fo, in the spiritual ingrafting, Christ apprehends the finner, and the finner being apprehended of Christ, apprehends him, and fo they become one, Phil. iii. 12.

Firſt, Christ apprehends the finner by his Spirit, and draws him to himfelf, 1 Cor. xii. 13. *For by one Spirit we are all baptized into one body.* The fame Spirit which is in the Mediator himfelf, he communicates to his elect in due time, never to depart from them, but to abide in them as a principle of life. Thus he takes hold of them by his own Spirit put into them; and fo the withered branch gets life. The foul is now in the hands of the Lord of life, and poffeffed by the Spirit of life: how can he then but live? The man gets a ravifhing fight of Chrift's excellency, in the glafs of the gofpel: he fees him a full, fuitable, and willing Saviour; and gets a heart to take him, for and inftead of all. The Spirit of faith furnifheth him with feet to come to Chrift, and hands to receive him. What by nature he could not do, by grace he can, the holy Spirit working in him the work of faith with power.

Secondly, The sinner thus apprehended, apprehends Christ by faith, and is one with the blessed stock, Eph. iii. 17. *That Christ may dwell in your hearts by faith.* The soul that before tried many ways of escape, but all in vain, now looks with the eye of faith, which proves the healing look. As Aaron's rod, laid up in the tabernacle, budded, and brought forth buds, Numb. xvii. 8. So the dead branch, apprehended by the Lord of life, put into, and bound up with the glorious quickening stock, by the Spirit of life, buds forth in actual believing on Jesus Christ, whereby this union is compleated. *We having the same Spirit of faith—believe,* 2 Cor. iv. 13. Thus the stock and the graft are united, Christ and the Christian are married, faith being the soul's consent to the spiritual marriage-covenant, which, as it is proposed in the gospel to mankind sinners indefinitely, so it is demonstrated, attested and brought home, to the man in particular, by the holy Spirit: and so he being joined to the Lord, is one Spirit with him. Hereby a believer lives in, and for Christ, and Christ lives in, and for the believer, Gal. ii. 20. *I am crucified with Christ. Nevertheless I live; yet not I, but Christ liveth in me.* Hos. iii. 3. *Thou shalt not be for another man, so will I also be for thee.* The bonds, then, of this blessed union are, the Spirit on Christ's part, and faith on the believer's part.

Now both the souls and bodies of believes are united to Christ. He that is joined to the Lord is one Spirit, 1 Cor. vi. 17. The very bodies of believers have this honour put upon them, that they are the temples of the Holy Ghost, ver. 19. and the members of Christ, ver. 15. When they sleep in the dust, they sleep in Jesus, 1 Thess. iv. 14. and it is in virtue of this union they shall be raised up out of the dust again, Rom. viii. 11. *He shall quicken your mortal bodies, by his Spirit that dwelleth in you.* In token of this mystical union, the church of believers is called by the name of her head and husband, 1 Cor. xii. 12. *For as the body is one, and hath many members—so also is Christ.*

Use. From what is said, we may draw the following inferences.

Head II. *Of the Union between Christ and Believers.* 243

1. The preaching of the law is most necessary. He that would ingraft, must needs use the prunning-knife. Sinners have many shifts to keep them from Christ; many things by which they keep their hold of the natural stock: therefore they have need to be closely pursued, and hunted out of their sculking holes, and refuges of lies.

2. Yet it is the gospel that crowns the work: the law makes nothing perfect. The law lays open the wound, but it is the gospel that heals. The law strips a man, wounds him, and leaves him half dead: the gospel binds up his wounds, pouring in wine and oil to heal them. By the law we are broken off, but it is by the gospel we are taken up, and implanted in Christ.

3. *If any man have not the Spirit of Christ, he is none of his,* Rom. viii. 9. We are told of a monster in nature, having two bodies differently animated, as appeared from contrary affections at one and the same time; but so united, that they were served with the self-same legs. Even so, however men may cleave to Christ, call themselves of the holy city, and stay themselves upon the God of Israel, Isa. xlviii. 2. and may be bound up as branches in him, John xv. 2. by the outward ties of sacraments: yet if the Spirit that dwells in Christ dwell not in them, they are not one with him. There is a great difference between adhesion and ingrafting. The ivy clasps and twists itself about the oak, but it is not one with it, for it still grows on its own root: so, to allude to Isa. iv. 1. many professors take hold of Christ, and eat their own bread, and wear their own apparel, only they are called by his name. They stay themselves upon him, but grow upon their own root: they take him to support their hopes, but their delights are elsewhere.

4. The union between Christ and his mystical members is firm and indissoluble. Were it so that the believer only apprehended Christ, and Christ apprehended not him, we could promise little on the stability of such an union; it might quickly be dissolved: but as the believer apprehends Christ by faith, so Christ appre-

hends him by his Spirit, and none shall pluck him out of his hand. Did the child only keep hold of the nurse, it might at length weary and let go its hold, and so fall away: but if she have her arms about the child, it is in no hazard of falling away, even though it be not actually holding by her. So whatever sinful intermissions may happen in the exercise of faith; yet the union remains sure, by reason of the constant indwelling of the Spirit. Blessed Jesus! *All his saints are in thy hand*, Deut. xxxiii. 3. It is observed by some, that the word *Abba* is the same, whether you read it forward or backward: whatever the believer's case be, the Lord is still to him *Abba, Father*.

Lastly, They have an unsure hold of Christ, whom he has not apprehended by his Spirit. There are many half marriages here, where the soul apprehends Christ, but is not apprehended of him. Hence many fall away, and never rise again: they let go their hold of Christ; and when that is gone, all is gone. These are the branches in Christ that bear not fruit, which the husbandman taketh away, John xv. 2. *Quest.* How can that be? *Answ.* These branches are set in the stock by a profession, or an unsound hypocritical faith; they are bound up with it, in the external use of the sacraments; but the stock and they are never knit; therefore they cannot bear fruit. And they need not be cut off, nor broken off; they are by the husbandman only taken away, or (as the word primarily signifies) lifted up, and so taken away, because there is nothing to hold them: They are indeed bound up with the stock, but were never united to it.

Quest. How shall I know if I am apprehended of Christ? *Answ.* You may be satisfied in this enquiry, if you consider and apply these two things.

First, When Christ apprehends a man by his Spirit, he is so drawn, that he comes away to Christ with his whole heart: for true believing is believing with all the heart, Acts viii. 37. Our Lord's followers are like those who followed Saul at first, men whose hearts God has touched, 1 Sam. x. 26. When the Spirit pours in overcoming grace, they pour out their hearts like water

Head II. *Of the Union between Christ and Believers.* 245
before him, Psal. lxii. 8. They flow unto him like a river, Isa. ii. 2. *All nations shall flow unto it,* namely, to *the mountain of the Lord's house*. It denotes not only the abundance of converts, but the disposition of their souls in coming to Christ: they come heartily and freely; *drawn with loving-kindness,* Jer. xxxi. 3. *Thy people shall be willing in the day of thy power,* Psal. cx. 3. i. e. free, ready, open hearted, giving themselves to thee as free-will offerings. When the bridegroom has the bride's heart, it is a right marriage: but some give their hand to Christ, who give him not their heart. They that are only driven to Christ by terror, will surely leave him again when that terror is gone. Terrors may break a heart of stone, but the pieces into which it is broken still continue to be stone: terrors cannot soften it into a heart of flesh. Yet terror may begin the work, which love crowns. The strong wind, the earthquake, and the fire going before, the still small voice, in which the Lord is, may come after them. When the blessed Jesus is seeking sinners to match with him, they are bold and perverse: they will not speak with him, till he hath wounded them, made them captives, and bound them with the cords of death. When this is done, then it is that he makes love to them, and wins their hearts. The Lord tells us, Hos. ii. 16. 20. that his chosen Israel shall be married unto himself. But how will the bride's consent be won? Why, in the first place, he will bring her into the wilderness, as he did the people when he brought them out of Egypt, ver. 14. There she will be hardly dealt with, scorched with thirst, and bitten of serpents: and then he will speak comfortably to her, or as the expression is, he will speak unto her heart. The sinner is first driven, and then drawn to Christ. It is with the soul as with Noah's dove; she was forced back again to the ark, because she could find nothing else to rest upon: but when she returned, she would have rested on the outside of it, if Noah had not put forth his hand, and pulled her in, Gen. viii. 9. The Lord sends the avenger of blood in pursuit of the criminal; who with a sad heart leaves his own city, and with tears in his eyes parts with his

old acquaintances, because he dare not stay with them, and he flees for his life to the city of refuge. This is not at all his choice, it is forced work; necessity has no law. But when he comes to the gates, and sees the beauty of the place, the excellency and loveliness of it charm him; then he enters it with heart and good will, saying, *This is my rest, and here I will stay:* and, as one said in another case, *I had perished, unless I had perished.*

Secondly, When Christ apprehends a soul, the heart is disengaged from, and turned against sin. As in cutting off the branch from the old stock, the great idol self is brought down, the man is powerfully taught to deny himself: so, in the apprehending of the sinner by the Spirit, that union is dissolved which was between the man and his lusts, while he was in the flesh, as the apostle expresses it, Rom. vii. 5. His heart is loosed from them, though formerly as dear to him as the members of his body; as his eyes, legs, or arms; and, instead of taking pleasure in them, as before, he longs to be rid of them. When the Lord Jesus comes to a soul, in the day of converting grace, he finds it like Jerusalem, in the day of her nativity, (Ezek. xvi. 4.) with its navel not cut, drawing its fulsome nourishment and satisfaction from its lusts; but he cuts off this communication, that he may set the soul on the breasts of his own consolations, and give it rest in himself. And thus the Lord wounds the head and heart of sin, and the soul comes to him, saying, *Surely our fathers have inherited lies, vanity, and things wherein there is no profit,* Jer. xvi. 19.

Of the Benefits flowing to true Believers from their Union with Christ.

V. And, *lastly*, I come to speak of the benefits flowing to true believers from their union with Christ. The chief of the particular benefits which believers have by it, are justification, peace, adoption, sanctification, growth in grace, fruitfulness in good works, acceptance of these works, establishment in the state of grace, support, and a special conduct of providence about

Head II. *Of the Union between Chrift and Believers.* 247

them. As for communion with Chrift, it is such a benefit, as being the immediate consequent of union with him, comprehends all the rest as mediate ones. For as the branch, immediately upon its union with the stock, hath communion with the stock, in all that is in it; so the believer, uniting with Chrift, hath communion with him; in which he launcheth forth into an ocean of happiness, is led into a paradise of pleasures, and has a saving intereft in the treafure hid in the field of the gofpel, the unfearchable riches of Chrift. As foon as the believer is united to Chrift, Chrift himfelf, in whom all fulnefs dwells, is his, Cant. ii. 16. *My beloved is mine, and I am his. And how fhall he not with him freely give us all things?* Rom. viii. 32. *Whether Paul, or Apollos, or Cephas, or the world, or life, or death, or things prefent, or things to come, all are yours,* 1 Cor. iii. 22. This communion with Chrift is the great comprehenfive blefling neceffarily flowing from our union with him. Let us now confider the particular benefits flowing from it, before mentioned.

The firft particular benefit which a finner hath by his union with Chrift, is juftification; for, being united to Chrift, he hath communion with him in his righteoufnefs, 1 Cor. i. 30. *But of him are ye in Chrift Jefus, who of God is made unto us wifdom and righteoufnefs.* He ftands no more condemned, but juftified before God, as being in Chrift, Rom. viii. 1. *There is therefore now no condemnation to them which are in Chrift Jefus.* The branches hereof are, pardon of fin, and perfonal acceptance.

Firft, His fins are pardoned, the guilt of them is removed. The bond obliging him to pay his debt is cancelled. God the Father takes the pen, dips it in the blood of his Son, crofieth the finners accounts, and blotteth them out of his debt book. The finner out of Chrift is bound over to the wrath of God: he is under an obligation in law to go to the prifon of hell, and there to lie till he hath paid the utmoft farthing. This arifeth from the terrible fanction with which the law is fenced; which is no lefs than death, Gen. ii. 18. So that the finner, paffing the bounds afligned him, is as

Shimei in another cafe, a man of death, 1 Kings ii. 42. But now, being united to Chrift, God faith, *Deliver him from going down to the pit; I have found a ranfom,* Job xxxiii. 24. The fentence of condemnation is reverfed, the believer is abfolved, and fet beyond the reach of the condemning law. His fins, which were fet before the Lord, Pfal. xc. 8. fo that they could not be hid, God now takes and cafts them all behind his back, Ifa. xxxvii. 17. Yea, he cafts them into the depths of the fea, Micah vii. 9. What falls into a brook may be got up again; but what is caft into the fea cannot be recovered. But there are fome fhallow places in the fea: true, but their fins are not caft there, but into the depths of the fea; and the depths of the fea are devouring depths, from whence they fhall never come forth again. But what if they do not fink? He will caft them in with force; fo that they fhall go to the ground, and fink as lead, in the mighty waters of the Redeemer's blood. They are not only forgiven, but forgotten, Jer. xxxi. 34. *I will forgive their iniquity, and I will remember their fins no more.* And though their afterfins do, in themfelves, deferve eternal wrath, and do actually make them liable to temporal ftrokes, and fatherly chaftifements, according to the tenor of the covenant of grace, Pfal. lxxxix. 3—33. yet they can never be actually liable to eternal wrath, or the curfe of the law; for they are dead to the law in Chrift, Rom. vii. 4. They can never fall away from their union with Chrift; neither can they be in Chrift, and under condemnation at the fame time, Rom. viii. 1. *There is therefore now no condemnation to them which are in Chrift Jefus.* This is an inference drawn from that doctrine of the believer's being dead to the law, fet forth by the apoftle, chap. vii. 1—6. as is clear from the 2d, 3d, and 4th verfes of this eighth chapter. In this refpect the juftified man is the bleffed man, unto whom the Lord imputeth not iniquity, Pfal. xxxii. 2. as one who has no intention to charge a debt on another, fets it not down in his account book.

Secondly, The believer is accepted as righteous in God's fight, 2 Cor. v. 21. *For he is found in Chrift, not*

Head II. *Of the Union between Christ and Believers.* 249

not having his own righteousness, but that which is through the faith of Christ, the righteousness which is of God by faith, Phil. ii. 9. He could never be accepted of God, as righteous, on account of his own righteousness; because, at best, it is but imperfect; and all righteousness, properly so called, which can abide a trial before the throne of God, is perfect. The very name of it implies perfection: for unless a work be perfectly conformable to the law, it is not right, but wrong; and so cannot make a man righteous before God, whose judgment is according to truth. Yet, if justice demands a righteousness of one who is in Christ, by which he may be accounted righteous before the Lord, *Surely, shall such an one say, in the Lord have I righteousness,* Isa. xiv. 24. The law is fulfilled, its commands are obeyed, its sanction is satisfied. The believer's Surety has paid the debt. It was exacted, and he answered for it.

Thus the person united to Christ is justified. You may conceive of the whole proceeding herein in this manner. The avenger of blood pursuing the criminal, Christ, as the Saviour of lost sinners, doth by the Spirit apprehend him, and draw him to himself; and he by faith lays hold on Christ: so the Lord our righteousness, and the unrighteous creature, unite. From this union with Christ results a communion with him in his unsearchable riches, and consequently in his righteousness, that white raiment which he has for cloathing the naked, Rev. iii. 18. Thus the righteousness of Christ becomes his: and, because it is his by unquestionable title, it is imputed to him; it is reckoned his in the judgment of God, which is always according to truth. So the believing sinner, having a righteousness which fully answers the demands of the law, is pardoned and accepted as righteous. See Isa. xlv. 22. 24. 45. Rom. iii. 24. and chap. v. 1. Now he is a free man. Who shall lay any thing to the charge of those whom God justifieth? Can justice lay any thing to their charge? No, for it is satisfied. Can the law? No, for it has got all its demands on them from Jesus Christ, Gal. ii. 20. *I am crucified with Christ.* What can the law require more, after it has wounded their head, poured in wrath in full meafure into their foul, and cut off their life, and brought it into the duft of death, by doing all this to Jefus Chrift, who is their head, Eph. i. 22. their foul, Acts ii. 25. 27. and their life ? Col. i. 4. What is become of the finner's own hand-writing, which would prove the debt againft him ? Chrift has blotted it out, Col. ii. 14. But it may be, juftice may get its eye upon it again. No, he took it out of the way. But O that it had been torn in pieces ! may the finner fay. Yea, fo it is ; the nails that pierced Chrift's hands and feet are driven through it; he nailed it. But what if the torn pieces be fet together again ? That cannot be ; for he nailed it to his crofs, and his crofs was buried with him, and will never rife more, feeing Chrift dieth no more. Where is the face-covering that was upon the condemned man ? Chrift has deftroyed it, Ifa. xxx. 7. Where is death, that ftood before the finner with a grim face, and an open mouth, ready to devour him ? Chrift has *fwallowed it up in victory*, ver. 8. Glory, glory, glory, to him that thus *loved us, and wafhed us from our fins in his own blood.*

The fecond benefit flowing from the fame fpring or union with Chrift, and coming by the way of juftification, is peace : peace with God, and peace of confcience, according to the meafure of the fenfe which the juftified have of their peace with God, Rom. v. 1. *Therefore, being juftified by faith, we have peace with God.* Chap. xiv. 17. *For the kingdom of God is not meat and drink, but righteoufnefs and peace, and joy in the Holy Ghoft*, Whereas God was their enemy before, now he is reconciled to them in Chrift : they are in a covenant of peace with him ; and as Abraham was, fo they are the friends of God ; he is well pleafed with them in his beloved Son. His word, which fpoke terror to them formerly, now fpeaks peace, if they rightly underftand its language. And there is love in all his difpenfations towards them, which makes all work together for their good. Their confciences are purged of that guilt and filthinefs that lay upon them : his confcience purifying blood ftreams through their fouls, by virtue of their

Head II. *Of the Union between Christ and Believers.* 251

union with him, Heb. ix. 14. *How much more shall the blood of Christ—purge your conscience from dead works, to serve the living God?* The bonds laid on their consciences, by the spirit of bondage, are taken off, never more to be laid on, Rom. viii. 15. *For ye have not received the spirit of bondage again to fear.* As soon as the soul becomes conscious of the application of that blood, the conscience is quieted, which falls out sooner or later, according to the measure of faith, and as the only wife God sees meet to time it. Unbelievers may have troubled consciences, which they may get quieted again: but alas! their consciences become peaceable before they become pure; so their peace is but the seed of greater horror and confusion. Carelesness may give ease for a while to a sick conscience; men neglecting its wounds, they close again of their own accord, before the filthy matter is purged out. Many bury their guilt in the grave of an ill memory: conscience smarts a little, at length the man forgets his sin, and there is an end of it: but this is only an ease before death. Business, or the affairs of life, often give ease in this case. When Cain is banished from the presence of the Lord, he begins building cities. When the evil spirit came upon Saul, he calls not for his Bible, nor for the priest, to converse with him about his case; but for music, to play it away. So many, when their consciences begin to be uneasy, they fill their heads and hands with business, to divert themselves, and to regain ease at any rate. Yea, some will run over the belly of their convictions, and so get some ease to their consciences, as Hazael gave his master ease by stifling him. Again, the performance of duties may give some ease to disquieted consciences: and this is all which legal professors have recourse to, for quieting their consciences. When conscience is wounded, they will pray, confess, mourn, and resolve to do so no more; and so they become whole again, without an application of the blood of Christ by faith. But they, whose consciences are rightly quieted, come for peace and purging to the blood of sprinkling. Sin is a sweet morsel, that makes God's elect sick souls, before they get it vomited up. It leaves a sting behind it, which one time or other, will create them no little pain.

Elihu shews us both the case and cure, Job xxxiii. Behold the case which a man may be in, whom God has thoughts of love to. He darteth convictions into his conscience; and makes them stick so fast, that he cannot rid himself of them, ver. 16. *He openeth the ears of men, and sealeth their instruction.* His very body sickens, ver. 19. *He is chastned also with pain upon his bed, and the multitude of his bones with strong pain.* He loseth his stomach, ver. 20. *His life abhorreth bread, and his soul dainty meat.* His body pines away, so that there is nothing on him but skin and bone, ver. 21. *His flesh is consumed away, that it cannot be seen, and his bones that were not seen stick out.* Though he is not prepared for death, he has no hopes of life, ver. 22. *His soul draweth near unto the grave,* (which is the height of his misery) *his life to the destroyers*; he is looking every moment when devils, these destroyers, Rev. ix. 11. these murderers, or manslayers, John viii. 44 will come and carry away his soul to hell. O dreadful case! Is there any hope for such? Yes, there is hope. God will *keep back his soul from the pit,* ver. 18. although he bring him forward to the brink of it. Now see how the sick man is cured. The physician's art cannot prevail here: the disease lies more inward, than that his medicines can reach. It is soul-trouble which has brought the body into his disorder: and therefore the remedies must be applied to the sick man's soul and conscience. The physician for this case, must be a spiritual Physician; the remedies must be spiritual, a righteousness, a ransom, an atonement. Upon the application of these; the soul is cured, the conscience is quieted; and the body recovers, ver. 23, 24, 25, 26. *If there be a messenger with him, an interpreter, one among a thousand, to shew unto man his uprightness: then he is gracious unto him, and saith, Deliver him from going down to the pit, I have found a ransom. His flesh shall be fresher than a child's; he shall return to the days of his youth; he shall pray unto God, and he shall be favourable unto him, and he shall see his face with joy.* The proper physician for this patient,

Head II. *Of the Union between Chriſt and Believers.* 253

is *a meſſenger, an interpreter,* ver. 23. that is, as ſome expoſitors, not without ground, underſtand it, the great Phyſician, Jeſus Chriſt, whom Job had called his Redeemer, chap. xix. 25. He is a Meſſenger, the *Meſſenger of the covenant of peace,* Mal. iii. 1. who comes ſeaſonably to the ſick man. He is an Interpreter, the great Interpreter of God's counſels of love to ſinners, John i. 8. *One among a thouſand, even the chief among ten thouſand,* Cant. v. 10. *One choſen out of the people,* Pſal. lxxxix. 29. One to whom *the Lord hath given the tongue of the learned—to ſpeak a word in ſeaſon to him that is weary,* Iſa. l. 4, 5, 6. It is he that is with him, by his Spirit, now to convince him of righteouſneſs, John xvi. 8. as he was with him before, to convince him of ſin and judgment. His work now is, to ſhew unto him his uprightneſs, or his righteouſneſs, i. e. the Interpreter, Chriſt's righteouſneſs; which is the only righteouſneſs, ariſing from the paying of a ranſom, and upon which a ſinner is delivered from going down to the pit, ver. 24. Thus Chriſt is ſaid to declare God's name, Pſal. xxii. 22. and to preach righteouſneſs, Pſal. lx. 9. The phraſe is remarkable: it is not to ſhew unto the man, but unto man, his righteouſneſs; which not obſcurely intimates, that he is more than a man, who ſhews or declareth this righteouſneſs. Compare Amos iv. 13. *He that formeth the mountains, and createth the wind, and declareth unto man what is his thought.* There ſeems to be in it a ſweet alluſion to the firſt declaration of this righteouſneſs unto man, or as the word is, unto Adam, after the fall, while he lay under terror from apprehenſions of the wrath of God: which declaration was made by the Meſſenger, the Interpreter, namely, the eternal Word, the Son of God, called, *the voice of the Lord God,* Gen. iii. 8. appearing, probably, in human ſhape. Now, while he, by his Spirit, is the preacher of righteouſneſs to the man, it is ſuppoſed that the man lays hold on the offered righteouſneſs; whereupon the ranſom is applied to him, and he is delivered from going down to the pit; for God hath a ranſom for him. Which is intimated to him by the words, *deliver him,* ver. 14. Hereupon his conſcience, being purged by the blood of atonment, is pacified, and sweetly quieted, *He shall pray unto God—and see his face with joy,* which before he beheld with horror, ver. 26. that is, in New-Testament language, *having an high priest over the house of God, he shall draw near with a true heart, in full assurance of faith, having his heart sprinkled from an evil conscience,* Heb. x. 21, 22. But then, what becomes of the body, the weak and weary flesh? Why, *his flesh shall be fresher than a child's, he shall return to the days of his youth,* ver. 25. Yea, *all his bones* (which were chastened with strong pain, ver. 19.) *shall say, Lord, who is like unto thee?* Psal. xxxv. 10.

A third benefit flowing from union with Christ, is adoption. Believers, being united to Christ, become children of God, and members of the family of heaven. By their union with him, who is the Son of God by nature, they become the sons of God by grace, John, i. 12. As when a branch is cut off from one tree, and grafted in the branch of another, the ingrafted branch, by means of its union with the adopting branch (as some not unfitly have called it), is made a branch of the same stock, with that into which it is ingrafted: So sinners, being ingrafted into Jesus Christ, whose name is the *Branch,* his Father is their Father, his God their God, John xx. 17. And thus they, who are by nature children of the devil, become the children of God. They have the Spirit of adoption, Rom. viii. 15. namely, the Spirit of the Son, which brings them to God, as children to a father; to pour out their complaints in his bosom, and to seek necessary supply, Gal. iv. 6. *Because ye are sons, God hath sent forth the Spirit of his Son into your hearts, crying, Abba Father.* Under all their weaknesses, they have fatherly pity and compassion shewn them, Psal. ciii. 13. *Like as a Father pitieth his children, so the Lord pitieth them that fear him.* Although they were but foundlings, found in a desert land; yet now *he keeps them as the apple of his eye,* Deut xxii. 10. Whoever pursues them, they have a refuge, Prov. xiv. 26. *His children shall have a place of refuge.* In a time of common calamity, they have chambers of pro-

Head II. *Of the Union between Christ and Believers.* 255
tection, where they may be hid, until the indignation be overpast, Isa. xxv. 20. And he is not only their refuge for protection, but their portion for provision, in that refuge, Psal. cxlii. 5. *Thou art my refuge and my portion in the land of the living.* They are provided for for eternity, Heb. xi. 16. *He hath prepared for them a city.* And what he sees they have need of for time, they shall not want, Mat. vi. 31, 32. *Take no thought, saying, What shall we eat? or what shall we drink? or wherewithal shall we be cloathed? for your heavenly Father knoweth that ye have need of all these things.* Seasonable correction is likewise their privilege as sons: so they are not suffered to pass with their faults, as others who are not children, but servants of the family, who at length will be turned out of doors for their miscarriages, Heb. xii. 7. *If ye endure chastening, God dealeth with you as with sons: for what son is he whom the Father chasteneth not?* They are heirs of, and shall inherit the promises, Heb. vi. 12. Nay, they are heirs of God, who himself is the portion of their inheritance, Psal. xvi. 5. and joint-heirs with Christ, Rom. viii. 17. And because they are the children of the great King, and heirs of glory, they have angels for their attendants, who are *sent forth to minister unto them that shall be heirs of salvation*, Heb. i. 14.

A fourth benefit is sanctification, 1 Cor. i. 30. *But of him are ye in Christ Jesus, who of God is made unto us wisdom, and righteousness, and sanctification.* Being united to Christ, they partake of his Spirit, which is the Spirit of holiness. There is a fulness of the Spirit in Christ, and it is not like the fulness of a vessel, which only retains what is poured into it; but it is the fulness of a fountain, for diffusion and communication, which is always sending forth its waters, and yet is always full. The Spirit of Christ, that spiritual sap, which is in the stock, and from thence is communicated to the branches, is the Spirit of grace, Zech. xii. 10. And where the Spirit of grace dwells, there will be found a confluence of all graces. Holiness is not one grace only, but all the graces of the Spirit: it is a constellation of graces; it is all the graces in their seed and root. And as the sap, conveyed from the stock into the branch, goes through it, and through every part of it; fo the Spirit of Chrift fanctifies the whole man. The poifon of fin was diffufed through the whole fpirit, foul, and body of the man; and sanctifying grace purfues it into every corner, 1 Theff. v. 23. Every part of the man is fanctified, though no part is perfectly fo. The truth we are fanctified by is not held in the head, as in a prifon; but runs, with his fanctifying influences, through heart and life. There are, indeed, fome graces, in every believer, which appears as top-branches above the reft; as meeknefs in Mofes, patience in Job; but feeing there is, in every child of God, a holy principle going along with the holy law, in all the parts thereof, loving, liking, and approving it; as appears from their univerfal refpect to the commands of God; it is evident that they are endowed with all the graces of the Spirit; becaufe there can be no lefs in the effect, than there was in the caufe.

Now this fanctifying Spirit, whereof believers partake, is unto them, (1.) A Spirit of mortification; *through the Spirit they mortify the deeds of the body*, Rom. viii. 13. fin is crucified in them, Gal. v. 24. They are planted together, (namely with Chrift) in the likenefs of his death, which was a lingering death, Rom. vi. 5. Sin, in the faint, though not quite dead, yet is dying. If it were dead, it would be taken down from the crofs, and buried out of his fight: but it hangs there as yet, working and ftruggling under its mortal wounds. Look, as when a tree has got fuch a ftroke as reaches the heart of it, all the leaves and branches begin to fade and decay: fo, where the fanctifying Spirit comes, and breaks the power of fin, there is a gradual ceafing from it, and dying to it, in the whole man; fo that he *no longer lives in the flefh to the lufts of men* He does not make fin his trade and bufinefs; it is not his great defign, to feek himfelf, and to fatisfy his corrupt inclinations: but he is for Immanuel's land; and is walking in the high-way to it, the way which is called the way of holinefs: though the wind from hell, that was on his back before, blows now full in his face, and makes his travelling uneafy, and often drives him off

Head II. *Of the Union between Christ and Believers.* 257

the high-way. (2.) This Spirit is a Spirit of vivification to them, for he is the Spirit of life, and makes them live unto righteousness, Ezek. xxxvi. 27. *And I will put my Spirit within you, and cause you to walk in my statutes.* Those that have been planted together with Christ, *in the likeness of his death, shall be also in the likeness of his resurrection,* Rom. vi. 5. At Christ's resurrection, when his soul was re-united with his body, every member of that blessed body was enabled again to perform the actions of life: so the soul, being influenced by the sanctifying Spirit of Christ, is enabled more and more to perform the actions of spiritual life. And as the whole of the law, and not some scraps of it only, is written on the holy heart; so believers are enabled to transcribe that law in their conversation. Although they cannot write one line of it without blots, yet God, for Christ's sake, accepts of the performances, in point of sanctification; they being disciples of his own Son, and led by his own Spirit.

This sanctifying Spirit, communicated by the Lord Jesus to his members, is the spiritual nourishment the branches have from the stock into which they are ingrafted; whereby the life of grace, given them in regeneration, is preserved, continued, and actuated. It is the nourishment whereby the new creature liveth, and is nourished up towards perfection. Spiritual life needs to be fed, and must have supply of nourishment: and believers derive the same from Christ their head, whom the Father has appointed the head of influences to all his members, Col. ii. 19. *And not holding the head, from which all the body, by joints and bands, having nourishment ministered, or supplied.* Now this supply is *the supply of the Spirit of Jesus Christ,* Phil. i. 19. The saints feed richly, *eating Christ's flesh, and drinking his blood,* for their spiritual nourishment: yet our Lord himself teacheth us, that it *is the Spirit that quickeneth,* even that Spirit who dwells in his blessed body, John vi. 63. The human nature is united to the divine nature, in the person of the Son, and so (like the bowl in Zechariah's candlestick, Zech. iv.) lies at the fountain-head, as the glorious means of conveyance of influences

L l

from the fountain of Deity. He receives not the Spirit by meafure, but ever hath a fulnefs of the Spirit, by reafon of that perfonal union. Hence believers, being united to the man Chrift, (as the feven lamps to the bowl, by their feven pipes, Zech. iv. 2.) his flefh is to them meat indeed, and his blood drink indeed: for feeding on that bleffed body, (*i. e.* effectually applying Chrift to their fouls by faith) they partake more and more of that Spirit, who dwelleth therein, to their fpiritual nourifhment. The holinefs of God can never admit of an immediate union with the finful creature, nor (confequently) an immediate communion with it: yet the creature could not live the life of grace, without communion with the Fountain of life. Therefore, that the honour of God's holinefs, and the falvation of finners, might jointly be provided for, the fecond Perfon of the glorious Trinity, took into a perfonal union with himfelf, a finlefs human nature; that fo this holy, harmlefs, and undefiled humanity, might immediately receive a fulnefs of the Spirit, of which he might communicate to his members, by his divine power and efficacy. Suppofe there were a tree, with its root in the earth, and its branches reaching to heaven, the vaft diftance between the root and the branches would not interrupt the communication between the root and the top-branch: even fo, the diftance between the man Chrift, who is in heaven, and his members, who are on earth, cannot hinder the communication between them. What though the parts of myftical Chrift (*viz.* the head and the members) are not contiguous, as joined together in the way of corporal union? the union is not therefore the lefs real and effectual. Yea, our Lord himfelf fhews us, that though we fhould eat his flefh, in a corporal and carnal manner, yet it would profit nothing, John vi. 63. We fhould not be one whit holier thereby. But the members of Chrift on earth are united to their head in heaven, by the invifible bond of the felf-fame Spirit dwelling in both; in him as the head, and in them as the members. The wheels in Ezekiel's vifion were not contiguous to the living creatures, yet were united to

Head II. *Of the Union between Christ and Believers.* 259
them by an invisible bond of one Spirit in both; so that *when the living creatures went, the wheels went by them, and when the living creatures were lift up from the earth, the wheels were lift up,* Ezek. i. 19. For, says the prophet, *the spirit of the living creatures was in the wheels,* ver. 20.

Hence we may see the difference between true sanctification, and that shadow of it, which is to be found amongst some strict professors of Christianity, who yet are not true Christians, are not regenerated by the Spirit of Christ, and is of the same kind with what has appeared in many sober heathens. True sanctification is the result of the soul's union with the holy Jesus, the first and immediate receptacle of the sanctifying Spirit; out of whose fullness his members do, by virtue of their union with him, receive sanctifying influences. The other is the mere product of the man's own spirit, which whatever it has, or seems to have of the matter of true holiness, yet does not arise from the supernatural principles, nor to the high aims and ends thereof: for, as it comes from self, so it runs out into the dead sea of self again; and lies as wide of true holiness as nature doth of grace. They who have this bastard holiness, are like common boat-men, who serve themselves with their own oars: whereas the ship bound for Immanuel's land, sails by the blowings of the Divine Spirit. How is it possible, that there should be true sanctification without Christ? Can there be true sanctification, without partaking of the Spirit of holiness? can we partake of that Spirit, but by Jesus Christ, *the way, the truth, and the life?* The falling dew can as soon make its way through the flinty rock, as influences of grace can come from God to sinners, any other way than through him whom the Father hath appointed the head of influences, Col. i. 19. *For it hath pleased the Father, that in him should all fullness dwell:* and chap. ii. 19. *And not holding the head, from which all the body by joints and bands having nourishment ministered and knit together, increaseth with the increase of God.* Hence see, how it comes to pass that many fall away from their seeming sanctification, and never recover: it is because they are not branches truly knit to the true vine. Mean while, others recover from their decays, becaufe of their union with the life-giving ſtock, by the quickening Spirit, 1 John ii. 19. *They went out from us, but they were not of us ; for if they had been of us, they would no doubt have continued with us.*

A fifth benefit is growth in grace. *Having nouriſhment miniſtered, they increaſe with the increaſe of God*, Col. ii. 19. *The righteous ſhall flouriſh like the palm-tree: he ſhall grow like a cedar in Lebanon*, Pſal. xcii. 12. Grace is of a growing nature: in the way to Zion they go from ſtrength to ſtrength. Though the holy man be at firſt a little child in grace, yet at length he becomes a young man, a father, 1 John ii. 13. Though he does but creep in the way to heaven ſometimes, yet afterwards " he walks, he runs, he mounts up with wings as eagles," Iſa. xl. 31. If a branch, grafted into a ſtock, never grows, it is a plain evidence of its not having knit with the ſtock.

But ſome may perhaps ſay, " If all true Chriſtians " be growing ones, what ſhall be ſaid of thoſe, who " inſtead of growing are going back?" I anſwer, 1ſt, There is a great difference between the Chriſtian's growing ſimply, and his growing at all times. All true Chriſtians do grow, but I do not ſay that they grow at all times. A tree, that has life and nouriſhment, grows to its perfection, yet it is not always growing; it grows not in the winter, Chriſtians alſo have their winters, wherein the influences of grace, neceſſary for growth, are ceaſed, Cant. v. 2. *I ſleep.* It is by faith the believer derives gracious influences from Jeſus Chriſt; as each lamp in the candleſtick received oil from the bowl, by the pipe going between them, Zech. iv. 2. Now, if that pipe be ſtopped, if the ſaint's faith lie dormant and inactive; then all the reſt of the graces will become dim, and ſeem ready to be extinguiſhed: in conſequence whereof, depraved nature will gather ſtrength, and become active. What then will become of the ſoul? Why, there is ſtill one ſure ground of hope. The ſaint's faith is not as the hypocrite's, like a pipe laid ſhort of the fountain, whereby

Head II. *Of the Union between Christ and Believers.* 261

there can be no conveyance : it still remains a bond of union between Christ and the soul : and therefore, because Christ lives, the believer shall live also, John xiv. 19. The Lord Jesus puts in his hand by the hole of the door, and clears the means of conveyance: and then influences for growth flow, and the believer's graces look fresh and green again, Hos. xiv. 7. *They that dwell under his shadow shall return : they shall revive as the corn, and grow as the vine.* In the worst of times, the saints have a principle of growth in them, 1 John iii. 9. *His seed remaineth in him.* Therefore, after decays they revive again; namely, when the winter is over, and the Sun of Righteousness returns to them with his warm influences. Mud thrown into a pool may lie there at ease, but if it be cast into a fountain, the spring will at length work it out, and run clear as formerly. 2*dly*, Christians may mistake their growth, and that two ways. (1.) By judging of their case according to their present feeling. They observe themselves, and cannot perceive themselves to be growing: but there is no reason thence to conclude they are not growing, Mark iv. 27. *The seed springs and grows up, he knoweth not how.* Were a person to fix his eye ever so stedfastly on the sun running his race, or on a growing tree, he would not perceive the sun moving, nor the tree growing: but if he compare the tree as it now is, with what it was some years ago; and consider the place in the heavens where the sun was in the morning; he will certainly perceive the tree has grown, and the sun has moved. In like manner may the Christian know whether he be in a growing or declining state, by comparing his present with his former condition. (2.) Christians may mistake their case, by measuring their growth by the advances of the top only, not of the root. Though a man be not growing taller, he may be growing stronger. If a tree be taking with the ground, fixing itself in the earth, and spreading out its roots, it is certainly growing, although it be nothing taller than formerly. So, although a Christian may want the sweet consolations, and flashes of affection which he had; yet, if he be growing in humility, self-denial, and sense of needy dependence on Jesus Christ, he is a growing Christian, Hos. xiv. 5. *I will be as the dew unto Israel, he shall cast forth his roots as Lebanon.*

Quest. But do hypocrites grow at all? and if so, how shall we distinguish between their growth, and true Christian growth? *Answ.* To the first part of the question; hypocrites do grow. The tares have their growth, as well as the wheat: the seed that fell among thorns did spring up, Luke viii. 7. only it did bring no fruit to perfection, ver. 14. Yea, a true Christian may have a false growth. James and John seemed to grow in the grace of holy zeal, when their spirits grew so hot in the cause of Christ, that they would have fired whole villages for not receiving their Lord and Master, Luke ix. 54. *They said, Lord, wilt thou that we command fire to come down from heaven, and consume them, even as Elias did?* But it was indeed no such thing; and therefore he turned and rebuked them, ver. 55. and said, *Ye know not what manner of spirit you are of.* To the second part of the question, it is answered, that there is a peculiar beauty in the Christian growth, distinguishing it from all false growth: it is universal, regular, proportionable. It is a *growing up unto him in all things, which is the head*, Eph. iv. 15. The growing Christian grows proportionably, in all the parts of the new-man. Under the kindly influences of the Sun of Righteousness, believers grow up as calves of the stall, Mal. iv. 2. You would think it a monsterous growth in these creatures, if you saw their heads grow, and not their bodies; or if you saw one leg grow, and another not; if all the parts do not grow proportionably. Ay, but such is the growth of many in religion. They grow like rickety children, who have a big head, but a slender body: they get more knowledge into their heads, but no more holiness into their hearts and lives. They grow very hot outwardly, but very cold inwardly; like men in the fit of the ague. They are more taken up about the externals of religion than formely; yet as great strangers to the power of godliness as ever. If a garden is watered with the hand, some of the plants will readily get much, some little, some no water at all;

Head II. *Of the Union between Christ and Believers.* 263
and therefore some wither, while others are coming forward: but after a shower from the clouds, all come forward together. In like manner, all the graces of the Spirit grow proportionably, by the special influences of divine grace. The branches ingrafted in Christ, growing aright, do grow in all the several ways of growth at once. They grow inward, growing into Christ, (Eph. iv. 15.) uniting more closely with him; and cleaving more firmly to him as the head of influences, which is the spring of all other true Christian growth. They grow outward in good works, in their life and conversation. They not only, with Naphtali, give goodly words; but, like Joseph, they are fruitful boughs. They grow upward in heavenly mindedness, and contempt of the world; for their conversation is in heaven, Phil. iii. 20. And, finally, they grow downward in humility and self-loathing. The branches of the largest growth in Christ, are, in their own eyes, less than the least of all saints, Eph. iii. 8. the chief of sinners, 1 Tim. i. 15. more brutish than any man, Prov. xxx. ii. They see that they cannot do any thing, no, not so much as to think any thing as of themselves, 2 Cor. iii. 5. that they deserve nothing, being not worthy of the least of all the mercies shewed unto them, Gen. xxx. 10. and that they are nothing, 2 Cor. xii. 2.

A sixth benefit is fruitfulness. The branch ingrafted into Christ is not barren, but brings forth fruit, John xv. 5. *He that abideth in me, and I in him, the same bringeth forth much fruit.* For that very end are souls married to Christ, that they may bring forth fruit unto God, Rom. vii. 4. They may be branches in Christ, by profession, but not by real implantation, that are barren branches. Whoever is united to Christ, brings forth the fruit of gospel obedience, and true holiness. Faith is always followed with good works. The believer is not only come out of the grave of his natural state; but he has put off his grave-cloaths, namely, reigning lusts, in the which he walked like a ghost; being dead while he lived in them, Col. iii. 7, 8. For Christ has said of him as of Lazarus, *Loose him, and let him go,* now he has put on Christ; he personates him (so to speak) as a beggar, in borrowed robes, represents a king on the stage, walking as he also walked. Now the fruit of the Spirit in him, is in all goodness, Eph. v. 9. The fruits of holiness will be found in the hearts, lips, and lives of those who are united to Christ. The hidden man of the heart is not only a temple built for God, and consecrated to him; but used and employed for him, where love, fear, trust, and all other parts of unseen religion are exercised, Phil. iii. 3. For we are the circumcision, which worship God in the Spirit. The heart is no more the devil's common, where thoughts go free; for there even vain thoughts are hated, Psal. cxix. 113. But it is God's inclosure, hedged about as a garden for him, Cant. iv. 16. It is true, there are weeds of corruption, because the ground is not perfectly healed: but the man, in the day of his new creation, is set to dress it, and keep it. A live coal from the altar has touched his lips, and they are purified, Psal. xv. 1, 2, 3. *Lord, who shall abide in thy tabernacle? who shall dwell in thy holy hill? He that speaketh the truth in his heart: he that backbiteth not with his tongue, nor taketh up a reproach against his neighbour.* There may be, indeed, a smooth tongue, where there is a false heart. The voice may be Jacob's, while the hands are Esau's. *If any man among you seem to be religious, and bridleth not his tongue, but deceiveth his own heart, this man's religion is vain,* James i. 26. The power of godliness will rule over the tongue, though a world of iniquity. If one be a Galilean, his speech will bewray him; he will speak, not the language of Ashdod, but the language of Canaan: he will neither be dumb in religion, nor will his tongue walk at random, seeing to the double guard, which nature hath given the tongue, grace hath added a third. The fruits of holiness will be found in his outward conversation; for he hath clean hands, as well as a pure heart, Psal. xxiv. 4. He is a godly man, and religiously discharges the duties of the first table of the law: he is a righteous man, and honestly performs the duties of the second table. In his conversation he is a good Christian, and a good neighbour too. He carries it towards God, as if men's

Head II. *Of the Union between Christ and Believers.* 265

eyes were upon him; and towards men, as believing God's eye to be upon him. Those things which God hath joined in his law, he dares not in his practice put asunder.

Thus the branches in Christ are full of good fruits. And those fruits are a cluster of vital actions, whereof Jesus Christ is the principle and end: the principle; for he lives in them, and the life they live is by faith in the Son of God, Gal. ii. 20. The end, for they live to him, and to them to live is Christ, Philip. i. 21. The duties of religion are in the world, like fatherless children, in rags: some will not take them in, because they never loved them, nor their Father: some take them in, because they may be serviceable to them: but the saints take them in for their Father's sake, that is, for Christ's sake; and they are lovely in their eyes, because they are like him. O! whence is this new life of the saints! Surely it could never have been hammered out of the natural powers of their souls, by the united force of all created power. In eternal barrenness would their womb have been shut up; but that being married to Christ, they bring forth fruit unto God, Rom. vii. 4.

If you ask me, "How your nourishment, growth, and fruitfulness may be forwarded?" I offer this advice. (1.) Make sure work, as to your knitting with the stock, by faith unfeigned; and beware of hypocrisy: a branch that is not found at the heart, will certainly wither. The trees of the Lord's planting are trees of righteousness, Isa. lxi. 3. So when others fade, they bring forth fruit. Hypocrisy is a disease in the vitals of religion, which will consume all at length. It is a leak in the ship, that will certainly sink it. Sincerity of grace will make it lasting, be it ever so weak: as the smallest twig, that is found at the heart, will draw nourishment from the stock, and grow; while the greatest bough that is rotten, can never recover, because it receives no nourishment. (2.) Labour to be stedfast in the truths and way of God. An unsettled and wavering judgment, is a great enemy to Christian growth and fruitfulness, as the apostle teaches, Eph.

M m

iv. 14, 15. *That we henceforth be no more children tossed to and fro, and caried about with every wind of doctrine: but speaking the truth in love, may grow up into him in all things, which is the head, even Christ.* A rolling stone gathers no moss, and a wavering judgment makes a fruitless life. Though a tree be never so sound, yet how can it grow, or be fruitful, if you be still removing it out of one soil into another? (3.) Endeavour to cut off the suckers, as gardeners do, that their trees may thrive. These are unmortified lusts; therefore *mortify your members that are upon the earth*, Col. iii. 5. When the Israelites got meat to their lusts, they got leanness to their souls. She that has many hungry children about her hand, and must be still putting into their mouths, will have much ado to get a bit put into her own. They must refuse the cravings of inordinate affections, who would have their souls to prosper. *Lastly*, Improve, for these ends, the ordinances of God. The courts of our God are the place where the trees of righteousness flourish, Psal. xcii. 13. The waters of the sanctuary are the means appointed of God to cause his people to grow as willows by the water courses. Therefore drink in with *desire the sincere milk of the word, that ye may grow thereby*, 1 Pet. ii. 2. Come to these wells of salvation; not to look at them only, but to draw water out of them. The sacrament of the Lord's supper is in a special manner appointed for these ends. It is not only a solemn public profession, and a seal of our union and communion with Christ; but it is a means of most intimate communion with him; and strengthens our union with him, our faith and love, repentance, and other graces, 1 Cor. x. 16. *The cup of blessing which we bless, is it not the communion of the blood of Christ? the bread which we break, is it not the communion of the body of Christ?* And chap. xii. 13. *We have been all made to drink into one Spirit.* Give yourselves unto prayer; open your mouths wide, and he will fill them. By these means the branches in Christ may be further nourished, grow up, and bring forth much fruit.

A seventh benefit is, the acceptance of their fruits of holiness before the Lord. Though they be very im-

Head II. *Of the Union between Christ and Believers.* 267
perfect, they are accepted, becaufe they favour of Christ, the bleſſed ſtock, which the branches grow upon; while the fruits of others are rejected of God, Gen. iv. 4, 5. *The Lord had reſpect unto Abel, and to his offering; but unto Cain and his offering he had no reſpect.* Comp. Heb. xi. 3. *By faith Abel offered unto God a more excellent ſacrifice than Cain.* O how defective are the ſaints du‑ ties in the eye of the law! The believer himſelf eſpies many faults in his beſt performances; yet the Lord graciouſly receives them. There is no grace planted in the heart, but there is a weed of corruption hard by its ſide, while the ſaints are in this lower world. Their very ſincerity is not without mixture of diſſimulation or hypocriſy, Gal. ii. 13. Hence there are defects in the exerciſe of every grace; in the performance of every duty: depraved nature always drops ſomething to ſtain their beſt works. There is ſtill a mixture of darkneſs with their cleareſt light. Yet this does not marr their acceptance, Cant. vi. 10. *Who is ſhe that looketh forth as the morning?* or as the dawning? Behold how Chriſt's ſpouſe is eſteemed and accepted of her Lord, even when ſhe looks forth as the morning, whoſe beauty is mixed with the blackneſs of the night! *When the morning was looking out,* as the word is, Judges xix. 26. i. e. *In the dawning of the day,* as we read it. So the very dawning of grace and good-will to Chriſt, grace peeping out from under a maſs of darkneſs in believers, is pleaſant and acceptable to him, as the break of day is to the weary traveller. Though the remains of unbelief make the hand of faith to ſhake and tremble; yet the Lord is ſo well pleaſed with it, that he employs it to carry away pardons and ſupplies of grace from the throne of grace, and the fountain of grace. His faith was effectual, who *cried out, and ſaid with tears, Lord, I believe, help thou mine unbelief,* Mark ix. 24. Though the remains of ſenſual affections make the flame of their love weak and ſmoky, he turns his eyes from the ſmoke, and beholds the flame, how fair it is, Cant. iv. 10. *How fair is thy love, my ſiſter, my ſpouſe! The ſmell of their* under *garment,* of inherint holineſs, as imperfect as it is, *is like the ſmell*

of Lebanon, ver. 11. and that becaufe they are covered with their elder brother's cloaths, which makes the fons of God to *fmell as a field which the Lord hath bleſſed.* Their good works are accepted : their cups of cold water, given to a difciple in the name of a difciple, fhall not want a reward. Though they cannot offer for the tabernacle, gold, filver, and brafs, and onyx-ſtones, let them come forward with what they have ; if it were but goats-hair, it fhall not be rejected : if it were but ram-ſkins, they fhall be kindly accepted ; for they are dyed red, dipped by faith in the Mediator's blood, and fo prefented unto God. A very ordinary work done in faith, and from faith, if it were but the building of a wall about the city, is a great work, Neh. vi. 3. If it were but the beſtowing of a box of ointment on Chriſt, it fhall never be forgotten, Mat. xxvi. 13. Even *a cup of cold water only, given to one of Chriſt's little ones, in the name of a difciple, ſhall be rewarded,* Mat. x. 42. Nay, not a good word for Chriſt fhall drop from their mouths, but it fhall be regiſtered in God's *book of remembrance,* Mal. iii. 16. Nor fhall a tear drop from their eyes for him, but he will put it in his bottle, Pfal. lvi. 8. Their will is accepted for the deed ; their forrow for the want of will, for the will itfelf, 2 Cor. viii. 12. *For if there be firſt a willing mind, it is accepted according to that a man hath, and not according to that he hath not.* Their groanings, when they cannot well word their defires, are heard in heaven ; the meaning of thofe groans is well known there, and they will be returned like the dove, with an olive branch of peace in her mouth. See Rom. vii. 26, 27. Their mites are better than other men's talents. Their lifping and broken fentences are more pleafant to their Father in heaven, than the moſt fluent and flouriſhing fpeeches of thofe that are not in Chriſt. Their voice is fweet, even when they are afhamed it fhould be heard ; their countenance is comely, even when they bluſh, and draw a veil over it, Cant. iii. 14. The Mediator takes their petitions, blots out fome parts, rectifies others, and then prefents them to the Father, in confequence whereof they pafs in the court of heaven.

Head II. *Of the Union between Chrift and Believers.* 269

Every true Chriftian is a temple to God. If you look for facrifices, they are not wanting there; they offer the facrifice of praife, and do good, with fuch facrifices God is well pleafed, Heb. xiii. 15, 16. Chrift himfelf is the altar that fanctifies the gift, ver. 10. But what comes of the fkins and dung of their facrifices? they are carried away without the camp. If we look for incenfe, it is there too. The graces of the Spirit are found in their hearts: and the Spirit of the crucified Chrift fires them, and puts them in exercife; as the fire was brought from the altar of burnt-offering, to fet the incenfe in a flame; then they mount heaven-ward, like pillars of fmoke, Cant. iii. 6. But the beft of incenfe will leave afhes behind it: yes, indeed; but as the prieft took away the afhes of the incenfe in a golden-difh, and threw them out; fo our great High-prieft takes away the afhes and refufe of all the faint's fervices, by his meditation in their behalf.

An eighth benefit, flowing from union with Chrift, is eftablifhment. The Chriftian cannot fall away, but muft perfevere unto the end, John x. 28. *They fhall never perifh, neither fhall any man pluck them out of my hand.* Indeed, if a branch do not knit with the ftock, it will fall away when fhaking winds arife: but the branch knit to the ftock ftands faft, whatever winds blows. Sometimes a ftormy wind of temptation blows from hell, and tofleth the brauches in Chrift the true vine: but their union with him, is their fecurity; moved they may be, but removed they never can be. The Lord *will with the temptation alfo make a way to efcape,* 1 Cor. x. 13. Calms are never of any continuance: there is almoft always fome wind blowing; and therefore branches are rarely altogether at reft. But fometimes violent winds arife, which threaten to rend them from off their ftock. Even fo it is with faints; they are daily put to it to keep their ground againft temptation: fometimes the wind from hell rifeth fo high, and blows fo furioufly, that it makes even top-branches to fweep the ground; yet being knit to Chrift, their ftock, they get up again, in fpight of the moft violent efforts of the prince of the power of the air, Pfal. xciv. 18. *When I faid my foot flippeth, thy mercy, O Lord, held me up.* But the Chriſtian improves by this trial; and is ſo far from being damaged, that he is benefited by it, as it diſcovers what hold the ſoul has of Chriſt, and what hold Chriſt has of the ſoul. As the wind in the bellows, which would blow out the candle, blows up the fire: even ſo it often comes to paſs, that ſuch temptations enliven the true Chriſtian, awakening the graces of the Spirit in him; and, by that means, diſcover both the reality and the ſtrength of grace in him. And hence, as Luther, that great man of God ſaith, " One Chriſtian, who hath had experience of temptation, is worth a thouſand others."

Sometimes a ſtormy wind of trouble and perſecution, from the men of the world, blows upon the vine, *i. e.* myſtical Chriſt: but union with the ſtock is a ſufficient ſecurity to the branches. In a time of the church's peace, and outward proſperity, while the angels hold the winds that they blow not, there are a great many branches taken up, and put into the ſtock, which never knit with it, nor live by it, though they be bound up with it, by the bonds of external ordinances. Now theſe may ſtand a while on the ſtock, and ſtand with great eaſe while the calm laſts. But when once the ſtorms ariſe, and the winds blow, they will begin to fall off one after another: and the higher the wind riſeth, the greater will the number be that falls. Yea, ſome ſtrong boughs of that ſort, when they fall, will, by their weight, carry others of their own kind quite down to the earth with them; and will bruiſe and preſs down ſome true branches in ſuch a manner, that they would alſo fall off, were it not for their being knit to the ſtock; in virtue whereof they get up their heads again, and cannot fall off, becauſe of that faſt hold which the ſtock has of them. Then it is that many branches, which before were high and eminent, are found lying on the earth withered, and fit to be gathered up and caſt into the fire, Matth. xiii. 6. *When the ſun was up, they were ſcorched: becauſe they had no root, they withered away.* John xv. 6. *If a man abide not in me, he is caſt forth as a branch, and is withered, and men gather them, and caſt*

Head II. *Of the Union between Christ and Believers.* 271

them into the fire, and they are burned. But however violently the winds blow, not any of the truly ingrafted branches, that are knit with the stock, are found missing, when the storm is changed into a calm, John xvii. 12. *Those that thou gavest me I have kept, and none of them is lost.* The least twig growing in Christ shall stand it out and subsist; when the tallest cedars growing on their own root, shall be laid flat on the ground, Rom. viii. 35. " Who shall separate us from the love " of Christ? shall tribulation, or distress, or persecu- " tion, or famine, or nakedness, or peril, or sword?" See ver. 36, 37, 38, 39. However severely Israel be *sifted, yet shall not the least grain* (or as it is in the original language, *a little stone) fall upon the earth,* Amos ix. 9. It is an allusion to the sifting of fine peble stones from among heaps of dust and sand; though the sand and dust fall to the ground, be blown away with the wind, and trampled under foot, yet there shall not fall on the earth so much as a little stone, such is the exactness of the sieve, and care of the sifter. There is nothing more ready to fall on the earth than a stone: yet, if professors of religion be lively stones, built on Christ, the chief corner stone, although they be little stones, they shall not fall to the earth, whatever storm beat upon them. See 1 Pet. ii. 4, 5, 6. All the good grain in the church of Christ is of this kind; they are stones, in respect of solidity, and lively stones, in respect of activity. If men be solid substantial Christians, they will not be like chaff, tossed to and fro with every wind; having so much of the liveliness, that they have nothing of the stone: and if they be lively Christians, whose spirit will stir in them, as Paul's did, when he saw the city wholly given to idolatry, Acts xvii. 16. they will not lie like stones, to be turned over, hither and thither, cut and carved, according to the lusts of men; having so much of the stones as leaves nothing of liveliness in them.

Our God's house is a great house, wherein are not only vessels of gold, but also of earth, 2 Tim. ii. 20. Both these are apt to contract filthiness; and therefore when God brings trouble upon the church, he hath an eye to both. As for the vessels of gold, they are not

272 *Of the Union between Christ and Believers.* State III.

destroyed, but purged by a fiery trial, in the furnace of affliction, as gold-smiths purge their gold, Isa. i. 25. *I will turn my hand upon thee, and purely purge away thy dross.* But destruction is to the vessels of earth; they shall be broken in shivers, as a potter's vessel, ver. 28. *And the destruction* (or *breaking*) *of the transgressors and of the sinners shall be together.* It seems to be an allusion to that law for breaking the vessels of earth, when unclean; while vessels of wood, and consequently vessels of gold, were only to be rinsed, Lev. xv. 12.

A ninth benefit is support. If thou be a branch ingrafted in Christ, the root beareth thee. The believer leans on Christ, as a weak woman in a journey, leaning upon her beloved husband, Cant. viii. 5. He stays himself upon him, as a feeble old man stays himself on his staff, Isa. l. 10. He rolls himself on him, as one rolls a burden, he is not able to walk under, off his own back, upon another who is able to bear it, Psal. xxii. 8. marg. There are many weights to hang upon, and press down the branches in Christ the true vine. But you know whatever weights hang on the branches, the stock bears all; it bears the branch and the weight that is upon it too.

First, Christ supports believers in him under a weight of outward troubles. This is a large promise, Isa. xliii. 2. *When thou passest through the waters, I will be with thee: and through the rivers, they shall not overflow thee.* See how David was supported under a heavy load, 1 Sam. xxx. 6. His city Ziklag was burnt, his wives were taken captives, his men spoke of stoning him: nothing was left him but his God and his faith; but by his faith he encouraged himself in his God. The Lord comes, and lays his cross on his people's shoulders; it presseth them down, they are like to sink under it, and therefore cry, *Master, save us, we perish:* but he supports them under their burden; he bears them up, and they bear their cross. Thus the Christian, with a weight of outward troubles upon him, goes lightly under his burden, having the everlasting arms underneath him. The Christian has a spring of comfort, which he cannot lose; and therefore never wants something to support him. If a

Head II. *Of the Union between Christ and Believers.* 273
man has all his riches in money, robbers may take these away; and then what has he more? But though the landed man be robbed of his money, yet his lands remain for his support. They that build their comfort on worldly goods, may quickly be comfortless: but they that are united to Christ shall find comfort, when all the streams of worldly enjoyments are dried up, Job vi. 13. *Is not my help in me? And is wisdom driven quite from me? q. d.* Though my substance is gone; though my servants, my children, my health, and soundness of body, are all gone; yet my grace is not gone too. Though the Sabeans have driven away my oxen and asses, and the Chaldeans have driven away my camels, they have not driven away my faith, and my hope too; these are yet in me, they are not driven from me; so that by them I can fetch comfort from heaven, when I can have none from earth.

Secondly, Christ supports his people under a weight of inward troubles and discouragements. Many times heart and flesh fail them, but then God is the strength of their heart, Psal. lxxiii. 26. They may have a weight of guilt pressing them. This is a load that will make the back bend, and the spirits sink: but he takes it off, and puts a pardon in their hand: while they cast their burden upon him. Christ takes the soul, as one marries a widow under a burden of debt; and so when the creditors come to Christ's spouse, she carries them to her husband, confesseth the debt, declares she is not able to pay, and lays all upon him. The Christian sometimes, through carelesness loseth his discharge; he cannot find it, however he search for it. The law takes that opportunity, and proceeds against him, for a debt paid already. God hides his face, and the soul is distressed. Many arrows go through the heart now; many long accounts are laid before the man, which he reads and acknowledges. Often does he see the officers coming to apprehend him, and the prison door open to receive him. What else keeps him from sinking utterly under discouragements in this case, but the everlasting arms of a Mediator underneath him, and that he relies upon the great Surety? Further, they
N n

may have a weight of ſtrong luſts preſſing them. They have a body of death upon them. Death is a weight that preſſeth the ſoul out of the body. A leg or an arm of death (if I may ſo ſpeak) would be a terrible load. (One lively luſt will ſometimes lie ſo heavy on a child of God, that he can no more remove it than a child could throw a giant from off him.) How then are they ſupported under a whole body of death? Their ſupport is from the root that bears them, from the everlaſting arm that is underneath them. His grace is ſufficient for them, 2 Cor. xii. 9. The great ſtay of the believer is not the grace of God within him; that is a well whoſe ſtreams ſometimes run dry: but it is the grace of God without him, the grace that is in Jeſus Chriſt; which is an ever-flowing fountain, to which the believer can never come amiſs. For the apoſtle tells us in the ſame verſe, it is *the power of Chriſt. Moſt gladly therefore*, ſaith he, *will I rather glory in my infirmities, that the power of Chriſt may reſt upon me*, or *tabernacle above me*, as the cloud of glory did on the Iſraelites, which God ſpread for a covering or ſhelter to them in the wildernefs, Pſal. cv. 39. compare Iſa. iv. 5, 6. So that the believer, in this combat, like the eagle, firſt flies aloft (by faith), and then comes down to the prey, Pſal. xxxiv. 5. *They looked to him, and were lightened.* Finally, They have a weight of weakneſs and wants upon them, but they caſt over that burden on the Lord, their ſtrength, and he ſuſtains them, Pſal. lv. 22. With all their wants and weakneſs, they are caſt upon him; as the poor, weak, and naked babe, coming out of the womb, is caſt into the lap of one appointed to take care of it, Pſal. xxii. 10. Though they be deſtitute (as a ſhrub in the wildernefs, which the foot of every beaſt may tread down) the Lord will regard them, Pſal. cii. 17. It is no marvel, that the weakeſt plant be ſafe in a garden: but our Lord Jeſus Chriſt is a hedge for protection to his weak and deſtitute ones, even in a wildernefs.

Object. But if the ſaints be ſo ſupported, how is it that they fall ſo often, under temptations and diſcouragements? *Anſw.* (1.) How long ſoever they fall at any time, they never fall off; and that is a great matter. They are *kept by the power of God, through faith unto falvation*, 1 Pet. i. 5. Hypocrites may fall, fo as to fall off, and fall into the pit, as a bucket falls into a well when the chain breaks. But though the child of God may fall, and that fo low as the waters go over his head; yet there is ſtill a bond of union between Chriſt and him; the chain is not broken; he will not go to the ground; he will be drawn up again, Luke xxii. 31, 32. *The Lord faid, Simon, Simon, Satan hath defired to have you, that he may fift you as wheat ; but I have prayed for thee, that thy faith fail not.* (2.) The falls of the faints flow from their not improving their union with Chriſt, their not making uſe of him by faith, for ſtaying or bearing them up, Pſal. xxvi. 13. *I had fainted, unleſs I had believed.* While the nurſe holds the child in her arms, it cannot fall to the ground: yet if the unwary child hold not by her, it may fall backwards in her arms, to its great hurt. Thus David's fall broke his bones, Pſal. li. 8. but it did not break the bond of union between Chriſt and him: the Holy Spirit, the bond of that union, was not taken from him, ver. 11.

The laſt benefit I ſhall name, is, the ſpecial care of the huſbandman, John xv. 12. *I am the true vine, and my Father is the huſbandman. Every branch that beareth fruit he purgeth, that it may bring forth more fruit.* Believers, by virtue of their union with Chriſt, are the objects of God's ſpecial care and providence. Myſtical Chriſt is God's vine; other ſocieties in the world are but wild olive-trees. The men of the world are but God's out-field; the faints are his vineyard, which he has a ſpecial property in, and a ſpecial concern for, Cant. viii. 12. *My vineyard, which is mine, is before me.* He that ſlumbers not nor ſleeps, is the keeper of it; he does keep it; left any hurt it, he will keep it night and day: he, in whoſe hands is the dew of heaven, will water it every moment, Iſa. xxvii. 3. He dreſſeth and purgeth it, in order to further fruitfulneſs, John xv. 2. He cuts off the luxuriant twigs, that mar the fruitfulneſs of the branch. This is done, eſpecially by the word, and by the croſs, or afflictions; the faints need the miniſtry of the word, as much as the vineyard needeth one to dreſs and prune the vines, 1 Cor. iii. 9. *We are labourers together with God; ye are God's huſbandry, ye are God's building.* And they need the croſs too, 1 Pet. i. 6.

Therefore, if we were to reckon the croſs amongſt the benefits flowing to belivevers from their union with Chriſt, I judge that we ſhould not reckon amiſs. Sure I am, in their ſufferings they ſuffer with him, Rom. viii. 17. The aſſurances which they have of the croſs, have rather the nature of a promiſe than of a threatening, Pſal. lxxxix. 30—33. *If his children forſake my law, then will I viſit their tranſgreſſion with the rod, and their iniquity with ſtripes. Nevertheleſs, my loving kindneſs will I not utterly take from him, nor ſuffer my faithfulneſs to fail.* This looks like a tutor's engaging to a dying father, to take care of the children left with him, and to give them both nurture and admonition for their good. The covenant of grace truly beats the ſpears of affliction into pruning hooks, to them that are in Chriſt, Iſa. xxvii. 9. *By this, therefore, ſhall the iniquity of Jacob be purged, and this is all the fruit, to take away his ſin.* Why, then, ſhould we be angry with our croſs? why ſhould we be frightened at it? The believer muſt take up his croſs, and follow his Leader, the Lord Jeſus Chriſt. He muſt take up his every day's croſs, Luke ix. 23. *If any man will come after me, let him deny himſelf, and take up his croſs daily.* Yea, he muſt take up his holy-days croſs too, Lam. iii. 22. *Thou haſt called, as in a ſolemn day, my terrors round about.* The church of the Jews had, for a long time, many a pleaſant meeting at the temple, on ſolemn days, for the worſhip of God; but they got a ſolemnity of another nature, when God called together, about the temple and city, the Chaldean army, that burnt the temple, and laid Jeruſalem on heaps. And as the church of God is yet militant in this lower region, how can it be but the clouds will return after the rain? But the croſs of Chriſt (which name the ſaint's troubles do bear) is a kindly name to the believer. It is a croſs indeed; not to the believer's graces, but to his corruptions. The hypocrite's ſeeming graces may indeed breathe out their last on a cross, as those of the stony-ground hearers did, Matt. xiii. 6. *When the sun* (of persecution, ver. 21.) *was up, they were scorched: and because they had not root, they withered away.* But never did one of the real graces in a believer die upon the cross yet. Nay, as the candle shines brightest in the night, and the fire burns fiercest in intense frost; so the believer's graces are ordinarily most vigorous in a time of trouble.

There is a certain pleasure and sweetness in the cross, to them who have their senses exercised to discern, and to find it out. There is a certain sweetness in a man's seeing himself upon his trials for heaven, and standing candidate for glory. There is a pleasure in travelling over those mountains, where the Christian can see the prints of Christ's own feet, and the footsteps of the flock, who have been there before him. How pleasant is it to a saint, in the exercise of grace, to see how a good God crosseth his corrupt inclinations, and prevents his folly! How sweet is it to behold those thieves upon the cross! How refined a pleasure is there in observing how God draws away provision from unruly lusts, and so pincheth them, that the Christian may get them governed! Of a truth, there is a paradise within this thorn-hedge. Many a time the people of God are in bonds, which are never loosed, till they be bound with cords of affliction. God takes them, and throws them into a fiery furnace, that burns off their bonds; and then, like the three children, Dan. iii. 25. they are loose, walking in the midst of the fire. God gives his children a portion with one bitter ingredient; if that will not work upon them, he will put in a second, a third, and so on, as there is need, that they may work together for their good, Rom. viii. 28. With cross-winds he hastens them to their harbour. They are often found in such ways, as that the cross is the happiest foot they can meet with: well may they salute it, as David did Abigail, saying, *Blessed be the Lord God of Israel, which sent thee this day to meet me,* 1 Sam. xxv. 32. Worldly things are often such a load to the Christian, that he moves but very slowly heaven-ward. God sends a wind of trouble that blows the burden off the man's back, and then he walks more speedily on his way, after God hath drawn some gilded earth from him, that was drawing his heart away from God, Zeph. iii. 12. *I will also leave in the midst of thee, an afflicted and poor people, and they shall trust in the name of the Lord.* It was an observation of an Heathen moralist, " That no history makes mention of any " man who hath been made better by riches." I doubt whether our modern histories can supply the defect of ancient histories in this point. But sure I am, many have been the worse for riches: thousands have been hugged to death, in the embraces of a smiling world; and many good men have got wounds from outward prosperity, that must be cured by the cross. I remember to have read of one, who having an impostume in his breast, had in vain used the help of physicians: but being wounded with the sword, the impostume broke; and his life was saved by that accident, which threatened immediate death. Often have spiritual impostumes gathered in the breasts of God's people, in time of outward prosperity, and been thus broken and discussed by the cross. It is kindly for believers to be healed by stripes: although they are usually so weak as to cry out for fear, at the sight of the pruning hook, as if it were the destroying ax; and to think that the Lord is coming to kill them, when he is indeed coming to cure them.

I shall now conclude, addressing myself in a few words, first to saints, and next to sinners.

I. To you that are saints, I say,

First, Strive to obtain and keep up actual communion and fellowship with Jesus Christ; that is, to be still deriving fresh supplies of grace, from the fountain thereof in him, by faith: making suitable returns of them, in the exercise of grace and holy obedience. Beware of estrangement between Christ and your souls. If it has got in already (which seems to be the case of many this day), endeavour to get it removed. There are multitudes in the world that slight Christ, though you should not slight him: Many have turned their

Head II. *Of the Union between Christ and Believers.* 279
backs on him, that looked fair for heaven. The warm sun of outward peace and prosperity, has caused some to cast their cloak of religion from them, who held it fast when the wind of trouble was blowing upon them: and *will ye also go away?* John vi. 67. The basest ingratitude is stampt on your slighting of communion with Christ, Jer. ii. 31. *Have I been a wilderness unto Israel: a land of darkness: wherefore say my people, We are lords, we will come no more unto thee?* Oh! beloved, *is this your kindness to your friend?* It is unbecoming any wife to slight converse with her husband, but her especially who was taken from a prison or a dunghill, as you were, by your Lord. But remember, I pray you, this is a very ill chosen time to live at a distance from God: it is a time in which Divine Providence frowns upon the land we live in; the clouds of wrath are gathering, and are thick above our heads? It is not a time for you to be out of your chambers, Isa. xxvi. 20. They that now are walking most closely with God, may have enough to do to stand when the trial comes: how hard will it be for others then, who are like to be surprised with troubles, when guilt is lying on their consciences unremoved! To be awakened out of a sound sleep, and cast into a raging sea, as Jonah was, will be a fearful trial. To feel trouble before we see it coming, to be past hope before we have any fear, is a very sad case. Wherefore break down your idols of jealousy, mortify these lusts, these irregular appetites and desires, that have stolen away your hearts, and left you like Sampson, without his hair, and say, *I will go and return to my first husband; for then was it better with me than now,* Hos. ii. 7.

Secondly, Walk as becomes those that are united to Christ. Evidence your union with him, by walking as he also walked, 1 John ii. 6. If you be brought from under the power of darkness, let your light shine before men. Shine as lights in the world, holding forth the word of life, as the lanthorn holds the candle, which being in it, shines through it, Philip. ii. 15, 16. Now that you profess Christ to be in you, let his image shine forth in your conversation, and remember that the bu-

280 *Of the Union between Christ and Believers.* State III.
finefs of your lives is, to prove by practical arguments what you profefs.

1. You know the character of a wife, *she that is married, careth how she may pleafe her hufband.* Go you and do likewife ; *walk worthy of the Lord unto all pleafing,* Col. i. 10. This is the great bufinefs of life : you muft pleafe him, though it fhould difpleafe all the world. What he hates muft be hateful to you, becaufe he hates it. Whatever lufts come in fuit of your hearts, deny them, feeing the grace of God has appeared, teaching us fo to do, and you are joined to the Lord. Let him be a covering to your eyes ; for you have not your choice to make, it is made already ; and you muft not difhonour your head. A man takes care of his feet, becaufe, if he catches cold there it flies up to his head. *Shall I take the members of Christ, and make them the members of an harlot ? God forbid,* fays the apoftle, 1 Cor. vi. 15. Wilt thou take that heart of thine, which is Chrift's dwelling place, and lodge his enemies there ? Wilt thou take that body, which is his temple, and defile it, by ufing the members thereof as inftruments of fin ?

2. Be careful to bring forth fruit, and much fruit. The branch well laden with fruit, is the glory of the vine, and of the hufbandman too, John xv. 8. *Herein is my Father glorified, that ye bear much fruit, fo shall ye be my difciples* A barren tree ftands fafer in a wood than in an orchard ; and branches in Chrift, that bring not forth fruit, will be taken away, and caft into the fire.

3. Be heavenly-minded, and maintain a holy contempt of the world. You are united to Chrift, he is your Head and Hufband, and is in heaven : wherefore your hearts fhould be there alfo, Col. iii. 1. *If ye then be rifen with Chrift, feek thofe things which are above, where Christ fitteth on the right hand of God.* Let the ferpent's feed go on their belly, and eat the duft of this earth : but let the members of Chrift be afhamed to bow down, and feed with them.

4. Live and act dependently, depending by faith on Jefus Chrift. That which grows on its own root is a tree, not a branch. It is of the nature of a branch, to

Head II. *Of the Union between Christ and Believers.* 281
depend on the stock for all, and to derive all its sap
from thence. Depend on him for life, light, strength,
and all spiritual benefits, Gal. ii. 20. *I live, yet not I,
but Christ liveth in me, and the life which I now live in the
flesh, I live by the faith of the Son of God.* For this cause,
in the mystical union, strength is united to weakness,
that death and earth may mount up on borrowed
wings. Depend on him for temporal benefits also;
Matth. vi. 2. *Give us this day our daily bread.* If we
have trusted him with our eternal concerns, let us be
ashamed to distrust him in the matter of our provision
in the world.

Lastly, Be of a meek disposition, and an uniting temper with the fellow members of Christ's body, as being united to the meek Jesus, the blessed centre of union. There is a prophecy to this purpose concerning the kingdom of Christ, Isa. ii. 6. *The wolf shall dwell with the lamb; and the leopard shall lie down with the kid.* It is an allusion to the beasts in Noah's ark. The beasts of prey, that were wont to kill and devour others, when once they came into the ark, lay down in peace with them: the lamb was in no hazard by the wolf there; nor the kid, by the leopard. There was a beautiful accomplishment of it in the primitive church, Acts iv. 32. *The multitude of them that believed were of one heart and of one soul.* And this prevails in all the members of Christ, according to the measure of the grace of God in them. Man is born naked, he comes naked into this world, as if God designed him for the picture of peace: and surely, when he is born again, he comes not into the new world of grace with claws to tear, a sword to wound, and a fire in his hand to burn up his fellow-members in Christ, because they cannot see with his light. Oh! it is sad to see Christ's lillies as thorns in one another's side, Christ's lambs devouring one another like lions, and God's diamonds cutting one another: yet it must be remembered, that sin is no proper cement for the members of Christ, though Herod and Pontius Pilate may be made friends that way. The apostle's rule is plain, Heb. xii. 14. *Follow peace with all men, and holiness.* To follow peace no further than our humour, credit, and such like things will allow us, is too short: to pursue it farther than holiness, that is, conformity to the Divine will, allows us, is too far. Peace is precious, yet it may be bought too dear: wherefore we must rather want it, than purchase it at the expence of truth or holiness. But otherwise it cannot be over dear bought, and it will always be precious in the eyes of the sons of peace.

II. And now, sinners, what shall I say to you? I have given you some view of the privileges of those in the state of grace: you have seen them afar off. But alas! they are not yours, because you are not Christ's. The sinfulness of an unregenerate state is yours; and the misery of it is yours also: you have neither part nor lot in this matter. The guilt of all your sins lies upon you; you have no part in the righteousness of Christ. There is no peace to you, no peace with God, no true peace of conscience: for you have no saving interest in the great Peace-maker. You are none of God's family: the adoption we spoke of belongs not to you. You have no part in the Spirit of sanctification; and, in one word, you have no inheritance among them that are sanctified. All I can say to you in this matter, is, that the case is not desperate, they may yet be yours, Rev. iii. 20. *Behold I stand at the door and knock: if any man hear my voice, and open the door, I will come in to him, and will sup with him, and he with me.* Heaven is proposing an union with earth still, the potter is making suit to his own clay, and the gates of the city of refuge are not yet closed. O that we could compel you to come in!

Thus far of the state of grace.

STATE IV.

NAMELY,

The ETERNAL STATE, or State of confummate Happiness or Misery.

HEAD I.

Of DEATH.

Job xxx. 23. *For I know that thou wilt bring me to death, and to the house appointed for all living.*

I Come now to discourse of man's eternal state, into which he enters by death. Of this entrance Job takes a solemn serious view, in the words of the text, which contain a general truth, and a particular application of it. The general truth is supposed, namely, that all men must, by death, remove out of this world; they must die. But whither must they go? They must go to the house appointed for all living; to the grave, that darksome, gloomy solitary house, in the land of forgetfulness. Wherever the body is laid up till the resurrection, thither, as to a dwelling-house, death brings us home. While we are in the body, we are but in a lodging-house; in an inn, on our way homeward. When we come to our grave, we come to our home, our long-home, Eccl. xii. 5. All living must be inhabitants of this house, good and bad, old and young. Man's life is a stream, running into death's devouring deeps. They who now live in palaces, must quit them, and go home to this house; and they who have not where to lay their heads, shall thus have a house at length. It is apppinted for all, by him whose counsel shall stand. This appointment cannot be shifted; it is a law, which mortals cannot transgress. Job's application of this general truth to himself, is expressed in these words; *I know that thou wilt bring me to death*, &c. He knew that he muſt meet with death, that his ſoul and body muſt part; that God, who had ſet the time, would certainly ſee it kept. Sometimes Job was inviting death to come to him, and carry him home to its houſe; yea, he was in hazard of running to it before the time. Job vii. 15. *My ſoul chooſeth ſtrangling and death, rather than my life.* But here he conſiders, God would bring him to it, yea, bring him back to it, as the word imports. Whereby he ſeems to intimate, that we have no life in this world, but as run-aways from death, which ſtretcheth out its cold arms to receive us from the womb: but though we do then narrowly eſcape its clutches, we cannot eſcape long; we ſhall be brought back again to it. Job knew this; he had laid it down as fixed, and was looking for it.

DOCTRINE, *All muſt die.*

Although this doctrine be confirmed by the experience of all former generations, ever ſince Abel entered into the houſe appointed for all living; and though the living know that they ſhall die; yet it is needful to diſcourſe of the certainty of death, that it may be impreſſed on the mind, and duly conſidered.

Wherefore conſider, firſt, There is an unalterable ſtatute of death, under which men are concluded. *It is appointed unto men once to die,* Heb. ix. 27. It is laid up for them, as parents lay up for their children: they may look for it, and cannot miſs it; ſeeing God has deſigned and reſerved it for them. There is no peradventure in it; *we muſt needs die,* 2 Sam. xiv. 14. Though ſome men will not hear of death, yet every man muſt ſee death, Pſal. lxxxix. 41. Death is a champion all muſt grapple with: we muſt enter the liſts with it, and it will have the maſtery. Eccl. viii. 8. *There is no man that hath power over the ſpirit, to retain the ſpirit, neither hath he power in the day of death.* They indeed, who are found alive at Chriſt's coming, *ſhall all be changed,* 1 Cor. xv. 51. But that change will be equivalent to death, will anſwer the purpoſes of it. All other perſons muſt go the common road, the way of all fleſh. *Secondly,* Let us conſult daily obſervation.

Every man seeth that wise men die, likewise the fool and brutish person, Psal. xlix. 10. There is room enough on this earth for us; notwithstanding the multitudes that were upon it before us: they are gone to make room for us; as we must depart to leave room for others. It is long since death began to transport men into another world, and vast shoals or multitudes are gone thither already: yet the trade is going on still; death is carrying off new inhabitants daily, to the house appointed for all living. Who could ever hear the grave say, *It is enough?* Long has it been getting, but still it asketh. The world is like a great fair, or market, where some are coming in, others going out; while the assembly that is in it is confused, and the most part know not wherefore they are come together: or like a town situated on the road to a great city, through which some travellers have passed, some are passing, while others are only coming in, Eccl. i. 4. *One generation passeth away, and another generation cometh: but the earth abideth for ever.* Death is an inexorable, irresistible messenger; who cannot be diverted from executing his orders, by the force of the mighty, the bribes of the rich, the entreaties of the poor. It doth not reverence the hoary head, nor pity the harmless babe. The bold and daring cannot out-brave it; nor can the faint-hearted obtain a discharge in this war. *Thirdly,* The human body consists of perishing principles, Gen. iii. 19. *Dust thou art, and unto dust shalt thou return.* The strongest are but brittle earthen vessels, easily broken in shivers. The soul is but meanly housed, while in this mortal body, which is not a house of stone, but a house of clay; the mud walls cannot but moulder away, especially seeing the foundation is not on a rock, but in the dust; they are crushed before the moth, though this insect be so tender, that the gentle touch of a finger will dispatch it, Job iv. 19. These principles are like gun-powder: a very small spark, lighting on them, will set them on fire, and blow up the house. The stone of a raisin, or a hair in milk, have choaked men and laid the house of clay in the dust. If we consider the frame and structure of our bodies, how fearfully and wonderfully we are made ; and on how regular and exact a motion of the fluids, and balance of humours, our life depends ; and that death hath as many doors to enter in by, as the body' hath pores; and if we compare the soul and body together, we may juſtly reckon, there is ſomewhat more aſtoniſhing in our life than in our death ; and that it is more ſtrange, to ſee duſt walking up and down on the duſt, than lying down in it. Though the lamp of our life be not violently blown out ; yet the flame muſt go out at length, for want of oil. What are thoſe diſtempers and diſeaſes which we are liable to, but death's harbingers, that come to prepare his way ? They meet us, as ſoon as we ſet our foot on earth, to tell us, at our entry, that we do but come into the world to go out again. Howbeit, ſome are ſnatched away in a moment, without being warned by ſickneſs or diſeaſe. *Fourthly*, We have ſinful ſouls, and therefore have dying bodies : Death follows ſin, as the ſhadow follows the body. The wicked muſt die, by virtue of the threatening of the covenant of works, Gen. ii. 17. *In the day thou eateſt thereof, thou ſhalt ſurely die.* And the godly muſt die too; that as death entered by ſin, ſin may go out by death. Chriſt has taken away the ſting of death, as to them ; though he has not as yet removed death itſelf. Wherefore, though it faſten on them, as the viper did on Paul's hand, it ſhall do them no harm : but becauſe the leproſy of ſin is in the walls of the houſe, it muſt be broken down, and all the materials thereof carried forth. *Laſtly*, Man's life in this world, according to the Scripture account of it, is but a few degrees removed from death. The Scripture repreſents it as a vain and empty thing, ſhort in its continuance, and ſwift in its paſſing away.

Firſt, Man's life is a vain and empty thing while it is : it vaniſheth away; and lo! it is not, Job vii. 6. *My days are vanity.* If you ſuſpect afflicted Job of partiality in this matter, hear the wiſe and proſperous Solomon's character of the days of his life, Eccl. vii. 15. *All things have I ſeen in the days of my vanity*; i. e. my vain days. Moſes, who was a very active man, com-

Head I. *Of Death.* 287

pares our days to a sleep, Psal. xc. 5. *They are as a sleep*; which is not noticed till it be ended. The resemblance is put: few men have right apprehensions of life, until death awakens them: then we begin to know that we were living. *We spend our years as a tale that is told,* ver. 9. When an idle tale is telling, it may affect a little; but when it is ended, it is forgot, and so is a man forgotten when the fable of his life is ended. It is as a dream, or vision of the night, in which there is nothing solid; when one awakes all vanisheth, Job xx. 8. *He shall fly away as a dream, and shall not be found; yea, he shall be chased away, as a vision in the night.* It is but a vain shew or image, Psal. xxxix. 6. *Surely every man walketh in a vain shew.* Man, in this world, is but as it were a walking statue: his life is but an image of life, there is so much of death in it.

If we look on our life, in the several periods of it, we shall find it a heap of vanities. *Childhood and youth are vanity,* Eccl. xi. 10. We come into the world, the most helpless of all animals; young birds and beasts can do something for themselves, but infant-man is altogether unable to help himself. Our childhood is spent in trifling pleasures, which become the scorn of our after-thoughts. Youth is a flower that soon withereth; a blossom that quickly falls off; it is a space of time in which we are rash, foolish, and inconsiderate, pleasing ourselves with a variety of vanities, and swimming, as it were, through a flood of them. But ere we are aware, it is past; and we are in middle age, encompassed with a thick cloud of cares, through which we must grope; and finding ourselves beset with pricking thorns of difficulties, through them we must force our way, to accomplish the projects and contrivances of our riper thoughts. The more we solace ourselves in any earthly enjoyment which we attain to, the more bitterness do we find in parting with it. Then comes old age, attended with its own train of infirmities, labour and sorrow, Psal. xc. 10. and sets us down next door to the grave. In a word, *All flesh is grass,* Isa. xl. 6. Every stage, or period of life, is vanity. *Man at his best state* (his middle age, when the heat of youth is spent, and the forrows of old age have not yet overtaken him) *is altogether vanity*, Pfal. xxxix. 5. Death carries off fome in the bud of childhood, others in the bloffom of youth, and others when they are come to their fruit; few are left ftanding till, like ripe corn, they forfake the ground : all die one time or other

Secondly, Man's life is a fhort thing : it is not only a vanity, but a fhort-lived vanity. Confider, *Firft*, How the life of man is reckoned in the Scriptures. It was indeed fometimes reckoned by hundreds of years: but no man ever arrived at a thoufand, which yet bears no proportion to eternity. Now, hundreds are brought down to fcores; threefcore and ten, or fourfcore, is its utmoft length, Pfal. xc. 10. But few men arrive at that length of life. Death does but rarely wait till men be bowing down, by reafon of age, to meet the grave. Yet, as if years were too big a word for fuch a fmall thing as the life of man on earth, we find it counted by months, Job xiv. 5. *The number of his months are with thee*. Our courfe, like that of the moon, is run in a little time; we are always waxing or waneing, till we difappear. But frequently it is reckoned by days; and thefe but few, Job xiv. 1. *Man, that is born of a woman, is of few days*. Nay, it is but one day in Scripture account; and that a hireling's day, who will precifely obferve when his day ends, and give over his work, ver. 6. *Till he fhall accomplifh as an hireling his day*. Yea, the Scripture brings it down to the fhorteft fpace of time, and calls it a moment, 2 Cor. iv. 17. *Our light affliction* (though it laft all our life long) *is but for a moment*. Elfewhere it is brought down yet to a lower pitch, farther than which one cannot carry it, Pfal. xxxix. 5. *Mine age is as nothing before thee*. Agreeable to this, Solomon tells us, Eccl. iii. 2. *There is a time to be born, and a time to die*; but makes no mention of a time to live, as if our life were but a fkip from the womb to the grave. *Secondly*, Confider the various fimilitudes by which the Scripture reprefents the fhortnefs of man's life. Hear Hezekiah, Ifa. xxxviii. 12. *Mine age is departed, and is removed from me as a fhepherd's tent; I have cut off like a weaver my life*. The fhepherd's tent is foon

Head I. *Of Death.* 289

removed; for the flocks muſt not feed long in one place: ſuch is a man's life on this earth, quickly gone. It is a web, which he is inceſſantly working; he is not idle ſo much as one moment: in a ſhort time it is wrought, and then it is cut off. Every breathing is a thread in this web; when the laſt breath is drawn, the web is woven out; he expires, and then it is cut off, he breathes no more. Man is like graſs, and like a flower, Iſa. xl. 6. *All fleſh* (even the ſtrongeſt and moſt healthy fleſh) *is graſs, and all the goodlineſs thereof is as the flower of the field.* The graſs is flouriſhing in the morning; but in the evening, being cut down by the mowers, it is withered. So man ſometimes is walking up and down at eaſe in the morning, and in the evening is lying a corpſe, being knocked down by a ſudden ſtroke, with one or other of death's weapons. The flower, at beſt, is but a weak and tender thing, of ſhort continuance, wherever it grows: but (obſerve) man is not compared to the flower of the garden; but to the flower of the field, which the foot of every beaſt may tread down at any time. Thus is our life liable to a thouſand accidents every day; any of which may cut us off. But though we ſhould eſcape all theſe, yet at length this graſs withereth, this flower fadeth of itſelf. It is carried off, *as the cloud is conſumed and vaniſheth away,* Job vii. 9. It looks big as the morning cloud, which promiſeth great things, and raiſeth the expectation of the huſbandman: but the ſun riſeth, and the cloud is ſcattered; death comes, and man vaniſheth. The apoſtle James propoſeth the queſtion, *What is your life?* Chap. iv. 14. Hear his anſwer, *It is even a vapour, that appeareth for a little time, and then vaniſheth away.* It is frail, uncertain, and laſteth not. It is as ſmoke, which goes out of the chimney, as if it would darken the face of the heavens; but quickly is ſcattered, and appears no more: thus goeth man's life, and *where is he?* It is a wind, Job vii. 7. *O remember that my life is wind.* It is but a paſſing blaſt, a ſhort puff, *a wind that paſſeth away, and cometh not again,* Pſal. lxxviii. 39. Our breath is in our noſtrils, as if it were always upon the wing to depart: ever paſſing and repaſſing like a traveller, until it be away, not to return till the heavens be no more.

P p

Lastly, Man's life is a swift thing; not only a passing, but a flying vanity. Have you not observed how swiftly a shadow hath run along the ground, in a cloudy and windy day, suddenly darkening the places beautified before with the beams of the sun, but as suddenly disappearing? Such is the life of man on earth; for *he fleeth as a shadow, and continueth not,* Job xiv. 2. A weaver's shuttle is very swift in its motion; in a moment it is thrown from one side of the web to the other; yet *our days are swifter than a weaver's shuttle,* ch. vii. 6. How quickly is man tossed through time into eternity! see how Job describes the swiftness of the time of life, chap. ix. 25, 26. *Now my days are swifter than a post; they flee away, they see no good. They are hasted away as the swift ships, as the eagle that hasteth to the prey.* He compares his days with a post, a foot-post; a runner, who runs speedily to carry tidings, and will make no stay. But though the post were like Ahimaaz, who over-ran Cushi, our days would be swifter than he; for they flee away, like a man fleeing for his life, before the pursuing enemy; he runs with his utmost vigour, yet our days run as fast as he: yet this is not all; even he who is fleeing for his life cannot run always: he must needs sometimes stand still, lie down, or turn in some where, as Sisera did into Jael's tent, to refresh himself: but our time never halts. Therefore it is compared to ships, which can sail night and day without intermission, till they be at their port; and to swift ships, ships of desire, in which men quickly arrive at their desired haven; or ships of pleasure, that sail more swiftly than ships of burden. Yet the wind failing, the ship's course is marred: but our time always runs with a rapid course. Therefore it is compared to the eagle flying; not with his ordinary flight, for that is not sufficient to represent the swiftness of our days; but when he flies upon his prey, which is with an extraordinary swiftness. And thus, even thus our days flee away.

Having thus discoursed of death, let us improve it, in discerning the vanity of the world, in bearing up, with Christian contentment and patience, under all troubles and difficulties in it, mortifying our lusts, in clearing unto the Lord with full purpose of heart, on all hazards, and in preparing for death's approach.

And *first*, Let us hence, as in a looking-glass, behold the vanity of the world, and of all those things in it which men so much value and esteem, and therefore set their hearts upon. The rich and the poor, are equally intent upon this world; they bow the knee to it; yet it is but a clay-god; they court the bulky vanity, and run keenly to catch this shadow: the rich man is hugged to death in its embraces; and the poor man wearies himself in the fruitless pursuit. (What wonder if the world's smiles overcome us, when we pursue it so eagerly, even while it frowns upon us?) But look into the grave, O man! consider and be wise; listen to the doctrine of death; and learn, (1.) That hold as fast as thou canst, thou shalt be forced to let go thy hold of the world at length. Though thou load thyself with the fruits of this earth, yet all shall fall off, when thou comest to creep into thy hole, the house, under ground, appointed for all living. When death comes, you must bid an eternal farewell to thy enjoyments in this world: thou must leave thy goods to another; and whose shall those things be which thou hast provided? Luke xii. 20. (2.) Thy portion of these things shall be very little ere long. If thou lie down on the grass, and stretch thyself at full length, and observe the print of thy body when thou risest, thou mayest see how much of this earth will fall to thy share at last. It may be thou shalt get a coffin, and a winding-sheet; but thou art not sure of that: many, who have had abundance of wealth, yet have not had so much when they took up their new house in the land of silence. But however that be, more you cannot expect. It was a mortifying lesson Saladine, when dying, gave to his soldiers. He called for his standard-bearer, and ordered him to take his winding-sheet upon his pike, and go out to the camp with it, and tell them, That of all his conquests, victories, and triumphs, he had nothing now left him but that piece of linen to wrap his body in for burial. *Lastly*, This world is a false friend, who leaves a man in time of greatest need; and flees from him when he has moſt to do. When thou art lying on a death-bed, all thy friends and relations cannot reſcue thee; all thy ſubſtance cannot ranſom thee; nor procure thee a reprieve for one day, nay, not for one hour. Yea, the more thou poſſeſſeſt of this world's goods, thy ſorrow at death is like to be the greater: for though one may live more commodiouſly in a palace than in a cottage, yet he may die more eaſily in the cottage, where he has very little to make him fond of life.

Secondly, It may ſerve as a ſtore-houſe, for Chriſtian contentment and patience, under worldly loſſes and croſ-ſes. A cloſe application of the doctrine of death, is an excellent remedy againſt fretting, and gives ſome eaſe to a troubled heart. When Job had ſuſtained very great loſſes, he ſat down contented, with this meditation, Job i. 21. *Naked came I out of my mother's womb, and naked ſhall I return thither: the Lord gave, and the Lord hath taken away, bleſſed be the name of the Lord.* When providence brings a mortality or murrain among your cattle, how ready are you to fret and complain! the ſerious conſideration of your own death (to which you have a notable help from ſuch providential occurrences) may be of uſe to ſilence your complaints, and quiet your ſpirits. Look to the houſe appointed for all living, and learn, (1.) That you muſt abide a ſorer thruſt than the loſs of worldly goods. Do not cry out for a thruſt in the leg or arm; for before long there will be a home-thruſt at the heart. You may loſe your deareſt relations: the wife may loſe her huſband, and the huſband his wife; and the parents may loſe their dear children, and the children their parents: but if any of theſe trials happen to you, remember, you muſt loſe your own life at laſt; and *wherefore doth a living man complain?* Lam. iii. 39. It is always profitable to conſider, under affliction, that our caſe might have been worſe than it is. Whatever be conſumed, or taken from us, *it is of the Lord's mercies that we ourſelves are not conſumed*, ver. 22. (2.) It is but a ſhort ſpace of time that we are to be in this world. It is but a little that our neceſſities require in ſo ſhort ſpace of time: when death comes, we ſhall ſtand in

Head I. *Of Death.* 293

need of none of these things. Why should men rack their heads with cares how to provide for to-morrow; while they know not if they shall need any thing to-morrow. Though a man's provision for his journey be near spent, he is not disquieted, if he thinks that he is near home. Are you working by candle-light, and is there little of your candle left? It may be there is as little sand in your glass; and if so, you have little use for it. (3.) You have matters of great weight, that challenge your care. Death is at the door, beware you lose not your souls. If blood breaks out at one part of the body, they generally open a vein in another part of it, to turn the stream of blood, and to stop it. Thus, the Spirit of God sometimes cures men of sorrow for earthly things, by opening the heart-vein to bleed for sin. Did we pursue heavenly things the more vigorusly that our affairs in this life prosper not, we should thereby gain a double advantage. Our worldly sorrow would be diverted, and our best treasure increased. (4.) Crosses of this nature will not last long. The world's smiles and frowns will quickly be buried together in everlasting forgetfulness. Its smiles go away as the foam on the water: and its frowns are as a passing stitch in a man's side. Time flees away with swift wings, and carries our earthly comforts, and crosses too, along with it: neither of them will accompany us into the house appointed for all living, Job iii. 17, 18, 19. *There the wicked cease from troubling, and there the weary be at rest; there the prisoners rest together, they hear not the voice of the oppressor: the small and great are there, and the servant is free from his master.* Cast a look into eternity, and you will see affliction here is but for a moment. The truth is, our time is so very short, that it will not allow either our joys or griefs to come to perfection. Wherefore, let them that weep be as though they wept not; and they that rejoice, as though they rejoiced not, &c. 1 Cor. vii. 29, 30, 31. (5.) Death will put all men on a level. The king and the beggar must dwell in one house, when they come to their journey's end; though their entertainment by the way be very different. The small and the great are there, Job iii. 19. We are all in this world as on a stage : it is no great matter whether a man act the part of a prince or a peasant ; for when they have acted their parts, they must both get behind the curtain, and appear no more. *Lastly*, If thou be not in Christ, whatever thy afflictions now be, troubles a thousand times worse are abiding thee in another world. Death will turn thy crosses into pure unmixed curses : and then how gladly wouldst thou return to thy former afflicted state, and purchase it at any rate, were there any possibility of such a return? If thou be in Christ, thou mayest well bear thy cross. Death will put an end to all thy troubles. If a man on a journey be not well accommodated, where he lodgeth only for a night, he will not trouble himself much about the matter ; because he is not to stay there, it is not his home. You are on the road to eternity ; let it not disquiet you that you meet with some hardships in the inn of this world. Fret not, because it is not so well with you as with some others. One man travels, with a cane in his hand ; his fellow traveller (perhaps) has but a common staff, or stick : either of them will serve the turn. It is no great matter which of them be yours ; both will be laid aside when you come to your journey's end.

Thirdly, It may serve for a bridle, to curb all manner of lusts, particularly those conversant about the body. A serious visit made to cold death, and that solitary mansion, the grave, might be of good use to repress them.

1*st*, It may be of use to cause men to remit their inordinate care for the body ; which is to many the bane of their souls. Often do these questions, What shall we eat ? What shall we drink ? And, Wherewithall shall we be clothed ? leave no room for another of more importance, *viz.* Wherewith shall I come before the Lord ? The soul is put on the rack, to answer these mean questions, in favour of the body, while its own eternal interests are neglected. But, ah ! why are men so busy to repair the ruinous cottage ; leaving the inhabitant to bleed to death of his wounds, un-

Head I. *Of Death.* 295

heeded, unregarded! Why so much care for the body, to the neglecting of the concerns of the immortal soul? O be not so anxious for what can only serve your bodies; since, ere long, the clods of cold earth will serve for back and belly too.

2dly, It may abate your pride on account of bodily endowments, which vain man is apt to glory in. Value not yourselves on the blossom of youth; for while you are in your blooming years, you are but ripening for a grave: death gives the fatal stroke, without asking any body's age. Glory not in your strength, it will quickly be gone: the time will soon be, when you shall not be able to turn yourselves on a bed; and you must be carried by your grieving friends to your long home. And what signifies your healthful constitution? Death doth not always enter in soonest, where it begins soonest to knock at the door; but makes as great a dispatch with some in a few hours, as with others in many years. Value not yourselves on your beauty, which shall consume in the grave, Psal. xlix. 14. Remember the change which death makes on the fairest face, Job xiv. 20. *Thou changest his countenance, and sendest him away.* Death makes the greatest beauty so loathsome, that it must be buried out of sight. Could a looking glass be used, in the house appointed for all living, it would be a terror to those who now look oftener into their glasses than into their Bibles. And what though the body be gorgeously arrayed? The finest clothes are but badges of our sin and shame; and in a little time will be exchanged for a winding-sheet; when the body will become a feast to the worms.

3dly, It may be a check upon sensuality and fleshly lusts, 1 Pet. ii. 11. *I beseech you as strangers and pilgrims, abstain from fleshly lusts, which war against the soul.* It is hard to cause wet wood to take fire; and when the fire doth take hold of it, it is soon extinguished. Sensuality makes men most unfit for divine communications, and is an effectual means to quench the Spirit. Intemperance in eating and drinking carries on the ruin of soul and body at once; and hastens death, while it makes the man most unmeet for it. Therefore, *take heed to your selves, left at any time your hearts be overcharged with surfeiting and drunkenness, and so that day come upon you unawares,* Luke xxi. 34. But O how often is the foul struck through with a dart, in gratifying the senses! At these doors destruction enters in. Therefore Job made a covenant with his eyes, chap. xxxi. 1. *The mouth of a strange woman is a deep pit ; he that is abhorred of the Lord shall fall therein,* Prov. xxii. 14. *Let him that standeth take heed lest he fall.* Beware of lasciviousness; study modesty in your apparel, words, and actions. The ravens of the valley of death will at length pick out the wanton eye : the obscene filthy tongue will at length be quiet in the land of silence: and grim death, embracing the body in its cold arms, will effectually allay the heat of all fleshly lusts.

Lastly, In a word: it may check our earthly-mindedness ; and at once knock down the lust of the flesh, the lust of the eyes, and the pride of life. Ah ! if we must die, why are we thus ? why so fond of temporal things ; so anxious to get them, so eager in the embraces of them, so mightily touched with the loss of them? Let me, upon a view of the house appointed for all living, bespeak the worldling in the words of Solomon, Prov. xxiii. 5. *Wilt thou set thine eyes upon that which is not ?* For riches certainly make themselves wings, *they flee away as an eagle towards heaven.* Riches, and all worldly things, are but a fair nothing : they are that which is not. They are not what they seem to be ; they are all but gilded vanities, that deceive the eye. Comparatively they are not ; there is infinitely more of nothingness and not-being, than of being or reality in the best of them. What is the world, and all that is in it, but a fashion, or fair show, such as men make on a stage, a passing show? 1 Cor. vii. 31. Royal pomp is but a gaudy show, or appearance, in God's account, Acts xxv. 23. The best name they get is good things : but observe it, they are only the wicked man's good things ; Luke xvi. 25. *Thou in thy life-time receivedst thy good things,* says Abraham, in the parable of the rich man in hell. Well may the men of the world call these things their goods ; for there is no other good in them, about them, nor attending them. Now, wilt thou set thine eyes upon empty shows and fancies? wilt thou cause thine eyes to fly on them, as the word is? shall men's hearts fly out at their eyes upon them, as a ravenous bird on its prey? if they do, let them know, that at length these shall flee as fast away from them, as ever their eyes flew upon them: like a flock of fair feathered birds, that settle on a fool's ground; the which, when he runs to catch them as his own, do immediately take wing, fly away, and, sitting down on his neighbour's ground, illude his expectation, Luke xii. 20. *Thou fool, this night thy soul shall be required of thee: then whose shall these things be?* Though you do not make wings to them, as many do; they make themselves wings, and fly away: not as a tame house-bird, which may be caught again; nor as an hawk, that will show where she is by her bells, and be called again with the lure: but as an eagle, which quickly flies out of sight, and cannot be recalled. Forbear thou to behold these things. O mortal! there is no reason thou should set thine eyes upon them. This world is a great inn, in the road to eternity, to which thou art travelling. Thou art attended by these things, as servants belonging to the inn, where thou lodgest; they wait upon thee while thou art there; and when thou goest away, they will convoy thee to the door. But they are not thine, they will not go away with thee; but return to wait on other strangers, as they did on thee.

Fifthly, It may serve as a spring of Christian resolution, to cleave to Christ, adhere to his truths, and continue in his ways, whatever we may suffer for so doing It would much allay the fear of man, that bringeth a snare. *Who art thou, that thou shouldst be afraid of a man that shall die!* Isa. li. 12. Look on persecutors as pieces of brittle clay, that shall be dashed in pieces; for then shall you despise them as foes that are mortal, whose terror to others in the land of the living, shall quickly die with themselves. The serious consideration of the shortness of our time, and the certainty of death, will teach us, that all the advantage which we can make by our apoſtacy, in time of trial, is not worth the while; it is not worth going out of our way to get it: and what we refuſe to forgo for Chriſt's ſake, may quickly be taken from us by death. But we can never loſe it ſo honourably, as for the cauſe of Chriſt and his goſpel: for what glory is it that you give up what you have in the world; when God takes it from you by death, whether you will or not? This conſideration may teach us to undervalue life itſelf, and chooſe to forgo it rather than to ſin. The worſt that men can do, is to take away that life which we cannot long keep, though all the world ſhould conſpire to help us to retain the ſpirit. If we refuſe to offer it up to God, when he calls for it in defence of his honour, he can take it from us another way; as it fared with him, who could not burn for Chriſt, but was afterwards burnt by an accidental fire in his houſe.

Laſtly, It may ſerve for a ſpur to incite us to prepare for death. Conſider, (1.) Your eternal ſtate will be according to the ſtate in which you die: death will open the doors of heaven or hell to you. As the tree falls, ſo it ſhall lie through eternity. If the infant be dead-born, the open world will not raiſe it to life again: and if one die out of Chriſt, in an unregenerate ſtate, there is no more hope of him for ever. (2.) Seriouſly conſider what it is to go into another world; a world of ſpirits, wherewith we are very little acquainted. How frightful is converſe with ſpirits to poor mortals in this life! And how dreadful is the caſe, when men are hurried away into another world, not knowing but devils may be their companions for ever! Let us then give all diligence to make and advance our acquaintance with the Lord of that world. (3.) It is but a ſhort time which you have to prepare for death: therefore now or never, ſeeing the time aſſigned for preparation will ſoon be over. Eccl. ix. 10. *Whatever thy hand findeth to do, do it with thy might: for there is no work, nor device, nor knowledge, nor wiſdom, in the grave, whither thou goeſt.* How can we be idle, having ſo great a work to do, and ſo little time to do it in? But if the time be ſhort, the work of preparation for death, though hard work, will not laſt long. The ſhadows of the evening make the labourer work chearfully, knowing the time to be at hand when he will be called in from his labour. (4.) Much of our ſhort time is over already; and the youngeſt of us all cannot aſſure himſelf that there is as much of his time to come as is paſt. Our life in the world is but a ſhort preface to long eternity; and much of the tale is told. Oh! ſhall we not double our diligence, when ſo much of our time is ſpent, and ſo little of our great work is done? (5.) The preſent time is flying away; and we cannot bring back time paſt, it hath taken an eternal farewell of us; there is no kindling the fire again that is burnt to aſhes. The time to come is not ours; and we have no aſſurance of a ſhare in it, when it comes. We have nothing we can call ours but the preſent moment; and that is flying away. How ſoon our time may be at an end we know not. Die we muſt, but who can tell us when? If death kept one ſet time for all, we were in no hazard of a ſurprize: but daily obſervation ſhews us, that there is no ſuch thing. Now the flying ſhadow of our life allows no time for loitering. The rivers run ſpeedily into the ſea, from whence they came; but not ſo ſpeedily as man to the duſt from whence he came. The ſtream of time is the ſwifteſt current, and quickly runs out to eternity. *Laſtly,* If once death carry us off, there is no coming back again to mend our matters, Job xiv. 14. *If a man die, ſhall he live again?* Dying is a thing we cannot get a trial of; it is what we can only do once, Heb. ix. 27. *It is appointed unto men once to die.* And that which can be but once done, and yet is of ſo much importance, that our all depends in our doing it right, we have need to uſe the utmoſt diligence, that we may do it well. Therefore prepare for death.

If you who are unregenerate aſk me, what you ſhall do to prepare for death, that you may die ſafely? I anſwer, I have told you already what muſt be done. Your nature and ſtate muſt be changed; you muſt be born again; you muſt be united to Jeſus Chriſt by faith. Till this is done, you are not capable of other directions, which belong to a person's dying comfortably; whereof we may discourse afterwards, in the due place.

HEAD II.

The Difference between the RIGHTEOUS and the WICKED in their Death.

Prov. xiv. 32. *The wicked is driven away in his wickedness: but the righteous hath hope in his death.*

THIS text looks like the cloud between the Israelites and Egyptians; having a dark side towards the latter, and a bright side towards the former. It represents death like Pharaoh's jaylor, bringing the chief butler and the chief baker out of prison; the one to be restored to his office, and the other to be led to execution. It shews the difference between the godly and ungodly in their death; who, as they act a very different part in life, so in death have a very different exit.

First, As to the death of a wicked man, here is, (1.) The manner of his passing out of the world: he is *driven away*; namely, in his death, as is clear from the opposite clause. He is forcibly thrust out of his place in this world; driven away as chaff before the wind. (2.) The state he passeth away in: he dies in a sinful and hopeless state. *First*, In a sinful state; he is driven away *in his wickedness*. He lived in it, and he dies in it: his filthy garments of sin, in which he wrapped up himself in his life, are his prison garments, in which he shall lie wrapped up for ever. *Secondly*, In a hopeless state; *but the righteous hath hope in his death:* which plainly imports the hopelessness of the wicked in their death. Whereby is not meant, that no wicked man shall have any hope at all when he is dying, but shall die in despair. No: sometimes it is so indeed; but frequently it is otherwise: foolish virgins may, and often do hope to the last breath. But the wicked man has no folid hope : as for the delufive hopes which he entertains himfelf with, death will root them up: and he fhall be for ever irretrivably miferable.

Secondly, As to the death of a righteous man, he hath hope in his death. This is ufhered in with a *but*, importing a removal of thefe dreadful circumftances, with which the wicked man is attended, who is driven away in his wickednefs : but the godly are not fo. Not fo, (1.) In the manner of their paffing out of the world. The righteous are not driven away, as chaff before the wind, but led away as a bride to the marriage chamber, carried away by the angels unto Abraham's bofom, Luke xvi. 22. (2.) Not fo as to their ftate, when paffing out of this life. The righteous man dies, (1.) Not in a finful, but in a holy ftate. He goes not away in his fin, but out of it. In his life he was putting off the old man, changing his prifon garments : and now the remaining rags of them are removed, and he is adorned with robes of glory. (2.) Not in a hopelefs, but a hopeful ftate. He hath hope in his death : he has the grace of hope, and the well-founded expectation of better things than ever he had in this world : and though the ftream of his hope at death may run fhallow, yet he has ftill as much of it as makes him venture his eternal interefts upon the Lord Jefus Chrift.

Doct. I. *The Wicked dying, are driven away in their Wickednefs, and in a hopelefs State.*

In fpeaking to this doctrine, (1.) I fhall fhew how, and in what fenfe, the wicked *are driven away in their wickednefs* at death. (2.) I fhall difcover the hopelefsnefs of their ftate at death. And, *laftly*, apply the whole.

I. How, and in what fenfe the wicked are *driven away in their wickednefs*. In difcourfing of this matter, I fhall briefly enquire, (1.) What is meant by their being *driven away*. (2.) Whence they fhall be driven, and whither. (3.) In what refpects they may be faid to be driven away *in their wickednefs*. But before I proceed, let me remark, that you are miftaken, if you think that no perfons are to be called *wicked*, but they who are avowedly vitious and profane; as if the devil could dwell in none, but thofe whofe name is legion. In Scripture account, all who are not righteous, in the manner hereafter explained, are reckoned wicked. Therefore the text divides the whole world into two forts, *the righteous and the wicked*; and you will fee the fame thing in Mal. iii. 18. *Then fhall ye return, and difcern between the righteous and the wicked.* Wherefore, if you be not righteous, you are wicked. If you have not an imputed righteoufnefs, and alfo an implanted righteoufnefs and holinefs; if you be yet in your natural ftate, unregenerated, not united to Chrift by faith, however moral, and blamelefs in the eyes of men your converfation may be, you are the wicked, who fhall be driven away in their wickednefs, if death finds you in that ftate. Now,

FIRST, As to the meaning of this phrafe, *driven away*; there are three things in it; the wicked fhall be taken away fuddenly, violently, and irrefiftibly.

Firft, Unrenewed men fhall be taken away fuddenly at death. Not that all wicked men die fuddenly; nor that they are all wicked that die fo; God forbid! but, (1.) Death commonly comes upon them unexpectedly, and fo furprifeth them; as the deluge furprifed the old world, though they were forewarned of it long before it came: and as travail cometh on a woman with child, with furprifing fuddennefs, although looked for and expected, 1 Theff. v. 3. Death feizeth them, as a creditor doth his debtor, to hale him to prifon, Pfalm iv. 15. and that when they are not aware. Death comes in, as a thief, at the window, and finds them full of bufy thoughts about this life, which that very day perifh. (2.) Death always feizeth them unprepared for it: the old houfe falls down about their ears, before they have another provided. When death cafts them to the door, they have not where to lay their heads; unlefs it be on a bed of fire and brimftone. The foul and body are as it were hugging one another in mutual embraces; when death comes like a whirlwind, and feparates them. (3.) Death hurries them away in a moment to deftruction, and makes a moft difmal change: the man for the moft part, never

Head II. *of the Righteous and the Wicked.*

knows where he is, till in hell he lift up his eyes, Luke xvi. 23. The floods of wrath suddenly overwhelm his soul; and ere he is aware, he is plunged into the bottomless pit.

Secondly, The unrenewed man is taken away out of the world violently. Driving is a violent action; he is chased out of the world, Job xviii. 18. Fain would he stay if he could; but death drags him away, like a malefactor to the execution. He sought no other portion than the profit and pleasures of this world; he hath no other, he really desires no other: how can he then go away out of it, if he were not driven?

QUEST. But may not a wicked man be willing to die? ANSW. He may indeed be willing to die; but, observe, it is only in one of three cases; (1.) In a fit of passion, by reason of some trouble, that he is impatient to be rid of. Thus many persons, when their passion has got the better of their reason; and when, on that account, they are most unfit to die, will be ready to cry, O to be gone! But should their desire be granted, and death come at their call, they would quickly shew, they were not in earnest; and that, if they go, they must be driven away against their wills. (2.) When they are brim-full of despair, they may be willing to die. Thus Saul murdered himself; and Spira wished to be in hell, that he might know the uttermost of what he believed he was to suffer. In this manner, men may seek after death, while it flees from them. But fearful is the violence which these undergo, whom the terrors of God do thus drive. (3.) When they are dreaming of happiness after death. Foolish virgins, under the power of delusion, as to their state, may be willing to die, having no fear of lying down in sorrow. How many are there, who can give no Scripture-ground for their hope, who yet have no bands in their death! many are driven to darkness sleeping; they go off like lambs, who would roar like lions, did they but know what place they are going to: though the chariot, in which they are, drive furiously to the deeps of hell, yet they fear not, because they are fast asleep.

Lastly, The unregenerate man is taken away irresistibly. He must go, though sore against his will. Death will take no refufal, nor admit of any delay, though the man has not lived half his days, according to his own computation. If he will not bow, it will break him. If he will not come forth, it will pull the houfe down about his ears; for there he muft not ftay. Although the phyfician help, friends groan, the wife and children cry, and the man himfelf ufe his utmoft efforts to retain the fpirit, his foul is required of him, yield he muft, and go where he fhall never more fee light.

Secondly, Let us confider, whence they are driven, and whither. When the wicked die, (1.) They are driven out of this world, where they finned, into the other world, where they muft be judged, and receive their particular fentences, Heb. ix. 27. *It is appointed unto men once to die, but after this the judgment.* They fhall no more return to their beloved earth. Though their hearts are wedded to their earthly enjoyments, they muft leave them, they can carry nothing hence. How forrowful muft their departure be, when they have nothing in view fo good as that which they leave behind them! (2.) They are driven out of the fociety of the faints on earth, into the fociety of the damned in hell, Luke xvi. 22, 23. *The rich man alfo died, and was buried. And in hell he lift up his eyes.* What a multitude of the devil's goats, now take their place among Chrift's fheep! but at death they fhall be led forth with the workers of iniquity, Pfal. cxxv. 5. There is a mixed multitude in this world, but no mixture in the other; each party is there fet by themfelves. Though hypocrites grow here, as tares among the wheat, death will root them up; and they fhall be bound in bundles for the fire. (3.) They are driven out of time into eternity. While time lafts with them, there is hope; but when time goes, all hope goes with it. Precious time is now lavifhingly fpent: it lies fo heavy on the hands of many, that they think themfelves obliged to take feveral ways to drive away time. But beware of being at a lofs what to do in life: improve time for eternity, whilft you have it; for ere long death will drive it from you, and you from it, fo as you fhall never meet again. (4.) They are driven out of their fpecious pretences to piety. Death ftrips them of the fplendid robes of a fair

Head II. *of the Righteous and the Wicked.*   305

profeffion, with which fome of them are adorned, and turns them off the ftage, in the rags of a wicked heart and life. The word *Hypocrite* properly fignifies a ftage player, who appears to be what indeed he is not. This world is the ftage, on which thefe children of the devil perfonate the children of God. Their fhew of religion is the player's coat, under which a perfon muft look, who will judge of them aright. Death turns them out of their coat, and they appear in their native drefs : it unveils them, and takes off their mafk. There is none in the other world who pretend to be better than they really are. Depraved nature acts in the regions of horror undifguifed. *Laftly,* They are driven away from all means of grace ; and are fet beyond the line, quite out of all profpect of mercy. There is no more an opportunity to buy oil for the lamp ; it is gone out at death, and can never be lighted again. There may be offers of mercy and peace made after they are gone ; but they are to others, not to them : there are no offers in the place to which they are driven ; thefe offers are only made in that place from which they are driven away.

LASTLY, In what refpects may they be faid to be driven away *in their wickednefs ? Anfwer,* (1.) In refpect of their being driven away in their finful unconverted ftate. Having lived enemies to God, they die in a ftate of enmity to him : for none is brought into the eternal ftate of confummate happinefs, but by the way of the ftate of grace in this life. The child that is dead in the womb, is born dead, and is caft out of the womb into the grave : fo he who is dead while he liveth, or is fpiritually dead, is caft forth of the womb of time, in the fame ftate of death, into the pit of utter mifery. O miferable death, to die in the gall of bitternefs and bond of iniquity ! it had been incomparably better for fuch as die thus, that they had never been born. (2.) In regard that they die finning, acting wickedly againft God, in contradiction to the divine law : for they can do nothing but fin while they live. So death takes them in the very act of finning ; violently draws them from the embraces of their lufts, and drives

R r

them away to the tribunal to receive their sentence. It is a remarkable expression, Job xxvi. 14. *They die in youth:* the marginal reading is, *their soul dieth in youth:* their lusts being lively, their desires vigorous, and expectations big, as is common in youth. *And their life is among the unclean;* or, *and the company*, (or herd) *of them* dieth among *the Sodomites,* i. e. is taken away in the heat of their sin and wickedness, as the Sodomites were, Gen. xix. Luke vii. 28, 29. (3.) As they are driven away loaded with the guilt of all their sins: this is the winding-sheet, that shall lie down with them in the dust, Job xx. 11. Their works follow them into the other world: they go away with the yoke of their transgressions wreathed about their necks. Guilt is a bad companion in life, but how terrible will it be in death! It lies now, perhaps, like cold brimstone on their benumbed consciences; but when death opens the way for sparks of divine vengeance, like fire, to fall upon it, it will make dreadful flames in the conscience, in which the soul will be as it were wrapped up for ever. *Lastly,* The wicked are driven away in their wickedness, for they die under the absolute power of their wickedness. While there is hope, there is some restraint on the worst of men: those moral endowments, which God gives to a number of men, for the benefit of mankind in this life, are so many restraints upon the imperious wickedness of human nature. But all hope being cut off, and those gifts withdrawn, the wickedness of the wicked will then arrive at its perfection. As the seeds of grace, sown in the hearts of the elect, come to their full maturity at death; so wicked and hellish dispositions, in the reprobate, come then to their highest pitch. Their prayers to God will then be turned to horrible curses; and their praises to hideous blasphemies, Matth. xxii. 13. *There shall be weeping and gnashing of teeth.* This gives a dismal but genuine view of the state of the wicked in another world.

II. I shall discover the hopelessness of the state of unrenewed men at death. It appears to be very hopeless, if we consider these four things:

First, Death cuts off their hopes and prospects of peace and pleasure in this life, Luke xii. 19, 20. *Soul, thou hast much goods laid up for many years, take thine ease, eat, drink, and be merry. But God said unto him, Thou fool, this night thy soul shall be required of thee: then whose shall those things be which thou hast provided?* They look for great matters in this world, they hope to increase their wealth, to see their families prosper, and to live at ease; but death comes like a stormy wind, and shakes off all their fond hopes, like green fruit from off a tree. *When he is about to fill his belly, God shall cast the fury of his wrath upon him,* Job xx. 23. He may begin a web of contrivances, for advancing his worldly interest; but before he gets it wrought out, death comes and cuts it out. His breath goeth forth, he returneth to his earth: in that very day his thoughts perish, Psal. cxlvi. 4.

Secondly, When death comes, they have no solid ground to hope for eternal happiness. *For what is the hope of the hypocrite, though he hath gained, when God taketh away his soul?* Job xxvii. 8. Whatever hopes they fondly entertain, they are not founded on God's word, which is the only sure ground of hope; if they knew their own case, they would see themselves only happy in a dream. And indeed what hope can they have? The law is plain against them, and condemns them. The curses of it (those cords of death) are about them already. The Saviour, whom they slighted, is now their judge; and their judge is their enemy. How then can they hope? They have bolted the door of mercy against themselves, by their unbelief. They have despised the remedy, and therefore must die without mercy. They have no saving interest in Jesus Christ, the only channel of conveyance through which mercy flows; and therefore they can never taste it. The sword of justice guards the door of mercy, so as none can enter in but the members of the mystical body of Christ, over whose head is a cover of atoning blood, the Mediator's blood. These indeed may pass without harm, for justice has nothing to require of them. But others cannot pass, since they are not in

Chrift: death comes to them with the fting in it, the fting of unpardoned guilt. It is armed againft them with all the force which the fanction of an holy law can give it, 1 Cor. xv. 56. *The fting of death is fin, and the ftrength of fin is the law.* When that law was given in Sinai, *the whole mount quaked greatly,* Exod. xix. 18. When the Redeemer was making fatisfaction for the elect's breaking it, *the earth did quake, and the rocks rent,* Matt. xxvii. 51. What poffible ground of hope, then, is there to the wicked man, when death comes upon him, armed with the force of this law? How can he efcape that fire, which *burnt into the midft of heaven?* Deut. iv. 11. How fhall he be able to ftand in that fmoke, that *afcended as the fmoke of a furnace?* Exod. xix. 18. How will he endure the terrible *thunders and lightnings,* ver. 19. and dwell in *the darknefs, clouds and thick darknefs?* Deut. iv. 11. All thefe refemblances, heaped together, do but faintly reprefent the fearful tempeft of wrath and indignation, which fhall purfue the wicked to the loweft hell; and for ever abide on them, who are driven to darknefs at death.

Thirdly, Death roots up their delufive hopes of eternal happinefs; then it is that their covenant with death, and agreement with hell, is broken. They are awakened out of their golden dreams, and at length lift up their eyes; Job viii. 14. *Whofe hope fhall be cut off, and whofe truft fhall be a fpider's web.* They truft that all will be well with them after death. But their truft is but a web woven out of their own bowels, with a great deal of art and induftry. They wrap themfelves up in their hope, as the fpider wraps herfelf in her web. But it is a weak and flender defence; for however it may whithftand the threatenings of the word of God, death, that befom of deftruction, will fweep them and it both away, fo as there fhall not be the leaft fhred of it left; and he, who this moment will not let his hope go, will next moment be utterly hopelefs. Death overturns the houfe built on the fand; it leaves no man under the power of delufion.

Laftly, Death makes their ftate abfolutely and for ever hopelefs. Matters cannot be retrieved and amended

Head II. *of the Righteous and the Wicked.* 309

after death. For, (1.) Time once gone can never be recalled. If cries or tears, price or pains, could bring time back again, the wicked man might have hope in his death. But tears of blood will not prevail; nor will his roaring for millions of ages cause it to return. The sun will not stand still, for the sluggard to awake, and enter on his journey; and when once it is gone down, he cannot expect the night to be turned into day for his sake: he must lodge through the long night of eternity, where his time left him. (2.) There is no returning to this life, to amend what is amiss; it is a state of probation and trial, which terminates at death, therefore we cannot return to it again; it is but once that we thus live, and once that we die. Death carries the wicked man to *his own place,* Acts i. 25. This life is our working day: death closeth our day and our work together. We may readily admit that the wicked might have some hope in their death, if, after death has opened their eyes, they could return to life, and have but the trial of one Sabbath, one offer of Christ, one day, or but one hour more, to make up their peace with God: but *man lieth down, and rifeth not till the heavens be no more; they shall not awake, nor be raised out of their sleep,* Job xiv. 12. *Lastly,* In the other world men have no access to get their ruined state and condition retrieved, though ever so desirous of it. *For there is no work nor device, no knowledge nor wisdom in the grave, whither thou goest,* Eccl. ix. 10. Now a man may flee from the wrath to come; he may get into a refuge; but when once death has done its work, the *door is shut*; there are no more offers of mercy, no more pardons; where the tree falls there it must lie.

Let what has been said be carefully pondered, and that it may be of use, let me exhort you,

First, To take heed that you entertain no hopes of heaven, but what are built on a solid foundation; tremble to think what fair hopes of happiness death sweeps away like cob-webs; how the hopes of many are cut off, when they seem to themselves to be at the very threshold of heaven; how, in the moment they expected to be carried by angels into Abraham's bosom, into the regions of bliss and peace, they are carried by devils into the society of the damned in hell, into the place of torment, and regions of horror. I beseech you beware, (1.) Of a hope built on ground that was never cleared. The wise builder digged deep, Luke vi. 48. Were your hopes of heaven never shaken; but have you had good hopes all your days? Alas for it! you may see the mystery of your case explained, Luke xi. 21. *When a strong man armed keepeth his palace, his goods are in peace.* But if they have been shaken, take heed left some breaches only have been made in the old building, which you have got repaired again, by ways and means of your own. I assure you, that your hope (however fair a building it is) is not to be trusted to, unless your old hopes have been razed, and you have built on a foundation quite new. (2.) Beware of that hope, which looks brisk in the dark, but loseth all its lustre when it is set in the light of God's word, when it is examined and tried by the touchstone of Divine revelation, John iii. 20, 21. *For every one that doth evil, hateth the light; neither cometh to the light, left his deeds should be reproved. But he that doth the truth, cometh to the light, that his deeds may be made manifest that they are wrought in God.* That hope which cannot abide Scripture-trial, but sinks when searched into by sacred truth, is a delusion, and not a true hope: for God's word is always a friend to the graces of God's Spirit, and an enemy to delusion. (3.) Beware of that hope which stands without being supported by Scripture-evidences. Alas! many are big with hopes, who cannot give, because they really have not any, Scripture-grounds for them. Thou hopest that all will be well with thee after death: but what word of God is it on which thou hast been caused to hope? Psal. cxix. 49. What Scripture-evidence hast thou to prove that thy hope is not the hope of the hypocrite? What hast thou, after impartial self-examination, as in the sight of God, found in thyself, which the word of God determines to be a sure evidence of his right to eternal life, who is possessed of it? Numbers are ruined with such hopes as stand unsupported by Scripture evidence. Men are fond and tenacious

Head II. *of the Righteous and the Wicked.*

of these hopes; but death will throw them down, and leave the self-deceiver hopeless. *Lastly*, Beware of that hope of heaven, which doth not prepare and dispose you for heaven, which never makes your soul more holy, 1 John iii. 3. *Every man that hath this hope in him, purifieth himself, even as he is pure.* The hope of the most part of men, is rather a hope to be free of pain and torment in another life, than a hope of true happiness, the nature whereof is not understood and discerned: therefore it rests in sloth and indolence, and does not excite to mortification, and a heavenly life. So far are they from hoping aright for heaven, that they must own, if they speak their genuine sentiments, removing out of this world into any other place whatever, is rather their fear than their hope. The glory of the heavenly city does not at all draw their hearts upwards to it; nor do they lift up their heads with joy, in the prospect of arriving at it. If they had the true hope of the marriage day, they would, as the bride, *the Lamb's wife*, be *making themselves ready for it*, Rev. xix. 7. But their hopes are produced by their sloth, and their sloth is nourished by their hopes. Oh, sirs, as you would not be driven away hopeless in your death, beware of these hopes! raze them now, and build on a new foundation, lest death leave not one stone of them upon another, and you never be able to hope any more.

Secondly, Hasten, O sinners, out of your wickedness, out of your sinful state, and out of your wicked life, if you would not at death be driven away in your wickedness. Remember the fatal end of the wicked man, as the text represents it. I know there is a great difference, in the death of the wicked, in respect of some circumstances: but all of them, in their death, agree in this, that they are driven away in their wickedness. Some of them die resolutely, as if they scorned to be afraid. Some in raging despair, so filled with horror, that they cry out, as if they were already in hell: others in sullen despondency, oppressed with fears, so that their hearts sink within them, on the remembrance of mis-spent time, and the view which they have of eternity, having neither head nor heart to do any thing for their own relief. And others die stupid: they lived like beasts, and they die like beasts, without any concern on their spirits about their eternal state. They groan under their bodily distress, but have no sense of the danger of their souls. One may, with almost as much prospect of success, speak to a stone, as speak to them: vain is the attempt to teach them; nothing that can be said moves them. To discourse to them, either of the joys of heaven, or the torments of hell, is to plough on a rock, or beat the air. Some die like the foolish virgins, dreaming of heaven: their foreheads are steeled against the fears of hell, with presumptuous hopes of heaven. Their business, who would be useful to them, is not to answer doubts about the case of their souls, but to dispute them out of their false hopes. But which way soever the unconverted man dies, he is *driven away in his wickedness.* O dreadful case! Oh! let the consideration of so horrible a departure out of this world, move you to flee to Jesus Christ, as the all-sufficient Saviour, and almighty Redeemer. Let it prevail to drive you out of your wickedness, to holiness of heart and life. Though you reckon it pleasant to live in wickedness, yet you cannot but own that it is bitter to die in it: if you leave it not in time, you must go in your wickedness to hell, the proper place of it, that it may be set there on its own base. For when you are passing out of this world, all your sins, from the eldest to the youngest of them, will swarm about you, hang upon you, accompany you to the other world, and as so many furies surround you there for ever.

Lastly, O be concerned for others, especially for your relations, that they may not continue in their sinful natural state, but be brought into a state of salvation; lest they be driven away in their wickedness at death. What would you not do to prevent any of your friends dying an untimely and violent death? But, alas! do not you see them in hazard of being driven away in their wickedness? is not death approaching them, even the youngest of them? and are they not strangers to true Christianity, remaining in that state in which they came

Head II. *of the Righteous and the Wicked.*

into the world? Oh! make haste to pluck the brand out of the fire, before it be burned to ashes. The death of relations often leaves a sting in the hearts of those they leave behind them, because they did not do for their souls as they had opportunity; and because the opportunity is for ever taken out of their hands.

DOCT. II. *The State of the Godly, in Death, is a hopeful State.*

We have seen the dark side of the cloud, looking towards ungodly men, passing out of the world: let us now take a view of the bright side of it, shining on the godly, as they enter on their eternal state. In discoursing on this subject, I shall confirm this doctrine, answer an objection against it, and then make some practical improvement of the whole.

For confirmation, let it be observed, that although the passage, out of this world by death, hath a frightful aspect to poor mortals, and to miscarry in it must needs be of fatal consequence, yet the following circumstances make the state of the godly, in their death, happy and hopeful.

First, They have a trusty good Friend before them in the other world. Jesus Christ, their best Friend, is Lord of that land, to which death carries them. When Joseph sent for his father to come down to him to Egypt, telling him, that *God had made him lord over all Egypt*, Gen. xlv. 9. and *Jacob saw the waggons Joseph had sent to carry him, the spirit of Jacob revived*, ver. 27. He resolves to undertake the journey. I think, when the Lord calls a godly man out of this world, he sends him such glad tidings, and such a kind invitation into the other world, that if he had faith to believe it, his spirit must revive, when he sees the waggon of death, which comes to carry him thither. It is true indeed, he has a weighty trial to undergo, after death the judgment. But the case of the godly is altogether hopeful; for the Lord of the land is their Husband, and their Husband is the Judge: *The Father hath committed all judgment unto the Son*, John v. 22. Surely the case of the wife is hopeful, when her own husband is her judge, even such a husband as hates putting away. No husband is so loving and so tender of his spouse, as the Lord Christ is of his. One would think it would be a very bad land, which a wife would not willingly go to, where her husband is the ruler and judge. Moreover, their judge is the advocate, 1 John ii. 1. *We have an advocate with the Father, Jesus Christ the righteous.* Therefore they need not fear their being put back, and falling into condemnation. What can be more favourable? Can they think, that he who pleads their cause, will himself pass sentence against them? Yet, further, their Advocate is their Redeemer; they are *redeemed with the precious blood of Christ*, 1 Pet. i. 18, 19. So when he pleads for them, he is pleading his own cause. Though an advocate may be careless of the interest of one who employs him, yet surely he will do his utmost to defend his own right, which he hath purchased with his money: and shall not their advocate defend the purchase of his own blood? But more than all that, their Redeemer is their Head, and they are his members, Eph. v. 23. 30. Though one were so silly as to let his own purchase go, without standing up to defend his right, yet surely he will not quit a limb of his own body. Is not their case then hopeful in death, who are so closely linked and allied to the Lord of the other world, who hath the keys of hell and of death?

Secondly, They shall have a safe passage to another world. They must indeed go through the valley of the shadow of death: but though it be in itself a dark and shady vale, it shall be a valley of hope to them: they shall not be driven through it, but walk through it; as men in perfect safety, who fear no evil, Psal. xxiii. 4. Why should they fear? They have the Lord of the land's safe conduct, his pass sealed with his own blood; namely, the blessed covenant, which is the saints deathbed comfort, 2 Sam. xxiii. 5. *Although my house be not so with God, yet he hath made with me an everlasting covenant, ordered in all things and sure: for this is all my salvation, and all my desire, although he make it not to grow.* Who then can harm them? It is safe riding in Christ's chariot, (Cant. ii. 9.) both through life and death. They

Head II. *of the Righteous and the Wicked.* 315

have good and honourable attendants, a guard, even a guard of angels. These encamp about them in the time of their life; and surely will not leave them in the day of their death. These happy ministering spirits are attendants on their Lord's bride, and will doubtless convey her safe home to his house. When friends, in mournful mood, stand by the saints bed-side, waiting to see him draw his last breath, his soul is waited for by holy angels, to be carried by them into Abraham's bosom, Luke xvi. 22. The Captain of the saints salvation is the Captain of this holy guard: he was their guide even unto death, and he will be their guide through it too, Psal. xxiii. 4. *Yea, though I walk through the valley of the shadow of death, I will fear no evil; for thou art with me.* They may without fear pass that river, being confident it shall not overflow them; and they may walk through that fire, being sure they shall not be burnt by it.

Death can do them no harm. It cannot even hurt their bodies: for though it separate the soul from the body, it cannot separate the body from the Lord Christ. Even death is to them but sleep in Jesus, 1 Thes. iv. 14. They continue members of Christ, though in a grave. Their dust is precious dust; laid up in the grave, as in their Lord's cabinet. They lie in a grave mellowing; as precious fruit laid up to be brought forth to him at the resurrection. The husbandman has corn in his barn, and corn lying in the ground: the latter is more precious to him than the former; because he looks to get it returned with increase. Even so the dead bodies of the saints are valued by their Saviour: they are *sown in corruption, to be raised in incorruption; sown in dishonour, to be raised in glory,* 1 Cor. xv. 42, 43. It cannot hurt their souls. It is with the souls of the saints at death, as with Paul and his company in their voyage, whereof you have the history, Acts xxvii. The ship was broke in pieces, but the passengers got all safe to land. When the dying saint's speech is stopped, his eyes set, and his last breath drawn, the soul gets safe away into the heavenly paradise, leaving the body to return to its earth, but in the joyful hope of a re-union at its glorious refurrection. How can death hurt the godly? It is a foiled enemy: if it caft them down, it is only that they may rife up more glorious. Our Saviour Jefus Chrift hath abolifhed death, 2 Tim i. 10. the foul and life of it is gone: it is but a walking fhade, that may fright, but cannot hurt faints: it is only the fhadow of death to them; it is not the thing itfelf: their dying is but as dying, or fomewhat like dying. The apoftle tells us, *It is Chrift that died*, Rom. viii. 34. Stephen, the firft Chriftian martyr, though ftoned to death, yet only fell afleep, Acts vii. 60. Certainly, the nature of death is quite changed, with refpect to the faints. It is not to them what it was to Jefus Chrift their Head: it is not the venomed ruinating thing, wrapt up in the fanction of the firft covenant, Gen. ii 17. *In the day thou eateft thereof, thou fhalt furely die*. It comes to the godly without its fting: they may meet it with that falutation, *O death, where is thy fting!* Is this *Mara!* is this bitter death! It went out full into the world, when the firft Adam opened the door to it! but the fecond Adam hath brought it again empty to his own people. I feel a fting, may the dying faint fay; yet it is but a bee-fting, ftinging only through the fkin: but, O death, where is thy fting, thine old fting, the ferpent's fting, that ftings to the heart and foul? The fting of death is fin: but that is taken away. If death arrefts the faint, and carries him before the judge, to anfwer for the debt he contracted, the debt will be found paid by the glorious Surety; and he has the difcharge to fhow. The thorn of guilt is pulled out of the man's confcience; and his name is blotted out-of the black roll, and written among the living in Jerufalem. It is true, it is a great journey to go through the valley of the fhadow of death; but the faint's burden is taken away from his back, his iniquity is pardoned, he may walk at eafe; *no lion fhall be there, nor any ravenous beaft;* The redeemed may walk at leifure there, free from all apprehenfions of danger.

Laftly, They fhall have a joyful entrance into the other world. Their arrival, in the regions of blifs, will be celebrated with rapturous hymns of praife to their glorious

Redeemer. A dying day is a good day to a godly man. Yea, it is his beft day; it is better to him than his birth-day, or than the moft joyous day which he ever had on earth. *A good name*, fays the wife man, is *better than precious ointment; and the day of death, than the day of one's birth*, Eccl. vii 1. The notion of the immortality of the foul, and of future happinefs, which obtained among fome Pagan nations, had wonderful effects on them. Some of them, when they mourned for the dead, did fit in women's apparel, that being moved with the indecency of the garb, they might the fooner lay afide their mourning. Others buried them without any lamentation or mourning; but had a facrifice and a feaft for friends upon the occafion. Some were wont to mourn at births, and rejoice at burials. But the practice of fome Indian nations is yet more ftrange, of whom it is reported, that upon the hufband's deceafe, his feveral wives contend before the judges, which of them was the beft beloved wife: and fhe, in whofe favour it was determined with a chearful countenance threw herfelf into the flames prepared for her hufband's corps, was burned with it, and reckoned happy, while the reft lived in grief, and were accounted miferable. But however lame notions of a future ftate, affifted by pride, affectation of applaufe, apprehenfions of difficulties in this life, and fuch like principles proper to depraved human nature, may influence rude uncultivated minds, when ftrengthened by the arts of hell; O what folid joy and confolation may they derive, who are true Chriftians, being in Chrift, who *hath brought life and immortality to light, through the gofpel!* 2 Tim. i. 10. Death is one of thofe *all things*, that *work together for good to them that love God*, Rom. viii. 28. When the body dies, the foul is perfected: the body of death goes off, at the death of the body. What harm did the jailor to Pharaoh's butler, when he opened the prifon-door to him, and let him out? Is the bird in worfe cafe, when at liberty, than when confined in a cage? Thus, and no worfe, are the fouls of the faints treated by death. It comes to the godly man, as Haman came to Mordecai, with the royal apparel and the horfe,

Efth. iv. 11. with commiſſion to do them honour, however aukwardly it be performed. I queſtion not but Haman performed the ceremony with a very ill mien, a pale face, a down look, and a cloudy countenance, and like one who came to hang him, rather than to honour him. But he whom the king delighted to honour, muſt be honoured; and Haman, Mordecai's grand enemy, muſt be the man employed to put this honour upon him. Glory, glory, glory, bleſſing and praiſe to our Redeemer, our Saviour, our Mediator, by whoſe death grim devouring death is made to do ſuch a good office to thoſe whom it might otherwiſe have hurried away in their wickedneſs, to utter and eternal deſtruction! A dying day is in itſelf a joyful day to the godly; it is their redemption-day, when the captives are delivered, when the priſoners are ſet free. It is the day of the pilgrims coming home from their pilgrimage; the day in which the heirs of glory return from their travels, to their own country, and their Father's houſe, and enter into actual poſſeſſion of the glorious inheritance. It is their marriage-day. Now is the time of eſpouſals; but then the marriage is conſummated, and the marriage-feaſt begun, which has no period. If ſo, is not the ſtate of the godly, in death, a hopeful ſtate?

Object. But if the ſtate of the godly, in their death, be ſo hopeful, how comes it to paſs that many of them, when dying, are full of fears, and have little hope? *Anſw.* It muſt be owned, that ſaints do not all die in one and the ſame manner; there is a diverſity among them, as well as among the wicked; yet the worſt caſe of a dying ſaint is indeed a hopeful one. Some die triumphantly, in full aſſurance of faith, 2 Tim. iv. 6, 7, 8. *The time of my departure is at hand. I have fought a good fight, I have finiſhed my courſe, I have kept the faith: Henceforth there is laid up for me a crown of righteouſneſs.* They get a taſte of the joys of heaven, while here on earth; and begin the ſongs of Zion, while yet in a ſtrange land. Others die in a ſolid fiducial dependence on their Lord and Saviour; though they cannot ſing triumphantly, yet they can and will

Head II. *of the Righteous and the Wicked.* 319
say confidently, *The Lord is their God.* Though they cannot triumph over death, with old Simeon, having Christ in his arms, and saying, *Lord, now lettest thou thy servant depart in peace, according to thy word; for mine eyes have seen thy salvation,* Luke ii. 29, 30. Yet they can say, with dying Jacob, *I have waited for thy salvation, O Lord,* Gen. xlix. 8. His left-hand is under their head, to support them, though his right-hand doth not embrace them; they firmly believe, though they are not filled with joy in believing. They can plead the covenant, and hang on the promise, although their house is not so with God as they could wish. The dying day of some saints may be like that day mentioned, Zech. xiv. 7. *Not day, nor night.* They may die under great doubts and fears; setting as it were in a cloud, and going to heaven in a mist. They may go mourning without the sun, and never put off their spirit of heaviness, till death strip them of it. They may be carried to heaven through the confines of hell; and may be pursued by the devouring lion, even to the very gates of the new Jerusalem; and may be compared to a ship almost wrecked in sight of the harbour, which yet gets safe into port, 1 Cor. iii. 15. *If any man's work shall be burnt, he shall suffer loss; but he himself shall be saved, yet so as by fire.* There is safety amidst their fears, but danger in the wicked's strong confidence; and there is a blessed seed of gladness in their greatest sorrows; *Light is sown for the righteous, and gladness for the upright in heart,* Psal. xcvii. 11.

Now saints are liable to such perplexity in their death, because, though they be Christians indeed, yet they are men of like passions with others; and death is a frightful object in itself, whatever dress it appears in; the stern countenance, with which it looks at mortals, can hardly miss of causing them to shrink. Moreover, the saints are of all men the most jealous of themselves. They think of eternity, and of a tribunal, more deeply than others do; with them it is a more serious thing to die than the rest of mankind are aware of. They know the deceits of the heart, the subtilties of depraved human nature, better than others do. Therefore they may have much to do to keep up hope on a death-bed; while others pafs off quietly, like fheep to the flaughter. Satan, who ufeth all his art to fupport the hopes of the hypocrite, will do his utmoft to marr the peace, and increafe the fears of the faint. Finally, the bad frame of fpirit, and ill condition, in which death fometimes feizeth a true Chriftian, may caufe this perplexity. By his being in the ftate of grace, he is indeed always habitually prepared for death, and his dying fafely is enfured; but there is more requifite to his actual preparation, and dying comfortably; his fpirit muft be in good condition too.

Wherefore, there are three cafes, in which death cannot but be very uncomfortable to a child of God. (1.) If it feize him at a time when the guilt of fome particular fin, unrepented of, is lying on his confcience; and death comes on that very account, to take him out of the land of the living; as was the cafe of many of the Corinthian believers, 1 Cor xi. 30. *For this caufe* (namely, of unworthy communicating) *many are weak and fickly among you, and many fleep.* If a perfon is furprized with the approach of death, while lying under the guilt of fome unpardoned fin, it cannot but caufe a mighty confternation. (2.) When death catches him napping. The mid-night cry muft be frightful to fleeping virgins. The man who lies in a ruinous houfe, and awakens not till the timber begins to crack, and the ftones to drop down about his ears, may indeed get out of it fafely, but not without fears of being crufhed by its fall. When a Chriftian has been going on in a courfe of fecurity and blackfliding, and awakens not till death comes to his bed-fide, it is no marvel that he gets a fearful awakening. *Laftly*, When he has loft fight of his faving intereft in Chrift, and cannot produce evidences of his title to heaven, it is hard to meet death, without fome evidence of a title of eternal life at hand: hard to go through the dark valley, without the candle of the Lord fhining upon the head. It is a terrible adventure, to launch out into eternity, when a man can make no better of it, than to leap in the dark, not knowing where he fhall light, whether in heaven or hell.

Head II. *of the Righteous and the Wicked.*

Neverthelefs, the ftate of the faints, in their death, is always in itfelf hopeful. The prefumptuous hopes of the ungodly, in their death, cannot make their ftate hopeful; neither can the hopeleffnefs of a faint make his ftate hopelefs: for God judgeth according to the truth of the thing, not according to men's opinion about it. Howbeit, the faints can no more be altogether without hope, than they can be altogether without faith. Their faith may be very weak, but it fails not; and their hope very low, yet they will, and do hope to the end. Even while the godly feem to be carried away with the ftream of doubts and fears, there remains ftill as much hope as determines them to lay hold on the tree of life, that grows on the banks of the river, Jonah ii. 4. *Then I faid, I am caft out of thy fight: yet I will look again toward thy temple.*

Use. This fpeaks comfort to the godly againft the fear of death. A godly man may be called a happy man before his death! becaufe, whatever befal him in life, he fhall certainly be happy at death. You who are in Chrift, who are true Chriftians, have hope in your end; and fuch a hope as may comfort you againft all thofe fears which arife from the confideration of a dying hour. This I fhall branch out, in anfwering fome cafes briefly.

Cafe I. The profpect of death (will fome of the faints fay) is uneafy to me, not knowing what fhall become of my family when I am gone. *Anfw.* The righteous hath hope in his death, as to his family, as well as himfelf. Although you have little, for the prefent, to live upon, which has been the condition of God's chofen ones, 1 Cor. iv. 11. *We,* (namely the apoftles) *both hunger and thirft, and are naked, and are buffeted, and have no certain dwelling place:* and though you have nothing to leave them, as was the cafe of that fon of the prophets, who did fear the Lord, and yet died in debt, which he was unable to pay; as his poor widow reprefents, 2 Kings iv. 1. yet you have a good friend to leave them to; a covenant God, to whom you may confidently commit them, Jer. xlix. 11. *Leave thy fatherlefs children; I will preferve them alive; and let thy widows trust in me.* The world can bear witness of signal settlements made upon the children of providence; such as by their pious parents have been cast upon God's providential care. It has been often remarked, that they wanted neither provision nor education. Moses is an eminent instance of this. He, though he was an outcast infant, (Exod. ii. 3.) yet was learned in all the wisdom of the Egyptians, Acts vii. 22. and became king in Jeshurun, Deut. xxxiii. 5. O! may we not be ashamed, that we do not confidently trust him with the concerns of our families, to whom, as our Saviour and Redeemer, we have committed our eternal interests.

Case II. Death will take us away from our dear friends; yea, we shall not see the Lord in the land of the living, in the blessed ordinances. *Answ.* It will take you to your best friend, the Lord Christ. The friends you leave behind you, if they be indeed persons of worth, you will meet again, when they come to heaven: and you will never be separated any more. If death takes you away from the temple below, it will carry you to the temple above. It will indeed take you from the streams, but it will set you down by the fountain. If it put out your candle, it will carry you where there is no night, where there is eternal day.

Case III. I have so much to do, in time of health, to satisfy myself as to my interest in Christ, about my being a real Christian, a regenerate man, I judge it is almost impossible that I should die comfortably. *Ans.* If it is thus with you, then double your diligence, to make your calling and election sure. Endeavour to grow in knowledge, and walk closely with God: be diligent in self-examination; and pray earnestly for the holy Spirit, whereby you may know the things freely given you of God. If you are enabled, by the power and Spirit of Christ thus diligently to prosecute your spiritual concerns, though the time of your life be neither day nor night, yet at evening-time it may be light. Many weak Christians indulge doubts and fears about their spiritual state, as if they had placed at least some part of religion in this imprudent practice:

but towards the period of life, they think and act in another manner. The traveller, who reckons that he has time to spare, may stand still debating with himself, whether this or the other be the right way: but when the sun begins to set, he is forced to lay aside his scruples, and resolutely to go forward in the road, which he judges to be the right one; left he lie all night in the open fields. Thus some Christians, who perplex themselves much, through the course of their lives, with jealous doubts and fears, content themselves, when they come to die, with such evidences of the safety of their state, as they could not be satisfied with before; and, by disputing less against themselves, and believing more, court the peace they formely rejected, and gain it too.

Case IV. I am under a sad decay, in respect of my spiritual condition. *Answ.* Bodily consumptions may make death easy: but it is not so in spiritual decays. I will not say that a godly man cannot be easy in such a case, when he dies; but I believe it is rarely so. Ordinarily, I suppose, a cry comes to awaken sleeping virgins, before death comes. Sampson is set to grind in the prison, till his locks grow again. David and Solomon fell under great spiritual decays; but before they died, they recovered their spiritual strength and vigour. However, bestir yourselves without delay, to strengthen the things that remain: your fright will be the less, for being awakened from spiritual sleep before death comes to your bed-side: and you ought to lose no time, seeing you know not how soon death may seize you.

Case V. It is terrible to think of the other world, that world of spirits, which I have so little acquaintance with. *Answ.* Thy best friend is Lord of that other world. Abraham's bosom is open even to those who never saw his face. After death, thy soul becomes capable of converse with the blessed inhabitants of the other world. The spirits of just men made perfect were once such as thy spirit now is. And as for the angels, however superior their nature in the rank of beings, yet our nature is dignified above theirs in the man Christ, and they are, all of them, thy Lord's servants, and so thy fellow-servants.

Case VI. *The pangs of death are terrible. Answ.* Yet not so terrible as pangs of conscience, caused by a piercing sense of guilt, and apprehensions of Divine wrath, with which I suppose thee to be not altogether unacquainted. But who would not endure bodily sickness, that the soul may become sound, and every whit whole? Each pang of death will set sin a step nearer the door; and with the last breath the body of sin will breathe out its last. The pains of death will not last long; and the Lord thy God will not leave, but support thee under them.

Case VII. But I am like to be cut off in the midst of my days. *Answ.* Do not complain, you will be the sooner at home: you hereby have the advantage of your fellow-labourers, who were at work before you, in the vineyard. God, in the course of his providence, hides some of his saints early in the grave, that they may be taken away from the evil to come. An early removal out of this world prevents much sin and misery. They have no ground of complaint, who get the residue of their years in Immanuel's land. Surely thou shalt live as long as thou hast work cut out for thee by the great Master, to be done for him in this world: and when that is at an end, it is high time to be gone.

Case VIII. I am afraid of sudden death. *Answ.* Thou mayest indeed die so. Good Eli died suddenly, 1 Sam. iv. 18. Yet death found him watching, ver. 13. *Watch, therefore, for ye know not at what hour the Lord doth come,* Matth. xxiv. 42. But be not afraid, it is an inexpressible comfort, that death, come when it will, can never catch thee out of Christ; and therefore can never seize thee, as a jailor, to hurry thee into the prison of hell. Sudden death may hasten and facilitate thy passage to heaven, but can do thee no prejudice.

Case IX. I am afraid that it be my lot to die wanting the exercise of reason. *Answ.* I make no question but a child of God, a true Christian, may die in this case. But what harm? There is no hazard in it, as to his eternal state: a disease at death may divest him of his reason, but not of his religion. When a man, going a long voyage, has put his affairs in order, and put all his goods aboard, he himself may be carried aboard the ship sleeping: all is safe with him, although he knows not where he is, till he awake in the ſhip. Even ſo the godly man, who dies in this caſe, may die uncomfortably, but not unſafely.

Caſe X. I am naturally timorous, and the very thoughts of death are terrible to me. *Anſw.* The leſs you think on death, the thoughts of it will be the more frightful: make it familiar to you by frequent meditations upon it, and you may hereby quiet your fears. Look at the white and bright ſide of the cloud: take faith's view of the city that hath foundations; ſo ſhall you ſee hope in your death. Be duly affected with the body of ſin and death, the frequent interruptions of your communion with God, and with the glory which dwells on the other ſide death: this will contribute much to remove ſlaviſh fear.

It is pity that ſaints ſhould be ſo fond of life as they often are: they ought to be always on good terms with death. When matters are duly conſidered, it might be well expected, that every child of God, every regenerate man, ſhould generouſly profeſs, concerning this life, what Job did, chap vii. 16. *I loath it, I would not live always.* In order to gain their hearts to this deſireable temper, I offer the following additional conſiderations.

Firſt, Conſider the ſinfulneſs that attends life in this world. While you live here, you ſin, and ſee others ſinning. You breathe infectious air. You live in a peſt-houſe. Is it at all ſtrange to loath ſuch a life? (1.) Your own plague-ſores are running on you. Doth not the ſin of your nature make you groan daily? Are you not ſenſible, that though the cure be begun, it is yet far from being perfected? Has not the leproſy got into the walls of the houſe, which cannot be removed without pulling it down? Is not your nature ſo vitiated, that no leſs than the ſeparation of the ſoul from the body can root out the diſeaſe? Have you not your ſores without, as well as your ſickneſs within? Do you not leave marks of your pollution on whatever paſſes through your hands? Are not all your actions tainted and blemiſhed with defects and imperfections? Who, then, ſhould be much in love with life, but ſuch whoſe ſickneſs is their health; and who glory in their ſhame?

(2.) The loathsome sores of others are always before your eyes, go where you will. The follies and wickedness of men are every where conspicuous, and make but an unpleasant scene. This sinful world is but an unsightly company, a disagreeable crowd, in which the most loathsome are the most numerous. (3.) Are not your own sores oft-times breaking out again, after healing? Frequent relapses may well cause us to remit of our fondness for this life. To be ever struggling, and anon falling into the mire again, makes weary work. Do you never wish for cold death, thereby effectually to cool the heat of those lusts, which often take fire again, even after a flood of godly sorrow has gone over them? (4.) Do not you sometimes infect others, and others infect you? There is no society in the world, in which every member of it doth not sometimes lay a stumbling-block before the rest. The best carry about with them the tinder of a corrupt nature, which they cannot be rid of while they live, and which is liable to be kindled at all times, and in all places: yea, they are apt to inflame others, and become the occasions of sinning. Certainly these things are apt to imbitter this life to the saints.

Secondly, Consider the misery and troubles that attend it. Rest is desireable, but it is not to be found on this side of the grave. Worldly troubles attend all men in this life. This world is a sea of trouble, where one wave rolls upon another. They who fancy themselves beyond the reach of trouble, are mistaken: no state, no stage of life, is exempted from it. The crowned head is surrounded with thorny cares. Honour many times paves the way to deep disgrace: riches, for the most part, are kept to the hurt of the owners. The fairest rose wants not prickles; and the heaviest cross is sometimes found wrapped up in the greatest earthly comfort. Spiritual troubles attend the saints in this life. They are like travellers travelling in a cloudy night, in which the moon sometimes breaks out from under one cloud, but quickly hides her head again under another: no wonder that they long to be at their journey's end. The sudden alterations which the best frame of spirit is liable to, the perplexing doubts, confounding fears, short-

Head II. *of the Righteous and the Wicked.* 327
lived joys, and long running sorrows, which have a certain affinity with the present life, must needs create in the saints a desire to be with Christ, which is best of all.

Lastly, Consider the great imperfections attending this life. While the soul is lodged in this cottage of clay, the necessities of the body are many; it is always craving. The mud-walls must be repaired and patched up daily, till the clay cottage fall down for good and all. Eating, drinking, sleeping, and the like, are in themselves but mean employments for a rational creature, and will be reputed such by the heaven-born soul. They are badges of imperfection, and, as such, unpleasant to the mind, aspiring unto that life and immortality which is brought to light through the gospel; and would be very grievous, if this state of things were of long continuance. Doth not the gracious soul often find itself yoked with the body, as with a companion in travel, unable to keep pace with it? when the spirit is willing, the flesh is weak. When the soul would mount upward, the body is a clog upon it, and as a stone tied to the foot of a bird attempting to fly. The truth is, O believer, thy soul in this body is, at best, but like a diamond in a ring, where much of it is obscured: it is far sunk in the vile clay, till relieved by death.

I conclude this subject with a few directions, how to prepare for death, so as we may die comfortably. I speak not here of habitual preparation for death, which a true Christian, in virtue of his gracious state, never wants, from the time he is born again, and united to Christ; but of actual preparation, or readiness in respect of his particular case, frame, and disposition of mind and spirit; the want of which makes even a saint very unfit to die.

First, Let it be your constant care to keep a clean conscience, *a conscience void of offence toward God, and toward man,* Acts xxiv 16. Beware of a standing controversy between God and you, on the account of some iniquity regarded in the heart. When an honest man is about to leave his country, and not to return, he settles accounts with those he had dealings with, and lays down methods for paying his debts in time, lest he be reckoned a bankrupt, and attacked by an officer when he is going off. Guilt, lying on the confcience, is a fountain of fears, and will readily fting feverely, when death ftares the criminal in the face. Hence it is, that many, even of God's children, when dying, wifh paffionately, and defire eagerly, that they may live to do what they ought to have done before that time. Wherefore, walk clofely with God; be diligent, ftrict, and exact in your courfe: beware of loofe, carelefs, and irregular converfation; as you would not lay up for yourfelves anguifh and bitternefs of fpirit in a dying hour. And becaufe, through the infirmity cleaving to us, in our prefent ftate of imperfection, in many things we offend all, renew your repentance daily, and be ever wafhing in the Redeemer's blood. As long as you are in the world, you will need to wafh your feet, John xiii. 10. that is, to make application to the blood of Chrift anew, for purging your confciences from the guilt of daily mifcarriages. Let death find you at the fountain; and, if fo, it will find you ready to anfwer its call.

Secondly, Be always watchful, waiting for your change, *Like unto men that wait for their lord—that when he cometh and knocketh, they may open unto him immediately*, Luke xii. 26. *Beware of flumbering and fleeping, while the bridegroom tarries*. To be awakened out of fpiritual flumber, by a fuprifing call to pafs into another world, is a very frightful thing: but he, who is daily waiting for the coming of his Lord, fhall comfortably receive the grim meffenger, while he beholds him ufhering him in to him, of whom he may confidently fay, *This is my God, and I have waited for him*. The way to die comfortably, is to die daily. Be often effaying (as it were) to die. Bring yourfelves familiarly acquainted with death, by making many vifits to the grave, in ferious meditations upon it. This was Job's practice, chap. xvii. 13, 14. *I have made my bed in darknefs*. Go thou and do likewife; and when death comes, thou fhalt have nothing to do but to lie down. *I have faid to corruption, Thou art my father: to the worm, Thou art my mother and my fifter*. Do thou fay fo too; and thou

Head II. *of the Righteous and the Wicked.*

wilt be the fitter to go home to their houſe. Be frequently reflecting upon your conduct, and conſidering what courſe of life you wiſh to be found in, when death arreſts you; and act accordingly. When you do the duties of your ſtation in life, or are employed in acts of worſhip, think with yourſelves, that it may be this is the laſt opportunity; and therefore do it as if you was never to do more of that kind. When you lie down at night, compoſe your ſpirits, as if you was not to awake till the heavens be no more. And when you awake in the morning, conſider that new day as your laſt; and live accordingly. Surely that night cometh, of which you will never ſee the morning; or that morning, of which you will never ſee the night. But which of your mornings or nights will be ſuch, you know not.

Thirdly, Employ yourſelves much in weaning your hearts from the world. The man who is making ready to go abroad, buſies himſelf in taking leave of his friends. Let the mantle of earthly enjoyments hang looſe about you, that it may be eaſily dropped when death comes to carry you away into another world. Moderate your affections towards your lawful comforts of life: let not your hearts be too much taken with them. The traveller acts unwiſely, who ſuffers himſelf to be ſo allured with the conveniences of the inn where he lodgeth, as to make his neceſſary departure from it grievous. Feed with fear, and walk through the world as pilgrims and ſtrangers. The ſame as, when the corn is forſaking the ground, it is ready for the ſickle; when the fruit is ripe, it falls off the tree eaſily: ſo, when a Chriſtian's heart is truly weaned from the world, he is prepared for death; and it will be the more eaſy to him. A heart diſengaged from the world, is an heavenly one: we are ready for heaven when our heart is there before us, Mat. vi. 21.

Fourthly, Be diligent in gathering and laying up evidences of your title to heaven, for your ſupport and comfort at the hour of death. The neglect hereof mars the joy and conſolation which ſome Chriſtians might otherwiſe have at their death. Wherefore, examine yourselves frequently, as to your spiritual state; that evidences, which lie hid unobserved, may be brought to light, and taken notice of. And if you would manage this work successfully, make solemn serious work of it. Set apart some time for it. And, after earnest prayer to God, through Jesus Christ, for the enlightening influences of his Holy Spirit, whereby you may be enabled to understand his own word, and to discern his own work in your souls; examine yourselves before the tribunal of your consciences, that you may judge yourselves in this weighty matter.

And, in the first place, let the marks of a regenerate state be fixed from the Lord's word: have recourse to some particular text for that purpose; such as Prov. viii. 17. *I love them that love me.* Comp. Luke xiv. 26. *If any man come to me, and hate not his father and mother, and wife, and children, and brethren, and sisters, yea, and his own life also, he cannot be my disciple.* Psal. cxix. 6. *Then shall I not be ashamed, when I have respect unto all thy commandments.* Psal. xviii. 23. *I was also upright before him; and I kept myself from mine iniquity.* Compare Rom. vii. 22, 23. *I delight in the law of God, after the inward man: but I see another law in my members, warring against the law of my mind.* 1 John iii. 3. *Every man that hath this hope in him, purifieth himself, even as he is pure.* Mat. v. iii. *Blessed are the poor in spirit, for theirs is the kingdom of heaven.* Phil. iii. 3. *We are the circumcision, which worship* (or serve) *God in the spirit, and rejoice in Christ Jesus, and have no confidence in the flesh.* The sum of the evidence arising from these texts lies here: a real Christian is one who loves God for himself, as well as for his benefits; and that with a supreme love, above all persons, and all things: he has an awful and partial regard to God's commands: he opposeth and wrestleth against that sin which of all others most easily besets him: he approveth and loveth the holy law, even in that very point wherein it strikes against his most beloved lust: his hope of heaven engageth him in the study of universal holiness; in the which he aims at perfection, though he cannot reach it in this life: he serves the Lord, not only in acts of worship, but in the

Head II. *of the Righteous and the Wicked.* 331
whole of his converfation: and as to both, is fpiritual in the principle, motives, aims, and ends of his fervice: yet he fees nothing in himfelf to truft to before the Lord: Chrift and his fullnefs is the ftay of his foul: his confidence is cut off from all that is not Chrift, or in Chrift, in point of juftification, or acceptance with God, and in point of fanctification too. Every one, in whom thefe characters are found, has a title to heaven, according to the word. It is convenient and profitable to mark fuch texts, for this fpecial ufe, as they occur, while you read the Scriptures, or hear fermons. The marks of a regenerate ftate thus fixed, in the next place, impartially fearch and try your own hearts thereby, as in the fight of God, with dependance on him for fpiritual difcernment, that you may know whether they be in you or not. When you find them, form the conclufion deliberately and diftinctly; namely, that therefore you are regenerated, and have a title to heaven. Thus you may gather evidences. But be fure to have recourfe to God in Chrift, by earneft prayer, for the teftimony of the Spirit, whofe office it is to bear witnefs with our fpirit that we are the children of God, Rom. viii. 16. Moreover, carefully obferve the courfe and method of providence towards you; and likewife, how your foul is affected under the fame, in the various fteps thereof: compare both with Scripture-doctrines, promifes, threatenings, and examples; fo fhall you perceive if the Lord deals with you as he ufeth to do unto thofe that love his name, and if you be going forth by the footfteps of the flock. This may afford you comfortable evidence. Walk tenderly and circumfpectly, and the Lord will manifeft himfelf to you, according to his promife, John xiv. 21. *He that hath my commandments, and keepeth them, he it is that loveth me; and he that loveth me, fhall be loved of my Father; and I will love him, and will manifeft myfelf to him.* But it is in vain to think of fuccefsful felf-examination, if you be loofe and irregular in your converfation.

Laftly, Difpatch the work of your day and generation with fpeed and diligence. *David, after he had ferved his own generation by the will of God, fell on fleep,*

Acts xiii. 36. God has allotted us certain pieces of work of this kind, which ought to be difpatched before the time of working be over, Eccl. ix. 10. *Whatfoever thy hand findeth to do, do it with thy might: for there is no work, nor knowledge, nor wifdom, in the grave, whither thou goeft.* Gal. vi. 10. *As we have, therefore, opportunity, let us do good unto all men, efpecially unto them who are of the houfehold of faith.* If a paffenger, after he is got on fhip board, and the fhip is getting under fail, remembers that he has omitted to difpatch a piece of neceffary bufinefs when he was afhore, it muft needs be uneafy to him: even fo, reflection in a dying hour, upon neglected feafons, and loft opportunities, cannot fail to difquiet a Chriftian. Wherefore, whatever is incumbent upon thee to do for God's honour, and the good of others, either as the duty of thy ftation, or by fpecial opportunity put into thy hand, perform it feafonably, if thou wouldft die comfortably

HEAD III.

The RESSURRECTION.

John v. 28, 29. *Marvel not at this: for the hour is coming, in which all that are in the graves fhall hear his voice, and fhall come forth, they that have done good, unto the refurrection of life; and they that have done evil, unto the refurrection of damnation.*

THESE words are part of the defence which our Lord Jefus Chrift makes for himfelf, when perfecuted by the Jews, for curing the impotent man, and ordering him to carry away his bed on the Sabbath; and for vindicating his conduct, when accufed by them of having profaned that day. On this occafion he profeffeth himfelf not only Lord of the Sabbath, but alfo Lord of life and death; declaring, in the words of the text, the refurrection of the dead to be brought to pafs by his power. This he introduces with thefe words, as

Head III. *Of the Resurrection.*

with a solemn preface, *Marvel not at this*, i. e. at this strange discourse of mine: do not wonder to hear me, whose appearance is so very mean in your eyes, talk at this rate; for the day is coming, in which the dead shall be raised by my power.

Observe in this text, (1.) The doctrine of the resurrection asserted: *All that are in the graves shall hear his voice, and shall come forth.* The dead bodies, which are reduced to dust, shall revive, and evidence life by hearing and moving. (2.) The author of it, Jesus Christ, *the Son of man*, ver. 27. The dead shall hear his voice, and be raised thereby. (3.) The number that shall be raised, *All that are in the graves*, i. e. all the dead bodies of men, however differently disposed of in different graves; or all the dead, good and bad. They are not all buried in graves, properly so called: some are burnt to ashes; some drowned, and buried in the bellies of fishes; yea, some devoured by man-eaters, called Canibals: but wherever the matter or substance of which the body was composed is to be found, thence they shall come forth. (4.) The great distinction that shall be made between the godly and the wicked. They shall indeed both rise again in the resurrection. None of the godly shall be missing, though, perhaps, they either had no burial, or a very obscure one: and all the wicked shall come forth; their vaulted tombs shall hold them no longer than the voice is uttered. But the former shall have a joyful resurrection to life, whilst the latter have a dreadful resurrection to damnation. *Lastly*, The set time of this great event: there is an hour, or certain fixed period of time, appointed of God for it. We are not told when that hour will be, but that is coming; for this, among other reasons, that we may always be ready.

DOCTRINE, *There shall be a resurrection of the dead.*

In discoursing on this subject, I shall, *first*, shew the certainty of the resurrection; *next*, I shall enquire into the nature of it; and, *lastly*, Make some practical improvement of the whole.

I. In shewing the certainty of the resurrection, I shall prove, (1.) That God can raise the dead. (2.) That he will do it ; which are the two grounds or topics laid down by Chrift himfelf, when difputing with the Sadducees, Mat. xxii. 29. *Jefus anfwered and faid unto them, Ye do err, not knowing the Scriptures, nor the power of God.*

Firſt, Seeing God is almighty, furely he can raife the dead. We have inftances of this powerful work of God, both in the Old and New Teftament. The fon of the widow in Sarepta was raifed from the dead, 1 Kings xvii. 22. The Shunamite's fon, Kings iv. 35. And the man caft into the fepulchre of Elifha, chap. xiii. 21. In which we may obferve a gradation, the fecond of thefe miraculous events being more illuftrious than the firft, and the third than the fecond. The firft of thefe perfons was raifed when he was but newly dead ; the prophet Elijah, who raifed him, being prefent at his deceafe. The fecond, when he had lien dead a confiderable time ; namely, while his mother travelled from Shunem to mount Carmel, (reckoned about the diftance of fixteen miles) and returned from thence to her houfe, with Elifha, who raifed him. The laft, not till they were burying him, and the corps was caft into the prophet's grave. In like manner, in the New Teftament, Jairus's daughter, (Mark v. 41.) and Dorcas, (Acts ix. 40.) were both raifed to life, when lately dead ; the widow's fon in Nain, when they were carrying him out to bury him, Luke vii. 11. 15. and Lazarus, when ftinking in the grave, John xi. 39. 44.

Can men make curious glaffes out of afhes, reduce flowers into afhes, and raife them again out of thefe afhes, reftoring them to their former beauty ; and cannot the great Creator, who made all things of nothing, raife man's body, after it is reduced into duft ? If it be objected, How can men's bodies be raifed up again, after they are turned into duft, and the afhes of many generations are mingled together ? Scripture and reafon furnifh the anfwer ; *With men it is impoſſible, but not with God.* It is abfurd for men to deny that God can do a thing, becaufe they fee not how it may be done. How fmall a portion do we know of his ways ! How abfolutely incapable are we of conceiving diftinctly of the extent of almighty power; and much more of comprehending its actings, and method of procedure ! I

Head III. *Of the Resurrection.* 335

question not, but many illiterate men are as great infidels to many chymical experiments, as some learned men are to the doctrine of the resurrection: and as these last are ready to deride the former, so the Lord will have them in derision. What a mystery was it to the Indian, that the Europeans could, by a piece of paper, converse together at the distance of some hundreds of miles! How much were they astonished to see them, with their guns, produce as it were thunder and lightening in a moment, and at pleasure kill men afar off! Shall some men do such things as are wonders in the eyes of others, because they cannot comprehend them! and shall men confine the infinite power of God within the narrow boundaries of their own shallow capacity, in a matter no ways contrary to reason ? An inferior nature has but a very imperfect conception of the power of a superior. Brutes do not conceive of the actings of reason in men ; and men have but lame notions of the power of angels : how low and inadequate a conception, then, must a finite nature have of the power of that which is infinite ! Though we cannot conceive how God acts, yet we ought to believe he can do above what we can think or conceive of.

Wherefore, let the bodies of men be laid in the grave ; let them rot there, and be reduced to the most minute particles : or let them be burnt, and the ashes cast into rivers, or thrown up into the air, to be scattered by the wind : let the dust of a thousand generations be mingled, and the stems of the dead bodies wander to and fro in the air : let birds or wild beasts eat the dead bodies, or the fishes of the sea devour them, so that the parts of human bodies, thus destroyed, pass into substantial parts of birds, beasts, or fishes : or, what is more than that, let man-eaters, who themselves must die, and rise again, devour human bodies ; and let others devour them again ; and then let our modern Sadducees propose the question in these cases, as the ancient Sadducees did in the case of the woman who had been married to seven husbands successively, Matt. xxii. 28. We answer, as our blessed Lord and Saviour did, verse 29. *Te do err, not knowing* the *Scriptures*, *nor the power of God*. We believe God to be omniscient, and omnipotent; infinite in knowledge and in power: and hence, agreeably to the dictates of reason, we conclude the possibility of the resurrection, even in the cases supposed.

Material things may change their forms and shapes, may be reduced to the principles of which they are formed: but they are not annihilated, or reduced to nothing; nor can they be so, by any created power. God is omniscient, his understanding is infinite: therefore he knows all things; what they were at any time, what they are, and where they are to be found. Though the country-man, who comes into the apothecary's shop, cannot find out the drug he wants; yet the apothecary himself knows what he has in his shop, whence it came, and where it is to be found. And in a mixture of many different seeds, the expert gardner can distinguish between seed and seed. Why then may not Omniscience distinguish between dust and dust? Can he, who knows all things to perfection, be liable to any mistake about his own creatures? Whoso believes an infinite understanding, must needs own, that no mass of dust is so jumbled together, but God perfectly comprehends, and infallibly knows, how the most minute particle, and every one of them, is to be matched. Therefore he knows where the particles of each dead body are; whether in the earth, sea, or air, how confused soever they are scattered. And particularly, he knows where to find the primitive substance of the man-eater, however evaporated or reduced, as it were, into the air or vapour, by sweat, or perspiration; and how to separate the parts of the body that was eaten, from the body of the eater, however incorporated or made one body with it: and so understands, not only how, but whence, he is to bring back the primitive substance of the man-eater to its proper place; and also to separate from the man-eater's body that part of the devoured body which goes into its substance, and is indeed but a very small part of it. It is certain that the bodies of men, as of all other animals or living creatures, are in a continual flux: they

Head III. *Of the Resurrection.*

grow and are sustained by daily food; so small a part whereof becomes nourishment, that the most part evaporates. It is reckoned that, at least, as much of the food evaporates insensibly by perspiration, as is voided by other perceptible ways. Yea, the nourishing part of the food, when assimilated, and hereby become a part of the body, evaporates by perspiration, through the pores of the skin, and is again supplied by the use of other food: yet the body is still reckoned one and the same body. Whence we may conclude, that it is not essential to the resurrection of the body, that every particle of the matter, which at any time was part of a human body, should be restored to it, when it is raised up from death to life. Were it so, the bodies of men would become of so huge a size, that they would bear no resemblance to the persons. It is sufficient to denominate it the same body that died, when it is risen again, if the body that is raised be formed in its former proportions, of the same particles of matter, which at any time were its constituent parts, however it be refined. The same as, we reckon it is the same body that was pined away by long sickness, which becomes fat and fair again after recovery.

Now, to this infinite understanding join infinite power, whereby he is able to subdue all things unto himself; and this gloriously great work appears most reasonable If Omniscience can discover every little particle of dust, where it is, and how it is to be matched, cannot Omnipotence bring them, and join them together in order? Can the watch-maker take up the several pieces of a watch, lying in a confused heap before him, and set each in its proper place; and cannot God put the human body into order, after its dissolution? Did he speak this world into being, out of nothing; and cannot he form man's body out of its pre-existent matter? If he calleth those things which be not, as though they were, surely he can call things that are dissolved, to be as they were, before the compound was resolved into its parts and principles. Wherefore, God can raise the dead. And *why should it be thought a thing incredible with you, that God should raise the dead?* Acts xxvi. 8.

X x

Secondly, God will do it. He not only can do it; but he certainly will do it, becaufe he has faid it. Our text is very full to this purpofe, *All that are in the graves fhall hear his voice : and fhall come forth ; they that have done good, unto the refurrection of life, and they that have done evil, unto the refurrection of damnation.* Thefe words relate to, and are an explanation of, that part of Daniel's prophecy, Dan. xii. 2. *Many of them that fleep in the duft of the earth fhall awake, fome to everlafting contempt;* which appears to be calculated to confront the doctrine of the Sadducees; which the Holy Ghoft knew was to be at a great height in the Jewifh church, under the perfecution of Antiochus. There are many other texts in the Old and New Teftament, that might be adduced fuch as Acts xxiv. 15. *And have hope towards God which they themfelves alfo allow, that there fhall be a refurrection of the dead, both of the juft and unjuft.* And Job xix. 26, 27. *Though after my fkin worms deftroy this body yet in my flefh fhall I fee God : whom I fhall fee for myfelf and mine eyes fhall behold, and not another ; though my reins be confumed within me.* But I need not multiply teftimonies, in a matter fo clearly and frequently taught in facred Scripture. Our Lord and Saviour himfelf proves it againft the Sadducees, in that remarkable text Luke xx. 37, 38. *Now that the dead are raifed, even Mofes fhewed at the bufh, when he calleth the Lord, th God of Abraham, and the God of Ifaac, and the God o Jacob. For he is not a God of the dead, but of the living for all live unto him.* Thefe holy Patriarchs were dead neverthelefs, the Lord JEHOVAH is called their God namely, in virtue of the covenant of grace, and in the fenfe thereof; in which fenfe the phrafe compre hends all bleffednefs, as that which by the covenant i fecured to them who are in it, Heb. xii. 16. *God is no afhamed to be called their God : for he hath prepared fo them a city.* He is not called the God of their fou only; but their God, the God of their perfons, fou and bodies; the which, by virtue of his truth an faithfulnefs, muft have its full effect : now it canno have its full effect on the dead, who, in as much they are dead, are far from all bleffednefs; but on t

Head III.   *Of the Resurrection.*   339

living, who alone are capable of it: therefore, since God is still called their God, they are living in respect of God [*], although their bodies are yet in the grave; for, in respect of him, who by his power can restore them to life, and in his covenant has declared his will and purpose so to do, and whose promise cannot fail, they all are to be reckoned to live; and, consistent with the covenant, their death is but a sleep, out of which, in virtue of the same covenant, securing all blessedness to their persons, their whole man, they must and shall certainly be awakened. The apostle Paul proves the resurrection at large, 1 Cor. xv. and shews it to be a fundamental article, the denial whereof is subversive of Christianity, ver. 13, 14, *If there be no resurrection of the dead, then is Christ not risen. And if Christ be not risen, then is our preaching vain, and your faith is also vain.*

To assist us in conceiving of it, the Scripture gives us types of the resurrection of the dead; as the dry bones living, Ezek. xxxvii. Jonah's coming out of the whale's belly, Matt. xii. 40. And nature affords us emblems and resemblances of it, as the sun's setting and rising again; night and day, winter and summer, sleeping and awaking; swallows in winter, lying void of all appearance of life, in ruinous buildings, subterraneous caverns, and reviving again in the springseason; the seed dying under the clod, and after springing up again: all which, and the like, may justly be admitted as designed by the God of nature, though not for proofs, yet for memorials of the resurrection; whereof we have assurance from the Scripture, 1 Cor. xv. 36. *Thou fool, that which thou sowest is not quickened, except it die.*

II. I shall enquire into the nature of the resurrection; shewing, *First*, Who shall be raised. 2*dly*, What shall be raised. 3*dly*, How the dead shall be raised.

I. Who shall be raised. Our text tells us who they are; namely, *All that are in the graves*, that is, all mankind who are dead. As for those persons who shall

---

[*] Their souls are actually so, and enjoy communion with him, and saints and angels.

be found alive, at the second coming of Christ, they shall not die, and soon after be raised again: but such a change shall suddenly pass upon them, as shall be to them instead of dying and rising again; so that their bodies shall become like to those bodies which are raised out of the graves, 1 Cor. xv. 51, 52 *We shall not all sleep, but we shall be changed. In a moment, in the twinkling of an eye.* Hence those who are to be judged at the great day, are distinguished into *quick* and *dead*, Acts x. 42. All the dead shall rise, whether godly or wicked, just or unjust, (Acts xxiv. 15.) old or young: the whole race of mankind, even those who never saw the sun, but died in their mother's belly, Rev. xx. 12. *And I saw the dead, small and great, stand before God.* The sea and earth shall give up their dead, without reserve; none shall be kept back.

II. What shall be raised. The bodies of mankind. A man is said to die, when the soul is separated from the body, *and returns unto God who gave it*, Eccl. xii. 7. But it is the body only which is laid in the grave, and can be properly said to be raised: wherefore the resurrection is, strictly speaking, competent to the body only. Moreover, it is the same body that dies, which shall rise again. At the resurrection, men shall not appear with other bodies, for substance, than those which they now have, and which are laid down in the grave; but with the self-same bodies, endowed with other qualities. The very notion of a resurrection implies this, since nothing can be said to rise again, but that which falls. But to illustrate it a little; *First*, It is plain from Scripture testimony. The apostle asserts, that it is *this mortal* which *must put on immortality*, 1 Cor. xv. 53. and that Christ *shall change our vile body, that it may be fashioned like unto his glorious body*, Phil. iii. 21. Death, in Scripture-language, is a sleep, and the resurrection an awakening out of that sleep, Job xvi. 12. which shews the body rising up to be the self-same that died. *Secondly*, The equity of the divine procedure, both with respect to the godly and the wicked, proves this. It is not reckoned equal among men, that one do the work, and another get the reward. Though the glori-

Head III. *Of the Resurrection.* 341

fying of the bodies of the saints is not, properly speaking, and in a strict sense, the reward of their services or sufferings on earth; yet this is evident, that it is not at all agreeable to the manner of the divine dispensation, that one body should serve him, and another be glorified; that one should fight, and another receive the crown. How can it be imagined, that *the temples of the Holy Ghost* (as the bodies of believers are termed, 1 Cor. vi. 19.) should always lie in rubbish, and others be reared up in their stead? That the members of Christ, (ver. 15.) should perish utterly, and other bodies come in their room? Nay, surely, as the bodies of the saints now bear a part in glorifying God, and some of them suffer in his cause, so they shall partake of the glory that is to be revealed. And the bodies of the wicked, which are laid in the dust, shall be raised again, that the same body which sinned may suffer. Shall one body sin here, and another suffer in hell for that sin? shall that body, which was the soul's companion in sin, lie for ever hid in the dust; and another body, which did not act any part in sinning, be its companion in torment? No, no; it is that body, which now takes up all their thoughts, to provide for its back and belly, that shall be raised up, to suffer in hell. It is that tongue that is now the swearing, lying tongue, which will need water to cool it, in eternal flames. The same feet, that now stand in the way of sinners, and carry men in their ungodly courses, shall stand in the burning lake. And the same covetous and lascivious eyes shall take part in the fire and smoke of the pit.

III. How the dead shall be raised. The same Jesus, who was crucified without the gates of Jerusalem, shall at the last day, to the conviction of all, be declared both Lord and Christ; appearing as judge of the world, attended with his mighty angels, 2 Thess. i. 7. He shall *descend from heaven with a shout, with the voice of the arch-angel, and with the trump of God*, 1 Thess. iv. 16. *The trumpet shall sound, and the dead shall be raised*, and those who are alive changed, 1 Cor. xv. 52. Whether this *shout, voice, and trumpet*, denote some audible voice, or only the workings of divine power, for the raising of the dead, and other awful purposes of that day, (though the former seems propable) I will not positively determine. There is no question, but this coming of the Judge of the world will be in greater majesty and terror than we can conceive: yet that awful grandeur, majesty and state, which was displayed at the giving of the law, *viz.* thunders heard, lightenings, and a thick cloud upon the mount seen, the Lord descending in fire, the whole mount quaking greatly, and the voice of the trumpet waxing louder and louder, (Exod. xix. 16. 18, 19.) may help us to form a becoming thought of it. However, the sound of this trumpet shall be heard all the world over; it shall reach to the depths of the sea, and into the bowels of the earth. At this loud alarm, bones shall come together, bone to his bone: the scattered dust of all the dead shall be gathered together, dust to his dust; neither shall one thrust another, they shall walk every one in his path: and meeting together again, shall make up that very same body which crumbled into dust in the grave. At the same alarming voice, shall every soul come again into its own body, never more to be separated. The dead can stay no longer in their graves, but must bid an eternal farewell to their long homes: they hear his voice, and must come forth, and receive their final sentence.

Now, as there is a great difference between the godly and the wicked, in their life, and in their death; so there will be also in their resurrection.

The godly shall be raised out of their graves, by virtue of the Spirit of Christ, the blessed bond of their union with him, Rom. viii. 11. *He that raised up Christ from the dead, shall also quicken your mortal bodies, by his Spirit that dwelleth in you.* Jesus Christ arose from the dead, as the *first fruits of them that slept,* 1 Cor. xvi. 20. So they that are Christ's, shall follow at his coming, ver. 23. The mystical head having got above the waters of death, he cannot but bring forth the members after him in due time.

They shall come forth with inexpressible joy: for then shall that passage of Scripture, which in its imme-

Head III. *Of the Resurrection.* 343

diate scope respected the Babylonish captivity, be fully accomplished in its extensive spiritual view, Isa. xxvi. 19. *Awake and sing, ye that dwell in the dust.* As a bride, adorned for her husband, goes forth from her bed-chamber unto the marriage; so shall the saints go forth from their graves, unto the marriage of the Lamb. Joseph had a joyful coming out from the prison, Daniel from the lion's den, and Jonah from the whale's belly; yet those are but faint representations of the saints coming forth from the grave at the resurrection. Then shall they sing the song of Moses and of the Lamb, in highest strains; death being quite swallowed up in victory. They had, while in this life, sometimes sung, by faith, the triumphant song over death and the grave, *O death, where is thy sting? O grave, where is thy victory?* 1 Cor. xv. 55. but then they sing the same, from sight and sense. The black band of doubts and fears, which frequently disturbed them, and disquieted their minds, is for ever disbanded, and driven away.

May we not suppose the soul and body of every saint, as in mutual embraces, to rejoice in each other, and triumph in their happy meeting again; and the body to address the soul thus? "O my soul, are we got together again, after so long a separation! Art thou come back to thine old habitation, never more to remove! O joyful meeting! how unlike is our present state, to what our case was when a separation was made between us at death! Now is our mourning turned into joy; the light and gladness sown before, are now sprung up, and there is a perpetual spring in Immanuel's land. Blessed be the day in which I was united to thee; whose chief care was to get Christ in us the hope of glory, and to make me a temple for his Holy Spirit. O blessed soul, which in the time of our pilgrimage kept thine eye to the land then afar off, but now near at hand! thou tookest me into secret places, and there madest me to bow these knees before the Lord, that I might bear a part in our humiliation before him: and now is the time that I am lifted up. Thou didst employ this tongue, in confessions, petitions, and thanksgivings, which henceforth shall be employed in praising for evermore. Thou madeſt theſe ſometimes weeping eyes, ſow that ſeed of tears, which is now ſprung up in joy, that ſhall never end. I was happily beat down by thee, and kept in ſubjection, while others pampered their fleſh, and made their bellies their gods, to their own deſtruction: but now I glorioully ariſe, to take my place in the manſions of glory, whilſt they are dragged out of their graves, to be caſt into fiery flames. Now, my ſoul, thou ſhalt complain no more of a ſick and pained body; thou ſhalt be no more clogged with weak and weary fleſh: I ſhall now hold pace with thee in the praiſes of our God for evermore." And may not the ſoul ſay, "O happy day in which I return to dwell in that bleſſed body, which was, and is, and will be for ever, a member of Chriſt, a temple of the Holy Spirit! Now I ſhall be eternally knit to thee: the ſilver cord ſhall never be looſed more: death ſhall never make another ſeparation between us. Ariſe, then, my body, and come away! and let theſe eyes, which were wont to weep over my ſins, behold, with joy, the face of our glorious Redeemer; lo! this is our God, and we have waited for him. Let theſe ears, which were wont to hear the word of life in the temple below, come and hear the hallelujahs in the temple above. Let theſe feet, that carried me to the congregation of ſaints on earth, take their place among thoſe in heaven. And let this tongue, which confeſſed Chriſt before men, and uſed to be ſtill dropping ſomething to his commendation, join the choir of the upper houſe, in his praiſes for evermore. Thou ſhalt faſt no more, but keep an everlaſting feaſt; thou ſhalt weep no more, neither ſhall thy countenance be overclouded; but thou ſhalt ſhine for ever, as a ſtar in the firmament. We took part together in the fight, come let us go together to receive and wear the crown."

But, on the other hand, the wicked ſhall be raiſed by the power of Chriſt, as a juſt Judge, who is to render vengeance to his enemies. The ſame divine power, which ſhut up their ſouls in hell, and kept their bodies in the grave, as in a priſon, ſhall bring them forth, that ſoul and body together may receive the dreadful ſentence of eternal damnation, and be ſhut up together in the priſon of hell.

Head III. *Of the Resurrection.*

They shall come forth from their graves, with unspeakable horror and consternation. They shall be dragged forth, as so many malefactors out of a dungeon, to be led to execution; crying to the mountains and to the rocks to fall on them, and hide them from the face of the Lamb. Fearful was the cry in Egypt, the night which the destroying angel went through, and slew their first-born. Dreadful were the shouts, at the earth's opening her mouth, and swallowing up Dathan and Abiram, and all that appertained to them. What hideous crying then must there be, when, at the sound of the last trumpet, the earth and sea shall open their mouths, and cast forth all the wicked world, delivering them up to the dreadful Judge! how will they cry, roar, and tear themselves! how will the jovial companions weep and howl, and curse one another! how will the earth be filled with their doleful shrieks and lamentations, while they are pulled out like sheep for the slaughter! they who, while they lived in the world, were profane debauchees, covetous worldlings, or formal hypocrites, shall then, in anguish of mind, wring their hands, beat their breasts, and bitterly lament their case, roaring forth their complaints, and calling themselves beasts, fools, and mad-men, for having acted so mad a part in this life, in not believing what they then heard. They were driven away in their wickedness, at death: and now all their sins rise with them, and, like so many serpents, twist themselves about their wretched souls, and bodies too, which have a frightful meeting, after a long separation.

Then we may suppose the miserable body thus to accost the soul: " Hast thou again found me, O mine enemy, my worst enemy, savage soul, more cruel than a thousand tygers? cursed be the day that ever we met. O that I had remained a lifeless lump, rotted in the belly of my mother, and had never received sense, life, nor motion! O that I had rather been the body of a toad or serpent, than thy body; for then had I lien still, and had not seen this terrible day! If I was to be necessarily thine, O that I had been thy ass! or one of thy dogs, rather than thy body; for then wouldst thou have taken more true care of me than thou didſt. O cruel kindneſs! haſt thou thus hugged me to death, thus nouriſhed me to the ſlaughter? is this the effect of thy tenderneſs for me? is this what I am to reap of thy pains and concern about me? what do riches and pleaſures avail now, when this fearful reckoning is come; of which thou hadſt fair warning? O cruel grave! why didſt thou not cloſe thy mouth upon me for ever? why didſt thou not hold faſt thy priſoner? why haſt thou ſhaken me out, while I lay ſtill, and was at reſt? Curſed ſoul, wherefore didſt thou not abide in thy place, wrapped up in flames of fire? wherefore art thou come back to take me alſo down to the bars of the pit? thou madeſt me an inſtrument of unrighteouſneſs; and now I muſt be thrown into the fire. This tongue was by thee employed in mocking at religion, curſing, ſwearing, lying, backbiting, and boaſting; and with-held from glorifying God: and now it muſt not have ſo much as a drop of water to cool it in the flames. Thou didſt withdraw mine ears from hearing the ſermons, which gave warning of this day. Thou foundeſt ways and means to ſtop them from attending to ſeaſonable exhortations, admonitions, and reproofs. But why didſt thou not ſtop them from hearing the ſound of this dreadful trumpet? why doſt thou not now rove and fly away on the wings of imagination, thereby, as it were, tranſporting me during theſe frightful tranſactions; as thou was wont to do, when I was ſet down at ſermons, communions, prayers, and godly conferences; that I might now have as little ſenſe of the one, as I formerly had of the other? But, ah! I muſt burn for ever, for thy love to thy luſts, thy profanity, thy ſenſuality, thy unbelief, and hypocriſy." But may not the ſoul anſwer? " Wretched and vile carcaſe, I am now driven back into thee, O that thou hadſt lien rotting for ever in thy grave! Had I not torment enough before? Muſt I be knit to thee again, that being joined together, as two dry ſticks for the fire, the wrath of God may burn us up? it was by caring for you, that I loſt myſelf. It was your back and your belly, and the gratifying of your ſenſes, which ruined me? How often was I enfnared by your ears? how often betrayed by your eyes? it was to fpare you, that I neglected opportunities of making peace with God, loitered away Sabbaths, lived in the neglect of prayer; went to the houfe of mirth, rather than the houfe of mourning; and that I chofe to deny Chrift, and forfake his caufe and interefts in the world; and fo am fallen a facrifice to your curfed eafe. When at any time my confcience began to awake, and I was fetting myfelf to think of my fins, and the mifery which I have felt fince we parted, and now feel, it was you that diverted me from thefe thoughts, and drew me off to make provifion for thee. O wretched flefh! by your filken cords of flefhly lufts, I was drawn to deftruction, over the belly of my light confcience: but now they are turned into iron chains, with which I am to be held under wrath for evermore. Ah wretched profits! ah curfed pleafures! for which I muft lie for ever in utter darknefs." But no complaints will then avail. *O that men were wife, that they underflood this, that they would confider their latter end.*

As to the qualities with which the bodies of the faints fhall be endowed at the refurrection, the apoftle tells us they fhall be raifed incorruptible, glorious, powerful, and fpiritual, 1 Cor. xv. 42, 43, 44. *It is fown in corruption, it is raifed in incorruption. It is fown in difhonour, it is raifed in glory. It is fown in weaknefs, it is raifed in power. It is fown a natural body, it is raifed a fpiritual body.*

Firft, The bodies of the faints fhall be raifed incorruptible. They are now as the bodies of others, a very mafs of corruption, full of the feeds of difeafes and death; and, when dead, become fo naufeous, even to their deareft friends, that they muft be buried out of their fight, in a grave, there to rot, and be confumed: yea, loathfome fores and difeafes make fome of them very unfightly, even while alive. But at the refurrection they leave all the feeds of corruption behind them in the grave; and rife incorruptible, incapable of the leaft indifpofition, ficknefs, or fore, and much more of dying. External violences, and inward caufes of pain, fhall for ever ceafe: they fhall feel it no more: yea, they fhall have an everlafting youth and vigour, being no more fubject to the decays which age produced in this life.

Secondly, They shall be glorious bodies; not only beautiful, comely, and well proportioned, but full of splendour and brightness. The most beautiful face, and best proportioned body, that now appears in the world, is not to be named in comparison with the body of the meanest saint at the resurrection; for *then shall the righteous shine forth as the sun*, Matt. xiii. 43. If there was a dazling glory on Moses's face, when he came down from the mount; and if Stephen's face was as *it had been the face of an angel*, when he stood before the council, how much more shall the faces of the saints be beautiful and glorious, full of sweet, agreeable majesty, when they shall have put off all corruption, and shine as the sun? But observe, this beauty of the saints is not restricted to their faces, but diffuses itself through their whole bodies: for the whole body is raised in glory, and shall be fashioned like unto their Lord and Saviour's glorious body; in whose transfiguration, not only did his face shine as the sun, but also his raiment was white as the light, Matt. xvii. 2. Whatever defects or deformities the bodies of the saints had, when laid in the grave, occasioned by accidents in life, or arising from secret causes in their formation in the womb, they shall rise out of the grave free of all these. But suppose the marks of the Lord Jesus, the scars or prints of the wounds and bruises which some of the saints received while on earth, for his sake, should remain in their bodies after the resurrection; the same as the print of the nails remained in the Lord Jesus's body after his resurrection; these marks will rather be badges of distinction, and add to their glory, than detract from their beauty. But however that be, surely Isaac's eyes shall not then be dim, nor will Jacob halt: Leah shall not be tender-eyed, nor Mephibosheth lame of his legs. For as the gold-smith melts down the old crazy vessel, and casts it over again in a new mould, bringing it forth with a new lustre; so shall the vile body, which lay dissolved in the grave, come forth at the resurrection, in perfect beauty and comely proportion.

Thirdly, They shall be powerful and strong bodies: the strongest man on earth, being frail and mortal, may justly be reckoned weak and feeble, in regard their

Head III. *Of the Resurrection.*

strength, however great, is quickly worn out and consumed. Many of the saints now have weaker bodies than others; but *the feeble among them* (to allude to Zech. xii. 8. *at that day shall be as David, and the house of David shall be as God.* A grave Divine says, That one shall be stronger, at the resurrection, than an hundred, yea, than thousands are now. Certainly, great, and vastly great, must the strength of glorified bodies be; for they shall bear up under an exceeding and eternal weight of glory. The mortal body is not at all adapted to such a state. Do transports of joy occasion death, as well as excessive grief does? and can it bear up under a weight of glory? can it subsist in union with a soul filled with heaven's raptures? Surely no. The mortal body would sink under that load, and such a fill would make the earthen pitcher to fly all in pieces. The Scripture has plainly told us, *That flesh and blood*, (namely, in their present frail state, though it were the flesh and blood of a giant) *cannot inherit the kingdom of God*, 1 Cor. xv. 50. How strong must the bodily eyes be, which, to the soul's eternal comfort, shall behold the dazling glory and splendour of the new Jerusalem; and stedfastly look at the transcendent glory and brightness of the man Christ, the Lamb, who is the light of that city, the inhabitants whereof shall shine as the sun? The Lord of heaven doth now, in mercy, hold back the face of his throne, and spreadeth his cloud upon it, that mortals may not be confounded with the rays of glory which shine forth from it, Job xxvi. 9. but then the veil shall be removed, and they be made able to behold it, to their unspeakable joy. How strong must their bodies be, who shall not rest night nor day, but be, without intermission, for ever employed in the heavenly temple, to sing and proclaim the praises of God without weariness, which is a weakness incident to the frail mortal, but not to the glorified body!

Lastly, They shall be spiritual bodies. Not that they shall be changed into spirits: but they shall be spiritual, in respect of their spirit-like qualities and endowments. The body shall be absolutely subservient to the soul, subject to it, and influenced by it; and therefore no more a clog to its activity, nor the animal appetites a snare to it. There will be no need to beat it down, nor to drag it to the service of God. The soul, in this life, is so much influenced by the body, that, in Scripture-style, it is said to be carnal: but then the body shall be spiritual, readily serving the soul in the business of heaven; and in that only, as if it had no more relation to earth than a spirit. It will have no further need of the now necessary supports of life, namely, food and raiment, and the like. *They shall hunger no more, neither thirst any more*, Rev. vii. 16. *For in the resurrection they neither marry nor are given in marriage, but are as the angels of God in heaven.* Then shall the saints be strong, without meat or drink, warm, without cloaths, ever in perfect health, without medicine, and ever fresh and vigorous, though they shall never sleep, but serve him night and day in his temple, Rev. vii. 15. They will need none of these things more than spirits do. They will be nimble and active as spirits, and of a most refined constitution. The body, that is now lumpish and heavy, shall then be most sprightly. No such thing as melancholy shall be found, to make the heart heavy, and the spirits flag and sink. Where the carcase is, there shall the saints, as so many eagles, be gathered together. I shall not further dip into this matter: the day will declare it.

As to the qualities of the bodies of the wicked, at the resurrection. I find that the Scripture speaks but little of them. Whatever they may need, they shall not get a drop of water to cool their tongues, Luke xvi. 24, 25. Whatever may be said of their weakness, it is certain they will be continued for ever in life, that they may be ever dying: they shall bear up, however unwilling, under the load of God's wrath, and shall not faint away under it. *The smoke of their torment ascendeth up for ever and ever.* *And they have no rest day nor night.* Surely they shall not partake of the glory and beauty of the saints. All their glory dies with them, and shall never rise again. Daniel tells us, they shall awake *to shame, and everlasting contempt*, chap. xii. 2. Shame follows sin, as the shadow followeth the body: but the wicked in this world walk in the dark,

Head III. *Of the Resurrection.*

and often under a disguise: nevertheless, when the Judge comes in flaming fire, at the last day, they will be brought to the light; their mask will be taken off, and the shame of their nakedness will clearly appear to themselves and others, and fill their faces with confusion. Their shame will be too deep for blushes: all their faces shall gather blackness at that day; when they shall go forth of their graves, as malefactors out of their prisons to execution: for their resurrection is the resurrection of damnation. The greatest beauties, who now pride themselves in their comeliness of body, not regarding their deformed souls, will then appear with a ghastly countenance, a grim and death-like visage. Their looks will be frightful, and they will be horrible spectacles, coming forth from their graves like infernal furies out of the pit. They shall rise also to everlasting contempt. They shall then be the most contemptible creatures, filled with contempt from God, as vessels of dishonour, whatever honourable employs they had in this world; and filled also with contempt from men. They will be most despicable in the eyes of the saints, even of those saints who gave them honour here, either for their high station, the gifts of God in them, or because they were of the same human nature with themselves. But then shall their bodies be as so many loathsome carcases, which they shall go forth and look upon with abhorrence: yea, *they shall be an abhorring unto all flesh*, Isa. lxvi. 24. The word here rendered *an abhorring*, is the same which in the other text is rendered *contempt*; and Isaiah and Daniel point at one and the same thing, namely, the loathsomness of the wicked at the resurrection. They will be loathsome in the eyes of one another. The unclean wretches were never so lovely to each other, as then they will be loathsome: dear companions in sin will then abhor each other; and the wicked, great and honourable men, shall be no more regarded by their wicked subjects, their servants, their slaves, than the mire in the streets.

Use I. Of comfort to the people of God. The doctrine of the resurrection is a spring of consolation and joy unto you. Think on it, O believers, when you are in the house of mourning, for the loss of your godly relations or friends, *that ye sorrow not even as others, which have no hope*; for you will meet again, 1 Thess. iv. 13, 14. they are but lain down to rest in their beds for a little while, (Isa. lvii. 2.) in the morning of the resurrection they will awake again, and come forth from their graves. The vessel of honour was but coarse, it had much alloy of base metal in it; it was too weak, too dim and inglorious, for the upper house, whatever lustre it had in the lower one. It was cracked, it was polluted; and therefore must be melted down to be refined, and fashioned more gloriously. Do but wait a while, and you shall see it come forth out of the furnace of earth, vying with the stars in brightness; nay, as the sun when he goeth forth in his might. Have you laid your infant children in the grave? you will see them again. Your God calls himself *the God of your seed*; which, according to our Saviour's exposition, secures the glorious resurrection of the body. Wherefore, let the covenant you embraced, for yourself and your babes now in the dust, comfort your heart in the joyful expectation, that, by virtue thereof, they shall be raised up in glory; and that as being no more infants of days, but brought to a full and perfect stature, as is generally supposed. Be not discouraged by reason of a weak and sickly body; there is a day coming when thou shalt be every whit whole. At the resurrection, Timothy shall be no more liable to his often infirmities; his body, that was weak and sickly, even in youth, shall be raised in power, Lazarus shall be healthy and sound, his body being raised incorruptible. Although, perhaps, thy weakness will not allow thee now to go one furlong to meet the Lord in public ordinances, yet the day cometh when thy body shall be no more a clog to thee, but thou shalt *meet the Lord in the air*, 1 Thess. iv. 17. It will be with the saints coming up from the grave, as with the Israelites, when they came out of Egypt, Psal. cv. 37. *There was not one feeble person among their tribes.* Hast thou an uncomely, or deformed body? There is a glory within, which will then set all right without, according to all the desire of thine heart. It shall rise a glorious, beautiful, handsome, and well proportioned body.

Head III.   *Of the Refurrection.*   353

Its uncomelinefs or deformities may go with it to the grave, but they fhall not come back with it O that thofe, who are now fo defirous to be beautiful and handfome, would not be too hafty to effect it with their foolifh and finful arts, but wait and ftudy the heavenly art of beautifying the body, by endeavouring now to become all glorious within, with the graces of God's Spirit! This would at length make them admirable and everlafting beauties. Thou muft indeed, O believer, grapple with death, and fhall get the firft fall: but thou fhalt rife again, and come off victorious at laft. Thou muft go down to the grave! but though it be thy long home, it will not be thine everlafting home. Thou wilt not hear the voice of thy friends there; but thou fhalt hear the voice of Chrift there. Thou mayeft be carried thither with mourning, but fhalt come up from it rejoicing. Thy friends, indeed, will leave thee there, but thy God will not. What God faid to Jacob, concerning his going down to Egypt, (Gen. xlvi. 3, 4.) he fays to thee, on thy going down to the grave, *Fear not to go down—I will go down with thee, and I will alfo furely bring thee up again.* O folid comfort! O glorious hope! *Wherefore comfort yourfelves, and one another with thefe words,* 1 Theff. iv. 18.

USE II. Of terror to all unregenerate men. You who are yet in your natural ftate, look at this piece of the eternal ftate; and confider what will be your part in it, if you be not in time brought into the ftate of grace. Think, O finner, on that day, when the trumpet fhall found, at the voice of which the bars of the pit fhall be broken afunder, the doors of the grave fhall fly open, the devouring depths of the fea fhall throw up their dead, the earth caft forth her's; and death every where, in the excefs of aftonifhment, fhall let go his prifoners; and thy wretched foul and body fhall be reunited, to be fummoned before the tribunal of God. Then, if thou hadft a thoufand worlds at thy difpofal, thou wouldft gladly give them all away, upon condition that thou mighteft lie ftill in thy grave, with the hundred part of that eafe wherewith thou haft fometimes lien at home on the Lord's day: or, if that cannot be obtained, that thou mighteſt be but a ſpectator of the tranſactions of that day; as thou haſt been at ſome ſolemn occaſions, and rich goſpel feaſts: or, if even that is not to be purchaſed, that a mountain or rock might fall on thee, and cover thee from the face of the Lamb. Ah! how are men infatuated, thus to trifle away the precious time of life, in almoſt as little concern about death, as if they were like the beaſts that periſh! Some will be telling where their corpſes muſt be laid, while yet they have not ſeriouſly conſidered whether their graves ſhall be their beds, where they ſhall awake with joy in the morning of the reſurrection; or their priſons, out of which they ſhall be brought to receive the fearful ſentence. Remember, now is your ſeed-time; and as you ſow, ſo you ſhall reap. God's ſeed-time begins at death; and at the reſurrection, the bodies of the wicked, that were ſown full of ſins, that lie down with them in the duſt, (Job xx. 11.) ſhall ſpring up again, ſinful, wretched, and vile. Your bodies, which are now inſtruments of ſin, the Lord will lay aſide for the fire at death, and bring them forth for the fire at the reſurrection. That body, which is not now employed in God's ſervice, but is abuſed by uncleanneſs and laſciviouſneſs, will then be brought forth in all its vileneſs, thenceforth to lodge with unclean ſpirits. The body of the drunkard ſhall then ſtagger, by reaſon of the wine of the wrath of God poured out on him, and poured into him, without mixture. Thoſe who now pleaſe themſelves in their revellings, will reel to and fro at another rate; when, inſtead of their ſongs and muſic, they ſhall hear the ſound of the laſt trumpet. Many toil their bodies for worldly gain, who will be loath to diſtreſs them for the benefit of their ſouls: by labour, unreaſonably hard, they will quite disfit them for the ſervice of God; and when they have done, will reckon it a very good reaſon for ſhifting duty, that they are already tired out with other buſineſs: but the day cometh, when they will be made to abide a yet greater diſtreſs. Many will go ſeveral miles for back and belly, who will not go half the way for the good of their immortal ſouls; many are ſickly and unable on the Lord's day, who will be tolerably

Head III.   *Of the Resurrection.*   355

well all the rest of the week. But when that trumpet sounds, the dead shall find their feet, and none shall be missing in that congregation. When the bodies of the saints shall shine as the sun, frightful will the looks of their persecutors be. Fearful will their condition be, who shut up the saints in nasty prisons, stigmatized, burned them to ashes, hanged them, and stuck up their heads and hands in public places, to frighten others from the way of righteousness, which they suffered for. Many faces, now fair, will then gather blackness. They shall be no more admired and caressed for that beauty, which has a worm at the root, that will cause it to issue in loathsomeness and deformity. Ah! what is that beauty, under which there lurks a monstrous, deformed, and graceless heart? What but a sorry paint, a slight varnish, which will leave the body so much the more ugly, before that flaming fire, in which the Judge shall be *revealed from heaven, taking vengeance on them that know not God, and that obey not the gospel,* 2 Thes. i. 7, 8. They shall be stripped of all their ornaments, and not have a rag to cover their nakedness: their carcases shall be an abhorring to all flesh, and serve as a foil to set off the beauty and glory of the righteous, and make it appear the brighter.

Now is the time to seek a part in the resurrection of the just: which, if you would do, unite with Jesus Christ by faith, rising spiritually from sin, and glorifying God with your bodies. He is *the resurrection and the life,* John xi. 25. If your bodies be members of Christ, temples of the Holy Ghost, they shall certainly arise in glory. Get into this ark now, and you shall come forth with joy into the new world. Rise from your sins; cast away these grave-cloaths, putting off your former lusts. How can any one imagine, that those who continue dead while they live, shall come forth at the last day unto the resurrection of life? That will be the privilege of those who, having first consecrated their souls and bodies to the Lord by faith, glorify him with their bodies as well as their souls; living and acting to him, and for him, yea, and suffering for him too, when he calls them to it.

HEAD IV.
The General JUDGMENT.

MATTH. xxv. 31, 32, 33, 34, 41. 46. *When the Son of Man shall come in his glory, and all the holy angels with him, then shall he sit upon the throne of his glory. And before him shall be gathered all nations; and he shall separate them one from another, as a shepherd divideth his sheep from his goats. And he shall set the sheep on his right-hand, but the goats on the left. Then shall the King say unto them on his right-hand, Come, ye blessed,* &c. ——*Unto them on the left-hand, Depart from me, ye cursed,* &c. *And these shall go away into everlasting punishment: but the righteous into life eternal.*

THE dead being raised, and those found alive at the coming of the Judge changed, follows the general judgment, plainly and awfully described in this portion of Scripture; in which we shall take notice of the following particulars: (1.) The coming of the Judge, *When the Son of man shall come in his glory,* &c. The Judge is Jesus Christ, the Son of man; the same by whose almighty power, as he is God, the dead will be raised. He is also called *the King,* ver. 34. the judging of the world being an act of the royal Mediator's kingly office. He will come in glory: glorious in his own person, and having a glorious retinue, even all the holy angels with him, to minister unto him at this great solemnity. (2.) The mounting the tribunal. He is a King, and therefore it is a throne, a glorious throne, *He shall sit upon the throne of his glory,* ver. 31. (3.) The appearance of the parties. These are all nations; all and every one, small and great, of whatever nation, who ever were, are, or shall be on the face of the earth: all shall be gathered before him; summoned before his tribunal. (4.) The sorting of them. He shall separate the elect sheep, and reprobate goats, setting each party by themselves: as a shepherd, who feeds his sheep and goats together all the day, separates them

Head IV. *Of the general Judgment.* 357
at night, ver. 32. The godly he will set on his right-hand, as the moſt honourable place; the wicked on the left, ver. 33. yet ſo as they ſhall be both before him, ver. 32. It ſeems to be an alluſion to a cuſtom in the Jewiſh courts, in which one ſat at the right-hand of the judge, who wrote the ſentence of abſolution, another at their left, who wrote the ſentence of condemnation. (5.) The ſentencing of the parties, and that according to their works; the righteous being abſolved, and the wicked condemned, ver. 34. 41. *Laſtly,* The execution of both ſentences, in the driving away of the wicked into hell, and carrying the godly to heaven, ver. 46.

Doct. There ſhall be a general judgment. This doctrine I ſhall, (1.) confirm; (2.) explain; and, (3.) apply.

I. For confirmation of this great truth, that there ſhall be a general judgment.

Firſt, It is evident from plain Scripture teſtimonies. The world has in all ages been told of it. Enoch, before the flood, taught it in his prophecy, related Jude 14, 15. *Behold, the Lord cometh with ten thouſands of his ſaints, to execute judgment upon all,* &c. Daniel deſcribes it, chap. vii. 9, 10. *I beheld till the thrones were caſt down, and the Ancient of Days did ſit, whoſe garment was white as ſnow, and the hair of his head like the pure wool: his throne was like the fiery flame, and his wheels as burning fire. A fiery ſtream iſſued and came forth before him : thouſand thouſands miniſtered unto him, and ten thouſand times ten thouſand ſtood before him : the judgment was ſet, and the books were opened.* The apoſtle is very expreſs, Acts xvii. 31. *He hath appointed a day, in the which he will judge the world in righteouſneſs, by that man whom he hath ordained.* See Mat. xvi. 27. 2 Cor. v. 10. 2 Theſſ. i. 7—10. Rev. xx. 11—15. God has not only ſaid it, but he has ſworn it, Rom. xiv. 10, 11. *We muſt all ſtand before the judgment ſeat of Chriſt.* For *it is written, As I live, ſaith the Lord, every knee ſhall bow to me, and every tongue ſhall confeſs to God.* So that the truth of God is moſt ſolemnly pledged for it.

Secondly, The rectoral juſtice and goodneſs of God, the ſovereign Ruler of the world, neceſſarily require it, inasmuch as they require its being well with the righteous, and ill with the wicked. Yet we often see wickedness exalted, while truth and righteousness fall in the streets; piety oppressed, while profanity and irreligion do triumph. This is so very common, that every one who sincerely embraceth the way of holiness, must and doth lay his account with the loss of all he has, which the world can take away from him, Luke xiv. 26. *If any man come to me, and hate not his father, and mother, and wife, and children, and brethren, and sisters, yea, and his own life also, he cannot be my disciple.* But it is inconsistent with the justice and goodness of God, that the affairs of men should always continue in the state which they appear in, from one generation to another; and that every man should not be rewarded according to his works: and since that is not done in this life, there must be a judgment to come; *Seeing it is a righteous thing with God to recompence tribulation to them that trouble you: and to you who are troubled, rest with us, when the Lord Jesus shall be revealed from heaven,* 2 Thess. i. 6, 7. There will be a day in which the tables will be turned; and the wicked shall be called to an account for all their sins, and suffer the due punishment of them; and the pious shall be prosperous: for, as the apostle argues for the happy resurrection of the saints, *If in this life only we have hope in Christ, we are of all men most miserable*, 1 Cor. xv. 19. It is true, God sometimes punisheth the wicked in this life, that men may know *he is a God that judgeth in the earth:* yet much wickedness remains unpunished, and undiscovered, to be a pledge of the judgment to come. If none of the wicked was punished here, they would conclude that God had utterly forsaken the earth: if all of them were punished in this life, men would be apt to think that there is no afterreckoning. Therefore, in the wisdom of God, some are punished now, and some not. Sometimes the Lord smites sinners in the very act of sin; to shew unto the world that he is witness to all their wickedness, and will call them to an account for it. Sometimes he delays long ere he strikes, that he may discover to the world that he forgets not men's ill deeds, though he

Head IV. *Of the general Judgment.* 359
does not prefently punifh them. Befides all this, the fins of many out-live them; and the impure fountain, by them opened, runs long after they are dead and gone. As in the cafe of Jeroboam, the firft king of the ten tribes, whofe fin did run on all along unto the end of that unhappy kingdom, 2 Kings xvii. 22, 23. *The children of Ifrael walked in all the fins of Jeroboam, which he did, they departed not from them, until the Lord removed Ifrael out of his fight.*

Thirdly, The refurrection of Chrift is a certain proof that there fhall be a day of judgment. This argument Paul ufeth to convince the Athenians that Jefus Chrift will be the Judge of the world; *Whereof,* fays he, *he hath given affurance to all men, in that he hath raifed him from the dead,* Acts xvii. 31. The Judge is already named, his patent written and fealed, yea, and read before all men, in his rifing again from the dead. He hath, by raifing Chrift from the dead, exhibited his credentials as Judge of the world. When, in the days of his humiliation, he was cited before a tribunal, arraigned, accufed, and condemned by men, he plainly told them of this judgment, and that he himfelf would be the Judge, Mat. xxvi. 64. *Hereafter fhall ye fee the Son of man fitting on the right-hand of power, and coming in the clouds of heaven.* And now he is raifed from the dead, though condemned as a blafphemer on this very head, is it not an undeniable proof from heaven of the truth of what he afferted? Moreover, this was one of the great ends of Chrift's death and refurrection; *For to this end Chrift both died, and rofe, and revived, that he might be the Lord,* (i. e. The Lord Judge, as is evident from the context) *both of the dead and of the living,* Rom. xiv. 9.

Laftly, Every man bears about with him a witnefs to this within his own breaft, Rom. ii. 15. *Which fhew the work of the law written in their hearts, their confcience alfo bearing witnefs, and their thoughts the mean while accufing, or elfe excufing one another.* There is a tribunal erected within every man, where confcience is accufer, witnefs, and judge, binding over the finner to the judgment of God. This fills the moft profligate wretches with horror, and inwardly stings them, upon the commission of some attrocious crime; in effect summoning them to answer for it before *the Judge of the quick and dead. And thus it doth, even when the crime is secret, and hid from the eyes of the world. It reacheth those whom the laws of men cannot reach, because of their power or craft. Men flee from the judgment of their fellow-creatures; yet, go where they will, conscience, as the supreme Judge's officer, still keeps hold of them, reserving them in its chains, to the judgment of the great day. And whether they escape punishment from men, or fall by the hand of public justice, when they perceive death's approach, they hear from within of this after-reckoning; being constrained to hearken thereto, in these the most serious minutes of their lives. If there be some, in whom nothing of this doth appear, we have no more ground thence to conclude against it, than we have to conclude, that because some men do not groan, therefore they have no pain; or that dying is a mere jest, because there have been some who seemed to make little else of it. A good face may be put upon an ill conscience: the more hopeless men's case is, they reckon it more their interest to make no reflections on their state and case. But every one, who will consult himself seriously, will find in himself the witness of the judgment to come. Even the heathens wanted not a notion of it, though mixed with fictions of their own. Hence, though some of the Athenians, *when they heard of the resurrection of the dead, mocked*, Acts xvii. 32. yet there is no account of their mocking when they heard of the general judgment, verse 31.

II. For explication, the following particulars may serve to give some view of the nature and transactions of that great day.

I. God shall judge the world by Jesus Christ. *He will judge the world in righteousness, by that man whom he hath ordained*, Acts xvii. 31. The Psalmist tells us that *God is Judge himself*, Psal. l. 6. The holy blessed Trinity, Father, Son, and Holy Ghost, is Judge, in respect of judiciary authority, dominion, and power:

Head IV.   *Of the general Judgment.*   361

but the Son incarnate is the Judge, in refpect of difpenſation, and ſpecial exerciſe of that power. The judgment ſhall be exerciſed or performed by him, as the royal Mediator; for he has a delegated power of judgment from the Father, as his Servant, *his King*, whom he hath *ſet upon his holy hill of Zion*, (Pſal. ii. 6.) and to whom he *hath committed all judgment*, John v. 22. This is a part of the Mediator's exaltation, given him in conſequence of his voluntary humiliation, Phil. ii. 8, 9, 10. *He humbled himſelf, and became obedient unto death, even the death of the croſs. Wherefore God alſo hath highly exalted him, and given him a name, which is above every name,* (i. e. power and authority over all, to wit,) *that at* (or *in*) *the name of Jeſus,* (not the name Jeſus; that is not the name above every name, being common to others, as to Juſtus, Col. iv. 11. and Joſhua, Heb. iv. 8.) *every knee ſhall bow.* The which is explained by the apoſtle himſelf of *ſtanding before the judgment-ſeat of Chriſt*, Rom. xiv. 10, 11. So he who was judged and condemned of men, ſhall be the Judge of men and angels.

II. Jeſus Chriſt, the Judge, deſcending from heaven into the air, (1 Theſſ. iv. 16, 17. *ſhall come in the clouds of heaven with power and great glory,* Mat. xxiv. 30. This his coming will be a mighty ſurprize to the world, which will be found in deep ſecurity; fooliſh virgins ſleeping, and the wiſe ſlumbering. There will then be much luxury and debauchery in the world, little ſobriety and watchfulneſs; a great throng of buſineſs, but a great ſcarcity of faith and holineſs. *As it was in the days of Noah, ſo alſo ſhall it be in the days of the Son of Man. They did eat, they drank, they married wives, they were given in marriage, until the day that Noah entered into the ark: and the flood came, and deſtroyed them all. Likewiſe alſo as it was in the days of Lot: they did eat, they drank, they bought, they ſold, they planted, they builded.— Even thus ſhall it be in the day when the Son of Man is revealed,* Luke xvii. 26, 27, 28. 30. The coming of the Judge will ſurpriſe ſome at markets, buying and ſelling; others at table, eating and drinking, and making merry; others buſy with their new plantings; ſome building

A a a

new houses; nay, some's wedding-day will be their own, and the world's judgment-day. But the Judge cometh! the markets are marred; the buyer throws away what he has bought; the seller casts down his money; they are raised from the table, and their mirth is extinguished in a moment; though the tree be set in the earth, the gardener cannot stay to cast the earth about it; the workmen throw away their tools, when the house is half built, and the owner regards it no more; the bridegroom, bride, and guests, must leave the wedding-feast, and appear before the tribunal: for, *Behold he cometh with clouds, and every eye shall see him*, Rev. i. 7. He shall come most gloriously; for he will *come in the glory of his Father, with the holy angels*, Mark viii. 38. When he came in the flesh, to die for sinners, he laid aside the robes of his glory, and was despised and rejected of men: but when he comes again, to judge the world, such shall be his visible glory and majesty, that it shall cast an eternal vail over all earthly glory, and fill his greatest enemies with fear and dread. Never had prince or potentate in the world such a glorious train, as will accompany this Judge: all the holy angels shall come with him, for his honour and service. Then he, who was led to the cross with a band of soldiers, will be gloriously attended to the place of judgment, by *(not a multitude of the heavenly host*, but) the whole host of angels; *all his holy angels*, says the text.

III. At the coming of the Judge, the summons is given to the parties, by the sound of the last trumpet; at which the dead are raised, and those found alive changed; of which before, 1 Thess. iv. 16, 17. O loud trumpet; that shall be heard at once, in all corners of the earth, and of the sea! O wonderful voice, that will not only disturb those who sleep in the dust, but effectually awaken, rouse them out of their sleep, and raise them from death! Were trumpets sounding now, drums beating, furious soldiers, crying and killing men, women, and children, running and shrieking, the wounded groaning and dying; those who are in the graves would have no more disturbance, than if the world were in most profound peace. Yea, were stormy winds to cast down the lofty oaks, the seas roar, and swallow up the ships, the moſt dreadful thunders to go along the heavens, lightenings every where to flaſh, the earth quake, tremble, open, and ſwallow up whole cities, and bury multitudes at once; the dead would ſtill enjoy a perfect repoſe, and ſleep ſoundly in the duſt, though their own duſt ſhould be thrown out of its place. But at the found of this trumpet they ſhall all awake. The morning is come, they can ſleep no longer; the time for the dead to be judged: they muſt get out of their graves, and appear before the Judge.

IV. The Judge ſhall fit down on the tribunal; he ſhall fit on the throne of his glory. He ſtood before a tribunal on earth, and was condemned as a malefactor: now he ſhall fit on his own tribunal, and judge the world. He once hung upon the croſs, covered with ſhame; now he ſhall fit on the throne of glory. What this throne ſhall be, whether a bright cloud, or what elſe, I ſhall not enquire. Our eyes will anſwer to that queſtion at length. John *ſaw a great white throne*, Rev. xx. 11. *His throne*, ſays Daniel, *was like the fiery flame, and his wheels as burning fire*, chap. vii. 9. Whatever it be, doubtleſs it will be a throne glorious beyond expreſſion; and in compariſon with which the moſt glorious throne on the earth is but a ſeat on a dunghill; and the ſight of it will equally ſurprize kings, who ſat on thrones in this life, and beggars who ſat on dunghills. It will be a throne, for ſtatelineſs and glory, ſuited to the quality of him who ſhall fit on it. Never had a judge ſuch a throne, and never had a throne ſuch a Judge on it.

Leaving the diſcovery of the nature of the throne until that day, it concerns us more nearly to conſider what a Judge will fit on it; a point in which we are not left to uncertain conjectures. The Judge on the throne will be, (1.) A viſible Judge, viſible to our bodily eyes, Rev. i. 7. *Every eye ſhall ſee him.* When God gave the law on mount Sinai, the people *ſaw no ſimilitude, only they heard a voice:* but when he calls the world to an account, how they have obſerved his law, the man Chriſt being Judge, we ſhall ſee our Judge with our eyes, either to our eternal comfort, or to our eternal confusion, according to the entertainment which we give him now. That very body which was crucified without the gates of Jerusalem, between two thieves, shall then be seen on the throne, shining in glory. We now see him symbolically, in the sacrament of his supper: the saints see him by an eye of faith: then all shall see him with the eyes now in their heads. (2.) A Judge having full authority and power to render unto every one according to his works. Christ, as God, hath authority of himself; and as Mediator he hath a judicial power and authority, which his Father has invested him with, according to the covenant between the Father and the Son, for the redemption of sinners. His divine glory will be a light, by which all men shall see clearly to read his commission, for his great and honourable employment. *All power is given unto him in heaven and in earth,* Matt. xxviii. 18. He hath *the keys of hell and of death,* Rev. i. 18. There can be no appeal from his tribunal: sentence once passed there, must stand for ever; there is no reversing it. All appeals are from an inferior to a superior court: but when God gives sentence against a man, where can he find a higher court to bring his process to? This judgment is the Mediator's judgment; and therefore the last judgment. If the intercessor be against us, who can be for us? If Christ condemn us, who will absolve us? (3.) A Judge of infinite wisdom. His eyes will pierce into, and clearly discern the most intricate cases. His omniscience qualifies him for judging of the most retired thoughts, as well as of words and works. The most subtle sinner shall not be able to outwit him, nor, by any artful management, to palliate the crime. He is the searcher of hearts, to whom nothing can be hid or perplexed; but all things are naked and open to his eyes, Heb. iv. 13. (5.) A most just Judge; a Judge of perfect integrity. He is the righteous Judge, 2 Tim. iv. 8. and his throne a great white throne, Rev. xx. 11. from whence no judgment shall proceed, but what is most pure and spotless. The Thebans painted justice blind, and without hands; for judges ought not to re-

Head IV.   *Of the general Judgment.*   365

spect persons, nor take bribes. The Areopagites judged in the dark, that they might not regard who spoke, but what was spoken. With the Judge on this throne there will be no respect of persons; he will neither regard the person of the rich nor of the poor: but just judgment shall go forth in every one's cause. *Lastly*, The omnipotent Judge; able to put his sentence in execution. The united force of devils and wicked men will be altogether unable to withstand him. They cannot retard the execution of the sentence against them one moment; far less can they stop it altogether. *Thousand thousands* (of angels) *minister unto him*, Dan. vii. 10. and by the breath of his mouth he can drive the cursed herd whither he pleaseth.

V. The parties shall appear. These are men and devils. Although the last, the fallen angels were, from the first moment of their sinning, subjected to the wrath of God, and were cast down to hell, and whereever they go, they carry their hell about with them: yet it is evident, that they are reserved unto judgment, (2 Pet. ii. 4.) namely, unto the judgment of the great day, Jude 6. then they shall be solemnly and publicly judged, 1 Cor. vi. 3 *Know ye not that we shall judge angels?* At that day they shall answer for their trade of sinning, and tempting to sin, which they have been carrying on from the beginning. Then many a hellish brat, which Satan has laid down at the saints door, but not adopted by them, shall be laid at the door of the true father of it, that is the devil. And he shall receive the due reward of all the dishonour which he has done to God, and of all the mischief which he has done to men. Those wicked spirits, now in chains (though not in such strait custody, but that they go about like roaring lions, seeking whom they may devour) shall then receive their final sentence, and be shut up in their den, namely, in the prison of hell; where they shall be held in extreme and unspeakable torment, through all eternity, Rev. xx. 10. *And the devil, that deceived them, was cast into the lake of fire and brimstone, where the beast and the false prophet are, and shall be tormented day and night for ever and ever.* In prospect of which the devils faid to Chrift, *Art thou come hither to torment us before the time ?* Mat. viii. 29.

But what we are chiefly concerned to take notice of, is the cafe of men at that day. All men muft appear before this tribunal. All of each fex, of every age, quality, and condition; the great and fmall, noble and ignoble: none are excepted. Adam and Eve, with all their fons and daughters (every one who has had, or to the end of the world fhall have a living foul united to a body), will make up this great congregation. Even thofe who refufed to come to the throne of grace, fhall be forced to the bar of juftice: for there can be no hiding from the all-feeing Judge, no flying from him who is prefent every where, no refifting of him, who is armed with almighty power. *We muſt all ſtand before the judgment-feat of Chriſt,* 2 Cor. v. 10. *Before him ſhall be gathered all nations,* fays the text. This is to be done by the miniftry of angels. By them fhall the elect be gathered, Mark xiii. 27. *Then ſhall he ſend his angels, and ſhall gather together his elect from the four winds.* And they alfo fhall gather the reprobate, Mat. xiii. 40, 41. *So ſhall it be in the end of this world. The Son of Man ſhall ſend forth his angels, and they ſhall gather out of his kingdom all things that offend, and them which do iniquity.* From all corners of the world fhall the inhabitants thereof be gathered, unto the place where he fhall fet his throne for judgment.

VI. There fhall be a feparation made between the righteous and the wicked; the fair company of the elect fheep being fet on Chrift's right hand, and the reprobate goats on his left. There is no neceffity to wait for this feparation till the trial be over; fince the parties will rife out of their graves with plain outward marks of diftinction, as was mentioned before. The feparation feems to be effected by that double gathering before mentioned; the one of the elect, Mark xiii. 27. the other of them that do iniquity, Matth. xiii. 41. The elect, being *caught up together in the clouds, meet the Lord in the air,* (1 Theff. iv. 17.) and fo are fet on his right-hand; and the reprobate left on the earth (Mat. xxiv. 40.) upon the Judge's left hand.

Head IV.   *Of the general Judgment.*   367

Here is now a total feparation of two parties, who were always oppofite to each other in their principles, aims, and manner of life, who, when together, were a burden the one to the other, under which the one groaned, and the other raged : but now they are freely parted, never to come together any more. The iron and clay (I allude to Dan. ii. 41. 43.) which could never mix, are quite feparated ; the one being drawn up into the air, by the attractive virtue of *the ftone cut out of the mountain*, namely, Jefus Chrift; and the other left upon its earth, to be trod under foot.

Now let us look to the right-hand, and there fhall we fee a glorious company of faints, fhining as fo many ftars in their orbs; and with a chearful countenance beholding him who fitteth upon the throne. Here will be two wonderful fights, which the world never faw. (1.) A great congregation of faints, in which there will not be fo much as one hypocrite. There was a bloody Cain in Adam's family, a curfed Ham in Noah's family, in the ark ; a treacherous Judas in Chrift's own family : but in that company there will be none but fealed ones, members of Chrift, having all one Father. This is a fight referved for that day. (2.) All the godly upon one fide. Seldom or ever do the faints on earth make fuch harmony, but there are fome jarring ftrings among them. It is not to be expected, that men who fee but in part, though they be all going to one city, fhould agree as to every ftep in the way : No, we muft not look for it in this ftate of imperfection. But at that day, Paul and Barnabas fhall meet in peace and unity, though once the contention was fo fharp between them, that they departed afunder, the one from the other, Acts xv. 39. There fhall be no more divifions, no more feparate ftanding amongft thofe who belong to Chrift. All the godly, of the different parties, fhall then be upon one fide; feeing, whatever were their differences in leffer things, while in the world, yet even then they met and concentered all in one Lord Jefus Chrift, by a true and living faith, and in the one way of holinefs, or practical godlinefs. And naughty hypocrites, of whatever party, fhall be led forth with the workers of iniquity.

Of the general Judgment. State IV.

Look to the left-hand, and there you will see the cursed goats (all the wicked ones from Cain to the last ungodly persons who shall be in the world) gathered together into one most miserable congregation. There are many assemblies of the wicked now; then there shall be but one: yet all of them shall be present there, brought together as one herd for the slaughter, bellowing and roaring, weeping and howling for the miseries come, and that are coming on them. (And remember, thou shalt not be a mere spectator, to look at these two so different companies ; but must thyself take thy place in one of the two, and shalt share with the company, whatever hand it be upon.) Those who now abhor no society so much, as that of the saints, would then be glad to be allowed to get in among them ; though it were but to lie among their feet. But then not one tare shall be found with the wheat; he will throughly purge his floor. Many of the right-hand men of this world, will be left-hand men in that day. Many, who must have the door on the right-hand of those who are better than they, (if the righteous be more excellent than his neighbour) shall then be turned to the left-hand, as most despicable wretches. O how terrible will this separation be to the ungodly ! how dreadful will this gathering them together into one company be! what they will not believe they will then see, namely, that but few are saved. They think it enough now to be neighbour like, and can securely follow the multitude: but the multitude on the left-hand will yield them no comfort. How will it sting the ungodly Christian, to see himself set on the same hand with Turks and Pagans ? How will it gall profane Protestants, to stand with idolatrous Papists ; praying people with their profane neighbours, who mocked at religious exercises ; formal professors, strangers to the new-birth, and the power of godliness, with persecutors ! Now there are many opposite societies in the world : but then all the ungodly shall be in one society. And how dreadful will the faces of companions in sin be to one another there ! What doleful shrieks, when the whoremonger and his whore shall meet ; when the drunkards,

Head IV.   *Of the general Judgment.*   369

who have had many a jovial day together, shall see one another in the face; when the husband and wife, the parents and children, masters and servants, and neighbours, who have been snares and stumbling-blocks to one another, to the ruin of their own souls, and those of their relatives, shall meet again in that miserable society? then will there be curses instead of salutations; and tearing of themselves, and raging against one another, instead of the wonted embraces.

VII. The parties shall be tried. The trial cannot be difficult, in regard the Judge is omniscient, and nothing can be hid from him. But, that his righteous judgment may be made evident to all, he will set the hidden things of darkness in the clearest light at that trial, 1 Cor. iv. 5.

Men shall be tried, *first*, upon their works; for *God shall bring every work into judgment, with every secret thing, whether it be good, or whether it be evil,* Eccles. xii. 14. The Judge will try every man's conversation, and set his deeds done in the body, with all the circumstances thereof, in a true light. Then will many actions, commended and applauded of men, as good and just, be discovered to have been evil and abominable in the sight of God: and many works now condemned in the world, will be approved and commended by the great Judge, as good and just. Secret things will be brought to light; and what was hid from the view of the world, shall be laid open. Wickedness, which hath kept its lurking place in spight of all human search, will then be brought forth to the glory of God, and the confusion of impenitent sinners, who hid it. The world appears now very vile in the eyes of those who are exercised to godliness: and it will then appear a thousand times more vile, when that which is done of men in secret comes to be discovered. Every good action shall then be remembered; and the hidden religion, and good works, most industriously concealed by the saints, from the eyes of men, shall no more lie hid: for though the Lord will not allow men to proclaim every man his own goodness, yet he himself will do it in due time. *Secondly,* Their words shall be judged,

B b b

Mat. xii. 37. *For by thy words thou shalt be justified, and by thy words thou shalt be condemned.* Not a word spoken for God and his cause in the world, from love to himself, shall be forgotten. They are all kept in remembrance, and shall be brought forth as evidences of faith, and of an interest in Christ, Mal. iii. 16, 17. *Then they that feared the Lord spake often one to another, and the Lord hearkened and heard it: and a book of remembrance was written before him—and they shall be mine, saith the Lord of hosts, in that day when I make up my jewels.* And the tongue, which did run at random, shall then confess to God; and the speaker shall find it to have been followed, and every word noted, that dropped from the unsanctified lips. *Every idle word that men shall speak, they shall give account thereof in the day of judgment*, Mat. xii. 36. And if they shall give account of idle words, that is, words spoken to no good purpose, neither for God's glory, one's own, nor one's neighbour's good; how much more shall men's wicked words, their sinful oaths, curses, lies, filthy communications, and bitter words, be called over again in that day? The tongues of many shall then fall upon themselves, and ruin them. *Thirdly*, Men's thoughts shall be brought into judgment: the Judge will make manifest the counsels of the heart, 1 Cor. iv. 5. Thoughts go free from man's judgment, but not from the judgment of the heart-searching God, who knows men's thoughts, without the help of signs to discern them by. The secret springs of men's actions will then be brought to light; and the sins, that never came further than the heart, will then be laid open. O what a figure will man's corrupt nature make, when his inside is turned out, and all his speculative impurities are exposed! The rottenness that is within many a whited sepulchre, the speculative filthiness and wantonness, murder and malignity, now lurking in the hearts of men, as in the chambers of imagery, will then be discovered, and what good was in the hearts of any shall no more lie concealed. If it was in their hearts to build a house to the Lord, they shall hear that they did well that it was in their heart.

Head IV.   *Of the general Judgment.*   371

This trial will be righteous and impartial, accurate and searching, clear and evident. The Judge is the righteous Judge, and he will do right to every one. He has a just balance for good and evil actions, and for honest and false hearts. The fig-leaf cover of hypocrisy will then be blown aside, and the hypocrite's nakedness will appear; as when the Lord came to judge Adam and Eve *in the cool* (or, as the word is, *in the wind) of the day*, Gen. iii. 8. *The fire* (which tries things most exquisitely) *shall try every man's work, of what sort it is*, 1 Cor. iii. 13. Man's judgment is often perplexed and confused: but here the whole process shall be clear and evident, as written with a sun-beam. It shall be clear to the Judge, to whom no case can be intricate; to the parties, who shall be convinced, Jude 15. And the multitudes on both sides shall see the Judge is clear when he judgeth; for then *the heavens shall declare his righteousness*, in the audience of all the world: and so it shall be universally known, Psal. l. 6.

On these accounts it is, that this trial is held out in the Scripture under the notion of *opening of books*; and men are said to be *judged out of those things written in the books*, Rev. xx. 12. The Judge of the world, who infallibly knoweth all things, hath no need of books to be laid before him, to prevent mistakes in any point of law or fact: but the expression points at his proceeding as most nice, accurate, just, and well grounded, in every step of it. Now there are four books which shall be opened in that day.

First, The book of God's remembrance, or omniscience, Mal. iii. 16. This is an exact record of every man's state, thoughts, words, and deeds, good or evil: it is, as it were, a day-book, in which the Lord puts down all that passeth in men's hearts, lips, and lives; and it is a-filling up every day that one lives. In it are recorded men's sins and good works, secret and open, with all their circumstances. Here are registered all their privileges, temporal and spiritual mercies, often made ready to their hand; the checks, admonitions, and rebukes, given by teachers, neighbours, afflictions, and men's own consciences; every thing in its due or-

B b b 2

der. This book will serve only as a bill of indictment, in respect of the ungodly: but it will be for another use in respect of the godly, namely, for a memorial of their good. The opening of it is the Judge's bringing to light what is written in it; the reading, as it were, of the bill and memorial respectively, in their hearing.

Secondly, The book of conscience will be opened, which will be as a thousand witnesses to prove the fact, Rom. i. 15. *Which shew the work of the law written in their hearts, their conscience also bearing witness.* Conscience is a censor, going with every man wherever he goes, taking an account of his deeds done in the body, and, as it were, noting them in a book. Much is written in it, which cannot be read now; the writing of conscience being, in many cases, like to that which is made with the juice of lemons, not to be read till it be held before the fire; but then men shall read it clearly and distinctly: the fire, which is to try every man's work, will make the book of conscience legible in every point. Though the book be sealed now (the conscience blind, dumb, and deaf), the seals will then be broken, and the book opened. There shall be no more a silent conscience, and far less a seared conscience, amongst all the ungodly crew: but their consciences shall be most quick-sighted, and most lively, in that day. None shall then call good evil, or evil good. Ignorance of what sin is, and what things are sins, will have no place among them: and the subtle reasonings of men, in favour of their lusts, will then be for ever baffled by their own consciences. None shall have the favour (if I may so speak) of lying under the soft cover of delusion: but they shall all be convicted by their conscience. Whether they will or not, they must look on this book, read, be confounded, and stand speechless, knowing that nothing is charged upon them by mistake; since this is a book which was always in their own custody. Thus shall the Judge make every man see himself in the glass of his own conscience, which will make quick work.

Thirdly, The book of the law shall be opened. This book is the standard and rule, by which is known what

Head IV.   *Of the general Judgment.*   373

is right and what is wrong; as alfo, what fentence is to be paffed accordingly, on thofe who are under it. As to the opening of the book, as a ftatute, which fhews what is fin, and what is duty, it agrees with the opening of the book of confcience: for confcience is fet, by the fovereign Lawgiver, in every man's breaft, to be his private teacher, to fhew him the law; and his private paftor, to make application of the fame; and at that day it will be perfectly fit for its office: So that the confcience, which is moft ftupid now, fhall then read to the man moft accurate, but dreadful lectures on the law. But what feems (mainly at leaft) pointed at by the opening of this book, is the opening of that part of it which determines the reward of men's works. Now the law promifeth life, upon perfect obedience: but none can be found on the right-hand, or on the left, who will pretend to that, when once the book of confcience is opened. It threateneth death upon difobedience, and will effectually bring it, upon all under its dominion. And this part of the book of the law, determining the reward of men's works, is opened only to fhew what muft be the portion of the ungodly, and that there they may read their fentence before it be pronounced. But it is not opened for the fentence of the faints; for no fentence abfolving a finner could ever be drawn out of it. The law promifeth life, not as it is a rule of actions, but as a covenant of works: therefore innocent man could not have demanded life upon his obedience, till the law was reduced into the form of a covenant: as was fhewn before. But the faints having been in this life brought under a new covenant, namely, the covenant of grace, were dead to the law as a covenant of works, and it was dead to them. Wherefore, as they fhall not now have any fears of death from it; fo they can have no hopes of life from it, fince they *are not under the law, but under grace*, Rom. vi. 14. but for their fentence *another book is opened*; of which in the next place.

Thus the book of the law is opened, to fentence againft all thofe on the left-hand: and by it they will clearly fee the juftice of the judgment againft them, and how the Judge proceeds therein according to law. Nevertheless, there will be this difference, namely, that those who had only the natural law, and lived not under any special revelation, shall be judged by that law of nature which they had in their hearts; which law declares, *That they which commit such things* (as they will stand convicted of) *are worthy of death*, Rom. i. 32. but those who had the written law, to whom the word of God came, founding in the visible church, shall be judged by that written law. So says the apostle, Rom. ii. 12. *For as many as have sinned without* (the written) *law, shall also perish without* (the written) *law: and as many as have sinned in the law, (i. e.* under the written law) *shall be judged by the* (written) *law.*

Lastly, Another book shall be *opened, which is the book of life,* Rev. xx. 12. In this the names of all the elect are written, as Christ said to his disciples, Luke x. 20. *Your names are written in heaven.* This book contains God's gracious and unchangeable purpose to bring all the elect to eternal life, and that, in order thereto, they be redeemed by the blood of his Son, effectually called, justified, adopted, sanctified, and raised up by him at the last day without sin. It is now lodged in the Mediator's hand, as the book of *the manner of the kingdom:* and having perfected the work which the Father gave him to do, he shall, on the great day, produce and open the book, and present the persons therein-named *faultless before the presence of his glory,* Jude, ver. 24. *Not having spot or wrinkle, or any such thing,* Eph. v. 27. Not one named in the book will be missing. They shall be found qualified, according to the order of the book, redeemed, called, justified, sanctified, raised up without spot: what remains, then, but, according to the same book, they obtain the great end, namely, everlasting life? This may be gathered from this precious promise, Rev. iii. 5. *He that overcometh, the same shall be cloathed in white raiment,* (being raised in glory) *and I will not blot out his name out of the book of life, but I will confess his name* (it shall be, as it were, read out among the rest of God's elect) *before my Father, and before his angels.* Here is the ground of the saint's absolution,

Head IV. *Of the general Judgment.*

and the ground of the blessed sentence which they shall receive. The book of life being opened, it will be known to all who are elected, and who are not. Thus far of the trial of the parties.

VIII. Then shall the Judge pronounce this blessed sentence on the saints, *Come, ye blessed of my Father, inherit the kingdom prepared for you from the foundation of the world,* Mat. xxv. 34. It is most probable, that the man Christ will pronounce it with an audible voice; which not only all the saints, but all the wicked likewise, shall hear and understand. Who can conceive the inexpressible joy with which these happy ones will hear these words? Who can imagine that fulness of joy which will be poured into their hearts, with these words reaching their ears? And who can conceive how much of hell shall break forth into the hearts of all the ungodly crew, by these words of heaven? It is certain that this sentence shall be pronounced before the sentence of damnation, Mat. xxv. 34. 41. *Then shall the King say to them on his right-hand, Come, ye blessed, &c. Then shall he also say to them on the left-hand, Depart from me, ye cursed, &c.* There is no need of this order, that the saints may, without fear or affrightment, hear the other sentence on the reprobate: they who are raised in glory, caught up to meet the Lord in the air, presented without spot, and whose souls (for the far greater part of them) have been so long in heaven before, shall not be capable of any such fear. But hereby they will be orderly brought in to sit in judgment, as Christ's assessors, against the ungodly, whose torment will be aggravated by it. It will be a hell to them to be kept out of hell, till they see the doors of heaven opened to receive the saints, who once dwelt in the same world with them, and perhaps in the same country, parish, or town, and sat under the same ministry with themselves. Thus will they see heaven afar off, to make their hell the hotter: like that unbelieving lord, 2 Kings viii. 20. They *shall see the plenty with their eyes, but shall not eat thereof.* Every word of the blessed sentence shall be like an envenomed arrow shot into their hearts, while they see what they have lost, and from thence gather what they are to expect.

Of the general Judgment. State IV.

This sentence passeth on the saints *according to their works*, Rev. xx. 12. but not for their works, nor for their faith, as if eternal life were merited by them. The sentence itself overthrows this absurd conceit. The kingdom which they are called to, was *prepared for them from the foundation of the world*; not left to be merited by themselves, who were but of yesterday. They inherit it as sons, and not procure it to themselves as servants do the reward of their work. They were redeemed by the blood of Christ, and cloathed with spotless righteousness, which is the proper cause of the sentence. They were also qualified for heaven, by the sanctification of his Spirit; and hence it is *according to their works*: so that the ungodly world shall see now, that the Judge of the quick and dead does good to them who were good. Therefore it is added to the sentence, *For I was an hungred, and ye gave me meat*, &c. ver. 35, 36. which doth not denote the ground, but the evidence of their right to heaven; as if a Judge should say, he absolves a man pursued for debt; for the witnesses depose that it is paid already. So the apostle says, 1 Cor. x. 5. *With many of them God was not well pleased, for they were over-thrown in the wilderness.* Their overthrow in the wilderness was not the ground of God's displeasure with them, but it was an evidence of it. And thus our Lord teacheth us the necessary connection between glory and good works, namely, works evangelically good; works having a respect to Jesus Christ, and done out of faith in him, and love to him, without which they will not be regarded in that day. And the saints will so far be judged according to such works, that the degrees of glory amongst them shall be according to these works: for it is an eternal truth, *He that soweth sparingly, shall reap sparingly*, 2 Cor. ix. 6.

Thus shall the good works of the godly have a glorious, but a gratuitous reward; a reward of grace, not of debt, which will fill them with wonder at the riches of free grace, and the Lord's condescending to take any notice, especially such public notice of their poor worthless works: which seems to be the import of what they are said to answer, *saying, Lord, when saw we thee an hungred*, &c. ver. 37, 38, 39. And may they not juftly wonder to fee themfelves fet down to the marriage-fupper of the Lamb, and hear him acknowledge a dinner or fupper, a little meat or drink, (fuch as they had) which they gave to a hungry or thirfty member of Chrift, for his fake? O plentiful harveft, following upon the feed of good works! Rivers of pleafures, in exchange for a cup of cold water, given to a difciple in the name of a difciple! eternal manfions of glory, in exchange for a night's lodging given to a faint, who was a ftranger! everlafting robes of glory in exchange for a new coat, or (it may be) an old one, beftowed on fome faint, who had not neceffary cloathing! a vifit to a fick faint, repaid by Chrift himfelf, coming in the glory of his Father, with all his holy angels! a vifit made to a poor prifoner, for the caufe of Chrift, repaid with a vifit from the Judge of all, taking away the vifitant with him to the palace of heaven, there to be ever with himfelf; thefe things will be matter of everlafting wonder; and fhould ftir up all to fow liberally in time, while the feed time of good works doth laft. But it is Chrift's ftamp on good works, that puts a value on them, in the eye of our gracious God; which feems to be the import of our Lord's reply, verfe 40. *Inafmuch as ye have done it unto one of the leaft of thefe my brethren, ye have done it unto me.*

IX. Now, the faints having received their own fentence, *they fhall judge the world,* 1 Cor. vi. 2, 3. This was not fulfilled, when the empire became Chriftian, and Chriftians were made magiftrates. No, the Pfalmift tells us, *This honour have all the faints,* Pfal. cxlix. 9. And the apoftle, in the forecited place, adds, *If the world fhall be judged by you, are ye unworthy to judge the fmalleft matters. Know ye not that we fhall judge angels?* Being called, they come to receive their kingdom, in the view of angels and men: they go, as it were, from the bar to the throne: *To him that overcometh, will I grant to fit with me in my throne,* Rev. iii. 21. They fhall not only judge the world, in Chrift their Head, by way of communion with him, by their works compared with them of the ungodly, or by way of teftimony againſt them; but they ſhall be aſſeſſors to Jeſus Chriſt the Judge, giving their voice againſt them, conſenting to his judgment as juſt, and ſaying *Amen* to the doom pronounced againſt all the ungodly: as is laid to the ſaints, upon the judgment of the great whore, Rev. xix. 1, 2. *Hallelujah—for true and righteous are his judgments.* Thus *the upright ſhall have dominion over them in the morning* of the reſurrection, Pſal. xlix. 14. Then, and not till then, ſhall that be fully accompliſhed in Pſalm cxlix. 6—9. *Let the high praiſes of God be in their mouth, and a two-edged ſword in their hand, to execute vengeance upon the Heathen, and puniſhments upon the people—this honour have all his ſaints.* O! what a ſtrange turn of affairs will appear here! what an aſtoniſhing ſight will it be, to ſee wicked churchmen and ſtateſmen, ſtanding as criminals before the ſaints, whom ſometimes they condemned as heretics, rebels, and traitors! to ſee men of riches and power ſtand pale faced before thoſe whom they oppreſſed! to ſee the mocker ſtand trembling before thoſe he mocked! the worldly wiſe man before thoſe whom he accounted fools! Then ſhall the deſpiſed faces of the ſaints be dreadful faces to the wicked: and thoſe, who ſometimes were the ſong of the drunkards, ſhall be a terror to them. All wrongs muſt be righted at length, and every one ſet in his proper place.

X. The Judge will pronounce the ſentence of damnation on all the ungodly multitude. *Then ſhall he ſay alſo unto them on the left-hand, Depart from me, ye curſed, into everlaſting fire, prepared for the devil and his angels,* verſe 41. Fearful doom! And that from the ſame mouth from whence proceeded the ſentence of abſolution before. It was an aggravation of the miſery of the Jews, when their city was deſtroyed, that they were ruined by one who was accounted the darling of the world. O what an aggravation of the miſery of the wicked will it be, that Chriſt will pronounce this ſentence alſo! to hear the curſe from mount Zion, muſt needs be moſt terrible. To be damned by him who came to ſave ſinners, muſt be double damnation. But thus it will be. The Lamb of God ſhall roar, as a

Head IV. *Of the general Judgment.* 379

lion, againſt them: he ſhall excommunicate, and caſt them out of his preſence for ever, by a ſentence from the throne, ſaying, *Depart from me, ye curſed:* he ſhall adjudge them to everlaſting fire, and the ſociety of devils for evermore. And this ſentence alſo, we ſuppoſe, will be pronounced with an audible voice by the man Chriſt. And all the ſaints ſhall ſay, *Hallelujah, true and righteous are his judgments.* None were ſo compaſſionate as the ſaints when on earth, during the time of God's patience: but now that time is at an end; their compaſſion on the ungodly is ſwallowed up in joy, in the Mediator's glory, and his executing of juſt judgment, by which his enemies are made his foot-ſtool. Though, when on earth, the righteous man wept in ſecret places for their pride, and becauſe they would not hear; yet he will *rejoice when he ſeeth the vengeance; he ſhall waſh his feet in the blood of the wicked,* Pſal. lviii. 10. No pity ſhall then be ſhewn to them from their neareſt relations. The godly wife ſhall applaud the juſtice of the Judge, in the condemnation of her ungodly huſband: the godly huſband ſhall ſay *Amen* to the damnation of her who lay in his boſom: the godly parent ſhall ſay *Hallelujah,* at the paſſing of the ſentence againſt their ungodly child: and the godly child ſhall, from his heart, approve the damnation of his wicked parents, the father who begat him, and the mother who bore him. The ſentence is juſt: they are judged *according to their works,* Rev. xx. 12.

There is no wrong done them, *For I was an hungry,* (ſaith our Lord) *and ye gave me no meat: I was thirſty, and ye gave me no drink: I was a ſtranger, and ye took me not in: naked, and ye cloathed me not: ſick, and in priſon, and ye viſited me not,* ver. 42, 43. Theſe are not only evidences of their ungodly and curſed ſtate, but moſt proper cauſes and grounds of their condemnation: for though good works do not merit ſalvation, yet evil works merit damnation. Sins of one kind only, namely of omiſſion, are here mentioned; not that theſe alone ſhall be then diſcovered, (for the books lay all open) but becauſe theſe, though there were no more, are ſufficient to damn unpardoned ſinners. And if men

C c c 2

are condemned for sins of omission, much more for sins of commission. The omission of works of charity and mercy, is mentioned in particular, to stop the mouths of the wicked; for it is most just, that he *have judgment without mercy, that hath shewed no mercy*, James ii. 13. Taking notice of the omission of acts of charity and mercy, towards the distressed members of Christ, intimates, that it is the judgment of those who have heard of Christ in the gospel, that is principally intended in this portion of Scripture; and that the slighting of Christ will be the great cause of the ruin of those who hear the gospel: but the enmity of the hearts of the wicked, against Christ himself, is discovered, by the entertainment which they now give to his members.

In vain will they say, *When saw we thee an hungred, or athirst?* &c. verse 44. For the Lord reckons, and will reckon, the world's unkindness to his people, unkindness to himself; *Inasmuch as ye did it not to one of the least of these, ye did it not to me*, ver. 45. O meat and drink unhappily spared, when a member of Christ was in need of it! O wretched neglect, that the stranger saint was not taken in! It had been better for them they had quitted their own room, and their own bed, than he had wanted lodging. O cursed cloathing, may the wicked say, that was in my house, locked up in my chest, or hanging in my wardrobe, and was not brought out to cloath such a one! O that I had stripped myself, rather than he had gone away without cloathing! Cursed business, that diverted me from visiting such a sick saint! O that I had rather watched whole nights with him. Wretch that I was! why did I sit at ease in my house, when he was in prison, and did not visit him? but now the tables are turned: Christ's servants shall eat, but I shall be hungry; his servants shall drink, but I shall be thirsty; they rejoice, but I am ashamed, Isa. lv. 13. They are taken in, but I cast out, and bid to depart; they are cloathed with robes of glory, but I *walk naked, and they see my shame*, Rev. xvi. 15. they are now raised up on high, beyond the reach of sickness or pain; but I must now lie down

Head IV.   *Of the general Judgment.*   381

in sorrow, Isa. l. 11. now they will go to the palace of heaven, but I must go to the prison of hell.

But if our Lord thus resents men's neglecting to help his people under these, and the like distresses, what may they expect who are the authors and instruments of them ? If they shall be fed with wrath, who fed them not when they were hungry ; what shall become of those who robbed and spoiled them, and took their bread away from them ? What a full cup of wrath shall be the portion of those, who were so far from giving them meat or drink, when hungry or thirsty, that they made it a crime for others to entertain them, and made themselves drunken with their blood ! They must lodge with devils for evermore, who took not in the Lord's people, when strangers : then what a lodging shall those have, who drave them out of their own houses, out of their native land, and made them strangers ? Men will be condemned for not cloathing them, when naked : then how heavy must the sentence of those be, who have stripped them, and made them go without cloathing ? Surely, if not visiting of them in sickness, or in a prison, shall be so severely punished ; they shall not escape a most heavy doom, who have cast them into prisons, and have put them under such hardships as have impaired their health, brought sickness on them, and cut short their days in prison, or out of prison.

To put a face upon such wicked practices, men will pretend to retain an honour for Christ and religion, while they thus treat his members, walking in his way, and keeping the truth. They are here represented to say, *When saw we thee an hungred, or athirst, or a stranger, or naked, or sick, or in prison, and did not minister unto thee ?* ver. 44. As if they should say, Our bread, drink, lodging, cloathing, and visits, were indeed refused, but not to Christ ; but to a set of men of bad character, men who *turned the world upside down*, Acts xvii. 6. who troubled Israel, Kings xviii. 17. a phantastic sort of people, having laws diverse from all people; factious and rebellious, (they did not keep the king's laws) and therefore a very dangerous set of men ; it was not for the king's profit to suffer them, Esther

iii. 8. But although men caft iniquity upon the godly, and give them ill names, that they may treat them as criminals, all thefe pretences will avail them nothing in the great day, before the righteous Judge, and their own confciences: but the real ground of their enmity againft the faints, will be found (to their own conviction) to be their enmity againft Chrift himfelf. This feems to be the import of the objection of the damned, ver. 44. and of the anfwer to it, ver. 45. *Inafmuch as ye did it not to one of the leaft of thefe, ye did it not to me.*

Laftly, Sentence being paffed on both parties, the full execution of the fame follows, ver. 46. *Thefe fhall go away into everlafting punifhment, but the righteous into life eternal.* The damned fhall get no reprieve, but go to their place without delay; they fhall be driven away from the judgment-feat, into hell: and the faints *fhall enter into the King's palace*, (Pfal. xlv. 15.) namely, into heaven, the feat of the bleffed. But our Lord Chrift, and his glorious company, fhall keep the field that day, and fee the backs of all their enemies; for the damned go off firft.

In this day of the Lord, the great day, fhall be the general conflagration; by which thefe vifible heavens, the earth, and fea, fhall pafs away. Not that they fhall be annihilated (or reduced to nothing), that is not the operation of fire: but they fhall be diffolved and purged by that fire, from all the effects of fin, and of the curfe upon them; and then renewed, and made more glorious and ftable. Of this conflagration the apoftle Peter fpeaks, 2 Pet. iii. 10. *The day of the Lord will come as a thief in the night; in the which the heavens fhall pafs away with a great noife, and the elements fhall melt with fervent heat; the earth alfo, and the works that are therein, fhall be burnt up.* See alfo ver. 7. 12. And of the renewing of the world, he adds, ver. 13. *Neverthelefs we, according to his promife, look for new heavens and a new earth, wherein dwelleth righteoufnefs.*

It feems moft agreeable to the Scriptures, and to the nature of the thing, to conceive this conflagration to follow after the general judgment; fentence being paffed on both parties before it. And I judge it pro-

Head IV. *Of the general Judgment.* 583

bable, that it will happen at the time of putting the sentence in execution against the damned; so as they shall (according to their sentence) depart, and the heavens and the earth pass away, together and at once, at that furious rebuke from the throne, driving away the damned out of the world (in this fire) to the everlasting fire prepared for the devil and his angels. Even as, in the deluge, with which the apostle Peter compares the conflagration, or burning of the world, 2 Pet. iii. 6, 7. the world itself, and the wicked upon it, perished together; the same water which destroyed the earth, sweeping away the inhabitants. For it is not likely that the wicked shall at all stand on the new earth, *wherein dwelleth righteousness*, 2 Pet. iii. 13. and as for this earth, it shall *flee away* (which seems to denote a very quick dispatch), and it shall *flee from his face who sits on the throne*, Rev. xx. 11. *And I saw a great white throne, and him that sat on it, from whose face the earth and the heaven fled away.* The execution of the sentence on the wicked is also thus expressed; *They shall be punished with everlasting destruction, from the presence*, or *from the face of the Lord*, 2 Thess. i. 9. The original word is the same in both texts, which being compared, seem to say, that these creatures, abused by the wicked, being left to stand as witnesses against them in the judgment, are, after sentence passed on their abusers, made to pass away with them from the face of the Judge. It is true, *the flying away* of the earth and heaven is narrated (Rev. xx. 11.) before the judgment; but that does not prove its going before the judgment; any more than the narrating of the judgment, ver. 12. before the resurrection, ver. 13. will prove the judgment to be before it. Further, it is remarkable, in the execution of the sentence, Rev. xx. 14, 15. that not only the reprobate are *cast into the lake*, but *death and hell* are cast into it likewise: all effects of sin, and of the curse, are removed out of the world (for which very cause shall the conflagration be), and they are confined to the place of the damned. Besides all this, it is evident that the end of the world is by the conflagration: and the apostle tells us, 1 Cor. xv. 24, 25. *Then cometh the end, when he shall have delivered up the kingdom to God, even the Father; when he shall have put down all rule, and all authority, and power. For he must reign till he hath put all his enemies under his feet.* Which last, as it must be done before the end, so it seems not to be done by putting the sentence in execution, passed in the day of judgment against the wicked.

Now, if the burning of Sodom and Gomorrah, that are set forth for an example, Jude 7. was so dreadful, how terrible will that day be, when the whole world shall be at once in flames! how will wretched worldlings look, when their darling world shall be all on fire? then shall strong castles, and towering palaces, with all their rich furniture, go up together, in one flame, with the lowest cottages. What heart can fully conceive the terror of that day to the wicked, when the whole fabric of heaven and earth shall at once be dissolved by the fire! when that miserable company shall be driven from the tribunal to the pit, with fire within them, and without on every hand of them; and fire awaiting them in the lake: whither the former fire (for ought which appears) may follow them.

As for the particular place of this judgment, though some point us to the valley of Jehoshophat for it, yet our Lord, who infallibly knew it, being asked the question, by his disciples, *Where Lord?* only said, *Wheresoever the body is, thither will the eagles be gathered together,* Luke xvii. 37. After which answer, it is too much for men to renew the question. As for the time when it shall be, in vain do men search for what the Lord has purposely kept secret, Acts i. 7., *It is not for you to know the times or the seasons, which the Father has put in his own power.* The apostle Paul, after having very plainly described the second coming of Christ, 1 Thess. iv. 16, 17. adds, chap. v. 1, 2. *But of the times and seasons, brethren, ye have no need that I write unto you : for yourselves know perfectly, that the day of the Lord so cometh as a thief in the night.* Nevertheless, some, in several ages, have made very bold with the time ; and several particular years, which are now past, have been given out to the world for the time of the end, by men who have pried into the se-

Head IV.   *Of the general Judgment.*

crets of God. Time has proclaimed to the world their rashness and folly: and it is probable that they will be no more happy in their conjectures, whose determinate time is yet to come. Let us rest in that he cometh. God hath kept the day hid from us, that we may be every day ready for it, Mat. xxv. 13. *Watch, therefore; for ye know neither the day nor the hour wherein the Son of Man cometh.* Let us remember, that the last day of our life will determine our state in the last day of the world: and as we die, so shall we be judged.

I shall now shut up this subject, with some application of what has been said.

USE I. Of comfort to all the saints. Here is abundance of consolation to all who are in the state of grace. Whatever be your afflictions in the world, this day will make up all your losses. *Though ye have lien among the pots: yet shall ye be as the wings of a dove, covered with silver, and her feathers with yellow gold,* Psal. lxviii. 13. Though the world reproach, judge, and condemn you, the Judge will at that day absolve you, and bring forth your righteousness as the light. The world's fools will then appear to have been the only wise men who were in it. Though the cross be heavy, you may well bear it, in expectation of the crown of righteousness, which the righteous Judge will then give you. If the world despise you, and treat you with the utmost contempt, regard it not: the day cometh wherein you shall sit with Christ on his throne. Be not discouraged by reason of manifold temptations. But resist the devil, in confidence of a full and compleat victory; for you shall judge the tempter at last. Though you have hard wrestling now, with the body of sin and death, yet you shall get all your enemies under your feet at length, and be presented faultless before the presence of his glory. Let not the terror of that day dispirit you, when you think on it. Let those who have slighted the Judge, and continue enemies to him, and to the way of holiness, droop and hang down their heads, when they think of his coming: but lift ye up your heads with joy, for the last day will be your best day. The Judge is your Head and Husband, your Redeemer, and your Advocate. You must appear before the judgment-seat, but you shall not come into condemnation, John v. 24. His coming will not be against you, but for you. He came in the flesh, to remove the lawful impediments of the spiritual marriage, by his death: he came in the gospel to you, to espouse you to himself: he will come, at the last day, to solemnize the marriage, and take the bride home to his Father's house. *Even so, come, Lord Jesus.*

USE. Of terror to all unbelievers. This may serve to awaken a secure generation, a world lying in wickedness, as if they were never to be called to an account for it; and slighting the Mediator, as if he were not to judge them. Ah! how few have the lively impressions of the judgment to come! most men live as if what is said of it, from the word, were but idle tales. The profane lives of many speak the thoughts of it to be far from their hearts, and in very deed make a mock of it before the world, saying, in effect, Where is the promise of his coming? The hypocrisy of others, who blind the eyes of the world with a splendid profession, being in appearance Christ's sheep, while they are indeed the devil's goats, proves, that the great separation of the sheep from the goats is very little laid to heart. How do many indulge themselves in secret wickedness, of which they would be ashamed before witnesses; not considering, that their most secret thoughts and actions will, at that day, be discovered before the great congregation! How eagerly are men's hearts set on the world, as if it were to be their everlasting habitation! The solemn assemblies, and public ordinances, wherein the Judge is upon a transaction of peace with the criminals, are undervalued: many hearts swim like feathers in the waters of the sanctuary, that sink like stones to the bottom in cares of this life: they will be very serious in trifles of this world, and trifle in the most serious and weighty things of another world. But, O consider the day that is approaching, in which Christ will come to judgment; the world shall be summoned, by the sound of the last trumpet, to appear before his tribunal. The Judge will sit on his throne,

Head IV. *Of the general Judgment.*

and all nations will be summoned before him; the separation will be made between the godly and the wicked; the books opened, and the dead judged out of them; one party will be adjudged to everlasting life, and the other to everlasting fire, according to their works.

It would be a sight of admirable curiosity, if thou couldst wrap up thyself in some dark cloud, or hide thyself in the clift of some high rock, from whence thou mightest espy wicked kings, princes, judges, and great ones of the earth, rising out of their marble tombs, and brought to the bar, to answer for all their cruelty, injustice, oppression, and profanity, without any marks of distinction, but what their wickedness puts upon them: profane, unholy, and unfaithful church-men, pursued with the curses of their ruined people, from their graves to the judgment-seat, and charged with the blood of souls, to whom they gave not faithful warning: mighty men standing trembling before the Judge, unable to recover their wonted boldness, to outwit him with their subtilties, or defend themselves by their strength: delicate women cast forth of their graves, as abominable branches, dragged to the tribunal, to answer for their ungodly lives: the ignorant, suddenly taught in the law to their cost; and the learned, declared before the world fools and laborious triflers; the Atheist convinced, the hypocrite unmasked; and the profane at length turned serious about his eternal state: secret murders, adulteries, thefts, cheats, and other works of darkness, which baffled all human search, discovered and laid open before the world, with their most minute circumstances: no regard had to the rich, no pity shewn to the poor: the scales of the world turned; oppressed and despised piety set on high; and prosperous wickedness at last brought low: all not found in Christ arraigned, convicted, and condemned, without respect of persons, and driven from the tribunal to the pit; while those found in him at that day, being absolved before the world, go with him into heaven. Nay, but thou canst not so escape. Whoever thou art, not being in Christ, thou must bear a part in this tragical and frightful action.

Sinner, that same Lord Christ, whom thou now despisest, whom thou woundest through the sides of his messengers, and before whom thou dost prefer thy lusts, will be thy Judge. The neglected Saviour will be a severe Judge. O! what mountain, what rock wilt thou get to fall on thee, and hide thee from the face of him who sitteth on the throne? Thou hast now a rock within thee, a heart of adamant, so that thou canst count the darts of the word as stubble, and laugh at the shaking of the spear: but that rock will rend at the sight of the Judge; that hard heart will then break, and thou wilt weep and wail, when weeping and wailing will be to no purpose. Death's bands will fall off, the grave will vomit thee out; the mountains shall skip from thee, and the rocks refuse to grind thee to powder. How will the cursed eyes abide the sight of the Judge! Behold, he cometh! Where is the profane swearer, who tore his wounds? the wretched worldling, now abandoned of his God? the formal hypocrite, who kissed him, and betrayed him? the despiser of the gospel, who sent him away in his messengers groaning, profaned his ordinances, and trampled under foot his precious blood? O murderer! the slain man is thy Judge: there is he whom thou didst so evil entreat: behold the neglected Lamb of God appearing as a lion against thee! How will thine heart endure the darts of his fiery looks! that rocky heart, which now holds out against him, shall then be blown up: that face, which refuseth to blush now, shall then gather blackness; arrows of wrath shall pierce, where arrows of conviction cannot enter now. What wilt thou answer him when he riseth up, and chargeth thee with thy unbelief and impatience? Wilt thou say thou wast not warned? Conscience within thee will give thee the lie: the secret groans and weariness of those who warned thee, will witness the contrary. If a child or a fool were to tell you that your house was on fire, you would immediately run to quench it; but, in matters of eternal concern, men will first fill their hearts with prejudices against the messengers, and then cast their message behind their backs. But these silly shifts and pretences will not avail in the day of the

Head IV. *Of the general Judgment.* 389
Lord. How will thefe curfed ears, now deaf to the call of the gofpel inviting finners to come to Chrift, hear the fearful fentence, *Depart from me, ye curfed, into everlafting fire, prepared for the devil and his angels?* No fleepy hearer fhall be there: no man's heart will then wander: their hearts and eyes will then be fixed on their mifery, which they will not now believe. O that we knew, in this our day, the things that belong to our peace!

Laftly, Be exhorted to believe this great truth; and believe it fo as you may prepare for the judgment betimes. Set up a fecret tribunal in your own breafts, and often call yourfelves to an account there. Make the Judge your friend in time, by clofing with him, in the offer of the gofpel; give all diligence, that you may be found in Chrift at that day. Caft off the works of darknefs; and live, as believing you are at all times, and in all places, under the eye of your Judge, who will *bring every work into judgment, with every fecret thing.* Be fruitful in good works, knowing, that as you fow you fhall reap. Study piety towards God, righteoufnefs and charity towards men. Lay up in ftore plenty of works of charity and mercy, towards them who are in diftrefs, efpecially fuch as are of the houfhold of faith; that they may be produced that day as evidences that you belong to Chrift. Shut not up your bowels of mercy now towards the needy; left you then find no mercy. Take heed, that in all your works you be fingle and fincere; aiming, in them all at the glory of your Lord, as a teftimony of your love to him, and in obedience to his command. Leave it to hypocrites, who have their rewards, to proclaim every man his own goodnefs; and to found a trumpet when they do their alms. It is a bafe and unchriftian fpirit, which cannot have fatisfaction in a good work, unlefs it be expofed to the view of others: it is utterly unworthy of one who believes that the laft trumpet fhall call together the whole world, before whom the Judge himfelf fhall publifh works truly good, how fecretly foever they were done. Live in a believing expectation of the coming of the Lord. Let your loins be always girt, and your lamps burning: fo when he comes, whether in the laſt day of your life, or in the laſt day of the world, you ſhall be able to ſay with joy, *Lo, this is our God, and we have waited for him.*

HEAD V.
The Kingdom of HEAVEN.

Mat. xxv. 34. *Then ſhall the King ſay unto them on his right-hand, Come, ye bleſſed of my Father, inherit the kingdom prepared for you from the foundation of the world.*

HAving from this portion of Scripture, which the text is a part of, diſcourſed on the general judgment; and being to ſpeak of the everlaſting happineſs of the ſaints, and the everlaſting miſery of the wicked, from the reſpective ſentences to be pronounced upon them in the great day, I ſhall take them in the order, wherein they lie before us; and the rather, as ſentence is firſt paſſed upon the righteous, ſo the execution thereof is firſt begun, though probably the other may be fully executed before it be compleated.

The words of the text contain the joyful ſentence itſelf, together with an hiſtorical introduction thereto, which gives us an account of the Judge pronouncing the ſentence, *the King*, Jeſus Chriſt; the parties on whom it is given, *them on his right-hand*; and the time when, *then*, as ſoon as the trial is over. Of theſe I have ſpoke already. It is the ſentence itſelf which we are now to conſider, *Come, ye bleſſed of my Father*, &c. Stand back, O ye profane goats! away all unregenerate ſouls, not being united to Jeſus Chriſt! this is not for you. Come, O ye ſaints, brought out of your natural ſtate, into the ſtate of grace! behold here the ſtate of glory awaiting you. Here is glory let down to us in words and ſyllables; a looking-glaſs, in which you may ſee your everlaſting happineſs; a ſcheme, (or draught) of Chriſt's Father's houſe, wherein there are many manſions.

The glorious ſentence bears two things. (1.) The compleat happineſs to which the ſaints are adjudged,

Head IV. *Of Heaven.* 391

the kingdom. (2.) Their folemn admiffion to it, *Come, ye bleſſed of my Father, inherit,* &c. *Firſt,* Their compleat happineſs is a kingdom. A kingdom is the top of worldly felicity; there is nothing on earth greater than a kingdom: therefore the hidden weight of glory in heaven is held forth to us under that notion. But it is not an ordinary kingdom, it is *the kingdom,* the kingdom of heaven, furpaſſing all the kingdoms of the earth, in glory, honour, profit, and pleafure, infinitely more than they do in thefe excel the low and inglorious condition of a beggar in rags, and on a dunghill. *Secondly,* There is a folemn admiffion of the faints into this their kingdom. *Come, ye, inherit the kingdom.* In view of angels, men, and devils, they are invefted with royalty, and folemnly inaugurated before the whole world, by Jefus Chriſt, the heir of all things, who hath *all power in heaven and in earth.* Their right to the kingdom is folemnly recognized and owned. They are admitted to it, as undoubted heirs of the kingdom, to poſſeſs it by inheritance or lot, as the word properly fignifies, becaufe, of old, inheritances were defigned by lot, as Canaan to Ifrael, God's *firſt-born,* as they are called, Exod. iv. 22. And becaufe this kingdom is the Father's kingdom, therefore they are openly acknowledged, in their admiffion to it, to be the bleſſed of Chriſt's Father; which bleſſing was given them long before this fentence, but is now folemnly recognized, and confirmed to them by the Mediator in his Father's name. It is obfervable, he fays not, ye bleſſed of *the* Father, but, ye bleſſed of *my* Father; to ſhew us, that all bleſſings are derived by us from the Father, the fountain of bleſſing, as he is *the God and Father of our Lord Jeſus Chriſt,* through whom we are bleſſed, Eph. i. 3. Finally, they are admitted to this kingdom, as that which was *prepared for them from the foundation of the world,* in God's eternal purpofe, before they or any of them were; that all the world may fee eternal life to be the free gift of God.

DocT. The faints ſhall be made compleatly happy, in the poſſeſſion of the kingdom of heaven.

Two things I ſhall here enquire into. (1.) The nature of this kingdom. (2.) The admiffion of the faints thereto. And then I shall make some practical improvement of the whole.

First, As to the nature of the kingdom of heaven, our knowledge of it is very imperfect; for, *eye hath not seen, nor ear heard, neither have entered into the heart of man, the things which God hath prepared for them that love him*, 1 Cor. ii. 9. As by familiar resemblances parents instruct their little children, concerning things of which otherwise they can have no tolerable notion; so our gracious God, in consideration of our weakness, is pleased to represent to us heaven's happiness, under similitudes taken from earthly things, glorious in the eyes of men; since naked discoveries of the heavenly glory, divested of earthly resemblances, would be too bright for our weak eyes, and in them we would but lose ourselves. Wherefore, now we can only speak as children of these things, which the day will fully discover.

The state of glory is represented under the idea of a kingdom; a kingdom, among men, being that in which the greatest number of earthly good things doth centre. Now every saint shall, as a king, inherit a kingdom. All Christ's subjects shall be kings, each one with his crown upon his head: not that the great King shall divest himself of his royalty, but he will make all his children partakers of his kingdom.

I. The saints shall have kingly power and authority given them. Our Lord gives not empty titles to his favourites; he makes them kings indeed. The dominion of the saints will be a dominion far exceeding that of the greatest monarch who ever was upon earth. They will be absolute masters over sin, which had the dominion over them. They will have a compleat rule over their own spirits; an entire management of all their affections and inclinations, which now create them so much molestation: the turbulent root of corrupt affections shall be for ever expelled out of that kingdom, and never be able any more to give them the least disturbance. They shall have power over the nations, the ungodly of all nations, *and shall rule them with a rod of iron*, Rev. ii. 26, 27. The whole world of the wicked shall be broken before them: *Satan shall*

Head IV. *Of Heaven.*

be bruised under their feet, Rom. xvi. 20. He shall never be able to fasten a temptation on them any more: but he will be judged by them: and, in their sight, cast, with the reprobate crew, into the lake of fire and brimstone. So shall they rule over their oppressors: Having fought the good fight, and got the victory, Christ will entertain them as Joshua did his captains, causing them to *come near, and put their feet on the necks of kings,* Josh. x. 24.

II. They shall have the ensigns of royalty. For a throne, Christ will grant them *to sit down with him on his throne,* Rev. iii. 21. They will be advanced to the highest honour and dignity that they are capable of; and in the enjoyment of it they will have an eternal undisturbed repose, after all the tossings which they met with in the world, in their way to the throne. For a crown, they shall *receive a crown of glory, that fadeth not away,* 1 Pet. v. 4. Not a crown of flowers, as subjects, being conquerors or victors, have got: such a crown quickly fades; but their crown never fades. Not a crown of gold, such as earthly kings wear. Even a crown of gold is often stained, and at the best can never make them happy who wear it. But it shall be a *crown of glory.* A crown of glory is *a crown of life,* (Rev. ii. 10.) that life which knows no end: a crown which death can never make to fall off one's head. It must be an abiding crown; for it is a *crown of righteousness,* 2 Tim. iv. 8. It was purchased for them by *Christ's righteousness,* which is imputed to them; they are qualified for it by inherent righteousness; God's righteousness, or faithfulness, secures it to them, they shall have *a sceptre, a rod of iron,* Rev. ii. 27. terrible to all the wicked world. And a sword too, *a two-edged sword in their hand, to execute vengeance upon the heathen, and punishments upon the people,* Psal. cxlix. 6, 7. They shall have royal apparel. The royal robes in this kingdom are *white robes,* Rev. iii. 4. *They shall walk with me in white:* which, in a very particular manner, point at the inconceivable glory of the state of the saints in heaven.

The Lord is pleafed often to reprefent unto us the glorious ftate of the faints, by fpeaking of them as cloathed in *white garments*. It is promifed to the overcomer, that he fhall be *cloathed in white raiment*, Rev. iii. 5. The elders about the throne are *cloathed in white raiment*, chap. iv. 4. The multitude before the throne are *cloathed with white robes*, chap. vii. 9. *arrayed in white robes*, ver. 13. *made white in the blood of the Lamb*, ver. 14. I own, the two laft teftimonies refpect the ftate of the faints on earth; yet the terms are borrowed from the ftate of the church in heaven. All garments, properly fo called, being badges of fin and fhame, fhall be laid afide by the faints, when they come to their ftate of glory. But if we confider on what occafions white garments were wont to be put on, we fhall find much of heaven under them.

Firft, The Romans, when they manumitted their bond-fervants, gave them a white garment, as a badge of their freedom. So fhall the faints, that day, get on their white robes; for it is the day of *the glorious liberty of the children of God*, (Rom. viii. 21.) the day of *the redemption of their body*, ver. 23. They fhall no more fee the houfe of bondage, nor lie any more among the pots. If we compare the ftate of the faints on earth, with that of the wicked, it is not indeed a ftate of freedom, whereas the other is a ftate of flavery: but, in comparifon with their ftate in heaven, it is but, a fervitude. A faint on earth is indeed a young prince, and heir to the crown; but his motto may be, I ferve; for *he differeth nothing from a fervant, though he be Lord of all*, Gal. iv. 1. What are the groans of a faint, the fordid and bafe work which he is fometimes found employed in, the black and tattered garments which he walks in, but badges of this comparative fervitude? But from the day the faints come to the crown, they receive their compleat freedom, and ferve no more. They fhall be fully freed from fin, which of all evils is the worft, both in itfelf; and in their apprehenfion too; how great then muft that freedom be, when thefe *Egyptians, whom they fee to-day, they fhall fee them again no more for ever?* They fhall be free from all temptation

Head IV.   *Of Heaven.*   395

to fin: Satan can have no accefs to tempt them any more, by himfelf, nor by his agents. A full anfwer will then be given to that petition they have fo often repeated, *Lead us not into temptation.* No hiffing ferpent can come into the paradife above: no fnare nor trap can be laid there to catch the feet of the faints: they may walk there without fear, for they can be in no hazard: there are no lions dens, no mountains of the leopards, in the promifed land. Nay, they fhall be fet beyond the poffibility of finning, for they fhall be confirmed in goodnefs. It will be the confummate freedom of their will, to be for ever unalterably determined to good. And they fhall be freed from all the effects of fin; *there fhall be no more death, neither forrow, nor crying, neither fhall there be any more pain,* Rev. xxi. 4. What kingdom is like unto death? Death makes its way now into a palace, as eafily as into a cottage: forrow fills the heart of one who wears a crown on his head: royal robes are no fence againft pain, and crying by reafon of pain. But in this kingdom no mifery can have place. All reproaches fhall be wiped off; and never fhall a tear drop any more from their eyes. They fhall not complain of defertions again; the Lord will never hide his face from them: but the Sun of Righteoufnefs, fhining upon them in his meridian brightnefs, will difpel all clouds, and give them everlafting day, without the leaft mixture of darknefs. A deluge of wrath, after a fearful thunder-clap from the throne, will fweep away the wicked from before the judgment-feat, into the lake of fire: but the faints are, in the firft place, like Noah, brought into the ark, and out of harms way.

Secondly, White raiment hath been a token of purity. Therefore *the Lamb's wife is arrayed in fine linen, clean and white,* Rev. xix. 8. Thofe who ftood before the throne, *wafhed their robes, and made them white in the blood of the Lamb,* chap. vii. 14. The faints fhall then put on the robes of perfect purity, and fhine in fpotlefs holinefs, like the fun in his ftrength, without the leaft cloud to intercept his light. Abfolute innocence fhall then be reftored, and every appearance of fin banifhed far from this kingdom. The guilt of fin, and the reigning power of it, are now taken away in the faints; neverthelefs fin dwelleth in them, Rom. vii. 20. but then it fhall be no more in them: the corrupt nature will be quite removed: that root of bitternefs will be plucked up, and no veftiges of it left in their fouls: their nature fhall be altogether pure and finlefs. There fhall be no darknefs in their minds; but the underftanding of every faint, when he is come to his kingdom, will be as a globe of pure and unmixed light. There fhall not be the leaft averfion to good, nor the leaft inclination to evil, in their wills: but they will be brought to a perfect conformity to the will of God; bleffed with angelical purity, and fixed therein. Their affections will not be liable to the leaft diforder or irregularity: it will coft them no trouble to keep them right: they will get fuch a fixed habit of purity, as they can never lofe. They will be fo refined from all earthly drofs, as never to favour more of any thing but heaven. Were it poffible for them to be fet again amidft the enfnaring objects of an evil world, they would walk among them without the leaft defilement; as the fun fhines on the dung-hill, yet untainted; and as the angels preferved their purity in the midft of Sodom. Their graces fhall then be perfected; and all the imperfection now cleaving to them done away. There will be no more ground for complaints of weaknefs of grace: none in that kingdom fhall complain of an ill heart, or a corrupt nature. *It doth not yet appear what we fhall be, but when he fhall appear, we fhall be like him*, 1 John iii. 2.

Thirdly, Among the Jews, thofe who defired to be admitted into the prieftly office, being tried, and found to be of the prieft's line, and without blemifh, were cloathed in white, and inrolled among the priefts. This feems to be alluded to, Rev. iii. 15. *He that overcometh, the fame fhall be cloathed in white raiment, and I will not blot out his name out of the book of life.* So the faints fhall not be kings only, but priefts alfo; for they are *a royal priefthood*, 1 Pet. ii. 9. They will be priefts upon their thrones. They are judicially found defcended

Head IV. *Of Heaven.*

from the great High-prieſt of their profeſſion, begotten of him by his Spirit, of the incorruptible ſeed of the word, and without blemiſh : ſo the trial being over, they are admitted to be prieſts in the temple above, that they may dwell in the houſe of the Lord for ever. There is nothing upon earth more glorious than a kingdom ; nothing more venerable than the prieſthood : and both meet together in the glorified ſtate of the ſaints. *The general aſſembly of the firſt born*, (Heb. xii. 23.) whoſe is the prieſthood and the double portion, appearing in their white robes of glory, will be a reverend and glorious company. That day will ſhew them to be the perſons whom the Lord hath choſen, out of all the tribes of the earth, to be near unto him, and to enter into his temple, even into his holy place. Their prieſthood, begun on earth, ſhall be brought to its perfection, when they ſhall be employed in offering the ſacrifice of praiſe to God and the Lamb for ever and ever. They got not their portion in the earth with the reſt of the tribes : but the Lord himſelf was their portion, and will be their double portion, through the ages of eternity.

Fourthly, They were wont to wear white raiment in a time of triumph ; to which alſo there ſeems to be an alluſion, Rev. iii. 5. *He that overcometh, the ſame ſhall be cloathed in white raiment.* And what is heaven, but an everlaſting triumph ? None get thither, but ſuch as fight and overcome too. Though Canaan was given to the Iſraelites as an inheritance, they muſt conquer it before they could be poſſeſſors of it. The ſaints, in this world, are in the field of battle ; often in red garments, garments rolled in blood : but the day approacheth, in which they ſhall *ſtand before the throne, and before the Lamb, cloathed with white robes, and palms in their hands*, Rev. vii. 9.) having obtained a compleat victory over all their enemies. The palm was uſed as a ſign of victory ; becauſe that tree, though oppreſſed with weight, yet yieldeth not, but rather ſhooteth upwards. And palm-trees were carved on the doors of the moſt holy place, (1 Kings vi. 32.) which was a ſpecial type of heaven ; for heaven is the place which the ſaints are received into, as conquerors,

Behold the joy and peace of the saints, in their white robes! The joys arising from the view of past dangers, and of riches and honours gained at the very door of death, do most sensibly touch one's heart: and this will be an ingredient in the everlasting happiness of the saints, which could have had no place in the heaven of innocent Adam, and his sinless offspring, supposing him to have stood. Surely the glorified saints will not forget the entertainment which they met with in the world: it will be to the glory of God to remember it, and will also heighten their joy. The Sicilian king, by birth the son of a potter, acted a wise part, in that he would be served at his table with earthen vessels; which could not but put an additional sweetness in his meals, not to be relished by one born heir to the crown. Can ever meat be so sweet to any as to the hungry man? Or can any have such a relish of plenty, as he who has been under pinching straits? The more difficulties the saints have passed through, in their way to heaven, the place will be the sweeter to them when they come at it. Every happy stroke, struck in the spiritual warfare, will be a jewel in the crown of glory. Each victory obtained against sin, Satan, and the world, will raise their triumphant joy the higher. The remembrance of the cross will sweeten the crown: and the memory of their travel through the wilderness, will put an additional verdure on the fields of glory, while they walk through them, minding the day when they went mourning without the sun.

And now they appear triumphing in white robes, it is a sign that they have obtained an honourable peace; such a peace as their enemies can disturb no more So every thing peculiarly adapted to their militant condition is laid aside. The sword is laid down! and they betake themselves to the pen of a ready writer, to commemorate the praises of him by whom they overcame. Public ordinances, preaching, sacraments, shall be honourably laid aside; there is no temple there, Rev. xx. 22. On earth these were sweet to them: but the travellers being all got home, the inns, appointed for

Head IV. *Of Heaven.*

their entertainment by the way, are shut up; the candles are put out, when the sun is risen; and the tabernacle used in the wildernefs is folded up, when the temple of glory is come in its room. Many of the faints duties will then be laid aside; as one gives his staff out of his hand, when he is come to the end of his journey. Praying shall then be turned to praising: and there being no sin to confefs, no wants to feek the supply of, confeffion and petition shall be swallowed up in everlafting thankfgiving. There will be no mourning in heaven: they have sown in tears. The reaping time of joy is come, *and God shall wipe away all tears from their eyes*, Rev. xxi. 4. No need of mortification there; and self-examination is then at an end. They will not need to watch any more; the danger is over. Patience has had its perfect work, and there is no ufe for it there. Faith is turned into fight, and hope is swallowed up in the ocean of senfible and full enjoyment. All the rebels are subdued, and the faints quietly sit on their thrones; and so the forces, needful in the time of the spiritual warfare, are difbanded; and they carry on their triumph in the profoundeft peace.

Lastly, White garments were worn on feftival days, in token of joy. So shall the faints be cloathed in white raiment; for they shall keep an everlafting Sabbath to the Lord; Heb. iv. 9. *There remaineth, therefore, a reft* (or *keeping of a Sabbath) to the people of God.* The Sabbath, in the efteem of faints, is the queen of days: and they shall have an endlefs Sabbatifm in the kingdom of heaven: fo shall their garments be always white. They will have an eternal reft, with an uninterrupted joy: for heaven is not a refting place, where men may fleep out an eternity; (there they reft not day nor night) but their work is their reft and continual recreation, and toil and wearinefs have no place there. They reft there in God, who is the centre of their fouls. Here they find the completion, or fatisfaction of all their defires; having the full enjoyment of God, and uninterrupted communion with him. This is the point unto which, till the foul come, it will always be restless: but that point reached, it rests; for he is the last end, and the soul can go no farther. It cannot understand, will, nor desire more; but in him it has what is commensurable to its boundless desires. This is the happy end of all the labours of the saints; their toil and sorrows issue in a joyful rest. The Chaldeans measuring the natural day, put the day first, and the night last; but the Jews counted the night first, and the day last. Even so the wicked begin with a day of rest and pleasure, but end with a night of everlasting toil and sorrow: but God's people have their gloomy night first, and then comes their day of eternal rest; which Abraham, in the parable, observed to the rich man in hell, Luke xvi. 25. *Son, remember, that thou in thy life-time receivedst thy good things, and likewise Lazarus evil things: but now he is comforted, and thou art tormented.*

III. If any inquire where the kingdom of the saints lies? It is not in this world; it lies in a better country, *that is an heavenly,* (Heb. xi. 16.) a country better than the best of this world; namely, the heavenly Canaan, Immanuel's land, where nothing is wanting to complete the happiness of the inhabitants. This is the happy country, blessed with perpetual spring, and which yieldeth all things for conveniency and delight. There men shall eat angel's food; they shall be entertained with *the hidden manna,* (Rev. ii. 17.) without being set to the painful task of gathering it: they will be fed to the full, with the product of the land falling into their mouths, without the least toil to them. That land enjoys everlasting day, for there is *no night there,* Rev. xxi. 25. Eternal sun-shine beautifies this better country, but there is no scorching heat there. No clouds shall be seen there for ever: yet it is not a land of drought; the trees of the Lord's planting are set by the rivers of water, and shall never want moisture, for they will have an eternal supply of the Spirit, by Jesus Christ, from his Father. This is the only country from whence our Lord came, and whither he is gone again; the country which all the holy patriarchs and prophets had their eye upon while on earth; and

Head V. *Of Heaven.*

which all the saints, who have gone before us, have fought their way to; and unto which the martyrs have joyfully swimmed through a sea of blood. This earth is the place of the saint's pilgrimage; that is their country, where they find their everlasting rest.

IV. The royal city is *that great city, the holy Jerusalem*, described at large, Rev. xxi. 10. to the end of the chapter. (It is true some learned divines place this city in the earth: but the particulars of this description seem to me to favour those most who point us to the other world for it.) The saints shall reign in that city, whose wall is of *jasper*, ver. 16. and *the foundations of the wall garnished with all manner of precious stones*, ver. 19. and the *street of pure gold*, ver. 21. So that their feet shall be set on that which the men of this world set their hearts upon. This is the city which God has *prepared for them*, Heb. xi. 16. *a city that hath foundations*, ver. 10. *a continuing city*, chap. xiii. 14. which shall stand and flourish, when all the cities of the world are laid in ashes; and which shall not be moved when the foundations of the world are overturned. It is a city that never changeth its inhabitants: none of them shall ever be removed out of it; for life and immortality reign there, and no death can enter into it. It is blessed with a perfect and perpetual peace, and can never be in the least disturbed. Nothing from without can annoy it; the gates therefore are not shut at all by day, and there is no night there, Rev. xxi. 25. There can nothing from within trouble it. No want of provision there; no scarcity; no discord amongst the saints now; no vestige of their former jarrings shall remain there. Love to God, and to one another, shall be perfected: and those of them who stood at the greatest distance here, will joyfully embrace and delight in one another there.

The royal palace is Christ's Father's house, in which *are many mansions*, John xiv. 2. There shall the saints dwell for ever. This is the house prepared for all the heirs of glory, even those of them who dwell in the meanest cottage now, or have not where to lay their heads. As the Lord calls his saints to a kingdom, he will provide them a house suitable to the dignity he puts upon them. Heaven will be a convenient, spacious, and glorious house, for those whom the King delighteth to honour. Never was a house purchased at so great a rate as this, being the purchase of the Mediator's blood; and no less could it be afforded for to them: never was there so much to do to fit inhabitants for a house. The saints were, by nature, utterly unfit for this house, and human art and industry could not make them meet for it. But the Father gives the designed inhabitants to the Son, to be by him redeemed: the Son pays the price of their redemption, even his own precious blood; Justice gives them access to the house: and the Holy Spirit sanctifies them by his grace: that they may be meet to come in thither, where no unclean thing can enter. And no marvel, for it is the King's palace they enter into, (Psal. xiv. 15.) the house of the kingdom, where the great King keeps his court, where he has set his throne, and shews forth his glory in a singular manner, beyond what mortals can conceive.

VI. Paradise is their palace garden. *This day shalt thou be with me in paradise*, said our Saviour to the penitent thief on the cross, Luke xxiii. 43. Heaven is a paradise for pleasure and delight, where there is both wood and water; *A pure river of water of life, clear as chrystal, proceeding out of the throne of God and of the Lamb, and on either side of the river, the tree of life, which bears twelve manner of fruits, and yields her fruit every month*, Rev. xxii. 1, 2. How happy might innocent Adam have been in the earthly paradise, where there was nothing wanting for use or delight! Eden was the most pleasant spot of the uncorrupted earth, and paradise the most pleasant spot of Eden: but what is earth in comparison of heaven? The glorified saints are advanced to the heavenly paradise. There they shall not only see, but *eat of the tree of life, which is in the midst of the paradise of God*, Rev. iii. 7. They shall behold the Mediator's glory, and be satisfied with his goodness. No flaming sword will be there, to keep the way of that tree of life; but they shall

Head V. *Of Heaven.*

freely eat of it, and live for ever. They shall drink *of the rivers of pleasures*, (Psal. xxxvi. 8.) the sweetest and purest pleasures which Immanuel's land affords; and shall swim in the ocean of unmixed delight for evermore.

VII. They shall have royal treasures, sufficient to support the dignity which they are advanced to. Since the street of the royal city is pure gold, and the twelve gates thereof are twelve pearls; their treasure must be of that which is better than gold or pearl. It is an *eternal weight of glory*, 2 Cor. iv. 17. O precious treasure! A treasure not liable to insensible corruption, by moths or rust; a treasure which none can steal from them, Matth. vi. 20. Never did any kingdom afford such a precious treasure, nor a treasure of such a variety; *for he that overcometh shall inherit all things*, Rev. xxi. 7. No treasures on earth are stored with all things: if they were all put together in one, there would be far more valuable things wanting in that one than found in it. This then is the peculiar treasure of the kings, who inherit the kingdom of heaven. They shall want nothing, that may contribute to their full satisfaction. Now they are rich in hope: but then they will have their riches in hand. Now all things are theirs in respect of right: then all shall be theirs in possession. They may go for ever through Immanuel's land, and behold the glory and riches thereof, with the satisfying thought, that all which they see is their own. It is pity they should ever be uneasy, under the want of earthly good things, who may be sure that they shall inherit all things at length.

VIII. Though there is no material temple therein, no serving of God in the use of ordinances, as here on earth; yet, as for this kingdom, *the Lord God Almighty and the Lamb are the temple of it*, Rev. xxi. 22. As the temple was the glory of Canaan, so will the celestial temple be the glory of heaven. The saints shall be brought in thither, as a royal priesthood, to dwell in the house of the Lord for ever; for Jesus Christ will then make every saint *a pillar in the temple of God, and he shall go no more out*, (Rev. iii. 12.) as the priests and Levites did, in their courses, go out of the material temple. There the saints shall have the cloud of glory, the divine presence, with most intimate, uninterrupted communion with God : there they shall have Jesus Christ, (as the true ark, wherein the fiery law shall be for ever hid from their eyes ;) and the mercy-seat, from which nothing shall be breathed but everlasting peace and good-will towards them : the cherubims, the society of holy angels, who shall join with them in eternal admiration of the mystery of Christ : the golden candlestick, with its seven lamps ; for *the glory of God* doth *lighten it, and the Lamb is the light thereof*, Rev. xxi. 23. The incense-altar, in the intercession of Christ, who *ever liveth to make intercession for them*, Heb. vii 25. eternally exhibiting the merit of his death and sufferings, and efficaciously willing for ever, that those whom the Father hath given him, be with him : and the shew-bread table, in the perpetual feast they shall have together in the enjoyment of God. This leads me more particularly to consider,

IX. The society in this kingdom. What would royal power and authority, ensigns of royalty, richest treasures, and all other advantages of a kingdom, avail, without comfortable society ? Some crowned heads have had but a sorry life, through the want of it : their palaces have been unto them as prisons, and their badges of honour as chains on a prisoner ; while hated of all, they had none they could trust in, or whom they could have comfortable fellowship with. But the chief part of heaven's happiness lies in the blessed society which the saints shall have there.

First, The society of the saints, among themselves, will be no small part of heaven's happiness. The communion of saints on earth is highly prized by all those who are travelling through the world to Zion : and companions in sin can never have such true pleasure and delight in one another, as sometimes the Lord's people have in praying together, and conversing about those things which the world is a stranger to. Here the saints are but few in company, at best : and some of

Head V. *Of Heaven.*

them are fo fituated, as to feem to themfelves to dwell alone; having no accefs to fuch as they could freely unbofom themfelves to in fpiritual matters. They figh and fay, *Wo is me, for I am as when they have gathered the fummer fruits—there is no clufter to eat—the good man is perifhed out of the earth,* Mic. vii. 1, 2. But in the general affembly of the firft-born in heaven, none of all the faints who ever were, or will be on the earth, fhall be miffing. They will be all of them together in one place, all poffefs one kingdom, and all fit down together to the marriage-fupper of the Lamb. Here the beft of the faints want not their finful imperfections, making their fociety lefs comfortable: but there they fhall be perfect, without *fpot or wrinkle, or any fuch thing,* Eph. v. 27. All natural, as well as finful imperfections, will be done away; they *fhall fhine as the brightnefs of the firmament,* Dan xii. 3.

There we fhall fee Adam and Eve in heavenly paradife, freely eating of the tree of life; Abraham, Ifaac, and Jacob, and all the holy patriarchs, no more wandering from land to land, but come to their everlafting reft; all the prophets, feeding their eyes on the glory of him of whofe coming they prophefied; the twelve apoftles of the Lamb, fitting on their twelve thrones; all the holy martyrs in their long white robes, with their crowns on their heads; the godly kings advanced to a kingdom, which cannot be moved; and them that turn many to righteoufnefs, fhining as the ftars for ever and ever. There we fhall fee our godly friends, relations, and acquaintances, pillars in the temple of God, to go no more out from us. And it is more than probable, that the faints will know one another in heaven; at leaft, they will know their friends, relatives, and thofe they were acquainted with on earth, and fuch as have been moft eminent in the church: yet that knowledge will be purged from all earthly thoughts and affections. This feems to be included in that perfection of happinefs to which the faints fhall be advanced. If Adam knew who and what Eve was, at firft fight, when the Lord God brought her to him, (Gen ii. 23, 24.) why fhould one queftion but hufbands and wives, parents and children, will know each other in glory? If the Theſſalonians, converted by Paul's miniſtry, ſhall be his *crown of rejoicing in the preſence of our Lord Jeſus Chriſt at his coming*, (1 Theſſ. ii. 19.) why may we not conclude, that miniſters ſhall know their people, and people their miniſters, in heaven? and if the diſciples, on the mount of transfiguration, knew Moſes and Elias, whom they had never ſeen before, (Mat. xviii. 4.) we have reaſon to think that we ſhall know them too, and ſuch as they, when we come to heaven. The communion of ſaints ſhall be moſt intimate there; *they ſhall ſit down with Abraham, Iſaac, and Jacob, in the kingdom of heaven*, Mat. viii. 11. Lazarus was carried by the angels into Abraham's boſom, (Luke xvi. 23.) which denotes moſt intimate and familiar ſociety. And though diverſity of tongues ſhall ceaſe, (1 Cor. xiii. 8.) I make no queſtion, but there will be the uſe of ſpeech in heaven; and that the ſaints will glorify God in their bodies there, as well as in their ſpirits, ſpeaking forth his praiſes with an audible voice. (As for the language, we ſhall underſtand what it is when we come thither.) When Paul was caught up to the third heaven, the ſeat of the bleſſed, he heard there *unſpeakable words, which it is not lawful for a man to utter*, 2 Cor. xii. 4. Moſes and Elias, on the mount with Chriſt, *talked with him*, Mat. xvii. 3. and *ſpake of his deceaſe which he ſhould accompliſh at Jeruſalem*, Luke ix. 31.

Secondly, The ſaints will have the ſociety of all the holy angels there. An innumerable company of angels ſhall be companions to them in their glorified ſtate. Happy were the ſhepherds, who heard the ſong of the heavenly hoſt when Chriſt was born: but thrice happy they, who ſhall join their voices with theirs, in the quire of ſaints and angels in heaven; when he ſhall be glorified in all who ſhall be about him there. Then ſhall we be brought acquainted with thoſe bleſſed ſpirits, who never ſinned. How bright will thoſe morning-ſtars ſhine in the holy place! they were miniſtring ſpirits to the heirs of ſalvation, loved them for their Lord and maſter's ſake; encamped round about them, to preserve them from danger: how joyful will they welcome them to their everlasting habitations; and rejoice to see them come at length to their kingdom, as the tutor doth in the prosperity of his pupils! The saints shall be no more afraid of them, as sometimes they were wont to be: they shall then have put off mortality, and infirmities of the flesh, and be themselves as the angels of God, fit to entertain communion and fellowship with them. And both being brought under one Head, the Lord Jesus Christ, they will join in the praises of God and of the Lamb, *saying, with a loud voice, Worthy is the Lamb that was slain,* &c. Rev. v. 11, 12. Whether the angels shall (as some think) assume ethereal bodies, that they may be seen by the bodily eyes of the saints, and be in a nearer capacity to converse with them, I know not: but as they want not ways of converse among themselves, we have reason to think, that conversation between them and the saints shall not be for ever blocked up.

Lastly, They shall have society with the Lord himself in heaven, glorious communion with God in Christ, which is the perfection of happiness. I choose to speak of communion with God and the man Christ together; because, as we derive our grace from the Lamb, so we shall derive our glory from him too, the man Christ being (if I may be allowed the expression) the centre of the divine glory in heaven, from whence it is diffused unto all the saints. This seems to be taught us by the Scriptures, which express heaven's happiness by *being with Christ*, Luke xxiii. 43. *This day shalt thou be with me in paradise.* John xvii. 24. *Father, I will that those also whom thou hast given me, be with me.* (And remarkable to this purpose is what follows, *that they may behold my glory*) 1 Thess. iv. 17. *So shall we ever be with the Lord*, to wit, the Lord Christ, whom we shall meet in the air. This also seems to be the import of the Scriptures, wherein God and the Lamb, the slain Saviour, are jointly spoken of, in point of the happiness of the saints in heaven, Rev. vii. 17. *For the Lamb, which is in the midst of the throne, shall feed them, and shall lead them unto living fountains of waters: and*

Of Heaven.

God shall wipe away all tears from their eyes. Chap. xxi. 3. *Behold, the tabernacle of God is with men, and he will dwell with them,* to wit, as in a tabernacle, (so the word signifies) that is, in the flesh of Christ, (comp. John i. 14.) and ver. 22. *The Lord God Almighty and the Lamb are the temple of it.* Here lies the chief happiness of the saints in heaven, without which they could never be happy, though lodged in that glorious place, and blessed with the society of angels there. What I shall venture to say of it, shall be comprized in three things.

First, The saints in heaven shall have the glorious presence of God and of the Lamb: God himself shall be with them, Rev. xxi. 3. And they shall ever be with the Lord. God is every where present, in respect of his essence; the saints militant have his special gracious presence: but in heaven they have his glorious presence. There they are brought near to the throne of the great King, and stand before him, where he shews his inconceivable glory. There they have the tabernacle of God, on which the cloud of glory rests, the all-glorious human nature of Christ, wherein the fulness of the God-head dwells; not vailed as in the days of his humiliation, but shining through that blessed flesh (that all the saints may behold his glory), and making that body more glorious than a thousand suns: so that the city has no need of the sun, nor of the moon, but *the glory of God doth lighten it, and the Lamb is the light thereof* (properly, *the candle thereof),* Rev. xxi. 23. *i. e.* The Lamb is the luminary or luminous body, which gives light to the city; as the sun and moon now give light to the world, or as a candle lightens a dark room: and the light proceeding from that glorious luminary of the city, is the glory of God. Sometimes on earth that candle burnt very dim, it was hid under a bushel, in the time of his humiliation; only now and then it darted out some rays of this light, which dazzled the eyes of the spectators: but now it is set on high, in the city of God, where it shines, and shall shine for ever, in perfection of glory. It was here laid aside, as a stone disallowed

Head V. *Of Heaven.* 409

of the builders: but now it is, and for ever will be *the light*, or luminary of that city; and that *like unto a stone most precious, even like a jasper stone, clear as chrystal*, ver. 11.

Who can conceive the happiness of the saints, in the presence chamber of the great King, where he sits in his chair of state, making his glory eminently to appear in the man Christ? His glorious presence makes a mighty change upon the saints in this world: his glorious presence in heaven, then, must needs raise their graces to perfection, and elevate their capacities. The saints experience that the presence of God, now with them, in his grace, can make a little heaven of a sort of hell. How great must the glory of heaven then be, by his presence there in his glory! If a candle, in some sort, beautifies a cottage or prison, how will the shining sun beautify a palace or paradise! the gracious presence of God made a wilderness lightsome to Moses, the valley of the shadow of death to David, a fiery furnace to the three children: what ravishing beauty shall then arise from the Sun of Righteousness, shining in his meridian brightness on the street of the city laid with pure gold! This glorious presence of God in heaven, will put a glory on the saints themselves. The pleasant garden hath no beauty, when the darkness of the night sits down on it; but the shining sun puts a glory on the blackest mountains: so those who are now as bottles in the smoke, when set in the glorious presence of God, will be glorious both in soul and body.

2*dly*, The saints in heaven shall have the full enjoyment of God and the Lamb. This is it that perfectly satisfies the rational creature; and here is the saints everlasting rest. This will make up all their wants and fill the desires of their souls, which, after all here obtained, still cry, *Give, give,* not without some anxiety; because though they do enjoy God, yet they do not enjoy him fully. As to the way and manner of his enjoyment, our Lord tells us, John xvii. 3. *This is life eternal that they might know thee the only true God, and Jesus Christ whom thou hast sent.* . Now there are two

G g g

ways, how a desireable object is known most perfectly and satisfyingly; the one is by sight, the other by experience: sight satisfies the understanding, and experience satisfies the will. Accordingly, one may say that the saints enjoy God and the Lamb in heaven, (1.) By an intuitive knowledge. (2.) By an experimental knowledge, both of them perfect, I mean, in respect of the capacity of the creature; for otherwise a creature's perfect knowledge of the infinite Being is impossible. The saints below enjoy God in that knowledge which they have of him by report, from his holy word, which they believe; they see him likewise darkly in the glass of ordinances, which do, as it were, represent the Bridegroom's picture or shadow, while he is absent: they have also some experimental knowledge of him, they taste that God is good, and that the Lord is gracious. But the saints above will not need a good report of the King; they shall see himself; therefore faith ceaseth; they will behold his own face; therefore ordinances are no more, there is no need of a glass. They shall drink, and drink abundantly of that whereof they have tasted; and so hope ceaseth, for they are at the utmost bounds of their desires.

I. The saints in heaven will enjoy God and the Lamb by sight, and that in a most perfect manner, 1 Cor. xiii. 12. *For now we see through a glass darkly, but then face to face.* Here our sight is but mediate, as by a glass, in which we see not things themselves, but the images of things: but there we shall have an immediate view of God and the Lamb. Here our knowledge is but obscure; there it shall be clear, without the least mixture of darkness. The Lord now converses with his saints, through the lattesses of ordinances; but then they will be in his presence-chamber with him. There is a vail now on the glorious face, as to us: but when we come to the upper-house, that vail, through which some rays of beauty are now darted, will be found entirely taken off; and then shall glorious excellencies and perfections, not seen in him by mortals, be clearly discovered, for we shall see his face, Rev. xxii. 4. The phrase seems to be borrowed from the honour put upon some in the courts of monarchs, to be attendants on the king's person. We read, Jer. liii. 25. of *seven men of them that were* (Heb. *seers of the king's face*, i. e. as we read it) *near the king's person.* O unspeakable glory! the great King keeps his court in heaven: and the saints shall all be his courtiers, ever near the King's person, seeing his face. *The throne of God and of the Lamb shall be in it, and his servants shall serve him. And they shall see his face.*

1. They shall see Jesus Christ, God and man, with their bodily eyes, since he will never lay aside the human nature. They will always behold that glorious blessed body, which is personally united to the divine nature, and exalted far above principalities and powers, and every name that is named. There we shall see, with our eyes, that very body which was born of Mary at Bethlehem, and crucified at Jerusalem between two thieves! the blessed head that was crowned with thorns; the face that was spit upon; the hands and feet that were nailed to the cross; all shining with inconceivable glory. The glory of the man Christ will attract the eyes of all the saints, and he will be for ever admired in all them that believe, 2 Thess. i. 10. Were each star in the heavens shining as the sun in its meridian brightness, and the light of the sun so encreased, for the stars to bear the same proportion to the sun, in point of light that they do now, it might possibly be some faint resemblance of the glory of the man Christ, in comparison with that of the saints: for though the saints *shall shine forth as the sun;* yet not they, but the Lamb shall be *the light of the city.* The wise men fell down and worshipped him, when they saw him a *young child with Mary his mother, in the house.* But O what a ravishing sight will it be to see him in his kingdom, on his throne, at the Father's right-hand! *The word was made flesh,* (John i. 14.) and the glory of God shall shine through that flesh, and joys of heaven spring out from it, unto the saints, who shall see and enjoy God in Christ. For since the union between Christ and the saints is never dissolved, but they continue his members for ever, and the members

cannot draw their life, but from their head, feeing that which is independent on the head, as to vital influence, is no member: therefore Jefus Chrift will remain the everlafting bond of union between God and the faints; from whence their eternal life fhall fpring, John xvii. 2, 3. 22, 23. *Thou haft given him power over all flefh, that he fhould give eternal life to as many as thou haft given him. And this is life eternal, that they might know thee the only true God,* &c. *And the glory which thou gaveft me, I have given them, that they may be one, even as we are one: I in them, and thou in me, that they may be made perfect in one.* Wherefore, the immediate enjoyment of God in heaven, is to be underftood in refpect of the laying afide of the word and facraments, and fuch external means as we enjoy God by in this world; but not as if the faints fhould then caft off their dependance on their Head for vital influences: nay, *the Lamb which is in the midft of the throne fhall feed them, and lead them unto living fountains of waters,* Rev. viii. 17.

Now when we fhall behold him, who died for us, that we might live for evermore, whofe matchlefs love made him fwim through the red-fea of God's wrath, to make a path in the midft of it for us, by which we might pafs fafely to Canaan's land; then we fhall fee what a glorious one he was, who fuffered all this for us; what entertainment he had in the upper-houfe; what hallelujahs of angels could not hinder him to hear the groans of a perifhing multitude on earth, and to come down for their help; and what glory he laid afide for us. Then fhall we be more able to *comprehend with all faints what is the breadth, length, and depth, and height; and to know the love of Chrift, which paffeth knowledge,* Eph. iii. 18, 19. When the faints fhall remember that the waters of wrath, which he was plunged into, are the wells of falvation, from whence they draw all their joy; that they have got the cup of falvation, in exchange for the cup of wrath which his Father gave him to drink, which his human nature fhivered at: how will their hearts leap within them, burn with feraphic love, and like coals of juniper, and the arch of heaven

Head V. *Of Heaven.* 413

ring with their fongs of falvation! The Jews celebrating the feaft of tabernacles (which was the moft joyful of all their feafts, and lafted feven days), went once every day about the altar, finging hofanna, with their myrtle, palm, and willow branches in their hand (the two former figns of victory, the laft of chaftity), in the mean time bending their boughs towards the altar. When the faints are prefented as a chafte virgin to Chrift, and as conquerors have got their palms in their hands, how joyfully will they compafs the altar evermore, and fing their hofannas, or rather their hallelujahs about it, bending their palms towards it; acknowledging themfelves to owe all unto the Lamb that was flain, and redeemed them with his blood! To this agrees what John faw, Rev. vii. 9, 10. *A great multitude flood before the throne, and before the Lamb, cloathed with white robes, and palms in their hands, and cried with a loud voice, faying,* Salvation *to our God, which fitteth upon the throne, and unto the Lamb.*

2. They fhall fee God, Matth. v. 8. They will be happy in feeing the Father, Son, and Holy Ghoft, (not with their bodily eyes, in refpect of which God is invifible, 1 Tim. i. 17.) but with the eyes of their underftanding; being bleffed with the moft perfect, full, and clear knowledge of God, and divine things, which the creature is capable of. This is called *the beatific vifion*; and is the perfection of underftanding, the utmoft term thereof. It is but an obfcure delineation of the glory of God that mortals can have on earth; a fight, as it were, of his *back parts*, Exod. xxxiii. 23. but there they will fee his face, Rev. xxii. 4. They fhall fee him in the fulnefs of his glory, and behold him fixedly; whereas it is but a paffing view which they can have of him here, Exod. xxxiv. 6. There is a vaft difference between the fight of a king in his night-clothes, quickly paffing by us, and a fixed leifure view of him, fitting on his throne in his royal robes, his crown on his head, and his fceptre in his hand: fuch a difference will there be between the greateft manifeftation of God that ever a faint had on earth, and the difplay of his glory in heaven. There the faints fhall eternally, without inter-

ruption, feed their eyes upon him, and be ever viewing his glorious perfections. And as their bodily eyes shall be strengthened and fitted to behold the glorious majesty of the man Christ, as eagles gaze on the sun, without being blinded thereby: so their minds shall have such an elevation, as will fit them to see God in his glory: their capacities shall be enlarged, according to the measure in which he shall be pleased to communicate himself unto them, for their complete happiness.

This blissful sight of God, being quite above our present capacities, we must needs be much in the dark about it. But it seems to be something else than the sight of that glory, which we shall see with our bodily eyes in the saints, and in the man Christ, or any other splendour or refulgence from the Godhead whatever; for no created thing can be our chief good and happiness, nor fully satisfy our souls; and it is plain that these things are somewhat different from God himself. Therefore I conceive that the souls of the saints shall see God himself: so the Scriptures teach us, that we shall *see face to face, and know even as we are known,* 1 Cor. xiii. 12. and that *we shall see him as he is,* 1 John iii. 2. yet the saints can never have an adequate conception of God: they cannot comprehend that which is infinite. They may touch the mountain, but cannot grasp it in their arms. They cannot with one glance of their eye behold what grows on every side: but the divine perfections will be an unbounded field, in which the glorified shall walk eternally, seeing more and more of God, since they can never come to an end of that which is infinite. They may bring their vessels to this ocean every moment, and fill them with new waters. What a ravishing sight would it be, to see all the perfections and lovely qualities, that are scattered here and there among the creatures, gathered together into one! But even such a sight would be infinitely below this blissful sight which the saints shall have in heaven. For they shall see God, in whom all these perfections shall eminently appear infinitely more, whereof there is no vestige to be found in the creatures. In him shall they see every thing desireable, and nothing but what is desireable.

Head V. *Of Heaven.* 415

Then shall they be perfectly satisfied as to the love of God towards them, which they are now ready to question on every turn. They will be no more put to it to persuade themselves of it, by marks, signs, and testimonies: they will have an intuitive knowledge of it. They shall (with the profoundest reverence be it spoken) look into the heart of God, and there see the love which he bore to them from all eternity, and the love and goodness which he will bear to them for evermore. The glorified shall have a most clear and distinct understanding of divine truths, for in his light we shall see light, Psal. xxxvi. 9. The light of glory will be a compleat commentary on the Bible, and untie all the hard and knotty questions in divinity. There is no joy on earth comparable to that which ariseth from the discovery of truth; no discovery of truth comparable to the discovery of Scripture truth, made by the Spirit of the Lord unto the soul. *I rejoice at thy word,* says the Psalmist, *as one that findeth great spoil,* Psal. cxix. 162. Yet it is but an imperfect discovery which we have of it while here: How ravishing then will it be, to see the opening of the whole treasure hid in that field! They shall also be led into the understanding of the works of God. The beauty of the works of creation and providence will then be set in due light. Natural knowledge will be brought to perfection by the light of glory. The web of Providence concerning the church, and all men whatever, will then be cut out, and laid before the eyes of the saints: and it will appear a most beautiful mixture, so as they shall all say together, on the view of it, *He hath done all things well.* But in a special manner, the work of redemption shall be the eternal wonder of the saints, and they will admire and praise the glorious contrivance for ever. Then shall they get a full view of its suitableness to the Divine perfections, and to the case of sinners; and clearly read the covenant that past between the Father and the Son, from all eternity, touching their salvation. They shall for ever wonder and praise, and praise and wonder at the mysteries of wisdom and love, goodness and holiness, mercy and justice, appearing in the glorious scheme. Their souls will be eternally satisfied with the sight of God himself, of their election by the Father, their redemption by the Son, and application thereof to them by the Holy Spirit.

II. The saints in heaven shall enjoy God in Christ by experimental knowledge, which is, when the object itself is given and possessed. This is the participation of the divine goodness in full measure; which is the perfection of the will, and utmost term thereof. *The Lamb shall lead them unto living fountains of waters*, Rev. vii. 17. These are no other but God himself, the *fountain of living waters*, who will fully and freely communicate himself unto them. He will pour out of his goodness eternally into their souls: then shall they have a most lively sensation, in the innermost part of their souls, of all that goodness which they heard of, and believed to be in him, and of what they see in him by the light of glory. This will be an everlasting practical exposition of that word, which men and angels cannot sufficiently unfold, to wit, God himself shall *be their God*, Rev. xxi. 3. God will communicate himself unto them fully: they will no more be set to taste of the streams of divine goodness in ordinances, as they were wont, but shall drink at the fountain-head. They will no more be entertained with sips and drops, but filled with all the fulness of God. And this will be the entertainment of every saint: for though in created things, what is given to one is withheld from another, yet the infinite Good can fully communicate itself to all, and fill all. Those who are heirs of God, the great heritage, shall then enter into a full possession of their inheritance: and the Lord will open his treasures of goodness unto them, that their enjoyment may be full. They shall not be stinted to any measure: but the enjoyment shall go as far as their enlarged capacities can reach. As a narrow vessel cannot contain the ocean, so neither can the finite creature comprehend the infinite Good. But no measure shall be set to the enjoyment, but what ariseth from the capacity of the creature. So that, although there be degrees of glory, yet all shall be filled, and have what they can hold; though some will be capable to hold more than others. There will be no want to any of them; all shall be fully satisfied, and perfectly blessed in the full enjoyment of divine goodness, according to their enlarged capacities. As when bottles of different sizes are filled, some contain more, others less; yet all of them have what they can contain. The glorified shall have all in God for the satisfaction of all their desires. No created thing can afford satisfaction to all our desires; cloaths may warm us, but they cannot feed us; the light is comfortable, but cannot nourish us. But in God we shall have all our desires, and we shall desire nothing without him. They shall be the happy ones, that desire nothing but what is truly desireable; they shall have all they desire. God will be all in all to the saints: he will be their life, health, riches, honour, peace, and all good things. He will communicate himself freely to them: the door of access to him shall never be shut again for one moment. They may, when they will, take of the fruits of the tree of life, for they will find it on each side the river, Rev. xxii. 2. There will be no vail between God and them, to be drawn aside; but his fulness shall ever stand open to them. No door to knock at in heaven; no asking to go before receiving: the Lord will allow his people an unrestrained familiarity with himself there.

Now they are in part made *partakers of the divine nature*; but then they shall perfectly partake of it; that is to say, God will communicate to them his own image, make all his goodness not only pass before them, but pass unto them, and stamp the image of all his own perfections upon them, so far as the creature is capable to receive the same; from whence shall result a perfect likeness to him, in all things in or about them; which compleats the happiness of the creature. This is what the Psalmist seems to have had in view, Psal. xvii. 15. *I shall be satisfied, when I awake, with thy likeness*; the perfection of God's image following upon the beatific vision. And so says John, 1 John iii. 2. *We shall be like him; for we shall see him as he is.* Hence there shall be a most close and intimate union between

God and the saints: God shall be in them, and they in God, in the way of a glorious and most perfect union; for then they shall dwell in love made perfect. *God is love, and he that dwelleth in love, dwelleth in God, and God in him,* 1 John iv. 16. How will the saints knit with God, and he with them, when he shall see nothing in them but his own image; when their love shall arrive at its perfection, no nature but the divine nature being left in them; and all imperfection swallowed up in their glorious transformation into the likeness of God! Their love to the Lord, being purged from the dross of self-love, shall be most pure: so as they will love nothing but God, and in God. It shall be no more faint and languishing, but burn like coals of juniper. It will be a light without darkness, a flaming fire without smoke. As the live coal, when all the moisture is gone out of it, is all fire; so will the saints be all love, when they come to the full enjoyment of God in heaven, by intuitive and experimental knowledge of him, by sight and full participation of the divine goodness.

Lastly, From this glorious presence and enjoyment shall arise an unspeakable joy, which the saints shall be filled with. *In thy presence is fulness of joy,* Psal. xvi. 11. The saints sometimes enjoy God in the world, but when their eyes are held, so as not to perceive it, they have not the comfort of the enjoyment: but then all mistakes being removed, they shall not only enjoy God, but rest in the enjoyment with inexpressible joy and satisfaction. The desire of earthly things breeds torment, and the enjoyment of them often ends in loathing. But though the glorified saints shall ever desire more and more of God, their desires shall not be mixed with the least anxiety, since the fulness of the Godhead stands always open to them; therefore they shall hunger no more, they shall not have the least uneasiness in their eternal appetite after the hidden manna; neither shall continued enjoyment breed loathing; they shall never think that they have too much; therefore it is added, *Neither shall the sun light on them, nor any heat,* Rev. vii. 16. The enjoyment of God and the Lamb will be ever fresh

Head V.   *Of Heaven.*   419

and new to them, through the ages of eternity; for they shall drink of living fountains of waters, where new waters are continually springing up in abundance, ver. 17. They shall eat of the tree of life, which, for variety, affords twelve manner of fruits, and these always new and fresh, for it yields every month, Rev xxii. 2. Their joy shall be pure and unmixed, without any dregs of sorrow; not slight and momentary, but solid and everlasting, without interruption. They will enter into joy, Matt. xxv. 21. *Enter thou into the joy of thy Lord.* The expression is somewhat unusual, and brings into my mind this word of our suffering Redeemer, Mark xvi. 34. *My soul is exceeding sorrowful unto death.* His soul was beset with sorrows, as the word there used will bear; the floods of sorrow went round about him, encompassing him on every hand; wherever he turned his eyes, sorrow was before him; it sprang in upon him from heaven, earth, and hell, at once: thus he entered into sorrow, and therefore saith, Psal. lxix. 2. *I am come into deep waters, where the floods overflow me.* Now wherefore all this, but that his own might enter into joy? Joy sometimes enters into us now, but has much to do to get access, while we are encompassed about with sorrows: but then joy shall not only enter into us, but we shall enter into it, and swim for ever in the ocean of joy; where we shall see nothing but joy wherever we turn our eyes. The presence and enjoyment of God and the Lamb will satisfy us with pleasures for evermore: and the glory of our souls and bodies, arising from thence, will afford us everlasting delight. The spirit of heaviness, how closely soever it cleaves to any of the saints now, shall drop off then: their weeping shall be turned into songs of joy, and bottles of tears shall issue in rivers of pleasures. Happy they who now sow in tears, which shall spring up in joy in heaven, which will encircle their heads with a weight of glory.

Thus far of the society in this kingdom of the saints

X. In the last place. The kingdom shall endure for ever. As every thing in it is eternal, so the saints shall have undoubted certainty and full assurance of the eternal duration of the fame. This is a neceſſary ingredient in perfect happineſs: for the leaſt uncertainty, as to the continuance of any good with one, is not without ſome fear, anxiety, and torment; and therefore is utterly inconfiſtent with perfect happineſs. But the glorified ſhall never have fear, or cauſe of fear, of any loſs; they ſhall be *ever with the Lord*, 1 Theſſ. iv. 17. They ſhall all attain to the full perſuaſion, that nothing ſhall be able to ſeparate them from the love of God; nor from the full enjoyment of him for ever. The inheritance *reſerved in heaven is incorruptible*; it hath no principle of corruption in itſelf, to make it liable to decay, but endures for evermore: it is undefiled; nothing from without can mar its beauty, nor is there any thing in itſelf to offend thoſe who enjoy it. Therefore it fadeth not away: but ever remains in its native luſtre, and primitive beauty, 1 Pet. i. 4. Hitherto of the nature of the kingdom of heaven.

SECONDLY, We now proceed to ſpeak of the admiſſion of the ſaints into this their kingdom. I ſhall briefly touch on two things. (1.) The formal admiſſion, in the call unto them from the Judge, to come to their kingdom. (2.) The quality in which they are admitted and introduced to it.

I. Their admiſſion, the text ſhews to be by a voice from the throne; the King calling to them from the throne, before angels and men, to come to their kingdom. *Come* and *go* are but ſhort words; but they will be ſuch as will afford matter of thought to all mankind, through the ages of eternity; ſince everlaſting happineſs turns upon one, and upon the other everlaſting miſery. Now our Lord bids the worſt of ſinners, who hear the goſpel, Come; but the moſt part will not come unto him. Some few, whoſe hearts are touched by his Spirit, who embrace the call, and their ſouls within them ſay, *Behold we come unto thee*, they give themſelves to the Lord, forſake the world and their luſts for him; they bear his yoke, and caſt it not off, no not in the heat of the day, when the weight of it, perhaps, makes them ſweat the blood out of their bodies. Behold the fools! ſaith the car-

Head V. *Of Heaven.* 421

nal world, whither are they going? But stay a little, O foolish world; from the same mouth, whence they had the call which they are now following, another call shall come, which will make amends for all. *Come, ye blessed of my Father, inherit the kingdom.*

The saints shall find an inexpressible sweetness in this call, Come. (1.) Hereby Jesus Christ shews his desire of their society in the upper-house, that they may be ever with him there. Thus he will open his heart unto them, as sometimes he did to his Father concerning them, saying, *Father, I will, that they—be with me, where I am,* John xvii. 24. Now the travail of his soul stands before the throne, not only the souls, but the bodies which he has redeemed; and they must come, for he must be compleatly satisfied. (2.) Hereby they are solemnly invited to the marriage-supper of the Lamb. They were invited to the lower table, by the voice of the servants, and the secret workings of the Spirit within them; and they came and did partake of the feast of divine communications in the lower-house; but Jesus Christ in person shall invite them, before all the world, to the highest table. (3.) By this he admits them into the mansions of glory. The key of heaven hangs at the girdle of our royal Mediator; *All power in heaven* is given to him, (Mat. xxviii. 18.) and none get in thither but whom he admits. When they were living on earth with the rest of the world, he opened the everlasting doors of their hearts, entered into them, and shut them again; so as sin could never re-enter, to reign there as formerly: now he opens heaven's doors to them, draws his doves into the ark, and shuts them in; so as the law, death, and hell, can never get them out again. The saints in this life were still labouring to enter into that rest; but Satan was always pulling them back, their corruption always drawing them down; insomuch that they have sometimes been left to hang by a hair of promise, (if I may be allowed the expression) not without fears of falling into the lake of fire: but now Christ gives the word for their admission; they are brought in, and put beyond all hazard. *Lastly,* He speaks to them as the person introducing them into the kingdom, into the prefence-chamber of the great King, and unto the throne. Jefus Chrift is the great Secretary of heaven, whofe office it is to bring the faints into the gracious prefence of God now; and to whom alone it belongs to bring them into the glorious prefence of God in heaven. Truly heaven would be a ftrange place to them, if Jefus was not there : but the Son will introduce his brethren into his Father's kingdom; they fhall go in *with him to the marriage*, Matt. xxv. 10.

II. Let us confider in what quality they are introduced by him.

Firft, He brings them in as the bleffed of his Father; fo runs the call from the throne, *Come, ye bleffed of my Father*, &c. It is Chrift's Father's houfe which they are to come into : therefore he puts them in mind that they are bleffed of his Father; dear to the Father, as well as to himfelf. This is it that makes heaven *home* to them ; namely, that it is Chrift's Father's houfe, where they may be affured of welcome, being married to the Son, and being his Father's choice for that very end. He brings them in for his Father's fake, as well as for his own : they are the bleffed of his Father; who, is the fountain of Deity, and of all bleffings conferred on the children of men. They are thofe whom God loved from eternity. They were bleffed in the eternal purpofe of God, being elected to everlafting life ; at the opening of the book of life, their names were found written therein. So that by bringing them to the kingdom, he doth but bring them to what the Father, from all eternity, defigned for them. Being faved by the Son, they are faved according to his (*i. e.* the Father's) purpofe, 2 Tim. i. 9. They are thofe to whom the Father has fpoken well. He fpoke well to them in his word, which muft now receive its full accomplifhment. They had his promife of the kingdom, lived and died in the faith of it ; and now they come to receive the thing promifed. Unto them he has done well. A gift is often in Scripture called a bleffing; and God's bleffing is ever real, like Ifaac's bleffing, by which Jacob became his heir; they were all by grace juftified, fanctified, and enabled to perfevere to the end ; now they are raifed up in glory,

Head V. *Of Heaven.*

and being tried, stand in the judgment: what remains, then, but that God crown his own work of grace in them, in giving them their kingdom, in the full enjoyment of himself for ever? *Finally*, They are those whom God has consecrated; which also is a Scripture term of blessing, 1 Cor. x. 16. God set them apart for himself, to be kings and priests unto him; and the Mediator introduceth them, as such, to their kingdom and priesthood.

Secondly, Christ introduceth them as heirs of the kingdom, to the actual possession of it. *Come, ye blessed, inherit the kingdom.* They are the children of God by regeneration and adoption; *and if children, then heirs, heirs of God, and joint heirs with Christ,* Rom. viii. 17. Now is the general assembly of the first-born before the throne: their minority is overpast, and the time appointed of the Father for their receiving of their inheritance is come. The Mediator purchased the inheritance for them with his own blood; their rights and evidences were drawn long ago, and regiftered in the Bible; nay, they have investment of their inheritance in the person of Jesus Christ, as their Proxy, when he ascended into heaven, *whither the Forerunner is for us entered,* Heb. vi. 20. Nothing remaineth, but that they enter into personal possession thereof, which, begun at death, is perfected at the last day, when the saints in their bodies, as well as their souls, go into their kingdom.

Lastly, They are introduced to it, as *those it was prepared for from the foundation of the world.* The kingdom was prepared for them in the eternal purpose of God, before they or any of them had a being, which shews it to be a gift of free-grace to them. It was, from eternity, the divine purpose, that there should be such a kingdom for the elect; and that all impediments, which might mar their access to it, should be removed out of the way; and also by the same eternal decree, every one's place in it was determined and set apart, to be referved for him; that each of the children coming home at length into their Father's house, might find his own place awaiting him, and ready for him; as at Saul's table, David's place was empty, when he was not there to occupy it himſelf, 1 Sam. xx. 25. And now the appointed time is come, they are brought in to take their ſeveral places in glory.

USE. I ſhall ſhut up my diſcourſe, on this ſubject, with a word of application. (1.) To all who claim a right to this kingdom. (2.) To thoſe who have indeed a right to it. (3.) To thoſe who have no right thereto.

Firſt, Since it is evident, there is no promiſcuous admiſſion into the kingdom of heaven, and none obtain it but thoſe whoſe claim to it is ſolemnly tried by the great Judge, and after trial ſupported as good and valid; it is neceſſary that all of us impartially try and examine, whether, according to the laws of the kingdom, contained in the holy Scriptures, we can verify and make good our claim to this kingdom? The hopes of heaven, which moſt men have, are built on ſuch ſandy foundations, as can never abide the trial; having no ground in the word, but in their own deluded fancy: ſuch hopes will leave thoſe who entertain them miſerably diſappointed at laſt. Wherefore it is not only our duty, but our intereſt, to put the matter to a fair trial in time. If we find we have no right to heaven, we are yet in the way; and what we have not, we may obtain: but if we find that we have a right to it, we ſhall then have the comfort of a happy proſpect into eternity; which is the greateſt comfort one is capable of in the world. If you enquire, How you may know whether you have a right to heaven or not? I anſwer, You may know that by the ſtate you are now in. If you are yet in your natural ſtate, you are children of wrath, and not children of this kingdom: for that ſtate, to them who live and die in it, iſſues in eternal miſery: If you be brought into the ſtate of grace, you have a juſt claim to the ſtate of glory; for grace will certainly iſſue in glory at length. This kingdom is an inheritance, which none but the children of God can juſtly claim: now we become the children of God by regeneration, and union with Chriſt his Son; *and if children, then heirs, heirs of God, joint heirs with Chriſt*, Rom. viii. 17. Theſe, then, are the great points upon which one's evidences for the ſtate of glory depend. Therefore I re-

Head V.   *Of Heaven.*   425

fer you to what is said on the state of grace, for satisfying you as to your right to glory.

If you be heirs of glory, *the kingdom of God is within you,* by virtue of your regeneration and union with Christ. (1.) The King of heaven has the throne in thy heart, if thou hast a right to that kingdom: Christ is in thee, and God is in thee; and having chosen him for thy portion, thy soul has taken up its everlasting rest in him, and gets no true rest but in him; as the dove, until she came unto the ark. To him the soul habitually inclines, by virtue of the new nature, the Divine nature, which the heirs of glory are partakers of, Psal. lxiii. 25. *Whom have I in heaven but thee? and there is none upon the earth that I desire besides thee.* (2.) The laws of heaven are in thy heart, if thou art an heir of heaven, Heb. viii. 10. *I will put my laws into their mind, and write them in their hearts.* Thy mind is enlightened in the knowledge of the laws of the kingdom, by the Spirit of the Lord, the instructor of all the heirs of glory; for whoever may want instruction, sure an heir to a crown shall not want it. *It is written in the prophets, And they shall all be taught of God,* John. vi. 45. Therefore, though father and mother leave them early, or be in no concern about their Christian education, and they be soon put to work for their daily bread, yet they shall not lack teaching. Withal, thy heart is changed, and thou bearest God's image, which consists in *righteousness and true holiness,* Eph. iv. 24. Thy soul is reconciled to the whole law of God, and at war with all known sin. In vain do they pretend to the holy kingdom, who are not holy in heart and life; for *without holiness no man shall see the Lord,* Heb. xii. 24. If heaven is a rest, it is for spiritual labourers, not for loiterers. If it is an eternal triumph, they are not in the way to it, who avoid the spiritual warfare, and are in no care to subdue corruption, resist temptation, and to cut their way through it, through the opposition made by the devil, the world, and the flesh. (3.) The treasure in heaven is the chief in thy esteem and desire; for it is your treasure, and *where your treasure is, there will your heart be also,* Mat.

I i i

vi. 21. If it is not the things that are seen, which thy heart is in greatest care and concern to obtain; if thou art driving a trade with heaven, and thy chief business lies there; it is a sign that thy treasure is there, for thy heart is there. But if thou art of those who wonder why so much ado about heaven and eternal life, as if less might serve the turn; thou art like to have nothing ado with it at all. Carnal men value themselves most on their treasures upon earth; with them the things that are not seen are weighed down by the things that are seen, and no losses so much affect them as earthly losses: but the heirs of the crown of glory value themselves most on their treasures in heaven, and will not put their private estate in the balance with their kingdom; nor will the loss of the former go so near their hearts, as the thoughts of the loss of the latter. Where these first-fruits of heaven are to be found, the eternal weight of glory will surely follow after; while the want of them must be admitted, according to the word, to be an incontestable evidence of an heir of wrath.

Secondly, Let the heirs of the kingdom behave themselves suitable to their character and dignity. Live as having the faith and hope of this glorious kingdom: let your conversation be in heaven, Phil. iii. 20. Let your souls delight in communion with God while you are on earth, since you look for your happiness in communion with him in heaven. Let your speech and actions favour of heaven: and in your manner of life look like the country to which you are going; that it may be said of you, as of Gideon's brethren, Judges viii. 18. *Each one resembled the children of a king.* Maintain a holy contempt of the world, and of the things of the world. Although others, whose earthly things are their best things, set their hearts upon them, yet it becomes you to set your feet on them, since your best things are above. This world is but the country through which lies your road to Immanuel's land. Therefore pass through it as pilgrims and strangers, and dip not into the incumbrances of it, so as to retard you in your journey. It is unworthy of one born to a palace, to set his heart on a cottage, to dwell there; and of one running for a prize of gold, to go off his way to gather the stones of the brook : but much more it is unworthy of an heir of the kingdom of heaven, to be hid among the stuff of this world, when he should be going on to receive his crown. The prize set before you challenges your utmost zeal, activity, and diligence: and holy courage, resolution, and magnanimity, become those who are to inherit the crown. You cannot come at it without fighting your way to it, through difficulties from without, and from within: but the kingdom before you is sufficient to balance them all, though you should be called to resist even unto blood. Prefer Christ's cross before the world's crown, and wants in the way of duty, before ease and wealth in the way of sin : *Choose rather to suffer affliction with the people of God, than to enjoy the pleasures of sin for a season,* Heb. xi. 25. In a common inn, strangers, perhaps, fare better than the children: but here lies the difference, the children are to pay nothing for what they have got, but the strangers get their bill, and must pay compleatly for all they have had. Did we consider the wicked's after-reckoning for all the smiles of common providence which they meet with in the world, we should not grudge them their good things here, nor take it amiss that God keeps our best things last. Heaven will make up all the saints losses, and all tears will be wiped away from their eyes there.

It is worth observing, that there is such a variety of Scripture notions of heaven's happiness, as may suit every afflicted case of the saints. Are they oppressed ? The day cometh, in which they shall have the dominion. Is their honour laid in the dust ? A throne to sit upon, a crown on their head, and a sceptre in their hand, will raise it up again. Are they reduced to poverty ? Heaven is a treasure. If they be forced to quit their own habitations, yet Christ's Father's house is ready for them. Are they driven to the wilderness ? There is a city prepared for them. Are they banished from their native country ? They shall inherit a better country. If they are deprived of public ordinances, the Lord God

Almighty and the Lamb are the temple there, whither they are going; a temple, the doors of which none can shut. If their life be full of bitterness, heaven is a paradise for pleasure. If they groan under the remains of spiritual bondage, there is a glorious liberty abiding them. Do their defiled garments make them ashamed? The day cometh in which their robes shall be made white, pure, and spotless. The battle against flesh and blood, principalities and powers, is indeed sore; but a glorious triumph awaits them. If the toil and labours of the Christian life be great, there is everlasting rest for them in heaven. Are they judged unworthy of society in the world? They shall be admitted into the society of angels in heaven. Do they complain of frequent interruptions of their communion with God? There they shall go no more out, but shall see his face for evermore. If they are in darkness here, eternal light is there. If they grapple with death, there they shall have everlasting life. And, to sum up all in one word, *He that overcometh shall inherit all things*, Rev. xxi. 7. He shall have peace and plenty, profit and pleasure, every thing desireable; full satisfaction to his most enlarged desires. Let the expectants of heaven, then, lift up their heads with joy, let them gird up their loins, and so run as they may obtain; trampling on every thing that may hinder them in the way to the kingdom. Let them never account any duty too hard, nor any cross too heavy, nor any pains too much, so they may attain the crown of glory.

Lastly, Let those, who have no right to the kingdom of heaven, be stirred up to seek it with all diligence. Now is the time, wherein the children of wrath may become heirs of glory: when the way to everlasting happiness is opened, it is no time to sit still and loiter. Raise up your hearts towards the glory that is to be revealed; and do not be always seeking rest in this perishing earth. What can all your worldly enjoyments avail you, while you have no solid ground to expect heaven after this life is gone? The riches and honours, profits and pleasures, that must be buried with us, and cannot accompany us into another world, are but a wretched

Head V.   *Of Heaven.*   429

portion, and will leave men comfortlefs at length. Ah! why are men fo fond, in their life-time, to receive their good things ? Why are they not rather careful to fecure an intereft in the kingdom of heaven, which would never be taken from them, but afford them a portion, to make them happy through the ages of eternity! If you defire honour, there you may have the higheft honour, which will laft when the world's honours are laid in the duft; if riches, heaven will yield you a treafure; and there are pleafures for evermore. O be not defpifers of the pleafant land, neither judge yourfelves unworthy of eternal life! But marry the Heir, and heaven fhall be your dowry; clofe with Chrift, as he is offered to you in the gofpel, and you fhall inherit all things. Walk in the way of holinefs, and it will lead you to the kingdom. Fight againft fin and Satan, and you fhall receive the crown. Forfake the world, and the doors of heaven will be opened to receive you.

HEAD VI.

Of HELL.

MATTH. xxv. 41. *Then fhall he fay alfo to them on the left hand, Depart from me, ye curfed, into everlafting fire, prepared for the devil and his angels.*

WERE there no other place of eternal lodging but heaven, I fhould here have clofed my difcourfe of man's eternal ftate: but feeing in the other world there is a prifon for the wicked, as well as a palace for the faints, we muft alfo enquire into that ftate of everlafting mifery; which the worft of men may well bear with, without crying, *Art thou come to torment us before the time?* fince there is yet accefs to flee from the wrath to come, and all that can be faid of it comes fhort of what the damned will feel; for *who knoweth the power of God's anger?*

The laft thing which our Lord did before he left the earth, was, *he lift up his hands, and bleffed his difciples,*

Luke xxiv. 50, 51. But the laſt thing which he will do, before he leaves the throne, is to curſe and condemn his enemies; as we learn from the text which contains the dreadful ſentence, wherein the everlaſting miſery of the wicked is wrapped up. In which three things may be taken notice of. *Firſt*, The quality of the condemned: *Ye curſed*. The Judge finds the curſe of the law upon them as tranſgreſſors, and ſends them away with it from his preſence into hell, there to be fully executed upon them. 2*dly*, The puniſhment which they are adjudged to, and to which they were always bound over, by virtue of the curſe; and it is two-fold, the puniſhment of loſs, in ſeparation from God and Chriſt; *Depart from me:* and the puniſhment of ſenſe, in moſt exquiſite and extreme torments: *Depart from me into fire.* 3*dly*, The aggravations of their torments. (1.) They are ready for them; they are not to expect a moment's re-ſpite. The fire is prepared, and ready to catch hold of thoſe who are thrown into it. (2.) They will have the ſociety of devils in their torments, being ſhut up with them in hell. They muſt depart into the ſame fire, prepared for Beelzebub the prince of devils, and his angels; namely, other reprobate angels, who fell with him, and became devils. It is ſaid to be prepared for them; becauſe they ſinned, and were condemned to hell, before man ſinned. This ſpeaks further terror to the damned, that they muſt go into the ſame torments, and place of torment, with the devil and his angels. They hearkened unto his temptations, and they muſt partake in his torments: his works they would do, and they muſt receive the wages, which is Death. In this life they joined with devils, in enmity againſt God and Chriſt, and the way of holineſs; and in the other they muſt lodge with them. Thus all the goats ſhall be ſhut up together; for that name is common to devils and wicked men in Scripture, Lev. xvii. 7. where the word rendered *devils* properly ſignifies *hairy ones*, or *goats*, in the ſhape of which creatures devils delighted much to appear to their worſhippers. (3.) The laſt aggravation of their torment is the eternal duration thereof; they muſt depart into everlaſting fire. This

Head VI.   *Of Hell.*   431

is what puts the top-ſtone upon their miſery, namely, that it ſhall never have an end.

DOCTRINE, *The wicked ſhall be ſhut up, under the curſe of God, in everlaſting miſery, with the devils in hell.*

After having proved that there ſhall be a reſurrection of the body, and a general judgment, I think it not needful to inſiſt on proving the truth of future puniſhments. The ſame conſcience which there is in men of a future judgment, bear witneſs alſo of the truth of future puniſhments. (And that the puniſhment of the damned ſhall not be annihilation, or a reducing them to nothing, will be clear in the progreſs of our diſcourſe.) In treating of this awful ſubject, I ſhall enquire into theſe four things: (1.) The curſe under which the damned ſhall be ſhut up. (2.) Their miſery under that curſe. (3.) Their ſociety with devils in this miſerable ſtate. (4.) The eternity of the whole.

I. As to the curſe, under which the damned ſhall be ſhut up in hell; it is the terrible ſentence of the law, by which they are bound over to the wrath of God, as tranſgreſſors. This curſe does not firſt ſeize them when ſtanding before the tribunal to receive their ſentence; but they were born under it, they led their lives under it in this world, they died under it, roſe with it out of their graves; and the Judge finding it upon them, ſends them away with it into the pit, where it ſhall lie on them through all the ages of eternity. By nature all men are under the curſe; but it is removed from the elect, by virtue of their union with Chriſt. It abides on the reſt of ſinful mankind, and by it they are devoted to deſtruction, *ſeparated to evil*, as one may deſcribe the curſe from Deut. xxxix. 21. *And the Lord ſhall ſeparate him unto evil.* Thus ſhall the damned for ever be perſons devoted to deſtruction, ſeparated and ſet apart from among the reſt of mankind unto evil, as veſſels of wrath, ſet up as marks for the arrows of Divine wrath; and made the common receptacle and ſhore of vengeance.

This curſe hath its firſt-fruits on earth, which are a pledge of the whole lump that is to follow. Hence it is, that as temporal and eternal benefits are bound up together, under the same expressions, in the promise to the Lord's people, as Isa. xxxv. 10. *And the ransomed of the Lord shall return, and come to Zion,* &c. relating both to the return from Babylon, and to the saints going to their eternal rest in heaven: even so, temporal and eternal miseries, on the enemies of God, are sometimes included under one and the same expression in the threatening, as Isa. xxx. 33. *For Tophet is ordained of old: yea, for the king it is prepared; he hath made it deep and large: the pile thereof is fire and much wood, the breath of the Lord, like a stream of brimstone, doth kindle it.* Which relates both to the temporal and eternal destruction of the Assyrians, who fell by the hand of the angel before Jerusalem. See also Isa. lxvi. 24. What is that judicial blindness to which many are given up, *whom the god of this world hath blinded,* (2 Cor. iv. 4.) but the first-fruits of hell and of the curse? Their sun is going down at noon-day; their darkness encreasing, as if it would not stop till it issue in utter darkness. Many a lash in the dark doth conscience give the wicked, which the world doth not hear of: and what is that, but the never dying worm already begun to gnaw them? And there is not one of these but they may call it Joseph, for *the Lord shall add another;* or rather Gad, for *a troop cometh.* These drops of wrath are terrible forebodings of the full shower which is to follow. Sometimes they are given up to their evil affections, that they have no more command over them, Rom. i. 26. So their lusts grow up more and more towards perfection, if I may so speak. As in heaven grace comes to its perfection, so in hell sin arrives at its highest pitch; and as sin is thus advancing upon the man, he is the nearer and liker to hell. There are three things which have a fearful aspect here. *First,* When every thing that might do good to men's souls is blasted to them; so that their blessings are cursed, (Mal. ii. 2.) Sermons, prayers, admonitions, and reproofs, which are powerful towards others, are quite inefficacious to them. 2*dly,* When men go on sinning still, in the face of plain rebukes from the Lord, in or-

Head VI. *Of Hell.* 433

dinances and providences; God meets them with rods in the way of their fin, as it were ftriking them back; yet they rufh forward. What can be more like hell, where the Lord is always fmitting, and the damned always finning againft him? *Laftly*, When every thing in one's lot is turned into fuel to one's lufts. Thus, adverfity and profperity, poverty and wealth, the want of ordinances, and the enjoyment of them, do all but nourifh the corruptions of many. Their vitious ftomachs corrupt whatever they receive, and all does but encreafe noxious humours.

But the full harveft follows, in that mifery which they fhall for ever lie under in hell; that wrath which, by virtue of the curfe, fhall come upon them to the uttermoft, which is the curfe fully executed. This black cloud opens upon them, and the terrible thunder-bolt ftrikes them, by that dreadful voice from the throne, *Depart from me, ye curfed*, &c. which will give the whole wicked world a difmal view of what is in the bofom of the curfe. It is, (1.) a voice of extreme indignation and wrath, a furious rebuke from the Lion of the tribe of Judah. His looks will be moft terrible to them: his eyes will caft flames of fire on them; and his words will pierce their hearts like envenomed arrows. When he will thus fpeak them out of his prefence for ever, and by his word chafe them away from before the throne, they will fee how keenly wrath burns in his heart againft them for their fins. (2.) It is a voice of extreme difdain and contempt from the Lord. Time was when they were pitied, admonifhed to pity themfelves, and to be the Lord's; yet they defpifed him, they would none of him: but now they fhall be buried out of his fight, under everlafting contempt. (3.) It is a voice of extreme hatred. Hereby the Lord fhuts them out of his bowels of love and mercy. *Depart, ye curfed*; *q. d.* I cannot endure to look at you; there is not one purpofe of good to you in mine heart; nor fhall you ever hear one word more of hope from me. *Laftly*, It is a voice of eternal rejection from the Lord. He commands them to be gone, and fo cafts them off for ever. Thus the doors of heaven are fhut againft them; the

K k k

gulf is fixed between them and it, and they are driven to the pit. Now were they to cry with all poffible earneftnefs, *Lord, Lord, open to us*; they will hear nothing but *Depart, depart, ye curfed*. Thus fhall the damned be fhut up under the curfe.

USE. *Firft*, Let all thofe who, being yet in their natural ftate, are under the curfe, confider this, and flee to Jefus Chrift in time, that they may be delivered from it. How can you fleep in that ftate, being wrapped in the curfe! Jefus Chrift is now faying unto you, " Come, ye curfed; I will take the curfe from off you, and give you the bleffing." The waters of the fanctuary are now running, to heal the curfed ground; take heed to improve them for that end to your own fouls, and fear it as hell, to get no fpiritual advantage thereby. Remember, that the *miry places* (which are neither fea nor dry land, a fit emblem of hypocrites) *and the marfhes* (that neither breed fifhes, nor bear trees, but the waters of the fanctuary leave them as they find them, in their barrennefs) *fhall not be healed* (feeing they fpurn the only remedy); *they fhall be given to falt*, (left under eternal barrennefs, fet up for the monuments of the wrath of God, and concluded for ever under the curfe), Ezek. xlvii. 11. 2*dly*, Let all curfers confider this, whofe mouths are filled with curfing themfelves and others. He who *cloaths himfelf with curfing*, fhall find the curfe *come into his bowels like water, and like oil into his bones*, (Pfal. cix. 18.) if the Lord prevent it not. He fhall get all his imprecations againft himfelf fully anfwered, in the day that he ftands before the tribunal of God; and fhall find the killing weight of the curfe of God, which he now makes light of.

II. I proceed to fpeak of the mifery of the damned under the curfe; a mifery which the tongues of men and angels cannot fufficiently exprefs. God always acts like himfelf: no favours can be compared to his, and his wrath and terrors are not to be equalled. As the faints in heaven are advanced to the higheft pitch of happinefs, fo the damned in hell arrive at the height of mifery. Two things here I fhall foberly enquire into, the punifhment of *lofs*, and the punifhment of *fenfe*, in

Head VI. *Of Hell.*

hell. But since these also are such things as eye hath not seen, nor ear heard, we must (as geographers do) leave a large void for the unknown land, which the day will discover.

First, The punishment of loss, which the damned shall undergo, is separation from the Lord, as we learn from the text, *Depart from me, ye cursed.* This will be a stone upon their graves mouth, as the talent of lead, Zech. v. 7, 8. that will hold them down for ever. They shall be eternally separated from God and Christ. Christ is the way to the Father: but the way, as to them, shall be everlastingly blocked up, the bridge shall be drawn, and the great gulf fixed; so shall they be shut up in a state of eternal separation from God, the Father, Son, and Holy Ghost. They will be locally separated from the man Christ, and shall never come into the seat of the blessed, where he appears in his glory, but be cast out into utter darkness, Matt. xxii. 13. They cannot, indeed, be locally separated from God, they cannot be in a place where he is not; since he is, and will be, present every where: *If I make my bed in hell,* says the Psalmist, *behold thou art there,* Psal. cxxxix. 8. But they shall be miserable, beyond expression, in a relative separation from God, Though he will be present in the very centre of their souls, (if I may so express it) while they are wrapped up in fiery flames, in utter darkness, it shall only be to feed them with the vinegar of his wrath, and to punish them with his revenging justice: but they shall never more taste of his goodness and bounty, nor have the least glimpse of hope from him. They will see his heart to be absolutely alienated from them, and that it cannot be towards them; but they are the party, against whom the Lord will have indignation for ever. They shall be deprived of the glorious presence and enjoyment of God; they shall have no part in the beatific vision, nor see any thing in God towards them, but one wave of wrath rolling at the back of another. This will bring upon them overwhelming floods of sorrow for evermore. They shall never taste of the rivers of pleasures, which the saints in heaven enjoy; but shall have an everlasting winter, and a perpetual night, becaufe the Sun of Righteoufnefs has departed from them, and fo they are left in utter darknefs. So great as heaven's happinefs is, fo great will their lofs be; for they can have none of it for ever.

This feparation of the wicked from God, will be, (1.) An involuntary feparation. Now they depart from him, they will not come to him; though they are called and entreated to come: but then they fhall be driven away from him, when they would gladly abide with him. Although the queftion, *What is thy beloved more than another beloved?* is frequent now, amongft the defpifers of the gofpel, there will be no fuch queftion among all the damned crew; for then they will fee that man's happinefs is only to be found in the enjoyment of God, and that the lofs of him is a lofs that can never be balanced. (2.) It will be a total and utter feparation. Though the wicked are, in this life, feparated from God, yet there is a kind of intercourfe between them: he gives them many good gifts, and they give him, at leaft, fome good words; fo that the peace is not altogether hopelefs. But then fhall there be a total feparation, the damned being caft into utter darknefs, where there will not be the leaft glimmer of light or favour from the Lord; which will put an end to all their fair words to him. *Laftly*, It fhall be a final feparation; they will part with him, never more to meet, being fhut up under everlafting horror and defpair. The match between Jefus Chrift and unbelievers, which has fo often been carried forward, and put back again, fhall then be broken up for ever: and never fhall one meffage of favour or good-will go between the parties any more.

This punifhment of *lofs*, in a total and final feparation from God, is a mifery beyond what mortals can conceive, and which the dreadful experience of the damned can only fufficiently unfold. But that we may have fome conception of the horror of it, let thefe following things be confidered.

Firft, God is the chief good, therefore to be feparated from him muft be the chief evil. Our native

Head VI.   *Of Hell.*   437

country, our relations, and our life, are good; and therefore to be deprived of them we reckon a great evil; and the better any thing is, fo much the greater evil is the lofs of it: wherefore, God being the chief good, and no good comparable to him, there can be no lofs fo great as the lofs of God. The full enjoyment of him is the higheft pinnacle of happinefs which the creature is capable of arriving at: to be fully and finally feparated from him, muft then be the loweft ftep of mifery which the rational creature can be reduced to. To be caft off by men, by good men, is heavy: what muft it then be to be rejected of God, of goodnefs itfelf!

Secondly, God is the fountain of all goodnefs, from which all goodnefs flows unto the creatures, and by which it is continued in them, and to them. Whatever goodnefs or perfection, natural as well as moral, is in any creature, it is from God, and depends upon him, as the light is from, and depends on, the fun; for every created being, as fuch, is a dependent one. Wherefore a total feparation from God, wherein all comfortable communications between God and a rational creature is abfolutely blocked up, muft of neceffity bring along with it a total eclipfe of all light, of comfort, and eafe whatever. If there is but one window, or open place, in a houfe, and that be quite fhut up, it is evident there can be nothing but darknefs in that houfe. Our Lord tells us, Mat. xix. 17. *There is none good but one, that is God*. Nothing good or comfortable is originally from the creature: whatever good or comfortable thing one finds in one's felf, as health of body, peace of mind; whatever fweetnefs, reft, pleafure, or delight one finds in other creatures, as in meat, drink, arts and fciences; all thefe are but fome faint rays of Divine perfections communicated from God unto the creature, and depending on a conftant influence from him, for their confervation, which failing they would immediately be gone; for it is impoffible that any created thing can be to us more or better than what God makes it to be. All the rivulets of comfort which we drink of, within or without ourselves, come from God as their spring-head; the course of which toward us being stopped, of necessity they must all dry up. So that when God goes, all that is good and comfortable goes with him; all ease and quiet of body and mind, Hof. ix. 12. *Wo also to them, when I depart from them.* When the wicked are totally and finally separated from him, all that is comfortable in them, or about them, returns to its fountain, as the light goes away with the sun, and darkness succeeds in the room thereof. Thus, in their separation from God, all peace is removed far away from them, and pain in body, and anguish of soul succeed to it: all joy goes, and unmixed sorrow settles in them: all quiet and rest separate from them, and they are filled with horror and rage: hope flies away, and despair seizeth them: common operations of the Spirit, which now restrain them, are withdrawn for ever, and sin comes to its utmost height. Thus we have a dismal view of that horrible spectacle of sin and misery, which a creature proves when totally separated from God, and left to itself; and we may see this separation to be the very hell of hell.

Being separated from God, they are deprived of all good. The good things which they set their hearts upon in this world, are beyond their reach there. The covetous man cannot enjoy his wealth there, nor the ambitious man his honours, nor the sensual man his pleasures, no, not a drop of water to cool his tongue, Luke xxi. 23. 25. no meat nor drink there to strengthen the faint; no sleep to refresh the weary; and no music, nor pleasant company, to comfort and chear up the sorrowful. And as for those good things which they despised in the world, they shall never more hear of them, nor see them. No offers of Christ there, no pardons, no peace; no wells of salvation in the pit of destruction. In one word, they shall be deprived of whatever might comfort them, being totally and finally separated from God, the fountain of all goodness and comfort.

Thirdly, Man naturally desires to be happy, being conscious to himself that he is not self-sufficient; he

Head VI. *Of Hell.*

has ever a defire of fomething without himfelf to make him happy, and the foul being, by its natural make and conftitution, capable of enjoying God, and nothing elfe being commenfurable to its defires, it can never have true and folid reft, till it refts in the enjoyment of God. This defire of happinefs the rational creature can never lay afide, no, not in hell. Now while the wicked are on earth, they feek their fatisfaction in the creature; and when one fails, they go to another: thus they fpend their time in the world, deceiving their own fouls with vain hopes. But in the other world, all comfort in the creatures failing, and the fhadows which they are now purfuing vanifhed in a moment, they fhall be totally and finally feparated from God, and fee they have thus loft him. So the doors of earth and heaven both are fhut up againft them at once. This will create them unfpeakable anguifh, while they fhall live under an eternal gnawing hunger after happinefs, which they certainly know fhall never be in the leaft meafure fatisfied, all doors being clofed on them. Who then can imagine how this feparation from God fhall cut the damned to the heart! how they will roar and rage under it! and how it will fting them and gnaw them, through the ages of eternity!

Fourthly, The damned fhall know that fome are perfectly happy, in the enjoyment of that God from whom they themfelves are feparated! and this will aggravate the fenfe of their lofs, that they can never have any fhare with thofe happy ones. Being feparated from God, they are feparated from the fociety of the glorified faints and angels. They may fee Abraham afar off, and Lazarus in his bofom, (Luke xvi. 23.) but can never come into their company; being as unclean lepers thruft out without the camp, and excommunicated from the prefence of the Lord, and of all his holy ones. It is the opinion of fome, that every perfon in heaven or hell fhall hear and fee all that paffeth in either ftate. Whatever is to be faid of this, we have ground from the word to conclude, that the damned fhall have a very exquifite knowledge of the happinefs of the faints in heaven; for what elfe can be meant by the rich man in hell seeing Lazarus in Abraham's bosom? One thing is plain, in this case, that their own torments will give them such notions of the happiness of the saints, as a sick man has of health, or a prisoner has of liberty. And as they cannot fail of reflecting on the happiness of those in heaven, without any hope of attaining to contentment with their own lot, so every thought of that happiness will aggravate their loss. It would be a mighty torment to a hungry man, to see others liberally feasting, while he is so chained up, as not to have one crumb to stay his gnawing appetite. To bring music and dancing before a man labouring under extreme pains, would but encrease his anguish: how then will the songs of the blessed, in their enjoyment of God, make the damned rore under their separation from him!

Fifthly, They will remember, that time was when they might have been made partakers of the blessed company of the saints, in their enjoyment of God: and this will aggravate their sense of the loss. All may remember, that there was once a possibility of it; that they were once in the world, in some corners of which the way of salvation was laid open to men's view; and may wish they had gone round the world till they had found it out. Despisers of the gospel will remember, with bitterness, that Jesus Christ, with all his benefits, was offered to them; that they were exhorted, entreated, and pressed to accept, but would not; and that they were warned of the misery which they feel, and exhorted to flee from the wrath to come, but they would not hearken. The gospel-offer slighted, will make a hot hell, and the loss of offered heaven will be a sinking weight on the spirits of unbelievers in the pit. Some will remember, that there was a probability of their being eternally happy; that once they seemed to stand fair for it, and were not far from the kingdom of God: that they had once almost consented to the blessed bargain; the pen was in their hand (as it were) to sign the marriage-contract between Christ and their souls; but unhappily they dropped it, and turned back from the Lord to their lusts again. Others will remember, that they thought themselves sure of heaven, but being blinded with pride and self-conceit, they were above ordinances, and beyond instruction, and would not examine their state, which was their ruin: but then they will in vain wish that they had reputed themselves the worst of the congregation in which they lived; and curse the fond conceit which they had of themselves, and that others had of them too. Thus it will sting the damned, that they might have escaped this loss.

Lastly, They will see the loss to be irrecoverable; that they must eternally lie under it, never, never to be repaired. Might the damned, after millions of ages in hell, regain what they have lost, it would be some ground of hope: but the prize is gone, and never can be recovered. There are two things which will pierce them to the heart: (1.) That they never knew the worth of it, till it was irrecoverably lost. Should a man give away an earthen pot full of gold for a trifle, never knowing what was in it, till it were quite gone from him, and past recovery, how would this foolish action gall him, upon the discovery of the riches in it! Such a one's case may be a faint resemblance of the case of despisers of the gospel, when in hell they lift up their eyes, and behold that to their torment, which they will not see now to their salvation. (2.) That they have lost it for dross and dung; sold their part of heaven, and not enriched themselves with the price. They lost heaven for earthly profits and pleasures, and now both are gone together from them. The drunkard's cups are gone, the covetous man's gain, the voluptuous man's carnal delights, and the sluggard's ease: nothing is left them to comfort them now. The happiness which they lost remains indeed, but they can have no part in it for ever.

USE. Sinners, be persuaded to come to God, through Jesus Christ, uniting with him through the Mediator; that you may be preserved from this fearful separation from him. O be afraid to live in a state of separation from God, lest that which you now make your choice, become your eternal punishment hereafter. Do not reject communion with God; caſt not off the communion of ſaints; for it will be the miſery of the damned to be driven out from that communion. Ceaſe to build up the wall of ſeparation between God and you, by continuing in your ſinful courſes: repent, rather, in time, and ſo pull it down; left the top-ſtone be laid upon it, and 'it ſtand for ever between you and happineſs. Tremble at the thoughts of rejection and ſeparation from God. By whoever men are rejected on earth, they ordinarily find ſome pity; but if you be thus ſeparated from God, you will find all doors ſhut againſt you. You will find no pity from any in heaven; neither ſaints nor angels will pity them whom God has utterly caſt off: none will pity you in hell, where there is no love but loathing; all being loathed of God, loathing him, and loathing one another. This is a day of loſſes and fears. I ſhew you a loſs you would do well to fear in time; be afraid left you loſe God; if you do, eternity will be ſpent in roaring out lamentations for this loſs. O horrid ſtupidity! Men are in a mighty care and concern to prevent worldly loſſes: but they are in hazard of loſing the enjoyment of God for ever and ever; in hazard of loſing heaven, the communion of the bleſſed, and all good things for ſoul and body in another world; yea, as careleſs in that matter, as if they were incapable of thought. O compare this day with the day which our text aims at. To-day heaven is opened for them who hitherto have rejected Chriſt; and yet there is room, if they will come: but that day the doors ſhall be ſhut. Now Chriſt is ſaying unto you, *Come:* then he will ſay, *Depart;* ſeeing you would not come when you were bidden. Now pity is ſhewn; the Lord pities you, his ſervants pity you, and tell you that the pit is before you, and cry to you, that you do yourſelves no harm: but then ſhall you have no pity from God or man.

SECONDLY, The damned ſhall be puniſhed in hell, w'th the puniſhment of *ſenſe;* they muſt depart from G)d into everlaſting fire. I am not diſpoſed to diſpute what kind of fire it is which they ſhall depart into, and

Head VI.   *Of Hell.*   443

be tormented by for ever, whether a material fire or not. Experience will more than fatisfy the curiofity of thofe who are difpofed rather to difpute about it, than to feek how to efcape it. Neither will I meddle with that queftion, Where is it? It is enough, that the worm which never dieth, and the fire that is never quenched, will be found fomewhere by impenitent finners. But, (1.) I fhall prove that whatever kind of fire it is, it is more vehement and terrible than any fire we on earth are acquainted with. (2.) I fhall fpeak of fome properties of thefe fiery torments.

As to the firft of thefe; burning is the moft terrible punifhment, and brings the moft exquifite pain and torment with it. By what reward could a man be induced to hold only his hand in the flame of a candle but for one hour? All imaginable pleafures on earth will never prevail with the moft vuluptuous man to venture to lodge but one half hour in a burning fiery furnace; nor would all the wealth in the world prevail with the moft covetous to do it. Yet, on much lower terms do moft men, in effect, expofe themfelves to everlafting fire in hell, which is more vehement and terrible than any fire we on earth are acquainted with; as will appear by the following confiderations.

Firft, As in heaven, grace being brought to its perfection, profit and pleafure alfo arrive at their height there; fo fin, being come to its height in hell, the evil of punifhment doth alfo arrive at its perfection there. Wherefore, as the joys in heaven are far greater than any joys which the faints obtain on earth, fo the punifhments of hell muft be greater than any earthly torments whatever; not only in refpect of the continuance of them, but alfo in refpect of vehemency and exquifitenefs.

Secondly, Why are the things of another world reprefented to us in an earthly drefs, in the word, but becaufe the weaknefs of our capacities in fuch matters (which the Lord is pleafed to condefcend unto) requires it; it being always fuppofed, that the things of the other world are in their kind more perfect than thofe by which they are reprefented? When heaven is represented to us under the notion of a city, with gates of pearl, and the street of gold, we expect not to find gold and pearls there, which are so mightily prized on earth, but something more excellent than the finest and most precious things in the world : when, therefore, we hear of hell-fire, it is necessary that we understand by it something more vehement, piercing, and tormenting, than any fire ever seen by our eyes. And here it is worth considering, that the torments of hell are held forth under several other notions than that of fire simply : and the reason of it is plain, namely, that hereby what of horror is wanting in one notion of hell, is supplied by another. Why is heaven's happiness represented under the various notions of *a treasure, a paradise, a feast, a rest,* &c. but that there is not one of these things sufficient to express it ? Even so, hell-torments are represented under the notion of fire, which the damned are cast into. A dreadful representation indeed ! Yet not sufficient to express the misery of the state of sinners in them. Wherefore, we hear also of *the second death,* Rev. xx. 6. for the damned in hell shall be ever dying : of *the wine-press of the wrath of God,* (chap. xiv. 19.) wherein they will be trodden in anger, trampled in the Lord's fury, (Isa. lxiii. 3.) pressed, broken, and bruised, without end : *the worm that dieth not,* (Mark ix. 44.) which shall eternally gnaw them : *a bottomless pit,* where they will be ever sinking, Rev. xx. 3. It is not simply called *a fire,* but *the lake of fire and brimstone,* (ver. 19.) *A lake of fire burning with brimstone,* (chap. xix. 20.) than which one can imagine nothing more dreadful. Yet, because fire gives light, and light (as Solomon observes, Eccl. xi. 7.) is sweet, there is no light there, but darkness, utter darkness, Mat. xxv. 30. For they must have an everlasting night, since nothing can be there which is in any measure comfortable or refreshing.

Thirdly, Our fire cannot affect a spirit, but by way of sympathy with the body, to which it is united : but hell-fire will not only pierce into the bodies, but directly into the souls of the damned : for it is prepared for the devil and his angels, those wicked spirits, whom

Head VI. *Of Hell.* 445

no fire on earth can hurt. Job complains heavily, under the chaftifement of God's fatherly hand, faying, *The arrows of the Almighty are within me, the poifon whereof drinketh up my fpirit,* Job vi. 4. But how will the fpirits of the damned be pierced with the arrows of revenging juftice! how will they be drunk with the poifon of the curfe on thefe arrows! how vehement muft that fire be, that pierceth directly into the foul, and makes an everlafting burning in the fpirit, the moft lively and tender part of a man, wherein wounds or pains are moft intolerable!

Laftly, The preparation of this fire proves the inexpreffible vehemency and dreadfulnefs of it. The text calls it *prepared fire,* yea, *the* prepared fire, by way of eminency. As the three children were not caft into an ordinary fire, but a fire prepared on a particular defign, which therefore was exceeding hot, the furnace being heated feven times more than ordinary, Dan. ii. 22. So the damned fhall find in hell prepared fire, the like to which was never prepared by human art: it is a fire of God's own preparing, the product of infinite wifdom, on a particular defign, to demonftrate the moft ftrict and fevere Divine juftice againft fin; which may fufficiently evidence to us the inconceivable exquifitenefs thereof. God always acts in a peculiar way, becoming his own infinite greatnefs, whether for or againft the creature. Therefore, as the things which he hath prepared for them that love him, are great and good beyond expreffion or conception; fo one may conclude, that the things he has prepared againft thofe who hate him, are great and terrible beyond what men can either fay or think of them. The pile of Tophet is *fire and much wood* (the coals of fire are *coals of juniper,* a kind of wood which, fet on fire, burns moft fiercely, Pfal. cxx. 4.) *and the breath of the Lord, like a ftream of brimftone, doth kindle it,* Ifa. xxx. 33. Fire is more or lefs violent, according to the matter of it, and the breath by which it is blown: what heart, then, can fully conceive the horror of coals of juniper, blown up with the breath of the Lord? Nay, God himfelf will be a confuming fire (Deut. iv. 24.) to the damned;

intimately present, as a devouring fire, in their souls and bodies. It is a fearful thing to fall into a fire, or to be shut up in a fiery furnace, on earth; but the terror of these vanisheth, when we consider how fearful it is to fall into the hands of the living God, which is the lot of the damned; for *who shall dwell with devouring fire? Who shall dwell with everlasting burnings?* Isa. xxxiii. 14.

As to the second point proposed, namely, the properties of the fiery torments in hell.

First, They will be universal torments, every part of the creature being tormented in that flame. When a person is cast into a burning fiery furnace, the fire makes its way into the very bowels, and leaves no member untouched: what part, then, can have ease, when the damned swim in a lake of fire burning with brimstone? There will their bodies be tormented, and scorched for ever. And as they sinned, so shall they be tormented in all the parts thereof, that they shall have no sound side to turn them to: for what soundness or ease can be to any part of that body, which being separated from God, and all refreshment from him, is still in the pangs of the second death, ever dying, but never dead? But as the soul was chief in sinning, it will be chief in suffering too, being brimful of the wrath of a sin-revenging God. The damned shall ever be under the deepest impressions of God's vindictive justice against them: and this fire will melt their souls within them like wax. Who knows the power of that wrath, which had such an effect on the Mediator, standing in the room of sinners? Psal. xxii. 14. *My heart is like wax, it is melted in the midst of my bowels.* Their minds shall be filled with the terrible apprehensions of God's implacable wrath. And whatever they can think upon, past, present, or to come, will aggravate their torment and anguish. Their will shall be crossed in all things for ever more: as their will was ever contrary to the will of God's precepts, so God, in his dealing with them in the other world, shall have war with their will for ever. What they would have, they shall not in the least obtain; but what they would not, shall be bound upon

Head VI.   *Of Hell.*   447

them without remedy. Hence, no pleafant affection fhall ever fpring up in their hearts any more: their love of complacency, joy, and delight, in any object whatever, fhall be plucked up by the roots; and they will be filled with hatred, fury, and rage, againft God, themfelves, and their fellow-creatures, whether happy in heaven, or miferable in hell, as they themfelves are. They will be funk in forrow, racked with anxiety, filled with horror, galled to the heart with fretting, and continually darted with defpair; which will make them weep, gnafh their teeth, and blafpheme for ever, Mat. xxii. 13. *Bind him hand and foot, and take him away, and caft him into utter darknefs: there fhall be weeping and gnafhing of teeth.* Rev. xvi. 21. *And there fell upon men a great hail out of heaven, every ftone about the weight of a talent: and men blafphemed God becaufe of the hail; for the plague thereof was exceeding great.* Confcience will be a worm to gnaw and prey upon them: remorfe for their fins fhall feize them, and torment them for ever, and they fhall not be able to fhake it off, as once they did; for *in hell—their worm dieth not,* Mark ix. 45, 46. Their memory will ferve but to aggravate their torment, and every new reflection will bring another pang of anguifh, Luke xvi. 25. *But Abraham faid,* (*viz.* to the rich man in hell) *Son, remember that thou in thy life-time receivedft thy good things.*

Secondly, The torments in hell are manifold. Put the cafe, that a man were, at one and the fame time, under the violence of the gout, gravel, and whatever difeafes and pains have ever met together in one body; the torment of fuch a one would be but light in comparifon with the torments of the damned: for as in hell there is an abfence of all that is good and defireable, fo there is the confluence of all evils there; since all the effects of fin and of the curfe take their place in it, after the laft judgment. Rev. xx. 14. *And death and hell were caft into the lake of fire.* There they will find a prifon they can never efcape out of; a lake of fire, wherein they will be ever fwimming and burning; a pit, whereof they will never find a bottom. The worm, that dieth not, fhall feed on them as on bodies which are interred: the fire that is not quenched shall devour them, as dead bodies which are burned. Their eyes shall be kept in blackness of darkness, without the least comfortable gleam of light; their ears filled with the frightful yellings of the infernal crew. They shall taste nothing but the vinegar of God's wrath, the dregs of the cup of his fury. . The stench of the burning lake of brimstone will be the smell there; and they shall feel extreme pains for evermore.

Thirdly, They will be most exquisite and vehement torments, causing *weeping, wailing, and gnashing of teeth*, Mat. xiii. 42. and xxii. 13. They are represented to us under the notion of pangs in travail, which are very sharp and exquisite. So says the rich man in hell, Luke xvi. 24. *I am tormented* (to wit, as one in the pangs of child-bearing) *in this flame*. Ah! dreadful pangs! horrible travel, in which both soul and body are in pangs together! helpless travail, hopeless and endless! The word used for hell, Mat. v. 22. and in diverse other places of the New Testament, properly denotes the valley of Hinnom; the name being taken from the valley of the children of Hinnom, in which was Tophet, (2 Kings xxiii. 10.) where idolaters offered their children to Molech. This is said to have been a great brazen idol, with arms like a man's: which being heated by fire within it, the child was set in the burning arms of the idol; and, that the parent might not hear the shrieks of the child burning to death, they beat drums in the time of the horrible sacrifice; whence the place had the name of Tophet. Thus the exquisiteness of the torments in hell are pointed out to us. Some have endured grievous tortures on earth, with surprising obstinacy, and undaunted courage: but men's courage will fail them there, when they find themselves fallen into the hands of the living God, and no escape to be expected for ever. It is true, that there will be degrees of torment in hell: *It shall be more tolerable for Tyre and Zidon, than for Chorazin and Bethsaida*, Matt. xi. 21, 22. But the least load of wrath there will be insupportable; for how can the heart of the creature endure, or his hands be strong, when God himself is consuming fire to him?

When the tares are bound in bundles for the fire, there will be bundles of covetous persons, of drunkards, profane swearers, unclean persons, formal hypocrites, unbelievers and despisers of the gospel, and the like: the several bundles being cast into hell fire, some will burn more keenly than others, according as their sins have been more heinous than those of others, a fiercer flame shall sieze the bundle of the profane, than the bundle of unsanctified moralists; the furnace will be hotter to those who sinned against light, than to those who lived in darkness, Luke xii. 47, 48. *That servant which knew his lord's will, and prepared not himself, neither did according to his will, shall be beaten with many stripes. But he that knew not, and did commit things worthy of stripes, shall be beaten with few stripes.* But the sentence common to them all, (Mat. xiii. 30.) *Bind them in bundles to burn them,* speaks the great vehemency and exquisiteness of the lowest degree of torment in hell.

Fourthly, They will be uninterrupted; there is no intermission there; no ease, no, not for a moment. They *shall be tormented day and night for ever and ever,* Rev. xx. 10. Few are so tossed in this world, but sometimes they get rest; but the damned shall get none; they took their rest in the time appointed of God for labour. No storms are rarely seen, without some space between showers: but no intermission in the storm that falls on the wicked in hell. There deep will be calling unto deep, and the waves of wrath continually rolling over them. There the heavens will be always black to them, and they shall have a perpetual night, but no rest, Rev. xiv. 11. *They have no rest day nor night.*

Fifthly, They will be unpitied. The punishments inflicted on the greatest malefactors on earth, draw forth some compassion from the spectators; but the damned shall have none to pity them. God will not pity them, but laugh at their calamity, Prov. i. 26. The blessed company in heaven shall rejoice in the execution of God's righteous judgment, and sing while the smoke riseth up for ever, Rev. xix. 3. *And again they said, Hallelujah: and her smoke rose up for ever and ever.* No compassion can be expected from the devil and his angels, who delight in the ruin of the children of men, and are and will be for ever void of pity. Neither will one pity another there, where every one is weeping and gnashing his teeth, under his own infupportable anguifh and pain. There natural affections will be extinguifhed : the parents will not love their children, nor children their parents : the mother will not pity the daughter in thefe flames, nor will the daughter pity the mother : the fon will fhew no regard to his father there, nor the fervant to his mafter, where every one will be roaring under his own torment.

Lafly, To compleat their mifery, their torments fhall be eternal, Rev. xiv. 11. *And the fmoke of their torment afcendeth up for ever and ever.* Ah ! what a frightful cafe is this, to be tormented in the whole body and foul, and that not with one kind of torment, but many; all of thefe moft exquifite, and all this without any intermiffion, and without pity from any ! What heart can conceive thofe things without horror ? Neverthelefs, if this moft miferable cafe were at length to have an end, that would afford fome comfort ; but the torments of the damned will have no end ; of which more afterwards.

Use. Learn from this, (1.) The evil of fin. It is a ftream that will carry down the finner, till he be fwallowed up in the ocean of wrath. The pleafures of fin are bought too dear, at the rate of everlafting burnings. What availed the rich man's purple cloathing and fumptuous fare, when in hell he was encircled by purple flames, and could not have a drop of water to cool his tongue ? Alas ! that men fhould indulge themfelves in fin, which will be fuch bitternefs in the end ; that they fhould drink fo greedily of the poifonous cup, and hug that ferpent in their bofom, that will fting them to the heart, and gnaw out their bowels at length ! (2.) What a God he is, with whom we have to do ! what hatred he bears to fin, and how feverely he punifheth it ! Know the Lord to be moft juft, as well as moft merciful ! and think not that he is fuch an one as you are : away with the fatal miftake, ere it be too late, Pfal. l. 21, 22. *Thou thoughteft that I was altogether fuch*

Head VI. Of Hell.

an one as thyself; but I will reprove thee, and set them in order before thine eyes. Now consider this, ye that forget God, lest I tear you in pieces, and there be none to deliver. The fire prepared for the devil and his angels, as dark as it is, will serve to discover God to be a severe revenger of sin. *Lastly,* The absolute necessity of flying to the Lord Jesus Christ by faith; the same necessity of repentance, and holiness of heart and life. The avenger of blood is pursuing thee. O sinner, haste and escape to the city of refuge. Wash now in the fountain of the Mediator's blood, that you may not perish in the lake of fire. Open thy heart to him, left the pit close its mouth on thee. Leave thy sins, else they will ruin thee: kill them, else they will be thy death for ever.

Let not the terror of hell-fire put thee upon hardening thy heart more, as it may do, if thou entertain that wicked thought, *viz. There is no hope,* Jer. ii. 25. which, perhaps, is more common among the hearers of the gospel than many are aware of. But there is hope for the worst of sinners, who will come unto Jesus Christ. If there are no good qualifications in thee (as certainly there can be none in a natural man, none in any man, but what are received from Christ in him), know, that he has not suspended thy welcome on any good qualifications: do thou take him and his salvation, freely offered unto all to whom the gospel comes. *Whosoever will, let him take of the water of life freely,* Rev. xxii. 17. *Him that cometh unto me, I will in no ways cast out,* John vi. 37. It is true, that thou art a sinful creature, and canst not repent; thou art unholy, and canst not make thyself holy: nay, thou hast attempted to repent, to forsake sin, and to be holy, but still missed of repentance, reformation, and holiness; and therefore, *thou saidst, There is hope. No, for I have loved strangers, and after them will I go.* Truly, no marvel that the success has not answered thy expectation, since thou hast always begun thy work amiss. But do thou, first of all, honour God, by believing the testimony which he has given of his Son, namely, that eternal life is in him: and honour the Son of God, by believing on him, that is, embracing and falling in with the free offer of Chrift, and of his falvation from fin and from wrath, made to thee in the gofpel, trufting in him confidently for righteoufnefs for thy juftification, and alfo for fanctification, feeing of God *he is made unto us* both *righteoufnefs and fanctification*, 1 Cor. i. 30. Then, if thou haft as much credit to give to the word of God, as thou wouldft allow to the word of an honeft man offering thee a gift, and faying, Take it, and it is thine, thou mayeft believe that God is thy God, Chrift is thine, his falvation is thine, thy fins are pardoned, thou haft ftrength in him for repentance and for holinefs; for all thefe are made over to thee in the free offer of the gofpel. Believing on the Son of God, thou art juftified, the curfe is removed. But while it lies upon thee, how is it poffible that thou fhouldeft bring forth the fruits of holinefs? But the curfe is removed, that death which feized on thee with the firft Adam, (according to the threatening, Gen. ii. 17.) is taken away. In confequence of which, thou fhalt find the bands of wickednefs (now holding thee faft in impenitency) broken afunder, as the bands of that death; fo as thou wilt be able to repent indeed, from the heart: thou fhalt find the Spirit of life, on whofe departure that death enfued, return to thy foul; fo as thenceforth thou fhall be enabled to live unto righteoufnefs. No man's cafe is fo bad, but it may be mended this way, in time, to be perfectly right in eternity: and no man's cafe is fo good, but, another way being taken, it will be marred for time and eternity too.

III. The damned fhall have the fociety of devils in their miferable ftate in hell: for they muft depart into fire prepared for the devil and his angels. O horrible company! O frightful affociation! Who would choofe to dwell in a place haunted with devils? To be confined to the moft pleafant fpot of earth, with the devil and his infernal furies, would be a moft terrible confinement. How would men's hearts fail them, and their hair ftand up, finding themfelves environed with the hellifh crew! But ah! how much more terrible muft

Head VI. *Of Hell.* 453

it be, to be caſt with the devils into one fire, locked up with them in one dungeon, ſhut up with them in one pit! To be cloſed up in a den of roaring lions, girded about with ſerpents, ſurrounded with venomous aſps, and to have the bowels eaten out by vipers, all together and at once, is a compariſon too low, to ſhew the miſery of the damned, ſhut up in hell with the devil and his angels. They go about now as roaring lions, ſeeking whom they may devour; but then ſhall they be confined in their den with their prey. They ſhall be filled to the brim with the wrath of God, and receive the full torment (Mat. viii. 29.) which they tremble in expectation of, (James ii. 19.) being caſt into the fire prepared for them. How will theſe lions roar and tear! how will theſe ſerpents hiſs! theſe dragons vomit out fire! What horrible anguiſh will ſeize the damned, finding themſelves in the lake of fire with the devil, who deceived them; drawn thither with the ſilken cords of temptation, by theſe wicked ſpirits; and bound with them in everlaſting chains under darkneſs! Rev. xx. 10. *And the devil that deceived them, was caſt into the lake of fire and brimſtone, where the beaſt and the falſe prophet are, and ſhall be tormented day and night for ever and ever.*

O that men would conſider this in time, renounce the devil and his luſts, and join themſelves to the Lord in faith and holineſs. Why ſhould men chooſe that company in this world, and delight in that ſociety, which they would not deſire to aſſociate with in the other world? Thoſe who like not the company of the ſaints on earth, will get none of it in eternity; but as godleſs company is their delight now, they will afterwards get enough of it, when they have eternity to paſs, in the roaring and blaſpheming ſociety of devils and reprobates in hell. Let thoſe, who invocate the devil to take them, ſoberly conſider, that the company ſo often invited will be terrible at laſt, when come.

IV. And Lastly, Let us conſider the eternity of the whole, the everlaſting continuance of the miſerable ſtate of the damned in hell.

Firſt, If I could, I would ſhew, what eternity is, I

mean the creature's eternity. But who can measure the waters of the ocean, or who can tell you the days, years, and ages of eternity, which are infinitely more than the drops of the ocean? None can comprehend eternity, but the eternal God. Eternity is an ocean whereof no one will ever see the shore; it is a deep, where we can find no bottom; a labyrinth, from whence we cannot extricate ourselves, and where we shall ever lose the door. There are two things we may say of it, (1.) It has a beginning. God's eternity has no beginning, but the creature's has. Once there was no lake of fire; and those who have been there, for some thousands of years, were once in time as we now are. But, (2.) It shall never have an end. The first who entered into eternity of woe, is as far from the end of it, as the last who shall go thither will be at his entry. They who have launched out furthest into that ocean, are as far from land, as they were the first moment they went into it: and thousands of ages after this, they will be as far from it as ever. Wherefore eternity, in respect of us, is a duration that hath a beginning, but no end. It is a beginning without a middle, a beginning without an end. After millions of years passed in it, still it is a beginning. God's wrath in hell, will ever be the wrath to come. But there is no middle in eternity. When millions of ages are past in eternity, what is past bears no proportion to what is to come; no, not so much as one drop of water, falling from the tip of one's finger, bears to all the waters of the ocean. There is no end of it: while God is, it shall be. It is an entry without any end to it, a continual succession of ages, a glass always running, which shall never run out.

Observe the continual succession of hours, days, months, and years, how one still follows upon another; and think of eternity, wherein there is a continual succession, without end. When you go out in the night, and behold the stars of heaven, how they can be numbered for multitude, think of the ages of eternity; considering also, that there is a certain definite number of stars, but no number of the ages of eternity. When

Head VI.   *Of Hell.*

you fee water running, think how vain a thing it would be to fit down by it, and wait till it fhould run out, that you may pafs over; obferve how new water ftill fucceeds to that which paffeth by you: and therein you have an image of eternity, which is a river that never dries up. They who wear rings, have an image of eternity on their fingers; and they who handle the wheel, have an emblem of eternity before them: for to which part foever of the ring or wheel we look, we ftill fee another part beyond it: and on whatever moment of eternity you meditate, there is ftill another beyond it. When you are abroad in the fields, and behold the blades of grafs on the earth, which no man can reckon; think for yourfelves, that were there as many thoufands of years to come, as there are blades of grafs on the ground, even thofe would have an end at length, but eternity will have none. When you look to a mountain, imagine in your hearts how long it would be ere that mountain fhould be removed, by a little bird coming but once every thoufand years, and carrying away but one grain of the duft thereof at once: the mountain would at length be removed that way, and brought to an end; but eternity will never end. Suppofe this with refpect to all the mountains of the earth; nay, with refpect to the whole globe of the earth; the grains of duft, of which the whole earth is made up, are not infinite, and therefore the laft grain would at length come to be carried away, as above; yet eternity would be in effect but beginning.

Thefe are fome rude drafts of eternity: and now add mifery and woe to this eternity, what tongue can exprefs it? What heart can conceive it? In what balance can that mifery and that woe be weighed?

Secondly, Let us take a view of what is eternal, in the ftate of the damned in hell. Whatever is included in the fearful torments of their ftate, is everlafting: therefore all the doleful ingredients of their miferable ftate will be everlafting; they will never end. The text exprefsly declares the fire, into which they muft depart, to be everlafting fire. And our Lord elfewhere tells us, that in hell the fire fhall never be quenched, (Mark

ix. 43.) with an eye to the valley of Hinnom, in which, befides the before-mentioned fire, for burning the children to Moloch, there was alfo another fire burning continually, to confume the dead carcafes, and filth of Jerufalem: fo the Scripture, reprefenting hell-fire, by the fire of that valley, fpeaks it not only to be moft exquifite, but alfo everlafting. Seeing, then, the damned muft depart, as curfed ones, into everlafting fire, it is evident that,

Firft, The damned themfelves fhall be eternal; they will have a being for ever, and will never be fubftantially deftroyed, or annihilated. To what end is the fire eternal, if thofe who are caft into it be not eternally in it? It is plain, that the everlafting continuance of the fire is an aggravation of the mifery of the damned. But, furely, if they are annihilated, or fubftantially deftroyed, it would be all the fame to them, whether the fire be everlafting, or not; nay, but they depart into everlafting fire, to be everlaftingly punifhed in it, Mat. xxv. 46. *Thefe fhall go away into everlafting punifhment.* Thus, the execution of the fentence is a certain difcovery of the meaning of it. The worm, that dieth not, muft have a fubject to live in. They who fhall have no reft day nor night, (Rev. xvi. 11.) but fhall be *tormented day and night, for ever and ever*, (chap. xx. 10.) will certainly have a being for ever and ever, and not be brought into a ftate of eternal reft in annihilation. Deftroyed indeed they fhall be: but their deftruction will be an everlafting deftruction, (2 Thef. i. 9.) a deftruction of their well-being, but not of their being. What is deftroyed, is not therefore annihilated: *Art thou come to torment us?* faid the devil unto Jefus Chrift, Luke iv. 34. The devils are afraid of torment, not of annihilation, Mat. viii. 29. *Art thou come hither to torment us before the time?* The ftate of the damned is indeed a ftate of death: but fuch a death it is, as is oppofite only to a happy life; as is clear from other notions of their ftate, which neceffarily include eternal exiftence, of which before. As they who are dead in fin, are dead to God and holinefs, yet live to fin: fo dying in hell, they live, but feparated from God and his favour, in

Head VI. Of Hell.

which is life, Pfal. xxx. 5. They shall ever be under the pangs of death; ever dying, but never dead, or absolutely void of life. How desireable would such a death be to them! but it will flee from them for ever. Could each one kill another there, or could they, with their own hands, tear themselves into lifeless pieces, their misery would quickly be at an end: but there they must live, who chose death, and refused life; for there death lives, and the end ever begins.

Secondly, The curse shall lie upon them eternally, as the everlasting chain, to hold them in the everlasting fire; a chain that shall never be loosed, being fixed for ever about them by the dreadful sentence of the eternal judgment. This chain, which spurns the united force of devils held fast by it, is too strong to be broken by men, who being solemnly anathematized, and devoted to destruction, can never be restored to any other use.

Thirdly, Their punishment shall be eternal, Matth. xxv. 46. *These shall go away into everlasting punishment.* They will be for ever separated from God and Christ, and from the society of the holy angels and saints; between whom and them an impassable gulph will be fixed, Luke xvi. 26. *Between us and you* (says Abraham, in the parable, to the rich man in hell) *there is a great gulf fixed, so that they which would pass from hence to you, cannot; neither can they pass to us, that would come from thence.* They shall for ever have the horrible society of the devil and his angels. There will be no change of company for ever, in that region of darkness. Their torment in the fire will be everlasting: they must live for ever in it. Several authors, both ancient and modern, tell us of earth-flax, or Salamander's hairs; that cloth made of it, being cast into the fire, is so far from being burnt or consumed, that it is only made clean thereby, as other things are by washing. But however that is, it is certain that the damned shall be tormented for ever and ever in hell-fire, and not substantially destroyed, Rev. xx. 10. Indeed nothing is annihilated by fire, but only dissolved. Of what nature soever hell-fire is, no question the same God, who kept the bodies of the three children from burning in

Nebuchadnezzar's fiery furnace, can also keep the bodies of the damned from any such dissolution by hell-fire, as may infer privation of life.

Lastly, Their knowledge and sense of their misery shall be eternal, and they shall assuredly know that it will be eternal. How desireable would it be to them, to have their senses for ever blocked up, and to lose the consciousness of their own misery: as one may rationally suppose it to fare at length with some, in the punishment of death inflicted on them on earth, and as it is with some mad people; but that agrees not with the notion of torment for ever and ever, nor the worm that dieth not. Nay, they will ever have a lively feeling of their misery, and the strongest impressions of the wrath of God against them. And that dreadful intimation of the eternity of their punishment, made to them by their Judge at their sentence, will fix such impressions of the eternity of their miserable state upon their minds, as they will never be able to lay aside, but it will continue with them evermore, to compleat their misery. This will fill them with everlasting despair, a most tormenting passion, which will continually rend their hearts, as it were, in a thousand pieces. To see floods of wrath ever coming, and never cease; to be ever in torment, and to know that there shall never, never be a release, will be the top-stone put on the misery of the damned. If *hope deferred maketh the heart sick*, Prov. xiii. 12. how killing will be hope rooted up, slain out-right, and buried for ever out of the creature's sight! This will fill them with hatred and rage against God, their known irreconcileable enemy: and under it they will roar for ever, like wild bulls in a net, and fill the pit with blasphemies evermore.

Lastly, I might here shew the reasonableness of the eternity of the punishment of the damned; but having already spoken of it, in vindicating the justice of God, in his subjecting men, in their natural state, to eternal wrath, I only re-mind you of three things. (1.) The infinite dignity of the party offended by sin requires an infinite punishment to be inflicted, for the vindication

Head VI. *Of Hell.* 459

of his honour; since the demerit of sin riseth according to the dignity and excellency of the person against whom it is committed. The party offended is the great God, the chief good: the offender a vile worm; in respect of perfection, infinitely distant from God, to whom he is indebted for all that ever he had, implying any good or perfection whatever. This then requires infinite punishment to be inflicted on the sinner, which, since it cannot in him be infinite in value, must be infinite in duration, that is to say, eternal. Sin is a kind of infinite evil, as it wrongs the infinite God: and the guilt and defilement thereof is never taken away, but endures for ever, unless the Lord himself in mercy removes it. God, who is offended, is eternal, his being never comes to an end: the sinful soul is immortal, and the man shall live for ever: the sinner being without strength (Rom. v. 6.) to expiate his guilt, can never put away the offence, therefore it ever remains, unless the Lord puts it away himself, as in the elect, by his Son's blood. Wherefore the party offended, the offender, and the offence, ever remaining, the punishment cannot but be eternal. (2.) The sinner would have continued the course of his provocations against God, for ever without end, if God had not put a check to it by death. As long as they were capable to act against him, in this world, they did it: and therefore justly will he act against them while he is; that is, for ever. God, who judgeth of the will, intents, and inclinations of the heart, may justly do against sinners, in punishing, as they would have done against him in sinning. *Lastly*, (though I put not the stress of the matter here, yet) it is just and reasonable, that the damned suffer eternally, since they will sin eternally in hell, gnashing their teeth (Mat. viii. 12.) under their pain, in rage, envy, and grudge, (compare Acts vii. 54. Psal. cxii. 10. Luke xiii. 28.) and blaspheming God there (Rev. xvi. 21.) while they are *driven away in their wickedness*, Prov. xiv. 32. That the wicked be punished for their wickedness, is just: and it is no ways inconsistent with justice, that the being of the creature be continued for ever: wherefore it is juft, that the damned, who continue wicked eternally, do fuffer eternally for their wickednefs. The mifery under which they fin, can neither free them from the debt of obedience, nor excufe their finning, and make it blamelefs. The creature, as a creature, is bound unto obedience to his Creator, and no punifhment inflicted on him can free him from it, any more than the malefactor's prifon, irons, whipping, and the like, fet him at liberty to commit again the crimes for which he is imprifoned or whipt. Neither can the torments of the damned excufe, or make blamelefs their horrible finning under them, any more than exquifite pains inflicted upon men on earth, can excufe their murmuring, fretting, and blafpheming againft God under them. It is not the wrath of God, but their own wicked nature, that is the true caufe of their finning under it; for the holy Jefus bore the wrath of God, without fo much as one unbecoming thought of God, and far lefs any one unbecoming word.

Use I. Here is a meafuring reed: O that men would apply it! *Firfl*, Apply it to your own time in this world, and you will find your time to be very fhort. A profpect of much time to come proves the ruin of many fouls. Men will be reckoning their time by years, (like the rich man, Luke xii. 19, 20.) when it may be there are not many hours of it to run. But reckon as you will, laying your time to the meafuring reed of eternity, you will fee your age is as nothing. What a fmall and inconfiderable point is fixty, eighty, or a hundred, in refpect of eternity? Compared with eternity, there is a greater difproportion, than between a hair's breadth and the circumference of the whole earth. Why do we fleep, then, in fuch a fhort day, while we are in hazard of lofing reft through the long night of eternity? *2dly*, Apply it to your endeavours for falvation, and they will be found very fcanty. When men are preffed to diligence in their falvation-work, they are ready to fay, To what purpofe is this wafte? Alas! if it were to be judged by our diligence, what it is which we have in view; as to the moft part,

Head VI. *Of Hell.* 461

of us, no man could thereby conjecture that we have eternity in view. If we duly confidered eternity, we could not but conclude, that we ought to leave no means appointed of God unemployed, till we get our falvation fecured: to refufe reft or comfort in any thing, till we are fheltered under the wings of the Mediator; to purfue our great intereft with the utmoft vigour; to cut off lufts, dear as right-hands and right-eyes; to fet our faces refolutely againft all difficulties, and fight our way through all oppofition made by the devil, the world, and the flefh; are all of them together little enough for eternity.

USE II. Here is a balance of the fanctuary, by which we may underftand the lightnefs of what is falfely thought weighty; and the weight of fome things, by many reckoned to be very light.

Firft, Some things feem very weighty, which, weighed in this balance, will be found very light. (1.) Weigh the world, and all that is in it, the luft of the flefh, the luft of the eyes, and the pride of life, and the whole will be found light in the balance of eternity. Weigh herein all worldly profits, gains, and advantages; and you will quickly fee, that a thoufand worlds will not be adequate to the coft of the eternity of woe. *For what is a man profited, if he fhall gain the whole world, and lofe his own foul?* Mat. xvi. 26. Weigh the pleafures of fin, which are but for a feafon, with the fire that is everlafting, and you fhew yourfelves to be fools and mad-men, to run the hazard of the one for the other. (2.) Weigh you afflictions in this balance, and you will find the heavieft of them very light, in refpect of the weight of eternal anguifh. Impatience under affliction, efpecially when worldly troubles fo imbitter men's fpirits, that they cannot relifh the glad tidings of the gofpel, fpeaks great regardlefnefs of eternity. As a fmall and inconfiderable lofs, will be very little at heart with him, who fees himfelf in danger of lofing his whole eftate: fo troubles in the world will appear but light, to him who has a lively view of eternity. Such a one will ftoop, and take up his crofs, whatever it be, thinking it enough to efcape eternal wrath.

(3.) Weigh the moſt difficult and uneaſy duties of religion here, and you will no more reckon the yoke of Chriſt inſupportable. Repentance and bitter mourning for ſin, on earth, are very light in compariſon of eternal weeping, wailing, and gnaſhing of teeth in hell. To wreſtle with God in prayer, weeping and making ſupplication for the bleſſing, in time, is far eaſier than to lie under the curſe through all eternity. Mortification of the moſt beloved luſt, is a light thing, in compariſon with the ſecond death in hell. *Laſtly*, Weigh your convictions in this balance. O how heavy do theſe lie upon many, till they get them ſhaken off! They are not diſpoſed to continue under them, but ſtrive to get clear of them, as of a mighty burden. But the worm of an ill conſcience will neither die nor ſleep in hell, though a man may now lull it aſleep for a time. And certainly it is eaſier to entertain the ſharpeſt convictions in this life, ſo as they lead us to Chriſt, than to have them fixed for ever in the conſcience, and to be in hell totally and finally ſeparated from him.

Secondly, But on the other hand, (1.) Weigh ſin in this balance; and, though now it ſeems but a light thing to you, you will find it a weight ſufficient to turn up eternal weight of wrath upon you. Even idle words, vain thoughts, and unprofitable actions, weighed in this balance, and conſidered as following the ſinner into eternity, will each of them be heavier than the ſand of the ſea. Time idly ſpent, will make a weary eternity. Now is your ſeed-time; thoughts, words, and actions, are the ſeed ſown; eternity is the harveſt: though the ſeed now lies under the clod, unregarded by moſt men, every the leaſt grain ſhall ſpring up at length; and the fruit ſhall be according to the ſeed, Gal. vi. 8. *For he that ſoweth to his fleſh, ſhall of the fleſh reap corruption* (i. e. deſtruction); *but he that ſoweth to the Spirit, ſhall of the Spirit reap life everlaſting.* (2.) Weigh in this balance your time and opportunities of grace and ſalvation, and you will find them very weighty. Precious time, and ſeaſons of grace, Sabbaths, communions, prayers, ſermons, and the like, are by

Head VI. Of Hell.

many, now a-days, made light of: but the day is coming, when one of these will be reckoned more valuable than a thousand worlds, by those who now have the least value for them. When they are gone for ever, and the loss cannot be retrieved, those will see the worth of them who will not now see it.

USE III. and *last*, Be warned and stirred up to flee from the wrath to come. Mind eternity, and closely ply the work of your salvation. What are you doing, while you are not so doing? Is heaven a fable, or hell a mere scare-crow? Must we live eternally, and shall we be at no more pains to escape everlasting misery? Will faint wishes take the kingdom of heaven by force? Will such drowsy endeavours, as most men satisfy themselves with, be accounted fleeing from the wrath to come? You who have already fled to Christ, up, and be doing: you have begun the work; go on, loiter not, but *work out your salvation with fear and trembling*, Philip. ii. 12. *Fear him which is able to destroy both soul and body in hell*, Mat. x. 28. Remember, you are not yet ascended into heaven: you are but in your middle state. The everlasting arms have drawn you out of the gulph of wrath you were plunged into, in your natural state; they are still underneath you, that you can never fall down into it again: nevertheless, you have not yet got up to the top of the rock; the deep below you is frightful; look at it, and hasten your ascent. You who are yet in your natural state, lift up your eyes, and take a view of the eternal state. Arise, ye profane persons, ye ignorant ones, ye formal hypocrites, strangers to the power of godliness, flee from the wrath to come. Let not the young venture to delay a moment longer, nor the old put off this work any more. To-day, if you will hear his voice, harden not your hearts; lest he swear in his wrath that you shall never enter into his rest. It is no time to linger in a state of sin, as in Sodom; when fire and brimstone are coming down on it from the Lord. Take warning in time: they who are in hell are not troubled with such warnings; but are enraged against themselves, because they slighted the warning when they had it.

Confider, I pray you, (1.) How uneafy it is to lie one whole night on a foft bed, in perfect health, when we very fain would have fleep, but cannot get it, fleep being departed from us. How often fhould we, in that cafe, wifh for reft! How full of toffings to and fro! But ah! how dreadful muft it then be, to lie in forrow, wrapped up in fcorching flames through eternity, in that place where they have no reft day nor night! (2.) How terrible would it be, to live under violent pains of the cholic or gravel, for forty or fixty years together, without any intermiffion! yet that is but a very fmall thing in comparifon of eternal feparation from God, the worm that never dieth, and the fire that is never quenched. (3.) Eternity is an awful thought! O long, long, endlefs eternity! but will not every moment, in eternity of woe feem a month, and every hour a year, in that moft wretched and defperate condition? Hence, *ever and ever*, as it were a double eternity. The fick man in the night, toffing to and fro on his bed, fays, It will never be day; complains, that his pain ever continues, never, never abates. Are thefe petty time-eternities, which men form to themfelves, in their own imaginations, fo very grievous? Alas! then how grievous, how utterly infupportable muft a real eternity of woe, and all manner of miferies be! *Laftly*, There will be fpace enough there, to reflect on all the ills of one's heart and life, which one cannot get time to think of now; and to fee that all that was faid of the impenitent finner's hazard was true, and that the half was not told. There will be fpace enough in eternity, to carry on delayed repentance, to rue one's follies, when it is too late; and in a ftate paft remedy, to fpeak forth thefe fruitlefs wifhes; "O that I never had been born! that the womb had been my grave, and I had never feen the fun! O that I had taken warning in time, and fled from this wrath, while the door of mercy was ftanding open to me! O that I had never heard the gofpel! that I had lived in fome corner of the world, where a Saviour and the great falvation were not once named!" But all in vain. What is done cannot be undone; the opportunity is

Head VI.   *Of Hell.*   465

loft, and cannot be retrieved; time is gone, and cannot be re-called. Wherefore improve time, while you have it, and do not wilfully ruin yourfelves, by ſtopping your ear to the goſpel-call.

And now, if you would be ſaved from the wrath to come, and never go into this place of torment, take no reſt in your natural ſtate; believe the ſinfulneſs and miſery of it, and labour to get out quickly, fleeing unto Jeſus Chriſt by faith. Sin in you is the ſeed of hell: and, if the guilt and reigning power of it be not removed in time, they will bring you to the ſecond death in eternity. There is no way to get them removed, but by receiving of Chriſt, as he is offered in the goſpel, for juſtification and ſanctification: and he is now offered to you, with all ſalvation, Rev. xxii. 12. 17. *Behold I come quickly, and my reward is with me, to give to every man according as his work ſhall be. And the Spirit and the Bride ſay, Come; and let him that heareth, ſay, Come; and let him that is athirſt, come; and whoſoever will, let him take of the water of life freely.* Jeſus Chriſt is the Mediator of peace, and the fountain of holineſs: he it is who delivereth us from the wrath to come. *There is no condemnation to them which are in Chriſt Jeſus, who walk not after the fleſh, but after the Spirit,* Rom. viii. 1. And the terrors of hell, as well as the joys of heaven, are ſet before you, to ſtir you up to cordial receiving of him, with all his ſalvation; and to incline you to the way of faith and holineſs: in which alone you can eſcape the everlaſting fire. May the Lord himſelf make them effectual to that end.

Thus far of man's eternal ſtate; which, becauſe it is eternal, admits no ſucceeding one for ever.

F I N I S.

O o o

A LIST of BOOKS Printed and Publifhed by
J. CHALMERS, No. 81, OLD-STREET.

A new and elegant Edition of
A View of the COVENANT of GRACE from the facred Records.

Alfo, a new and elegant Edition of
The CROOK in the LOT; or the Sovereignty and Wifdom of God difplayed in the Afflictions of Men; together with a Chriftian Deportment under them.

The above two by the Author of this Work. The former is printed in nine fixpenny Numbers; and the latter in three; and may be had by one or more Numbers at a Time, or elegantly bound together, or feparate.

The CROOK in the LOT may be, and by many is, bound with the FOUR-FOLD STATE.

An entire new Spelling-Book; or, a Sure Guide for all Youth. By. E. Dearle, Scchoolmafter, Golden-Lane. With Recommendatory Prefaces, by the Rev. Mr. Romaine, A.M. Mr. Platt, Mr. Towers, Mr. Crole, &c. Particularly adapted for Sunday-Schools, or religious Mafters; the Leffons being entirely taken from the Scriptures of the Old and New Teftaments. Price 1s. Good Allowance to thofe who take a Quantity.

A new Edition of Mr. Hart's Hymns, printed in a fmaller Size than before, on Writing Paper. Price 2s.

Religious Courtfhip; being hiftorical Difcourfes on the Neceffity of marrying religious Hufbands and Wives only; as alfo of Hufbands and Wives being of the fame Opinions in Religion. Price 1s. 6d. fewed.

The Advantages and Difadvantages of the Marriage State, as entered into with religious and irreligious Perfons, reprefented under the Similitude of a Dream. Very ufeful for ferious young People. Price 3d.

A LIST of BOOKS Printed and Publiſhed by J. CHALMERS, No. 81, Old-Street.

The laſt Farewell Sermon, preached at the Tabernacle, near Moorfields, April 1, 1792. By the Rev. John Berridge, M. A. Late Vicar of Everton, Bedfordſhire. To which is added, A Short Account of Mr. Berridge's Death, in a Letter from a Friend, who was with him the Day he died. Alſo a Narrative of the Reſpect ſhewed to him by his Friends in London. Price 6d.

An Elegy on the Death of Mr. Berridge, Price 1d.

A Short Account of the laſt days of the Counteſs of Huntingdon, by the Rev. T. Haweis, LL. B. her Chaplain. Price 6d.

The Watchman's Anſwer to the Queſtion, What of the Night?

The Practical Improvement to the Watchman's Anſwer.

The Glory of the Church in the latter Day.

Faith in God, and his Word, the Eſtabliſhment of his People.

> The above four Sermons by Dr. Gill, 6d. each. They are juſtly called his Prophetic Sermons, as they point out, and refer to, the Time we live in, though they were preached above forty Years ago.

A Serious Letter; with a Word to the Backſlider; another to the unfeeling Brother; and one to the Formaliſt and Phariſee. Price 2d.

The Pauſe; Where ſhall I be in Eternity? Price 2d.

A ſerious and important Queſtion, Am I in the Road that leads to Heaven; or in that which leads to Deſtruction? Price 1d.

The Roſe of Sharon, a Poem. Price 1d.

A Letter to a Methodiſt, on Degrees of Glory. Price 1d.

A Picture of Popery. By the late Rev. J. Ryland, Price 2d.

The Experience of Miſs F. M. Price 1d.

The Life of Faith, a Letter found in the Study of a late eminent Divine. Price 1d.

A LIST of BOOKS Printed and Publifhed by
J. CHALMERS, No. 81, OLD-STLEET.

THE
FEMALE PILGRIM;
OR, THE
Travels of HEPHZIBAH,
Under the Similitude of a DREAM.

In which is given

An hiftorical Account of the PILGRIM's Defcent, and a Defcription of her native Country, with the State of the Inhabitants thereof; the Reafon why, and Manner how, fhe left the Place of her Nativity, in Search of a better Country; the kind Entertainment fhe met with on the Road; the Dangers fhe went through, with her fafe Arrival at the Country fhe travelled in Search of.

Interfperfed with Variety of REFLECTIONS, DIALOGUES, SONGS, &c.

ILLUSTRATED WITH COPPER-PLATES.

N. B. The above is publifhing in Twelve Sixpenny Numbers.

Grofvenor's Mourner; or, the Afflicted Relieved. Recommended by Mr. Hervey. Price 1s. 6d.

Apocalyptical Key. Publifhed in 1702, in a Difcourfe on the Death of King William. By Robert Fleming, V. D. M. Being a vindication and enlargement of that Difcourfe, on the Rife and Fall of Papacy, publifhed in 1701. The various Periods are inferted, the pouring out of the Vials, the final Deftruction of Papacy, and the Commencement of the Millenium State. Price 6d.

www.ingramcontent.com/pod-product-compliance
Lightning Source LLC
Chambersburg PA
CBHW051849300426
44117CB00006B/324